MW01283460

SUMMER BY THE SEASIDE

Summer by the Seaside

The Architecture of New England Coastal Resort Hotels, 1820–1950

BRYANT F. TOLLES, JR.

UNIVERSITY PRESS OF NEW ENGLAND   HANOVER & LONDON

To the memory of
my Tolles and Ludden grandparents
who savored the summer life
of the New England costal resort hotels

Published by University Press of New England,

One Court Street, Lebanon, NH 03766

www.upne.com

© 2008 by Bryant F. Tolles, Jr.

Printed in Singapore

5   4   3   2   1

Frontispiece: Sea View House, Oak Bluffs, Martha's Vineyard, Mass.
Photograph, c. 1885. Courtesy of the Martha's Vineyard Museum.

Library of Congress Cataloging-in-Publication Data

Tolles, Bryant Franklin, 1939–
  Summer by the seaside : the architecture of New England coastal resort
hotels, 1820–1950 / Bryant F. Tolles, Jr.
      p.   cm.
  Includes bibliographical references and index.
  ISBN-13: 978–1–58465–576–3 (cloth : alk. paper)
  ISBN-10: 1-58465-576-3 (cloth : alk. paper)
  1. Hotels—New England—History—19th century. 2. Hotels—New
England—History—20th century. 3. Resort architecture—New England.
4. Hotels—Atlantic Coast (U.S.)—Guidebooks. I. Title.
  TX909.T616 2008
  917.406—dc22   2007049127

Contents

List of Illustrations — vi

Preface — xv

Acknowledgments — xix

1. Introduction: The American Resort Hotel and Its Expression on the New England Coast — 1

2. Connecticut: The Long Island Sound Shoreline — 15

3. Rhode Island: Narragansett Bay, Watch Hill, and Block Island — 35

4. Massachusetts: The South Shore, Cape Cod, and the Islands — 63

5. Massachusetts: The North Shore — 87

6. New Hampshire: The Beaches, New Castle, and the Isles of Shoals — 109

7. Maine: From Kittery to Cape Elizabeth — 124

8. Maine: From Casco Bay to New Brunswick — 151

Notes — 183

Bibliography — 201

Index — 223

Illustrations

Plates (color section follows page 104)

1. Ocean House (south view), Watch Hill, R.I., photograph, 2004
2. Ocean House (southwest view), Watch Hill, R.I., photograph, 2004
3. Spring House Hotel (main building), Block Island, R.I., photograph, c. 2006
4. Chatham Bars Inn, Chatham, Cape Cod, Mass., photograph, 2007
5. Harbor View Hotel, Edgartown, Martha's Vineyard, Mass., photograph, 2007
6. The Farragut House, Rye Beach, N.H., photograph, 1973
7. Wentworth-By-The-Sea, New Castle, N.H., photograph, 1968
8. Wentworth-By-The-Sea, New Castle, N.H., photograph, 1999
9. Wentworth-By-The-Sea, New Castle, N.H., photograph, 2004
10. Second Oceanic Hotel (Star Island Conference Center), Star Island, Isles of Shoals, N.H., photograph, 2007
11. Narragansett Hotel (Condominiums), Kennebunk Beach, Maine, photograph, 2006
12. The Colony Hotel (Breakwater Court), south façade, Kennebunkport, Maine, photograph, 2006
13. Ocean View Hotel (Marie Joseph Spiritual Center), Biddeford Pool, Maine, photograph, 2006
14. The second Asticou Inn, Northeast Harbor, Mount Desert Island, Maine, photograph, 2006

Figures

1-1.	"Indian Harbor Hotel, Greenwich, Conn.," trade advertisement, 1884	2
1-2.	"Pequot House, New London, Conn.," lithograph from photograph, F. W. Beers, *Atlas of New London County, Connecticut* (1868)	2
1-3.	"Ocean House Polka," sheet music cover, c. 1860	3
1-4.	The Mathewson Hotel, Narragansett Pier, R.I., photograph, c. 1898, from the southeast with the Casino and Towers	3
1-5.	"The Hotel Nantasket and Rockland Café," Nantasket Beach, Hull, Mass., lithograph from *King's Handbook of Boston Harbor* (1882)	4
1-6.	"Chatham Bars Inn, Chatham, Mass.," photograph from *DeLuxe Hotels of New England* (1915 ed.)	4
1-7.	"Aerial View, New Ocean House and Puritan Hall, Swampscott, Mass.," colored postcard, c. 1925	5
1-8.	The Oceanside Hotel, Magnolia, Mass., lithograph, c. 1910	5
1-9.	Harbor Façade, Colonial Arms Hotel, Eastern Point, Gloucester, Mass., photograph, c. 1905	6

1-10. "The Wentworth, New Castle, N.H.," 7
sheet music cover, 1892

1-11. Appledore House, Appledore Island, Isles 8
of Shoals, Maine, photograph, c. 1900

1-12. Ocean Bluff Hotel, Cape Arundel, 9
Kennebunkport, Maine, photograph,
c. 1890

1-13. "Old Orchard House, Old Orchard Beach, 10
Me.—E. C. Staples, Proprietor," lithograph
from booklet, *Boston & Maine and Maine
Central Summer Resorts* (c. 1891)

1-14. Hotel Cushing's Island (Ottawa House), 11
Cushing's Island, Casco Bay, Maine,
lithograph from booklet, *Summer Resorts
Reached by the Grand Trunk Railroad and
Its Connections* (1888)

1-15. "The Algonquin Hotel, St. Andrews, N.B.," 12
Canada, lithograph from booklet, *New
England's Summer and America's Leading
Winter Resorts* (1897)

2-1. The Indian Harbor Hotel (view from the 16
south), Indian Point, Greenwich, Conn.,
photograph, c. 1890

2-2. The Indian Harbor Hotel (view from the 17
west), Indian Point, Greenwich, Conn.,
photograph, c. 1890

2-3. Edgewood Inn (front view), Edgewood 19
Park, Greenwich, Conn., photograph, n.d.

2-4. Edgewood Inn (rear view, main entrance), 19
Edgewood Park, Greenwich, Conn.,
photograph, n.d.

2-5. Dining Room, Edgewood Inn, Edgewood 20
Park, Greenwich, Conn., photograph from
booklet, *Edgewood Inn, Greenwich,
Connecticut* (c. 1910)

2-6. George Hotel, Black Point, Bridgeport, 21
Conn., photograph, c. 1890

2-7. "Savin Rock House, West Haven, Conn.," 21
hotel menu engraving, 19 July 1861

2-8. "Sea View House," Savin Rock, West Haven, 21
Conn., engraving from Thursty McQuill
[Wallace Bruce], *The White and Green
Mountains and Routes There* (1873 ed.)

2-9. Branford Point House, Branford Point, 22
Branford, Conn., photograph, n.d.

2-10. "The Montowese House, Indian Neck, 23
Conn.," colored postcard, c. 1910

2-11. Front elevation plan, annex (east wing), 23
Montowese House, Indian Neck, Branford,
Conn., from booklet, *The Montowese,
Indian Neck, Branford, Conn.* (c. 1905)

2-12. "Interior Assembly Room," Montowese 23
House, Indian Neck, Branford, Conn.,
from booklet, *The Montowese* (n.d.)

2-13. "Sachem's Head Hotel, Guilford, Conn.," 24
broadside wooden engraving, 1862

2-14. "Fenwick Hall, Saybrook Point, Conn.," 24
engraving from *History of Middlesex
County, Connecticut* (1884)

2-15. First floor, Fenwick Hall, Saybrook Point, 25
Conn., promotional brochure, c. 1902

2-16. Second floor, Fenwick Hall, Saybrook 25
Point, Conn., promotional brochure, c. 1902

2-17. "Pequot House, New London, Conn.," 26
engraving from *Pleasant Days in Pleasant
Places* (1886)

2-18. Fire at the Pequot House, New London, 27
Conn., photograph, 7 May 1908

2-19. Fort Griswold House (Edgecomb House), 28
Eastern Point, New London [Groton],
Conn., photograph, c. 1900

2-20. Parlor floor and first floor plans, Fort 28
Griswold House, Eastern Point, New
London [Groton], Conn., Fort Griswold
House brochure (1886)

2-21. "The Griswold, Eastern Point," New 29
London [Groton], Conn., photograph
from *Views of New London* (1908)

2-22. "The New Hotel Griswold As It Will Look 30
When Completed," Eastern Point, New
London [Groton], Conn., drawing from
The Architectural Record 19, no. 5 (May 1906)

2-23. Office floor, the Griswold, Eastern Point, 30
New London [Groton], Conn., plan from
The Architectural Record 19, no. 5
(May 1906)

2-24. First floor, the Griswold, Eastern Point, 30
New London [Groton], Conn., plan from
The Architectural Record 19, no. 5
(May 1906)

2-25. The kitchen and its dependencies — Hotel   31
Griswold, Eastern Point, New London
[Groton], Conn., plan from *The Architectural
Record* 19, no. 5 (May 1906)

2-26. Lounge, Hotel Griswold, Eastern Point,   32
New London [Groton], Conn., photograph
from booklet, *The Griswold, New London,
Conn.* (c. 1909)

2-27. Mansion House, Fishers Island, Long   33
Island Sound, N.Y., postcard, n.d.

2-28. Mononotto Inn, Fishers Island, Long   34
Island Sound, N.Y., postcard, n.d.

3-1. "Belle Vue House," Newport, R.I., engraving   36
from *Hand-Book of Newport* (1852)

3-2. "Ocean House. Newport. Rhode Island."   37
Lithograph, c. 1844

3-3. "Atlantic House, Newport R.I.," lithograph,   37
c. 1845

3-4. "Ocean House," Newport, R.I., lithograph   37
from [John Collins], *The City and Scenery
of Newport, Rhode Island* (1857)

3-5. "Grand Veranda of the Ocean House,   38
Newport," R.I., photograph, c. 1890

3-6. Ocean House, Bellevue Avenue, Newport,   39
R.I., photograph, c. 1890

3-7. Rocky Point Hotel, Rocky Point, Warwick,   39
R.I., photograph, c. 1875

3-8. "Oakland Beach Hotel, Warwick Neck,   40
R.I.," photoengraving from Wilfred H.
Munro, *Picturesque Rhode Island* (1881)

3-9. Looking north past the hotels, Jamestown,   41
R.I., photograph, c. 1910.

3-10. Bay View House, Jamestown, R.I.,   42
photograph, c. 1900

3-11. Plans of the Bay View House (first floor),   42
Jamestown, R.I., from booklet, *Bay View
House* (n.d.)

3-12. Bay View Condominiums (c. 1987–89),   43
Jamestown, R.I., photograph, 2004

3-13. Gardner House, Jamestown, R.I.,   43
photograph, c. 1900

3-14. Hotel Thorndike, Jamestown, R.I.,   44
photograph from *Newport, R.I.* (1907)

3-15. Narragansett Pier, R.I., from Steamboat Pier,
photograph, 1883   45

3-16. "Atlantic House, Abijah Browning, Esq.,   46
Prop., Narragansett Pier, R.I.," lithograph
from *History of the State of Rhode Island*
(1878)

3-17. Metatoxet House, Narragansett Pier, R.I.,   46
photograph from *Views of Narragansett
Pier* (1884)

3-18. Continental Hotel, Narragansett Pier, R.I.,   46
photograph, c. 1875

3-19. "Mount Hope House, Hon. W. G. Caswell,   47
Prop., Narragansett Pier, R.I.," lithograph
from *History of the State of Rhode Island*
(1878)

3-20. Tower Hill House, Narragansett Heights,   47
R.I., advertisement engraving, *A Guide to
Narragansett Bay* (1878)

3-21. "The Rockingham, Narragansett Pier," R.I.,   47
engraving from Robert Grieve, *The New
England Coast* (1892)

3-22. The Casino and Rockingham Hotel,   48
Narragansett Pier, R.I., photograph, c. 1895

3-23. Fire at the Rockingham Hotel, Narragansett   48
Pier, R.I., photograph, 12 September 1900

3-24. Gladstone Hotel, Narragansett Pier, R.I.,   48
photograph, c. 1889

3-25. The Mathewson Hotel, Narragansett Pier,   49
R.I., photograph, June 1883

3-26. "Greene's Inn," Narragansett Pier, R.I.,   50
drawings from *American Architect and
Building News* 23 (28 January 1888)

3-27. "The Mathewson, Narragansett Pier, R.I.,"   50
front elevation perspective drawing from
The Woods, Lakes, Sea-Shore and Mountains
(1896)

3-28. The Mathewson Hotel, Narragansett Pier,   51
R.I., construction photograph, c. 1896

3-29. "The Imperial Hotel. Narragansett Pier,   52
R.I.," colored postcard, c. 1900

3-30. Plimpton House and annex, Watch Hill,   52
R.I., engraving from Robert Grieve,
Picturesque Narragansett (c. 1889)

3-31. Southwest view, Ocean House, Watch Hill,   53
R.I., photograph, 2004

3-32. Southeast view, Ocean House, Watch Hill,   54
R.I., photograph, 2004

3-33. Southwest veranda, c. 1905, Ocean House, Watch Hill, R.I., photograph, 2004   54

3-34. Larkin House, Watch Hill, R.I., photograph, 1889   55

3-35. New Watch Hill House (with Atlantic House to the left), Watch Hill, R.I., photograph, c. 1889   56

3-36. "Plan of First Floor," Watch Hill House, Watch Hill, R.I., from booklet, *Watch Hill House, Watch Hill, R.I.* (c. 1890)   56

3-37. The National Hotel (*left*) and the Surf Hotel (Cottage) (*right*), Old Harbor, Block Island, R.I., photograph, 2005   57

3-38. Hotel Manisses, Old Harbor, Block Island, R.I., photograph, 2005   58

3-39. "The Spring House, Block Island, R.I.," engraving from Samuel T. Livermore, *Block Island* (1886 ed.)   58

3-40. The Spring House, Old Harbor, Block Island, R.I., photograph, 2005   58

3-41. "Ocean View Hotel, Block Island. Hon. Nicholas Ball, Prop.," lithograph from *History of the State of Rhode Island* (1878)   59

3-42. Ocean View Hotel, Old Harbor, Block Island, R.I., photograph, c. 1883   60

3-43. "Plan of First Floor of Ocean View Hotel, Block Island, R.I., 1882," from Samuel T. Livermore, *Block Island Guide* (1882 ed.)   60

3-44. "The Hygeia," Block Island, R.I., photograph from viewbook, *Block Island: Hotels, Residences* (1900)   61

4-1. "The Oregon House, Hull," Mass., photolithograph from Moses F. Sweetser, *King's Handbook of Boston Harbor* (1882)   64

4-2. "Rockland House, Nantasket Beach," Hull, Mass., lithograph from sheet music, "Rockland Echoes Waltzes," 1870   64

4-3. "Hotel Nantasket, Nantasket Beach," Hull, Mass., drawing by J. Pickering Putnam, Boston, from *American Architect and Building News* 6, no. 196 (27 September 1879)   65

4-4. "The Hotel Pemberton, Windmill Point, Hull," Mass., photolithograph from Moses F. Sweetser, *King's Handbook of Boston Harbor* (1882)   66

4-5. "Atlantic House, Nantasket Beach, Mass.," postcard view, c. 1920   67

4-6. "Old Colony House, Hingham, Mass.," drawing by Bradlee & Winslow, Architects, Boston, from *American Architect and Building News* 9, no. 279 (30 April 1881)   68

4-7. Rose Standish House, Hingham, Mass., engraving from the *New Columbian Railroad Atlas and Pictorial Album of American Industry* (1884)   68

4-8. Black Rock House, North Cohasset, Mass., photograph, c. 1960   69

4-9. Hotel Humarock, Humarock Beach, Scituate, Mass., photograph, c. 1897   69

4-10. The Cliff Hotel, Minot Beach, North Scituate, Mass., postcard photograph, c. 1925   70

4-11. Churchill Hotel, Brant Rock Village, Marshfield, Mass., photograph, c. 1900   71

4-12. Peace Haven Hotel, Brant Rock Village, Marshfield, Mass., photograph, c. 1925   71

4-13. Hotel Pilgrim (Clifford House), Plymouth, Mass., photograph before renovations, c. 1890   72

4-14. Hotel Pilgrim, Plymouth, Mass., photograph, c. 1940   72

4-15. Mayflower Hotel, Plymouth, Mass., photograph, c. 1920   73

4-16. "The Mayflower Inn, Manomet Point, Plymouth, Massachusetts," drawing by J. Williams Beal, Architect, Boston, from the *Old Colony Memorial*, 26 January 1917   73

4-17. The Sippican Hotel, Marion, Mass., photograph from *DeLuxe Hotels of New England* (1915)   74

4-18. "Vineyard Sound Hotel, Falmouth, Mass.," colored postcard view, c. 1925   74

4-19. Sippewissett (Cape Codder) Hotel, Falmouth, Cape Cod, Mass., photograph after the 1902 addition   75

4-20. "First Floor Plan," Sippewissett Hotel, Falmouth, Cape Cod, Mass., from booklet, *The Sippewissett, Falmouth, Mass.* (n.d.)   75

4-21. "The Nobscussett House, Dennis, Mass.," lithograph from Simeon L. Dejo, *History of Barnstable County, Massachusetts* (1890)   76

4-22. Hotel Belmont, West Harwich, Cape Cod, Mass., photograph from *DeLuxe Hotels of New England* (1915)   77

4-23. Hotel Chatham, Chatham, Cape Cod, Mass, photograph, c. 1890   78

4-24. "Hotel Mattaquason, Chatham, Mass.," colored postcard view, c. 1905   79

4-25. Chatham Bars Inn, Chatham, Cape Cod, Mass., construction photograph, 1917   79

4-26. Chatham Bars Inn, Chatham, Cape Cod, Mass., photograph, 2007   79

4-27. Lounge, Chatham Bars Inn, Chatham, Cape Cod, Mass., postcard view, c. 1920   79

4-28. "The Nantucket, Nantucket, Mass.," engraving from Robert Grieve, *The New England Coast and Its Famous Resorts* (1892)   80

4-29. Sea Cliff Inn, Nantucket Island, Mass., photograph, c. 1910   81

4-30. The Beach House, Siasconset, Nantucket Island, Mass., photograph, c. 1930   82

4-31. "Oak Bluffs Galop [Sea View House — Oak Bluffs — Martha's Vineyard]," sheet music illustration, J. H. Bufford's Lith., Boston, 1872   83

4-32. Highland House, Vineyard Highlands, Martha's Vineyard, Mass., stereo view, c. 1880   84

4-33. "Mattakeset Lodge, Katama, Martha's Vineyard," Mass., engraving from John Bachelder, *Popular Resorts, Routes to Reach Them* (1873)   85

4-34. Harbor View Hotel, Edgartown, Cape Cod, Mass., photograph, 2007   86

5-1. "Beach View at the Point of Pines," Hotel Pines, Revere, Mass., lithograph, Forbes Litho. Co., c. 1890   88

5-2. "Nahant Hotel," Nahant, Mass., engraving from promotional broadside (1 May 1825)   89

5-3. "Nahant House" from "Nahant Polka" sheet music cover, J. H. Bufford's Lith., 1854   90

5-4. Eastern façade of the Lincoln House, Swampscott, Mass., photograph, c. 1895   91

5-5. "First Floor Plan," Lincoln House, from booklet, *The Lincoln House, Swampscott, Mass.* (c. 1895)   92

5-6. "The New Office," Lincoln House, photograph from booklet, *The Lincoln House, Swampscott, Mass.* (c. 1895)   92

5-7. The Hotel Preston, Beach Bluff, Swampscott, Mass., photograph, c. 1925   93

5-8. "Ocean House, Swampscott, Mass.," lithograph from *New England's Summer and America's Leading Winter Resorts* (1897)   94

5-9. New Ocean House, Swampscott, Mass., letterhead lithograph, c. 1902   94

5-10. "Impressive Façade of the New Ocean House, Swampscott, Massachusetts, Since its Recent Additions and Improvements," photograph from *The North Shore Reminder* 7, no. 1 (14 July 1908)   94

5-11. "The Foyer," New Ocean House, Swampscott, Mass., photograph from *The North Shore Reminder* 6, no. 3 (13 July 1907)   94

5-12. "The Nanepashemet: Marblehead, Great Neck," Mass., drawing from *American Architect and Building News* 12 (15 July 1882)   95

5-13. Rockmere Inn from Crocker Point, Marblehead, Mass., postcard photograph, 1906   96

5-14. "Part of the Foyer, Rock-mere Inn," Marblehead, Mass., photograph from booklet, *Rock-mere Inn, Marblehead* (c. 1907)   96

5-15. The Gun Deck, Fo'cas'le, Rockmere Inn, Marblehead, Mass., postcard photograph, c. 1930   97

5-16. Lowell Island House, Lowell (Cat) Island, Salem Harbor, Mass., photograph, n.d.   97

5-17. "The Queen," Beverly, Mass., photo-engraving from Benjamin D. Hill and Winfield S. Nevins, *The North Shore of Massachusetts Bay* (1891 ed.)   98

5-18. "Masconomo, Manchester By The Sea," Mass., photograph from *North and South Shore Views* (188?)   98

5-19. "Office Floor," Hotel Masconomo, Manchester, Mass., plan from booklet, *The Masconomo, Manchester-by-the-Sea* (1906)   99

5-20. "The Hesperus, Magnolia, Mass.," carte-de-visite, 1908   100

5-21. The Oceanside (early state), Magnolia, Mass., photograph, c. 1880   100

5-22. The Oceanside, Magnolia, Mass., photograph, c. 1905   101

5-23. "The Magnolia, Magnolia, Mass.," lithograph from *New England's Summer and America's Leading Winter Resorts* (1897)   102

5-24. Pavilion Hotel, Crescent Beach, Gloucester, Mass., etching, c. 1875   103

5-25. The main building and wings, Hawthorne Inn and Cottages, East Gloucester, Mass., photograph, Eben Parsons, 1913   104

5-26. "Bass Rock House," Gloucester, Mass., engraving from Benjamin D. Hill and Winfield S. Nevins, *The North Shore of Massachusetts Bay* (1881 ed.)   104

5-27. "Hotel Moorland, Gloucester, Mass.," colored postcard, c. 1930   105

5-28. "Bass Rocks, Mass. The Thorwald Hotel," colored postcard, c. 1930   105

5-29. The Colonial Arms under construction with work crew, Eastern Point, Gloucester, Mass., photograph, 1904   106

5-30. The Colonial Arms, Eastern Point, Gloucester, Mass., photograph, c. 1905   107

5-31. Turk's Head Inn, Rockport, Mass., photograph, n.d.   108

6-1. Boar's Head Hotel, Hampton, N.H., stereo, n.d.   110

6-2. First Ocean House, Hampton Beach, N.H., stereo, n.d.   110

6-3. "Ocean House, Rye Beach, N.H., Job Jenness, Proprietor," lithograph, c. 1855   111

6-4. Second Ocean House, Rye Beach, N.H., engraving from John B. Bachelder, *Popular Resorts, Routes to Reach Them* (1873)   111

6-5. The first Farragut House, Rye Beach, N.H., photograph, c. 1880   112

6-6. "Farragut House, Rye Beach, N.H.," front elevation perspective drawing from *American Architect and Building News* 13, no. 374 (24 February 1883)   113

6-7. Tower, northeast corner, Farragut House, Rye Beach, N.H., photograph, n.d.   113

6-8. The Farragut House, Rye Beach, N.H., photograph, 1973   113

6-9. The Sea View Hotel, Rye Beach, N.H., photograph, c. 1890   114

6-10. The Wentworth Hotel, New Castle, N.H., panorama engraving from brochure, c. 1880   115

6-11. The Wentworth, New Castle, N.H., ground floor plan from brochure, 1888   116

6-12. Hotel Wentworth, New Castle, N.H., cabinet view, c. 1883   116

6-13. "Hotel Wentworth, New Castle-By-The-Sea, Portsmouth, N.H.," photoengraving from *DeLuxe Hotels of New England* (1914)   117

6-14. Wentworth-By-The-Sea, New Castle, N.H., photograph, 1973   118

6-15. "Interior Views," photographs from booklet, *The Wentworth, New Castle, New Hampshire* (c. 1900)   118

6-16. Wentworth-By-The-Sea, New Castle, N.H., photograph, 2004   119

6-17. Appledore House, Appledore Island, Isles of Shoals, Maine, engraving from William C. Gage, *"The Switzerland of America"* (1879)   120

6-18. First Oceanic Hotel, Star Island, Isles of Shoals, N.H., hotel stationery logo, c. 1876   121

6-19. "The Oceanic," Star Island, Isles of Shoals, N.H., lithograph from *Town and City Atlas of the State of New Hampshire* (1892)   122

6-20. The second Oceanic Hotel (Star Island Conference Center), Star Island, Isles of Shoals, N.H., photograph, 2007   122

6-21. "Piazza of the Oceanic," second Oceanic Hotel, Star Island, Isles of Shoals, N.H., photograph from booklet, *Oceanic Hotel, Star Island, Isles of Shoals* (1907)   122

7-1. The Champernowne Hotel, Kittery Point, Maine, photograph, c. 1900   125

7-2. "The Pocahontas, Kittery Point, Me.," photoengraving from booklet, *Hotel Pocahontas* (n.d.)   126

7-3. "Marshall House — Edward S. Marshall, Proprietor," lithograph from [W. W. Clayton], *History of York County* (1880)   126

7-4.   "The Marshall House," York Harbor, Maine, lithograph from booklet, *The Marshall House* . . . (n.d.)   127

7-5.   Floor plans, Marshall House, York Harbor, Maine, John Calvin Stevens, architect   128

7-6.   "The Lounge, Marshall House," York Harbor, Maine, photograph from booklet, *The Marshall House* (n.d.)   129

7-7.   "The New Marshall House, York Harbor, Me.," perspective drawing, John Calvin Stevens, architect   129

7-8.   "Entrance Front," Marshall House, York Harbor, Maine, drawing, 1916, John Calvin Stevens, architect   130

7-9.   Passaconaway Inn, York, Maine, photograph, c. 1925   131

7-10.   Passaconaway Inn, York, Maine, with construction workers, photograph, 1893   131

7-11.   Hotel Abracca, York, Maine, postcard photograph, n.d.   131

7-12.   Ocean House, York Beach, Maine, photograph, n.d.   132

7-13.   Young's Hotel, York Beach, Maine, photograph from *DeLuxe Hotels of New England* (1914)   132

7-14.   "Island Ledge Hotel," Wells Beach, Maine, engraving from John B. Bachelder, *Popular Resorts, Routes to Reach Them* (1873)   133

7-15.   Sparhawk Hall, Ogunquit, Maine, photograph, n.d.   134

7-16.   Lookout Hotel (Condominiums), Ogunquit, Maine, photograph, 2006   134

7-17.   Atlantis Hotel, Kennebunk Beach, Maine, photograph, n.d.   135

7-18.   Narragansett Hotel (Condominiums), Kennebunk Beach, Maine, photograph, 2006   135

7-19.   Ocean Bluff Hotel, Kennebunkport, Maine, photograph, n.d.   136

7-20.   Cliff House, Kennebunkport, Maine, photograph, n.d.   136

7-21.   Oceanic Hotel, Kennebunkport, Maine, photograph, n.d.   137

7-22.   First and second floor plans, Oceanic Hotel, Kennebunkport, Maine, from broadside, "The Oceanic and Cottages" (n.d.)   138

7-23.   Old Fort Inn (first stage), Kennebunkport, Maine, photograph, c. 1902   139

7-24.   The Colony Hotel (Breakwater Court), south façade, Kennebunkport, Maine, photograph, 2006   139

7-25.   The Colony Hotel (Breakwater Court), north entrance façade, Kennebunkport, Maine, photograph, 2006   139

7-26.   "Highland House, . . . Biddeford Pool, Me.," engraving from J. S. Locke, *Shores of Saco Bay* (1880)   140

7-27.   Ocean View Hotel, Biddeford Pool, Maine, photograph, n.d.   140

7-28.   Ocean View Hotel (Marie Joseph Spiritual Center), Biddeford Pool, Maine, photograph, 2006   140

7-29.   Old Orchard Beach, Maine. Panorama from *Guide to the Sea-Shore, Mountains and Lakes* (1877)   141

7-30.   "Ocean House, Old Orchard Beach, Me.," engraving from J. S. Locke, *Shores of Saco Bay* (1880)   141

7-31.   "Old Orchard House, Old Orchard Beach, Me.," advertisement from *Saratoga Illustrated: The Visitor's Guide to Saratoga Springs* (1880)   142

7-32.   "Ground Floor Plan," Old Orchard Beach House, from booklet, *Old Orchard Beach House, Old Orchard Beach, Maine* (1910)   142

7-33.   "Section of Main Dining Room," Old Orchard Beach House, from booklet, *Old Orchard Beach House, Old Orchard Beach, Me.* (c. 1900)   143

7-34.   "Seashore House, Old Orchard Beach," photograph from booklet, *Old Orchard Beach, Maine* (1900)   143

7-35.   "Blanchard House, Old Orchard Beach, Me.," engraving from J. S. Locke, *Shores of Saco Bay* (1880)   143

7-36.   Central House, Old Orchard Beach, Maine, photograph, n.d.   143

7-37.   Hotel Fiske, Old Orchard Beach, Maine, photograph, n.d.   144

7-38.   "Hotel Fiske, Old Orchard Beach, Me.," broadside, n.d.   144

7-39. Hotel Velvet, Old Orchard Beach, Maine, 145
lithograph from booklet, *Hotel Velvet,
Old Orchard Beach, Maine* (c. 1900)

7-40. Room plans, first and second sleeping 146
floors, Hotel Velvet, Old Orchard Beach,
Maine, from brochure, *Hotel Velvet . . .* (1902)

7-41. Hotel Alberta (*left*) and Hotel Velvet (*right*), 147
Old Orchard Beach, Maine, photograph, 1903

7-42. "The Hotel Everett, Old Orchard Beach, 147
Me.," advertisement from booklet, *The
Vacation Route* (1891)

7-43. The Jocelyn House, Prouts Neck, Scar- 148
borough, Maine, photograph, n.d.

7-44. "The Checkley House from the Ocean 149
Side," Prouts Neck, Scarborough, Maine,
photograph from booklet, *The Checkley* (n.d.)

7-45. Cape Cottage, Cape Elizabeth, Maine, 150
photograph, n.d.

8-1. First Ottawa House, Cushing's Island, 152
Casco Bay, Maine, engraving from Edward
H. Elwell, *Portland and Vicinity* (1876)

8-2. Ottawa House, Cushing's Island, Casco Bay, 153
Maine, photograph, n.d.

8-3. "Hotel Cushing's Island, Maine," front 153
elevation perspective drawing by Clarence
Luce, Architect, New York City, from
Building 8, no. 4 (23 July 1887)

8-4. "Granite Spring Hotel and Casino, Long 154
Island, Portland Harbor, Me.," photograph
from *The Island & Shore Gems of Beautiful
Casco Bay, Portland, Maine* (1895)

8-5. Peak's Island House, Peak's Island, Casco 154
Bay, Maine, photograph, c. 1900

8-6. Casco Castle, South Freeport, Maine, 155
photograph, c. 1900

8-7. "Ocean View House and 'Annex,' Popham 156
Beach, Maine," engraving from W. B.
Lapham, *Popham Beach as a Summer
Resort . . .* (1888)

8-8. Oake Grove Hotel, Boothbay Harbor, 156
Maine, cover illustration from brochure,
Oake Grove Hotel, Boothbay Harbor, Me.
(c. 1905)

8-9. Samoset House, Mouse Island, Boothbay 157
Harbor, Maine, broadside engraving, c. 1881

8-10. "Squirrel Inn — Keyes H. Richards, Prop.," 158
photograph from Francis B. Greene, *History
of Boothbay, Southport and Boothbay Harbor,
1623–1905* (1906)

8-11. "Holly Inn," with Rutherford House (*right*), 158
Christmas Cove, Maine, photograph from
booklet, *Holly Inn, Christmas Cove, Maine*
(n.d.)

8-12. "Bay Point Hotel, Rockland Breakwater, 159
Rockland, Me.," lithograph from *The Woods,
Lakes, Sea-Shore and Mountains* (1896)

8-13. "Samoset Hotel Rockland, Me.," photograph, 160
c. 1910

8-14. Office, Samoset Hotel, Rockland, Maine, 161
photograph from booklet, *The SamOset
By the Sea* (1914)

8-15. Dining room, Samoset Hotel, Rockland, 161
Maine, photograph from booklet, *The
SamOset By the Sea* (1914)

8-16. "Third Floor Plan, The Samoset, Rockland 161
Breakwater, Penobscot Bay, Rockland, Me.,"
from booklet, *The SamOset* (1902)

8-17. "Islesborough Inn — Westerly View," 162
Islesboro Island, Penobscot Bay, Maine,
photograph from John P. Farrow, *History
of Islesborough, Maine* (1893)

8-18. "First Floor Plan — Islesboro Inn," Islesboro 163
Island, Penobscot Bay, Maine, from John P.
Farrow, *History of Islesborough, Maine* (1893)

8-19. Second Islesboro Inn, Islesboro Island, 164
Penobscot Bay, Maine, photograph, n.d.

8-20. Wassaumkeag Hotel, Fort Point, Stockton 165
Springs, Maine, photograph, c. 1880

8-21. "The Acadian, Castine, Maine," booklet 165
cover lithograph, 1905

8-22. Bar Harbor from Bar Island, Frenchman's 166
Bay, Maine, photograph, c. 1890

8-23. The Rodick Hotel, Bar Harbor, Mount 167
Desert Island, Maine, photoelectric
engraving from [W. B. Lapham], *Bar
Harbor and Mount Desert Island* (1886)

8-24. "Newport House and Cottages," Bar 167
Harbor, Mount Desert Island, Maine,
photograph from W. H. Sherman, *A
Souvenir of Bar Harbor* (1896)

8-25. St. Sauveur Hotel, Bar Harbor, Mount   167
       Desert Island, Maine, photograph from
       W. H. Sherman, *A Souvenir of Bar Harbor*
       (1896)

8-26. Louisburg Hotel, Bar Harbor, Mount   168
       Desert Island, Maine, lithograph from
       *New England's Summer and America's
       Leading Winter Resorts* (1897)

8-27. Grand Central Hotel, Bar Harbor, Mount   168
       Desert Island, Maine, photograph, c. 1895

8-28. "West End • Hotel • Bar Harbor • Mt.   169
       Desert • Me. Bruce Price • Archt. N.Y.,"
       front elevation perspective drawing from
       American Architect and Building News 5
       (25 January 1879)

8-29. "Malvern Hotel, Kebo Street," Bar Harbor,   170
       Mount Desert Island, Maine, photograph
       from W. H. Sherman, *A Souvenir of Bar
       Harbor* (1896)

8-30. The Island House, Southwest Harbor,   171
       Mount Desert Island, Maine, photograph,
       c. 1886

8-31. The second Asticou Inn, Northeast Harbor,   172
       Mount Desert Island, Maine, photograph,
       2006

8-32. Rock End Hotel, Northeast Harbor,   173
       Mount Desert Island, Maine, photograph,
       c. 1910

8-33. Kimball House, Northeast Harbor,   174
       Mount Desert Island, Maine, photograph,
       c. 1890

8-34. The Seaside Inn, Seal Harbor, Mount   174
       Desert Island, Maine, photograph, c. 1910

8-35. "The Bluffs, Mt. Desert Ferry, Me.,"   175
       engraving, Philadelphia, c. 1890

8-36. "Hotel Sorrento," Sorrento, Maine,   175
       engraving from booklet, *A Summer at
       Sorrento* (c. 1893)

8-37. Grindstone Inn, Winter Harbor, Maine,   176
       photograph from booklet, *The Grindstone
       Inn* (c. 1910)

8-38. "Tyn-y-Coed, Campobello Island, New   177
       Brunswick," front elevation perspective
       drawing from booklet, *Campobello Island*
       (1881)

8-39. "The Algonquin Hotel, St. Andrews,   178
       New Brunswick," front elevation
       perspective drawing from *American
       Architect and Building News* 26
       (14 December 1889)

Preface

The publication of *Summer by the Seaside: The Architecture of New England Coastal Resort Hotels, 1820–1950* represents the eminently satisfying culmination of my long-term efforts to research and compile a trilogy of illustrated books treating the architecture and related economic, social, cultural, and intellectual history of the large hotel building type in major resort regions of New England and upstate New York. The primary inspiration for these book projects has been my keen interest since the early 1990s in the history of tourism, leisure, and recreation in North America, with primary emphasis on the northeastern United States. On several occasions over the years, I have had the pleasure of teaching a course in this subject area to undergraduate as well as graduate students as a professor of history and art history at the University of Delaware.

The first of the three books was published in 1998 by David R. Godine of Boston and is titled *The Grand Resort Hotels of the White Mountains: A Vanishing Architectural Legacy*. In 2003, the second appeared under the imprint of the University Press of New England bearing the title *Resort Hotels of the Adirondacks: The Architecture of a Summer Paradise, 1850–1950*. Furthermore, I would be remiss not to mention that all three books stem from broad interests developed as a deeply committed, long-time resident of New England, as a graduate of the American and New England Studies doctoral program at Boston University, and as a past visitor to virtually all the long list of summer vacation communities along the New England coastline.

The vast majority of New England's pre-1950 seaboard resort hotels were highly functional buildings constructed of wood and vulnerable to destruction as a result of fire, obsolescence, and lack of profitability, often leading to demolition. Consequently, as in the White Mountain and Adirondack regions, the record of preservation, conditioned by the realities of the hospitality industry, has been extremely poor. Only a handful of structures remain on the New England coast today to serve as invaluable historical documents of the past architecture and life of the summer resort hotel. While there were well over 150 built within this book's time frame, accommodating 150 to 200 or more guests, fewer than 10 have survived, currently satisfying tourism and other demands. The most widely recognized and oldest of the large hotel complexes, often referred to as "grand," is the Hotel Wentworth (Wentworth-by-the-Sea) at New Castle, New Hampshire, the original core of which has been modernized and greatly enlarged in size since 2000 (see chapter 6). Another more recent structure, also in the grand hotel category, is the Colony Hotel (formerly Breakwater Court) at Kennebunkport, Maine (see chapter 7). Among the other extant large hostelries, all discussed in the following chapters, are the Spring House at Block Island, Rhode Island; the Chatham Bars Inn at Chatham, Cape Cod, and the Harbor View Hotel at Edgartown, Martha's Vineyard, both in Massachusetts; and the second Oceanic Hotel, today a conference center at Star Island, the Isles of Shoals, New Hampshire. The small group of survivors alone suggests the importance of developing this book topic while some historic hotel building examples still exist to be studied, analyzed, recorded, and appreciated.

Considering the importance of the topic and the great volume of published literature treating the New England region, it is surprising that a book has not been previously written treating the architecture and related history of New England coastal resort hotels. For the most part, even general studies developing other regional history topics fail to discuss the resort hotel phenomenon in a broader New England and American national context, if it is even mentioned at all. In recent years, however, several outstanding works (see bibliography) devoted to specific localities and/or architects/architectural firms have been published, in each instance containing references to significant hotel buildings, other forms of resort architecture, and their financiers and planners. A major factor discouraging extensive research on the topic is the dearth of pertinent manuscript source materials (business records, correspondence, guest registers, architectural drawings and specifications, etc.), many of which have been destroyed in numerous hotel fires or simply thrown out, without proper comprehension of their documentary value. While I have utilized a small number of manuscript and other unpublished items for research, and I have conducted some oral history interviews, the major sources consulted for the book are printed materials falling into the category of secondary literature. These include monographic works; state, county, and local histories; guidebooks and travel accounts; diaries; pictorial publications; scholarly journal, magazine, and newspaper articles; reference work entries; hotel booklets and other informational/promotional materials; travel flyers, brochures, and broadsides; and, indispensable to students and connoisseurs of architecture, printed views, photographs, and other forms of artistic creativity. These varied, highly eclectic sources are listed in the bibliography and/or are identified in the endnote citations.

Another challenge in successfully developing a book project of this kind is determining the most appropriate definition of subject, as well as organizational structure. Initially I considered arranging the text chronologically and topically. After much thought, however, I decided to relate the story of New England's coastal resort hotels by geographical location. Following an introductory contextual chapter treating the origins and evolution of tourism and the resort hotel industry in the eastern United States, concentrating on New England, separate chapters are devoted to shore regions commencing with Connecticut and proceeding to the northeast, concluding with northeastern Maine above Portland and Casco Bay. As a result of this decision, the reader will undergo a trip through time and subject matter, as well as geography along coastal land and to islands for over four thousand miles from New York City to New Brunswick, Canada. Considering the geographic scope of the project, and the number of buildings to be discussed, this seemed the most logical and comprehensible approach to take. I also believe that it will offer the most gratifying reading experience.

As for date span, the book begins in the early nineteenth century, when resort hotel development began to take root along the New England coast. It then proceeds through the period of greatest growth, prosperity, and architectural expression from the 1840s to World War I. While there is commentary in the text about the current era, surviving hotel examples, and modern-day hospitality tourism trends, the book essentially concludes with the mid–twentieth century and the precipitous decline and transformation of the regional resort-hotel industry caused by the two world wars, the Depression, altered leisure-time living patterns, and changing means of transportation and other technological advancements (see chapter 1).

In addition, I have made the decision to focus on "large" hotels accommodating roughly 200 or more guests, possessing unusual architectural character and integrity, and providing a broad range of visitor experiences. Those complexes which I have deemed of greatest architectural significance have received the most extensive description and analysis, coupled with pictorial illustration. Present in this fascinating group are a number of massive, luxurious resort establishments that have been traditionally termed "grand" hotels — distinctive, high-style structures, recognized for their sumptuous accommodations and public spaces, the most up-to-date technology, beautifully manicured grounds and recreation/athletic venues, generous socializing opportunities, and food/beverage and entertainment program offerings of the same high quality found in major American urban settings. The large hotels, including the grand category, were impressive in scale and expressed a wide variety of architectural styles. While a great many were ornate and sophisticated in appearance and layout, most were rather subdued, conventional examples of their respective styles or style amalgams, and some could be most accurately described as vernacular, lacking recognizable style attributes. Intentionally omitted from this study are the numerous smaller hotels, inns, and boardinghouses, most of which lacked architectural quality, offered relatively modest hospitality services and experiences, and hence said little about hospitality tourism and its building legacy.

As I have done with my other two books on resort hotels, I have intended this undertaking to reach a scholarly as well as a general reading audience. To accomplish this objective I have attempted to present the narrative in a comfortable, readable style, meeting high scholarly standards entailing the use of varied sources, extensive endnotes, and the inclusion of an exhaustive bibliography and index. An essential visual supplement to the text are the many black-and-white and color illustrations, most of which are based on originals housed at libraries, historical societies, museums, and other organizations cited in the acknowledgments section and the illustration credit lines. Without such pictorial documentation, a book such as this one could not achieve its stated objectives.

In conclusion, I wish to underscore two key points. First, this book is intended as a general survey highlighting the most important and representative of coastal New England's large, pre-1950 resort-hotel buildings. Second, the principal focus is on architectural history. The book, while it draws upon and references several other areas of history, is *not* intended as a chronicle of hotel life, with broad social and cultural history underpinnings. Such a study is another book to be written at a future time by another author. I remain satisfied with the thought that readers of this book will gain a better understanding of the New England coastal hospitality industry, the tourism economy that sustained it, and the resort hotel and its glorious, distinctive, and conspicuous architectural statement.

Center Sandwich, New Hampshire   B.F.T., Jr.
May 2007

Acknowledgments

The subject complexity and broad geographical scope of this book necessitated extensive research over a three-year period at a wide variety of libraries, museums, and historical organizations in the Northeast. While I conducted the bulk of this research in person at these repositories, I was also the beneficiary of extensive assistance through postal mail, e-mail, and telephone communications. I wish to express my deep gratitude, therefore, to the many repositories and their staff members and volunteers, as well as to individuals for invaluable aid that made possible the successful researching, writing, and illustration of the final book manuscript.

For materials pertaining to hospitality tourism and resort hotels in all five of the New England coastal states, I consulted relevant collections at the following institutions and organizations: the Hugh M. Morris Library, University of Delaware, Newark (Susan Brynteson, director, and staff); the Fine Arts Library, University of Pennsylvania, Philadelphia (William B. Keller, fine arts librarian); the Winterthur Museum Library, Winterthur, Del. (Emily Guthrie, librarian, printed book and periodical collection); the Athenaeum of Philadelphia, Pa. (Bruce Laverty, curator of architecture); the American Antiquarian Society, Worcester, Mass. (Georgia B. Barnhill, curator of graphics arts, and library staff; Jackie Donovan, rights and reproductions); Historic New England (S.P.N.E.A.) Library, Boston (Lorna Condon, director; Jeanne Gamble, assistant, library and archives); New England Historic Genealogical Society, Boston; the Frances Loeb Design Library, Harvard University, Cambridge, Mass.; the Boston Athenaeum (Sally Pierce, curator of prints); the Benson Ford Research Center, the Henry Ford, Dearborn, Mich. (Jim Orr, images services coordinator); the Hagley Museum and Library, Wilmington, Del.; and the Wilmington Public Library, Del.

I conducted research for the Connecticut chapter of the book primarily at the Connecticut Historical Society Museum, Hartford, with the assistance of library staff and Nancy Finlay, curator of graphics, supplemented by visits to or contacts with numerous libraries and historical societies along the Long Island Sound coastline. These repositories included Mystic Seaport, Mystic (Wendy Schnur and staff, G. W. Blunt White Library; Phillip L. Budlong, associate curator, graphics; Louisa Watrous, intellectual property manager); the New Haven Museum & Historical Society, New Haven (James Campbell and library staff); the New London County Historical Society, New London (Pat Schaeffer); the Historical Society of the Town of Greenwich (Amy Briggs and Anne H. Young, archivists); the Greenwich Library (Karl White, Cathy Ogden, Mary Coff); the Groton Public Library; Carol Kimball, Groton (local historian); New London Landmarks (Sylvia Malizia, archivist); the New London Public Library (Marcia Stuart and staff); the Mystic River Historical Society, Mystic (Dorothy Hanna); the Bridgeport Public Library (Mary Witkowski, head, historical collections); the Guilford Free Library (Penny Colby, Suellen Croteau, Edith Meddleton); the Mystic and Noank Public Library; the Westbrook Public Library; the Fairfield Historical Society (Dennis Barrow, librarian); the Westport

Historical Society (Barbara Raymond); the Westport Public Library (Suzanne Bush, reference); DeForest W. Smith, Milford; the James Blackstone Memorial Library, Branford (Joel Ettinger, reference librarian); the Branford Historical Society (Jane Bouley); the Acton Public Library, Old Saybrook (Michelle Van Epps); the Old Saybrook Historical Society; the Ferguson Library, Stamford (Kate Sheehan, reference); the Stamford Historical Society Library (Ronald Marcus, librarian; Irene Hahn, photo archivist); the Norwalk Museum, South Norwalk (Linda Hayes, archives and reference); the Stonington Free Library (Nancy Young, director); the West Haven Public Library (Peggy Dolan, reference assistant); and the Henry L. Ferguson Museum, Fishers Island, N.Y. (Pierce Rafferty, director).

For assistance in locating and utilizing Rhode Island source materials, I contacted and/or visited the Rhode Island Historical Society, Providence (Karen Eberhart and library staff; Jennifer J. Betts, graphics assistant; J. D. Kay); the John Hay Library, Brown University, Providence (Holly Snyder); the Rhode Island Preservation and Heritage Commission, Providence (Mack Woodward and Jeffry Emidy); the Newport Historical Society (Bertram Lippincott, III, librarian, and staff; N. Joan Youngken, curator of graphics; Kimberly A. Hanrahan, registrar); the Redwood Library and Athenaeum, Newport (Lisa Long and Stacey Lyon, special collections and archives); the Newport Public Library (Sandra Allen, reference assistant); Marlen Scalzi, director of sales and marketing, Hotel Viking, Newport; the Warwick Public Library (Sonita Cummings, reference assistant); Donald DaMotto, Warwick (local historian); the Essex Library, Tiverton (Manny Leite, reference librarian); the Jamestown Philomenian Library (Deborah Homer, reference librarian); the Jamestown Historical Society (Mary Miner and Rosemary Enright); Sue Maden, Jamestown (local historian); the North Kingston Free Library (Susan Berman, assistant director); the South Kingston Public Library, Peacedale (Janice Wilson, librarian); the East Greenwich Free Library (Diane Hogan, reference); the Narragansett Public Library (Joyce Brothers); the Westerly Public Library; the Westerly Historical Society; James Buffum, Weekapaug Inn, Westerly; the Uriah B. Dodge Block Island Free Library (Christine Bowman and staff); the Block Island Historical Society (Ray Batcher); and the Spring House Hotel (David M. Houseman, managing director), Block Island.

I consulted resource materials for the Massachusetts chapters from the Phillips Library, Peabody Essex Museum, Salem (Kathy Flynn, head of reference and public services; Irene Axelrod, head manuscript librarian; Ruth Stewart, head catalogue librarian; Christine G. Michelini, photo services manager); the Massachusetts Historical Society, Boston; the Cape Ann Historical Association, Gloucester (Stephanie Buck, librarian/archivist); the Nantucket Historical Association (Georgen Gilliam Charnes, curator of library and archives; Marie Henke, photo archives specialist); the Wilkens Library, Cape Cod Community College, West Barnstable (Mary Sicchio, archivist); the Edgartown Public Library, Martha's Vineyard (Danguole Budris, reference librarian); the Martha's Vineyard Museum, Edgartown (Peter Van Tassell, librarian; Keith Gorman; Linda Wilson); the Harbor View Hotel of Martha's Vineyard, Edgartown (Karen Candee, director of sales); the Oak Bluffs Library, Martha's Vineyard (Mat Bose and Sally Barker); the Old Dartmouth Historical Society, New Bedford Whaling Museum; the Chatham Historical Society (Spencer Gray, director; Mary Ann Gray, archivist; Nancy Barr, administrator); the Eldredge Public Library, Chatham (Amy Andreasson, reference librarian); the Chatham Bars Inn, Chatham (Linda Kelleher, director of marketing); the Falmouth Public Library; the Falmouth Historical Society (Mary Sicchio, archivist); the Woods Hole Historical Collection and Museum (Susan Witzell, assistant curator); the Brooks Free Library, Harwich (Jo Ann Latimer, reference librarian); the Harwich Historical Society at Brooks Academy Museum, Harwich (Betty Szberenyi, cataloguer); the Dennis Memorial Library Association; the Dennis Historical Society (Burt Derick, librarian); the Cotuit Library (Kathleen Pratt and Barbara Burrow, director); the Jonathan Bourne Public Library, Bourne; the West Yarmouth Public Library (Martha Powers, reference librarian); the Historical Society of Old Yarmouth (Dorothy Henion and Roy Morton); the Sippican Historical and Preservation Society, Marion (Pete Smith); the Hyannis Public Library Association (Carol Saunders, reference librarian); Pilgrim Hall Museum, Plymouth (Peggy M. Baker, librarian); the Plymouth Public Library (Lee Regan, librarian; Christine Cook, history room; Herman Hunt and Sharon LaRosa); the Ventress Memorial Library, Marshfield (Chris Woods, head, reference department); the Marshfield Historical Society (Dottie McMullen); Cynthia H. Krusell, Marshfield town historian; the Scituate Historical Society (Carol Miles, archivist); the Pratt Memorial Library, Cohasset (Gale Walsh, reference); the Cohasset Historical Society (David Wadsworth and Laura Abrams); the Hingham Public Library (Anne Dalton, reference librarian); the Hull Public Library (Daniel Johnson, director; Christina Frederick); John Galluzzo, Hull town historian; the Chelsea Public Library (George Ostler); the Revere Public Library (Robert Rice); the Nahant Public Library (Daniel DeStefano, library director); the Nahant Historical Society (Bonnie D'Orlando, assistant curator); the Lynn Public Library (Joseph Coffill, reference librarian); the Lynn Historical Society (Diane Shephard, librarian); the Swampscott Public Library (Susan M. Conner, assistant director); the Swampscott Historical Society (Mary Cassidy); the Swampscott Historical Commission (Louis Gallo); the Abbot Public Library, Marblehead (Jonathan Randolph, reference); the Marblehead Museum & Historical Society (Karen MacInnis, curator of collections); the Beverly Historical Society & Museum (Sharon Spieldenner, librarian); the Manchester-by-the-Sea Public Library; the Manchester Historical Society (Esther Proctor, librarian); the Magnolia Historical Society, Gloucester (Judy Ann Gilliss, curator; James A. Cook, president); the Gloucester City Archives (Jane Walsh); the Gloucester Lyceum and Sawyer Free Library (Judy Oski); Judy Peterson, Gloucester; the Rockport Public Library (Camilla Ayers); the Sandy Bay Historical Society, Rockport (Cynthia Peckham, curator); Eugene Castellano, Sharpley, Del. (Rockport materials); Kenneth R. Nickerson, Rockport (postcard collection); and the Salisbury Public Library (Terry Kzvos).

For New Hampshire source materials, I sought research assistance from the New Hampshire Historical Society, Concord (William Copeley, librarian; David Smolen, special collections); the New Hampshire Division of Historical Resources, Concord (James L. Garvin, state architectural historian); the Historical Society of Seabrook (Evelyn Foster); the Lane Memorial Library, Hampton (William Teschek); the Hampton Historical Society; the Hampton Falls Free Public Library (Carol Sanborn);

the North Hampton Public Library (Susan J. Tidd); the North Hampton Historical Society (Janet Taylor, director; Priscilla Leavitt, curator); the Rye Public Library; the Rye Historical Society (Bonnie Goodwin, Alex Herlihy); the Portsmouth Public Library (Michael Huxtable, reference); and the Portsmouth Athenaeum (Marcia Jebb, reference; Susan Stowe Kindstedt, archivist).

My research for the Maine chapters was completed largely at the Maine Historic Preservation Commission, Augusta (Earle G. Shettleworth, Jr., director); the Maine State Library, Augusta; and the Maine Historical Society, Portland (Nicholas Noyes, librarian; Christine Albert and Gabrielle Daniello, image services). I also made visits to or had contacts with the Rice Public Library, Kittery (Rachael Armstrong, library director); the Old York Historical Society, York (Tom Johnson, curator; Virginia Spiller, librarian/archivist); the York Public Library (Frank Dahler); the Kennebunkport Historical Society (Sharon Cummins, curator); the Louis T. Graves Memorial Library, Kennebunkport (Linda Wade); the Brick Store Museum, Kennebunk (Rosalind Magnuson, archivist); the Kennebunk Free Library (Janet Cate, director); the Colony Hotel (Dona Kabay, general manager), Kennebunkport; the Old Orchard Beach Historical Society (Evelyn Cooper); the Edith Belle Libby Memorial Library, Old Orchard Beach; the McArthur Public Library, Biddeford (Sally Leahey, assistant director); the Biddeford Historical Society (Charles Butler); the Ogunquit Memorial Library; the Historical Society of Wells and Ogunquit (Jane Edgecomb and Hope Shelley); the Wells Public Library; the Scarborough Public Library (Carolyn Brownhill, reference assistant); the Scarborough Historical Society (Anna M. Delaware); the Black Point Inn, Prout's Neck, Scarborough; the Thomas Memorial Library, Cape Elizabeth; the Cape Elizabeth Historical Preservation Society (Barbara Sanborn); the Portland Public Library, Portland Room; Greater Portland Landmarks, Inc., Portland (Gabrielle Daniello); the Museum of Chebeague History, Chebeague Island, Casco Bay (Donna Daman); the Chebeague Island Library, Casco Bay (Deborah Bowman, director; Martha Hamilton); the Freeport Historical Society (Randall Thomas, director); the Pejepscot Historical Society, Brunswick (Brian Banton, coordinator of education); the Phippsburg Historical Society (Ada Haggett); the Boothbay Harbor

Historical Society (Barbara Rumsey); the Skidompha Public Library, Damarscotta; the Pemaquid-Bristol Area Library, New Harbor (Mimi Aldrich and staff); the South Bristol Historical Society (Ellen Wells, president); the Rutherford Library Association, South Bristol; the Rockland Public Library (Neil Crochetiere, reference); the Rockport Public Library (Priscilla Wood); the Belfast Historical Society and Museum (Megan Pinette); the Belfast Free Library (Betsy Paradis); the Penobscot Marine Mueum, Searsport (John Arrison, director of library and education); the Castine Historical Society (Sara Foote, collections); the Witherle Memorial Library, Castine; the Islesboro Historical Society (Melissa Olson, registrar; Rowland E. Logan, archivist); the Blue Hill Public Library (Erich Reed, assistant librarian); the Mount Desert Island Historical Society (Charlotte Singleton, director); the Jesup Memorial Library, Bar Harbor (Mae Corrion); the Bar Harbor Historical Society (Deborah M. Dyer, director, and Clair Lambert); the Southwest Harbor Public Library, Mount Desert Island (Candy Emlen, Julie Russell, and Charlotte R. Morrill); the Northeast Harbor Library, Mount Desert Island (Tina Hawes and Anna C. Carr); the Winter Harbor Public Library (Janet Fickett and Allan Smallidge); Sanford E. Phippen, Hancock; the Fairmount Algonquin Hotel, St. Andrews, New Brunswick, Canada (Lisa Sampson); and David Sullivan, St. Andrews, New Brunswick (author of *The Algonquin, St. Andrews, N.B.*, 2005).

I would also like to acknowledge with much appreciation the assistance of the following individuals: Alison Brayfield, administrative assistant, Museum Studies Program, University of Delaware; and George Freeman, Image Master, associated with the Art History Department, University of Delaware, for his superb photographic print work. In addition, I am most grateful to the following good friends who provided accommodations and hospitality to my wife and me while I was on research visits to New England: John and Joan Butler (Mystic, Conn.), Charles and Ethel Hamann (Belmont, Mass.), Stephanie Woolf (Rockport, Mass.), Jim and Felicity Bowditch (Camden, Maine), Greg and Sandy Downes (Milton, Mass.), Chuck and Joanne Gibson (Concord, Mass.), Sandy Armentrout (Kennebunk, Maine), George and Sandy Esser (Fishers Island, N.Y.), Dick and Beverly Hughes (West Hartford, Conn.), John and Deanie Davison (West Hartford, Conn.), and my wife's sister, Cynthia Kimball (Lexington, Mass.). Lastly and most significantly, I would like to offer profuse thanks to my wife, Carolyn, for her useful critical comments, for listening to my readings of the text, for orchestrating the illustrations permission process, and for her enthusiastic support and encouragement, which helped make this book project such a pleasant and rewarding undertaking. I also would like to extend my appreciation to those individuals whom I did not name specifically or whom I inadvertently overlooked.

SUMMER BY THE SEASIDE

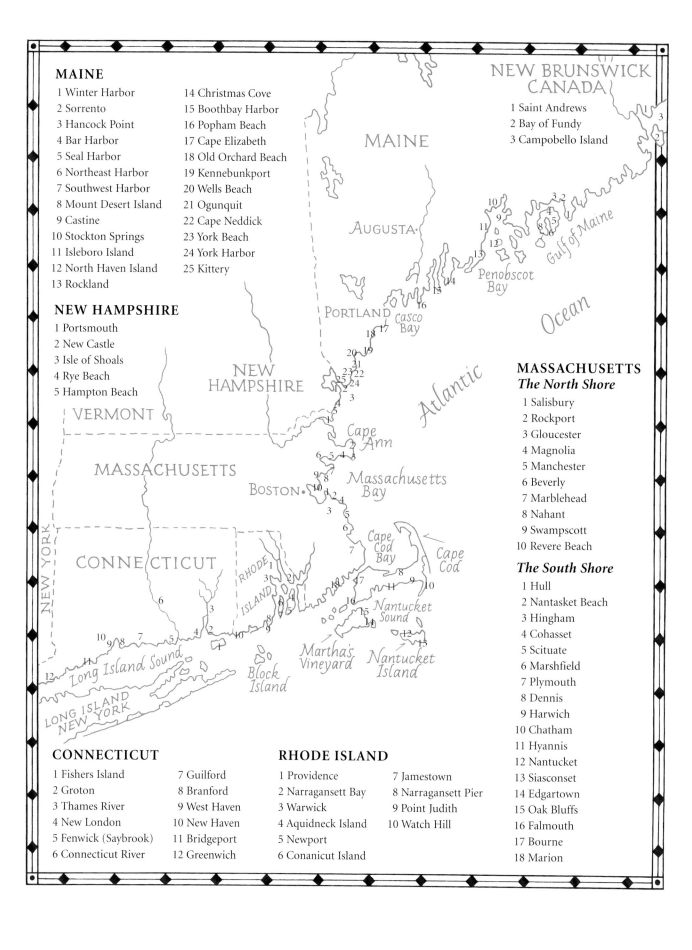

MAINE

1 Winter Harbor
2 Sorrento
3 Hancock Point
4 Bar Harbor
5 Seal Harbor
6 Northeast Harbor
7 Southwest Harbor
8 Mount Desert Island
9 Castine
10 Stockton Springs
11 Isleboro Island
12 North Haven Island
13 Rockland
14 Christmas Cove
15 Boothbay Harbor
16 Popham Beach
17 Cape Elizabeth
18 Old Orchard Beach
19 Kennebunkport
20 Wells Beach
21 Ogunquit
22 Cape Neddick
23 York Beach
24 York Harbor
25 Kittery

NEW HAMPSHIRE

1 Portsmouth
2 New Castle
3 Isle of Shoals
4 Rye Beach
5 Hampton Beach

NEW BRUNSWICK CANADA

1 Saint Andrews
2 Bay of Fundy
3 Campobello Island

MASSACHUSETTS
The North Shore

1 Salisbury
2 Rockport
3 Gloucester
4 Magnolia
5 Manchester
6 Beverly
7 Marblehead
8 Nahant
9 Swampscott
10 Revere Beach

The South Shore

1 Hull
2 Nantasket Beach
3 Hingham
4 Cohasset
5 Scituate
6 Marshfield
7 Plymouth
8 Dennis
9 Harwich
10 Chatham
11 Hyannis
12 Nantucket
13 Siasconset
14 Edgartown
15 Oak Bluffs
16 Falmouth
17 Bourne
18 Marion

CONNECTICUT

1 Fishers Island
2 Groton
3 Thames River
4 New London
5 Fenwick (Saybrook)
6 Connecticut River
7 Guilford
8 Branford
9 West Haven
10 New Haven
11 Bridgeport
12 Greenwich

RHODE ISLAND

1 Providence
2 Narragansett Bay
3 Warwick
4 Aquidneck Island
5 Newport
6 Conanicut Island
7 Jamestown
8 Narragansett Pier
9 Point Judith
10 Watch Hill

INTRODUCTION

The American Resort Hotel and Its Expression
on the New England Coast

NEARLY TWO CENTURIES have passed since the first resort communities and their most conspicuous architectural expression, the resort hotel, began to appear along the New England coast, providing opportunities for leisure, social interaction, recreation, intellectual engagement, and other forms of pleasure and relaxation. In recent years, the story of their beginnings and subsequent development has become recognized more than ever before as essential to our understanding of nineteenth- and early twentieth-century American life, and its social, cultural, economic, intellectual, and artistic heritage. Furthermore, there is broad agreement that without full appreciation of the resort phenomenon and its hotel centerpiece, a proper perception of American tourism and the hospitality industry cannot be fully achieved. In the most general terms, an examination of the resort hotel can lead to "a better understanding of themes and patterns associated with America's evolution as a society, national cultural qualities, and national values."[1] Architect/scholar Jeffery W. Limerick has offered a further perspective of value in the coauthored book *America's Grand Resort Hotels*, the first publication of real substance to be written on the topic:

By looking at the resorts, one can appreciate the impact of new means of transportation and technological innovations; the American attraction to novelty and fashion; the changes in American attitudes toward nature and landscape; and the connection between architectural styles and cultural aspirations.[2]

As I have stated in my other books (see bibliography) treating resort hotels in the Northeast since the late eighteenth century, Americans, following the earlier European example, have embraced the travel and vacation ritual with the aim of providing "aesthetic and intellectual stimulation, religious enlightenment, improved physical and mental well-being, social interaction, recreational involvement and change from routine life habits."[3] Resort life and its trappings were of particular appeal to the financially secure who sought contact with other people from comparable economic and social backgrounds, or who aspired to improve their social position. The larger hotels, especially the immense, lavish establishments classified as "grand" (see preface), tended to attract "the affluent and career accomplished, such as socialites, the leaders of business and industry, high government officials, representatives of the professions, and also opportunists with a variety of motivations."[4] Hence, in most instances, the Ameri-

Fig. 1-1. "Indian Harbor Hotel, Greenwich, Conn." Trade advertisement, 1884. William E. Finch, Jr. Archives, Historical Society of the Town of Greenwich.

can resort hotel, with its extensive verandas (also often referred to as "piazzas"), other large public spaces, and recreational areas offered guests a stagelike environment for display of wealth, social position, and fashion, and for critical observation of others who shared their motivations. Certain New England seaside hotels, like many in other regions of the country, placed great emphasis on this social ritual and its attendant lifestyle, while others were more self-contained and retreat-like, offering their patrons greater privacy and independence. As they continue to do today, Americans then, depending on personal preferences, chose from a variety of social settings provided by the hospitality industry. Over time, however, there has been general agreement that exclusiveness, and an aura of romance and escape, are highly important components of the resort hotel experience.

As a building type, American resort hotels, almost without exception, were planned to provide their clients with a sense of privacy and insularity in an environment that was comfortable, visually appealing, and highly efficient, as well as invigorating and entertaining. As Limerick has pointed out, though resort hotels shared many common qualities, most were planned "to answer the needs of a particular time and place and to live up to the expectations of a particular clientele."[5] In considering American resort-hotel history, however, it must be understood that the structures themselves, largely erected in short time frames for quick profit, were highly vulnerable to fire or demolition, ever-changing guest preferences, competition within the tourism industry, and the inevitable ups and downs of the national econ-

omy. As was the case with most other resort hotels in the Northeast, those situated along the New England shoreline, with only a few exceptions, were of fragile wood construction, suggesting that they would have limited life spans. It should not be a surprising disclosure, therefore, that the great majority of the country's large resort hotels (as defined in the preface) that were built before 1950 have failed to survive into the twenty-first century. Those that exist in our time, and still serve hospitality needs, have successfully combined older architectural, environmental, and operational traditions with the need for constant change, a reality that is reflected in their physical appearance, interior décor, services, amenities, and the surrounding outdoor landscape or seascape. Along the New England seacoast, fewer than ten large resort-hotel buildings predating World War II still exist, though in modified form, and only four of these continue to house active hospitality enterprises.

Again referencing Limerick's groundbreaking work, it should be understood that grand hotels, including those of somewhat smaller capacity, possessed what he refers to as "two seemingly contradictory characteristics."[6] First, these notable guest establishments were committed to offering their customers novel visitation experiences that were in stark contrast to their standardized, ritualistic urban and suburban lives, and satisfied their vision of the ideal summer vacation experience. Those drawn

Fig. 1-2. "Pequot House, New London, Conn." Lithograph from a photo by Bolles & Frisbie, New London, Conn., from F. W. Beers, *Atlas of New London County, Connecticut* (1868). The Connecticut Historical Society Museum, Hartford, Connecticut.

to New England shoreline resorts sought to achieve the pure, relaxed, and unspoiled life, if only momentarily, through physical and sensory contact with the sea and its unique attributes and offerings. Second, as hotels focused on the expectations of their guests, they had to meet the highest business standards, maintaining high advertising visibility and generating profits for their owners. To survive in the fiercely competitive hotel marketplace and satisfy customer demand, nineteenth-century resort hotels adopted and marketed the most current technology in equipment and other conveniences—elevators, telegraph communications, telephone and signal bell systems, gas and ultimately electric lighting, improved fireplaces, steam heat, box-spring mattresses, improved sanitation systems, and hot and cold running water, the latter sometimes fresh from lakes or mountain streams or salt water piped directly from the ocean. Amazingly, many of these technological advances were present in hotel settings before they appeared in American homes or other places of business enterprise.

Ever since their initial appearance, the large American resort hotels, particularly the luxurious grand examples, have had great appeal, not only to guests, but also to general aficionados, students of business administration and tourism, and scholars of architectural and general history. As my other books have noted, the most compelling reasons for this are the hotels' unique architectural character, romantic associations, and engrossing natural surroundings. Influenced by foreign cultures, hotel complexes were frequently designed in a variety of intriguing eclectic styles, which, while strong architectural statements, were successfully integrated into the landscape. In many instances, they embodied national, and even regional and local, cultural traditions. On the New England coastline, the first hotels, dating from the 1820s to the 1850s, were conceived either as strongly vernacular, expanded residential-type buildings, or incorporated early revival styles such as the Greek, Gothic, or Italian, or amalgamations of these design modes. Resort hotel architecture following the Civil War incorporated a variety of mid- and late Victorian eclectic styles, the most common being the French Second Empire (Mansard), Stick, English Queen Anne, late Italianate, Shingle, Colonial Revival, and Arts and Crafts (Craftsman). On the New England seaboard, most of these styles were

Fig. 1-3. "Ocean House Polka." Sheet music cover (c. 1860), with J. H. Bufford's lithograph of the second Ocean House, Newport, R.I. Courtesy of The Newport Historical Society, R.I.

Fig. 1-4. The Mathewson Hotel, Narragansett Pier, R.I. Photograph, c. 1898, from the southeast with the Casino and Towers. North Kingston Free Library, Lawrence Collection.

Fig. 1-5. "The Hotel Nantasket and Rockland Café," Nantasket Beach, Hull, Mass. Lithograph from *King's Handbook of Boston Harbor* (1882), p. 57. Courtesy The Winterthur Library Printed Book and Periodical Collection.

Fig. 1-6. "Chatham Bars Inn, Chatham, Mass." Photograph from *DeLuxe Hotels of New England* (1915 ed.). Author's collection.

represented, with unusually outstanding examples in all five ocean states. Although the Second Empire style was most frequently employed, also present were sterling examples of the Stick, Queen Anne, Shingle, and Colonial Revival vernaculars. By and large, coastal hotel structures, unlike many located at inland areas of the Northeast, were planned to be impressive, forceful, and skillfully articulated architectural standouts, dominating yet usually relating positively to the local environment. Among the most prominent and representative grand hotel examples were the Hotel Griswold, Groton, Connecticut; the Mathewson, Narragansett Pier, Rhode Island; the Colonial Arms, Gloucester, and the second New Ocean House, Swampscott, both in Massachusetts; the Wentworth Hotel, New Castle, New Hampshire; and the Colony Inn (formerly Breakwater Court), Kennebunkport, and the Samoset Hotel, Rockland, both in Maine. All are discussed in depth and illustrated in subsequent chapters of this book.

Traditionally, the siting and design of American resort hotels has been strongly influenced by qualities of landscape or seascape, with special accounting for unusually fine natural settings and panoramic viewpoints. As much if not even more so than the hotels of the interior lake and mountain regions, those located on the coast had a singular frontal focus on a paramount natural fea-

Fig. 1-7. "Aerial View, New Ocean House and Puritan Hall, Swampscott, Mass." Colored postcard, c. 1925. Author's collection.

Fig. 1-8. The Oceanside Hotel, Magnolia, Mass. Lithograph, c. 1910. The Magnolia Historical Society.

ture—the ocean, with its infinite, constantly changing visual forms, weather patterns, and evidence of human utilization and enjoyment. Recognizing this primary focus, the developers and architects/builders of New England shoreline hostelries positioned them close to and oriented their main or front façades toward the sea, concentrating the primary architectural elements and decorative features on the façades themselves. Adopting the practice of southern plantation and town houses, the coastal hotels, commencing with the first examples, displayed extensive verandas or piazzas attached to their front façades and other walls. These provided patrons with protected outdoor space for relaxation and social and physical activity, as well as opportunities to connect through sound and sight with the natural world. In addition, as illustrated throughout this book, architects and contractors, in determining floor plans for public areas and guest quarters, customarily arranged rooms along central, double-loaded corridors in an effort to maintain outside window views of the seascape and the life of the resort community. Essential to the success of the shoreline hotel was the positive interrelationship between the man-made and the features and powers of nature, where the "tourist's experience of nature . . . [was] tempered by the comfort and luxury of the resort hotel itself."[7]

As previously alluded to, resort hotels, for the most part, were operated as conservative business enterprises, with constant attention to the "bottom line." An understandable outgrowth of this concern was the effort by local developers to construct architecturally conservative, low-cost structures of the vernacular type that still provided an aesthetically pleasing and socially gratifying, service-oriented environment for their patrons. This practice did not, of course, preclude the possibility of the highest-quality architectural design and structural engineering, as was evident at so many New England coastal hotels. "The key to successful aesthetic and functional impact and a pleasurable guest experience was the combination of imposing size, visual appeal, and properly configured and furnished interior spaces."[8] Along the New England shoreline, this was achieved in an extraordinary number of instances, whether buildings were designed by professional architects or by those who doubled as planners and contractors, working directly with owners and financiers to successfully realize building projects. Resort hotels, or additions to them, were often a direct product of prosperous economic times, available investment capital, and the desire to enter the hospitality market as quickly as possible and maximize occupancy. Frequently, those structures erected over short time frames were unsophisticated and vernacular in form, and lacked the design quality of those built less hurriedly over longer periods. Excellent regional examples formerly existed at Narragansett Pier, Rhode Island, and Old Orchard Beach, Maine, where numerous, modest, quasi-vernacular hotels, influenced by the Second Empire and other styles, were built between the late 1860s and 1880s. Such conventional, very functional structures, when combined with their high-style counterparts, comprise a worthy architectural legacy, which is best viewed from a broader regional and national historical perspective.

Fig. 1-9. Harbor Façade, Colonial Arms Hotel, Eastern Point, Gloucester, Mass. Photograph, Ernest L. Blatchford Collection, c. 1905. CAPE ANN HISTORICAL ASSOCIATION, Gloucester, Massachusetts.

Therefore, to establish a firm contextual foundation for an intensive discussion of pre-1950 New England coastal resort hotels in the ensuing chapters, it is essential to briefly trace the origins and development of the hotel building type in the United States over a century-long period beginning in the early 1800s. From this building type's initial appearance in this country, America assumed a leadership role on a worldwide basis. With the much older city, town, and highway inns or taverns establishing precedent, the first hotels of the nation appeared in the late eighteenth century. Quickly becoming centers of community life, these new, expanded facilities contained lounges, dining halls, ballrooms, and other public spaces, in addition to more traditional areas devoted to guest lodging and food service. As travel increased and the hospitality business expanded, the need arose for larger and more specialized guest establishments modeled on European urban prototypes. Usually cited as early, prominent examples of the building type are the New York City Hotel (1794), Asher Benjamin's Exchange Coffee House (1807) in Boston,

the City Hotel in Baltimore (1824), and Isaiah Rogers' Tremont House, also in Boston (1829). On the New England coastline, forerunners to the later, more modern resort hotels began to appear as early as the 1820s, but they lacked the influence of such urban-based hotels and the new thinking that determined both their form and function. This would gradually change, however.

Because of their groundbreaking contribution to innovative and efficient hotel design, two hotel structures, both in the Northeast, merit close scrutiny. Historians are in general agreement that the construction and opening of Rogers' Tremont House signaled the beginning of U.S. preeminence in the development of the modern hotel. Among its most innovative features, the Tremont contained the world's first self-contained lobby (lounge) and adjacent office, a spacious dining room, a self-contained barroom, a subscription library, other elegant public rooms, private lockable bedrooms, indoor privies and bathing rooms, and a garden supplanting the traditional horse stable yard. Soon after the Tremont was premiered to the public, fur and real estate mogul John Jacob As-

Fig. 1-10. "The Wentworth, New Castle, N.H." Sheet music cover, Bournique's, Chicago, 1892. Wentworth-by-the-Sea Collection, Portsmouth Athenaeum.

tor contracted with Rogers to design and supervise the construction of an even larger, better appointed hotel in New York City. Known as the Astor House, as expected it displayed many of the same features as the Tremont House but also introduced an astounding innovation for its time—a new version of the steam pump that raised water vertically to the privies and bathing rooms on the upper guest bedroom floors. As pioneering enterprises, these two building projects "established the arenas for competition among hotels that have lasted to the present: size, fashionable styling and décor, and the latest in technical and convenience gadgetry."[9] In the Tremont and the Astor, and the more ambitious hotels that followed them, architectural style, building technology, and site were combined to provide stimulating, enriching venues for myriad expressions of human activity.

Although modest numbers of Americans pursued leisure-time travel to mineral springs, spas, and other rural attractions prior to 1820, during the next two decades vacation lifestyle habits underwent change as a result of improved means of transportation and new attitudes toward nature, recreation, and social interaction. During the 1830s and 1840s, hotels, adopting many features of the Tremont, the Astor, and other urban examples, began to appear at the most desirable and accessible mountain, lake, and seaside locations, principally in the Northeast. People seeking tourism and the resort experience were drawn by "a new romantic fascination in spirituality, ethical and moral standards, healthfulness and landscape."[10] Among the most recognized of the new focal points of summer resort life were Cape May and Long Branch, New Jersey; Saratoga Springs and Ballston Spa, New York; Nahant, Massachusetts (see chapter 5); and Newport, Rhode Island (see chapter 3). Perhaps the most prominent and representative early resort center was a single hotel, the Catskill Mountain House (1822–23, etc.), just west of New York's Hudson River Valley, which developed in stages in the Greek Revival mode to achieve a status equivalent to that of the best city hostelries in the Northeast. This legendary establishment, and the few other hotels of its size and type, shared common characteristics that set the stan-

Fig. 1-11. Appledore House, Appledore Island, Isles of Shoals, Maine.
Photograph, c. 1900. Courtesy of Peabody Essex Museum.

dard for the larger and even more extravagant hotels that would eventually follow them — multifaceted and nearly self-contained operations; corporate ownership or partnership, as opposed to individual ownership; imposing physical size and architectural presence; wooden frame construction, siding, and detailing; and interiors reflecting assiduous planning and concern for the wishes of the vacation consumer.

The national interest in tourism and the leisure-time experience continued to grow in the 1840s and 1850s, largely because of the introduction of new and efficient forms of transportation, providing greatly improved linkages with areas removed from major population centers. Vital to the success of the coastal resorts of New England was the establishment of steamboat service connecting New York City and other, smaller cities with burgeoning resort communities all along the coast and on the offshore islands. At the same time, inland access was achieved through several waterways, the primary being from New York up the Hudson River to Lake George, Lake Champlain, the Adirondacks, the Saint Lawrence

River, and the Thousand Islands. Having an even greater impact on the growing tourism economy and supplementing gravel roads were new railroad routes that extended along the coastline between Maine and Georgia and also reached inland areas with resort potential such as the southern and central Appalachian Mountains, and the lakes and mountains of upstate New York and northern New England. Later in the nineteenth century, major rail lines like the New York and New Haven, the Eastern, the Boston and Maine, and the Maine Central ran along the New England seacoast and linked major population centers and resort communities, thereby enhancing resort development. Aided by such transportation innovation, pioneering resort communities like Saratoga Springs, Long Branch, and Cape May established their own special identities, attracting distinct groups of tourists seeking the atmosphere and social, recreational, and entertainment options that each one promoted and made available. Correspondingly, resort hotel complexes became much more lavish and larger in size, the most often cited and extreme being the Mount Vernon Hotel

(1852–53) at Cape May, in fully developed form boasting space for 2,000 guests. Departing from their initial rectangular, single-corridor configuration, floor plans became far more expansive and complicated, assuming L, E, T, U, and H shapes. On the New England coast, this pre–Civil War advancing concept of the large resort hotel could be observed in several examples, including the second Ocean House (1845–46, etc.) at Newport, Rhode Island (see chapter 3), the Appledore House (1847–48, etc.) at the Isles of Shoals off New Hampshire (see chapter 6), the Rockland House (1854, etc.) at Nantasket Beach, Massachusetts (see chapter 4), and the first Old Orchard House (1860, etc.) at Old Orchard Beach, Maine (see chapter 7).

In the years immediately following the Civil War, the United States entered an era of all-encompassing change, marked by rapidly advancing industrialization, growth in areas of business enterprise, and urbanization, broadly affecting American society and lifestyle attitudes and habits. Personal wealth grew, which caused people to pursue more materialistic existences, and social as well as economic power. As a consequence, leisure-time pursuits became possible for an enlarged segment of the American population. Recovering from the trauma of the war, the American citizenry looked for cultural inspiration from Europe and the idealized, democratic American past. Blessed with newly found financial security, status, as well as leisure time, many sought to escape the now highly competitive and faster-paced lifestyle by immersion in more idealized, rewarding, optimistic, and relaxing environments offered by the developing resort communities and their specialized type of hotel building. Not surprisingly, resort architecture of all classifications dating from the mid-1860s to the late 1870s conveyed images of "the unusual, the cosmopolitan, the exotic and the picturesque."[11] Most often mentioned as best representative of this trend is Saratoga Springs, which during this era became the nation's most visible, popular, and sumptuous inland resort center — a magnet for an eclectic blend of summer visitors seeking to display their economic and social prominence, engage in the summer vacation ritual, and immerse themselves in the customary array of recreational and entertainment pursuits. Satisfying the needs of this demanding clientele were several immense, wooden guest establishments, led by the largest, the mansard-roofed Grand Union Hotel

Fig. 1-12. Ocean Bluff Hotel, Cape Arundel, Kennebunkport, Maine. Photograph, c. 1890. The Brick Store Museum, Kennebunk, ME.

Fig. 1-13. "Old Orchard House, Old Orchard Beach, Me.—E. C. Staples, Proprietor." Lithograph from booklet, *Boston & Maine and Maine Central Summer Resorts* (c. 1891), p. 88. Author's collection.

(1874, etc.), consistently promoted as the grandest hotel of its time in the country. Its primary rival at Saratoga for elaborate architecture and extravagant ambience was the United States Hotel, coincidentally reopened the same year.[12] In the five New England states with ocean coastline, the most illustrious examples of this period, intended to satisfy the vacation urge for self-display, included Fenwick Hall (1870–71, etc.) at the Fenwick Colony in Saybrook, Connecticut (see chapter 2); the Larkin House (1869, etc.) at Watch Hill, Rhode Island (see chapter 3); the Oceanside and Cottages (1877, etc.) at Magnolia, Gloucester, Massachusetts (see chapter 4); the Wentworth Hotel (1873–74, etc.) at New Castle, New Hampshire (see chapter 6); and the first Marshall House (1870–71) at York and the Rodick House (1866, etc.) at Bar Harbor, both in Maine (see chapters 7 and 8).

An influential Victorian eclectic style in vogue from the 1860s to 1890 was the Stick, characterized by wood-frame construction, asymmetrical plan and cross section, balloon framing, and applied exterior ornamentation intended to reflect the inner structure of build-

ings. Although it was employed primarily in American residential architecture, it also appeared in other building types, including resort hotels, related pavilions, and other outbuildings. Used very selectively in hotel design, resulting in a modest number of quality examples, it still left a significant legacy. Open and airy, with a proliferation of porches and verandas, it was well suited to the seaside environment with its constant, presumed healthful sun exposure and cooling ocean breezes. Formerly, the New England seaboard boasted several superlative Stick-style resort-hotel structures: Fenwick Hall in Connecticut (see above); the Sea View House (1871–72) at Oak Bluffs, Martha's Vineyard, and the Hotel Nantasket (1879, etc.) at Nantasket Beach, both in Massachusetts (see chapter 4); and the Hotel Fiske (1882, etc.) at Old Orchard Beach and the West End Hotel (c. 1870, etc.) at Bar Harbor, both in Maine (see chapters 7 and 8).

In the fifteen years following the Civil War, numerous Americans, seeking to identify with the less complex, morally uplifting life of the colonial era, developed an interest in older resort communities, particularly those situated in the inland and seacoast regions of New England. In their quest for the best of the romanticized colonial past and pristine retreats from life's daily demands, people were inevitably attracted to vacation hotels and cottages that were plain and often quite vernacular in both form and style, and that satisfied their desires for nostalgia and identification with the historical past. A contrasting architectural style to the popular Second Empire and the Stick, and drawing from a different cultural tradition, was the American version of the English Queen Anne, in many respects ideal for the period and lifestyle desired by increasing numbers of American citizens. Characterized by irregularity in plan and massing, this vibrant design mode featured imaginative mixtures of different roof shapes, gables, brackets, turrets, towers, cupolas, complex chimneys, pinnacles, balconies, and wide verandas, occasionally on two or more levels. Wall siding consisted of various juxtaposed materials such as wood shingles and/or clapboards, stone, brick, lattice screening, and stickwork. In the Northeast, notable hotel buildings adopting this predominantly residential style were the Manhattan Beach (1877, etc.) and Oriental (1879, etc.) at Coney Island, New York; the Chalfonte (1867, etc.) at Cape May, New Jersey; Wentworth Hall and Cottages (1869, 1880s, etc.) and the second Glen House (1885–87) in New Hampshire's White Mountains; and the Prospect House (1880–82) and the first (1882–83) and second (1893–94) Sagamore Hotels in the Adirondack region of New York State. Although the numerous expressions of the Queen Anne in New England coastal hotel architecture were more modest-size structures, one can point to six well-executed, large examples: Farragut House (1882–83) at Rye Beach, New Hampshire (see chapter 6); the new Magnolia Hotel (1890–91) and the Oceanside and Cottages (1877, etc.) at Magnolia, Gloucester, in Massachusetts (see chapter 5); and the Jocelyn House (1890, etc.) at Prouts Neck, the Bluffs (c. 1885) at Mount Desert Ferry, and the Seaside Inn (1891) at Seal Harbor, Mount Desert Island, all three in Maine (see chapters 7 and 8).

From the late 1870s to the mid-1880s, as competition in the hospitality industry accelerated, hotel construction increased, particularly that of the larger grand resort hotels, as the building type and the vacation ritual became more a part of mainstream American life. This golden era of American vacation resorts would last until the arrival of the twentieth century. Over these two eventful decades, hotels of all types, whether they were located in urban or rural settings, assumed larger proportions than ever before and displayed new interpretations, some in combination, of design styles. Following the 1876 national centennial, the United States saw accelerated economic and population growth, along with further advances in technology and increased personal mobility. There was also evidence of increasing social stratification. In the hospitality tourism business, the combination of the newly wealthy and the older social elite significantly broadened the resort hotel customer base. Like their pre–Civil War forerunners, the hostelries of the eighties and nineties also functioned as perfect staging grounds for social competition and, in contrast, as retreats where people could find relief from the stressful, less desirable aspects of their lives brought on by more demanding living patterns.

After experiencing the economic downturn of the 1870s and the subsequent recovery, Americans embraced the resort hotel experience for reasons that were well beyond the traditional list of guest offerings and amenities. By the 1880s, the public interest in sound health and physical fitness, pursued through outdoor recreation and athletic participation, became a national passion. Resort hotels with inland as well as seaside locations proved to be ideal venues for fulfillment of romanticized versions of these activities. Supplementing the older, entrenched practices of veranda promenading, the seeking of cures,

Fig. 1-14. Hotel Cushing's Island (Ottawa House), Cushing's Island, Casco Bay, Maine. Lithograph from booklet, *Summer Resorts Reached by the Grand Truck Railroad and Its Connections* (1888), p. 11. Author's collection.

Fig. 1-15. "The Algonquin Hotel, St. Andrews, N.B.," Canada. Lithograph from booklet, *New England's Summer and America's Leading Winter Resorts* (1897). Author's collection.

and other equally sedentary pursuits was an eclectic array of outdoor activities, namely hiking, swimming, bicycling, horseback riding, hunting, fishing, rowing, and sailing. Listed among the more organized and competitive sports were golf, tennis, bowling, croquet, baseball, archery, polo, and badminton. Beginning in the mid-1890s, many of the coastal New England hotels owned and maintained, or had access to, golf courses on or within easy distance of their properties. Another major public interest, for which the hotels made appropriate physical and programmatic adjustments, was automobile touring, appearing about 1900 and widely advertised in travel literature.

At the ocean resorts, however, the all-pervading obsession was the sea — its mental and physical benefits and swimming, surfing, sunbathing, boating, fishing, and other pursuits that captivated the visiting public. Not surprisingly, the healthful qualities of seawater and sea air were strongly emphasized by the hotels themselves. For many, particularly city dwellers, such resorts offered "a return to the pristine charms of nature in their most harmonious setting."[13]

As competition within the summer resort field continued to increase in the 1880s and 1890s, American resort hotels, most notably those of "grand" proportions and pretense, strived to achieve individual identity by abandoning the Queen Anne and most older styles for new, "modern" expressions of architectural design. Still, they maintained many traditional characteristics in common such as low-rise, horizontal massing and interior floor plans where the main or first floor contained public and staff work spaces, and the floors above private sleeping rooms, some arranged in suites, and bathrooms, configured along double-loaded corridors. To describe this phase of resort hotel history, Limerick has employed the phrase "visual age," as owners, financiers, managers, architects, and contractors concerned with aesthetics and atmosphere endeavored "to create unique, pleasure-providing hotel complexes that embodied fantasy, glamour, picturesqueness, remoteness and affinity with the natural world."[14]

During this time, resort hotels in the United States demonstrated a rather remarkable facility in marketing and information dissemination, taking full advantage of new methods of graphic reproduction. The New England seaboard hostelries, consistent with the national practice, successfully connected with their potential customer base through self-generated broadsides, brochures, booklets, and viewbooks, as well as newspaper, magazine, and tourist guidebook essays, entries, and advertising. Supplementing the printed word was generous visual illustration (engravings, lithographs, and photographs) that conveyed selective and stylized images that built on the printed word and further captured the attention and imagination of the reading and viewing public. Artist-conceived landscape and seascape paintings, as well as printed views, played a similar role. This form of outreach, when combined with the appealing realism of the resort hotel environment, proved to be a highly effective educational resource, attracting many to commit to the lure, mystique, and practical benefits of resort life. By marketing through publications, hotels presented themselves as symbolic centers of national as well as personal culture and accomplishment, underscoring the best in technology, building techniques, and management practices upon which their creation and subsequent success were founded. An outstanding New England coastline example was the huge Samoset Hotel (1888–89, etc.) at Rockland, Maine (see chapter 8), during its lengthy tenure a master at advertising and information circulation, an embodiment of the best and most up-to-date physical plant and operational practices, and an industry leader in orchestrating the optimal visitor experience.

By the end of the 1880s, American architects, departing from the Queen Anne and other styles then current, began to show in their work the influence of more palatial and older architectural styles of Europe, modifying them to fit the American cultural scene. In returning to traditional architectural standards and perceptions of beauty, they emulated the classical, academic design principles of Richard Morris Hunt and the Ecole des Beaux-Arts in Paris and applied them to a range of large building types, including office and commercial complexes, government facilities, libraries, academic structures, railroad stations, and hotels. At certain American resort centers, most notably in the Southwest, California, and Florida, hotels raised after 1890 often took the form of Mediterranean country villas, Italian or Spanish Renaissance palaces, Moorish castles, or French châteaux. The Northeast, however, did not generally follow this trend, and hotels along the New England coast continued to reflect the legacy of the Queen Anne and other time-tested styles, often in combination.

Choosing not to adhere to the new interest in European-originated styles, many American architects of the period, most certainly in New England, adhered to American national design traditions. Reflecting pride in their country's cultural heritage, they employed colonial-era motifs in imaginative ways to create building forms in a novel and popular new style, the "Shingle," the formal name conceived by architectural historian Vincent J. Scully, Jr., during the 1950s.[15] These architects, as well as other professional colleagues, also launched the Colonial Revival, which expressed certain traits of the Ecole des Beaux-Arts, the Shingle style, and even the more recent Arts and Crafts movement. This second, widely influential style, so popular in residential and particularly summer cottage architecture, became best known for its well-conceived proportions and beautifully articulated classical features. Both the Shingle and the Colonial Revival were impressively represented in numerous hotels on the New England coast well into the twentieth century. Superlative regional examples of the Shingle style were the Edgewood Inn (1901–2) at Greenwich, Connecticut (see chapter 2); the Mathewson (1868, 1895–96, etc.) at Narragansett Pier, and the Hotel Thorndike (1889–90) at Jamestown, both in Rhode Island (see chapter 3); the Hotel Chatham (1889–90, etc.) at Chatham, Cape Cod, Massachusetts (see chapter 4); and, the second Ottawa House (1888) on Cushing's Island, Casco Bay near Portland, and the Passaconaway Inn (1893) at York Cliffs, both in Maine (see chapters 7 and 8). The Colonial Revival displayed its best features, sometimes in combination with the Shingle, at the Chatham Bars Inn (1913–14, etc.) at Chatham, the Rockmere Inn (1901, etc.) at Marblehead, the Turk's Head Inn (c. 1889–90, etc.) at Rockport, the New Ocean House (c. 1883–84, etc.) at Swampscott, and the Colonial Arms (1903–4) at Eastern Point, Gloucester, all in Massachusetts (see chapters 4 and 5).

At the same time that American resort hotels were adopting new styles and taking on greater planning complexity and size, ownership, particularly of the grand hotels, passed increasingly to wealthy investors and management groups. Many hotel ventures, nevertheless, remained under the control of families or individuals, continuing traditional ownership patterns. The clientele of the larger, more opulent guest establishments became more affluent and cosmopolitan, including people from all across the country as well as abroad. To satisfy the resulting high expectations, social, cultural, recreational, dining, and other services became more extensive and sophisticated. Many resort hotels transitioned to virtual self-contained, independent communities, and expanding an older practice, main complexes became supplemented by a variety of smaller outbuildings performing specialized functions. This group comprised guest annexes and cottages, staff dormitories, manager's residences, horse barns and automobile garages, kitchen and storage facilities, and other building types. Such insular cities of hospitality were unmistakable reflections of the growing, more complicated nature of large-hotel operations (and, in many instances, of much smaller hotels) as the resort industry attempted to further advance its fortunes in the twentieth century. Figuratively speaking, however, storm clouds were forming on the horizon. Ironically, this expansion trend and the financial pressures it created became a major factor in the long and arduous decline of the large resort-hotel industry in the New England coastal region and other areas of the United States from 1900 to 1950 (see chapter 8).[16]

The remarkable era of large resort hotels on the New England coast has all but ended, but it can be stated with certitude that it has constituted a major phenomenon in the economic, social, cultural, intellectual, and architectural history of the New England region since the early nineteenth century. As a prominent and multifaceted architectural statement, the resort hotel and the various images it conjures up will long be with us, and will continue to influence our perceptions of our regional and national past. While the hospitality tourism–based economy continues to remain dominant on New England's Atlantic seaboard, its origins remain forever lodged in another time, when the resort industry, based on leisure, recreation, and pleasure, was in its earliest but advancing stages. Organized by geographical districts, the remaining seven chapters of this book systematically treat New England coastal resort communities, their highly specialized large-hotel architecture, and the continuing legacy that has provided guidance and inspiration to modern regional hospitality enterprise.

CONNECTICUT

The Long Island Sound Shoreline

FORMING THE SOUTHERN BOUNDARY of New England, the Connecticut shore-line stretches for over 130 miles from West Chester County, New York, to Rhode Island. While less extensive than in the other New England coastal states, nineteenth- and early twentieth-century resort-hotel development there was still much in evidence. Primary factors favoring this growth were the close proximity of the coast to the large New York City population base, the presence there of key population centers (e.g., Stamford, Bridgeport, New Haven, New London), and the creation of efficient and convenient transportation access, first by gravel roads and subsequently by steamboat lines and railroad routes (New York and New Haven; Shore Line) connecting New York City, Providence, and Boston.[1]

While pre–World War I American tourist guidebooks highlight the positive features of Connecticut coastal resort life, they also cite conditions that inhibited resort development and the growth of hospitality tourism. In many of these publications, the shoreline of the state is described as forming the "northern limit of Long Island Sound . . . quite different in character from the shore opposite . . . to a great extent rocky, though not, as a general rule, bold."[2] To be sure, there were notable exceptions to this characterization, but for the most part it may be considered accurate. Swimming and sunbathing, the favorite activities of summer shore visitors, were thus limited by the sloping granite ledges often present. In addition, Long Island, extending nearly the entire length of the Connecticut shoreline, provided shieldlike protection, resulting in generally calm waters unfavorable to surf bathing. Taintor's *American Seaside Resorts* (1882) contains the following observation:

Surf-bathing is not to be had on the Connecticut coast, for although some hotel proprietors prefer to consider the short seas which dance in from the sound as "surf," no one who has bathed on an ocean beach will . . . admit the justice of the title.[3]

Nevertheless, the virtues of "still-bathing" in the waters of the Sound were actively promoted, along with superb fishing and boating opportunities, active social life, and cool and invigorating summer air. While modest in scale, resort hotel development along the Connecticut shoreline responded to these attractions. The resulting large-hotel architecture is most systematically treated by geographical location, commencing with Fairfield County and proceeding eastward toward Rhode Island.

Fig. 2-1. The Indian Harbor Hotel (view from the south), Indian Point, Greenwich, Conn. Photograph, c. 1890. William E. Finch, Jr. Archives, Historical Society of The Town of Greenwich.

Greenwich: Indian Harbor Hotel and Edgewood Inn

Situated about thirty miles northeast of New York City, the town of Greenwich became a popular summer resort as well as commuting suburb for affluent New Yorkers during the decades after the Civil War. Summer tourists visiting the community from New York and elsewhere, typically for lengthy stays, were accommodated in hotels and rooming houses along the shore. In some instances, after being introduced to resort life, these people built substantial summer cottages adjacent to the hostelries. Most of the Greenwich hotels were modest in size (under 150 guest capacity) and design features but included such well-known names as the Old Greenwich Inn, the Lennox House, the Maples, and the Crossways Inn.[4] Two larger complexes, the Indian Harbor Hotel and the Edgewood Inn, were architectural standouts, thereby commanding our close attention.

Formerly situated on Indian Point, the Indian Harbor Hotel (figs. 2-1 and 2-2) originated from 1870 to 1871 as the lavish Americus Club, a country retreat for William Marcy "Boss" Tweed and his Tammany Hall "gang," a political organization from New York City. With Tweed's downfall, the complex was abandoned in 1873, and it reverted to the Mead family, the owners of the tract on which it was initially built. Soon thereafter, a New York partnership, Ashman and Morton, leased the complex and in c. 1874 it was remodeled, enlarged, and reopened as a summer hotel, "Morton House." Accommodating up to 400 guests, this new business enterprise advertised its elegantly furnished apartments, "gas and running water," and the availability of fishing, sea bathing, horseback riding, billiards, archery, boating, and bowling. In the mid-eighties, it became the Indian Harbor Hotel and operated under that name until the property was purchased by Commodore Eliss C. Benedict. In May

Fig. 2-2. The Indian Harbor Hotel (view from the west), Indian Point, Greenwich, Conn. Photograph, c. 1890. William E. Finch, Jr. Archives, Historical Society of the Town of Greenwich.

1895, after selling the contents at auction, Benedict had the complex demolished and his own home erected on the site.[5]

As first conceived and then expanded, the Indian Harbor Hotel was arguably the most outstanding example of Second Empire–style hotel architecture to be erected along the entire New England coastline. Of substantial, richly embellished wood-frame construction, this elegant, L-shaped, three-story structure stood on a bluff with broad, raised, delicately crafted verandas extending over one thousand feet along the front and side walls.[6] The most pronounced feature was the dominant, five-story, square corner tower topped by a tall, flat mansard roof. This roof was capped by decorative metalwork cresting, its surfaces broken by tall, hooded, corner, segmental arch windows, the latter set in their own elongated corner dormers positioned

above a narrow balustrade and bracketed cornice extending around all four sides of the tower. Mimicking the form and adornment of this principal tower were two four-story end towers possessing lower, flat mansard roofs. The flat wooden wall surfaces of the building were accented by ornamental flat pilasters and pierced by double-sash windows with low triangular pediments.

Adjacent to the north end tower was a six-story, flat-roof wooden annex (c. 1880) for guest quarters, displaying decorative details similar to those of the original Americus Club but also a roof balustrade and wall balconies reflecting the impact of the Colonial Revival. Next to the annex was a small, square, two-story structure of late Italian Revival inspiration housing bar, billiard, and pool rooms. Connected to the east end tower by a covered walkway was a raised dining pavilion protected by an intriguing, rounded convex roof capped by an elongated, pitched-roof monitor with center and end cupolas. The placement of dining facilities in a structure removed from the main complex was highly unusual in nineteenth-century American resort-hotel architecture.

Of more recent vintage and in a strikingly contrasting architectural vernacular was the Edgewood Inn (figs. 2-3 and 2-4), a massive, brilliantly executed, Shingle-style edifice formerly located above the Post Road on a knoll in Edgewood Park, with panoramic views of Greenwich village and Long Island Sound. Raised from 1901 to 1902 by Nathaniel Witherell at a cost of $200,000, the Edgewood, long regarded as one of the most fashionable hotels on the Connecticut coast, deserves recognition as one of New England's most outstanding examples of the Shingle-style design mode. Of its many guest offerings, the most appealing were the associated casino building (containing a dance hall, reading room, bowling alleys, and dressing rooms); private golf course; tennis courts; nearby bathing, sailing, and other water sports; tree-shrouded park; and vegetable garden and pasture with Jersey cows to supply the hotel with produce. Despite its architectural distinction and seeming popularity, however, the hostelry underwent numerous ownership changes over the years. In 1932, the Edgewood ceased operations as a hotel, and the physical plant was leased to Edgewood Park Junior College. This educational venture was also unsuccessful, and in July 1940, after an auction disposed of the interior contents, the complex was leveled by a Bridgeport wrecking company.[7]

Designed by a relatively unknown architect, J. T. Weir, the Edgewood Inn was three stories tall with two attic levels, the first-story walls of rubble stone masonry and those above with shingle sheathing. Characteristic of its style, the rambling, V-shaped floor plan was asymmetrical, with generous single- and two-story verandas attached to the front and rear façades. A five-story octagonal tower covered by a flared, angled roof cap penetrated by pitched-roof ventilators and dormers served as the primary visual ordering point for the entire structure. Connected main building blocks were protected by flared, steep-pitched gable roofs pierced by corbeled brick chimneys, and gable and truncated gable roof ventilators and dormers. The wide gable ends displayed

impressive, broad roof cornices with heavy, arched support brackets held in place by stepped wall brackets. Attached to the main building in the rear center was an ell containing on the first level the main entrance protected by a spacious, open, balustraded porch easily accessed by automobile and opening into the main office/reception hall. Etched in gold letters on the green tiles of the mantel in this warm, welcoming space were appropriate words of cordial greeting — "Shall I Not Take Mine Ease in Mine Inn?"[8]

An excerpt from a c. 1910 promotional booklet captures the owner's vision for the Edgewood, as well as its primary amenities (including the latest in technology) intended to attract and satisfy visitors:

The ideal of an American country hotel is found in Edgewood Inn. It unites every city comfort with every country charm. It has well-lighted and perfectly ventilated rooms, wide hallways, fire-proof elevator shafts and stairways, fire-alarms, [steam heat,] large closets, pure water, open plumbing and excellent drainage, and a fire sprinkling system in all working departments and the entire basement. The Inn has 150 bedrooms, all outside and well-ventilated, an automatic fire-alarm and telephone in each room. The majority of these rooms are arranged so that they can be had *en suite* with private bath. Just below the main floor is the spacious and well-equipped billiard room. The green alcove for smoking opens from it and two cardrooms. Adjoining the billiard-room is a first-class barber shop. Hotel automobiles meet all trains. Express, telephone and telegraph service.

Additional spaces serving guest needs included Ye Colonial Tea Room, the ladies' reception room, the ballroom (music room), the Dutch Room for private dining, the men's reading and writing room, the main dining room (fig. 2-5) with separate space for children and nurses, and the Palm Court Piazza, popular for outdoor dancing and entertainment on evenings. In addition to the aforementioned casino, adjacent freestanding buildings included a one-story, low-pitched-roof automobile garage with a chauffeurs' waiting room and an attractive two-and-one-half-story dormitory for hotel staff containing sleeping quarters, a laundry room, and other guest services. Without question, the Edgewood represented the ultimate in luxury, unmatched by the great majority of pre-1950 resort hotels on the New England seaboard.[9]

Fig. 2-3. Edgewood Inn (front view from the southeast), Edgewood Park, Greenwich, Conn. Photograph, n.d. William E. Finch, Jr. Archives, Historical Society of the Town of Greenwich.

Fig. 2-4. Edgewood Inn (rear view, main entrance, from the northwest), Edgewood Park, Greenwich, Conn. Photograph, n.d. William E. Finch, Jr. Archives, Historical Society of the Town of Greenwich.

Fig. 2-5. Dining Room, Edgewood Inn, Edgewood Park, Greenwich, Conn. Photograph from booklet, *Edgewood Inn, Greenwich, Connecticut* (c. 1910). William E. Finch, Jr. Archives, Historical Society of Town of Greenwich.

The Coast from Greenwich to Saybrook

From Greenwich to Saybrook, along more than two-thirds of the Connecticut coastline, several resort communities with excellent shore frontage sprung up between 1820 and 1950. For the most part these contained boardinghouses and small to medium-size hotel enterprises that came and went, but there were notable exceptions. Although only a few fit the definition of large resort hotels advanced for this book, those that were constructed in the region contributed significantly to the hospitality industry and the legacy of New England resort-hotel architecture.

Another exemplary Second Empire–style summer resort building was the George Hotel (fig. 2-6), named after its developer and first proprietor, George A. Wells, who had honed his business skills as P. T. Barnum's public relations director in Bridgeport. It was located along Grover Hill overlooking the beach at Black Rock Harbor, two miles to the west of downtown Bridgeport toward Fairfield. Opened in 1874, this renowned hostelry drew guests to the main complex, grounds, and associated cottages primarily from New York City and the Bridgeport area but also from other locations along the Northeast coast and interior New England. Topped by a ponderous hipped-on-steep-mansard roof with ventilators and dormers, the nicely proportioned main building block was four stories in height with three-story wings, the east wing over twice the length of the west, and both were later expanded. The principal visual ordering point at-

tached to the façade of the main block was an elaborately detailed three-stage tower, the upper stage with a concave mansard roof cap. Accessed by several stairways, a ten-foot-wide veranda extended around the entire structure, offering guests the constantly promoted opportunity to experience a healthy, invigorating, and highly social outdoor environment. The hotel proper had a capacity of about 175 people, while the several contiguous rental cottages increased this figure by well over 100 beds. Adjacent to the hotel was a large barn and stable complex, and situated at the water's edge was the hotel's "Shore House" (later the Black Rock Yacht Club) containing a bar and dining room. The George was closed circa 1896, a couple of years after Wells' death, and the Black Rock Pearsall-Thorne-Watson syndicate, which acquired the entire property, ultimately tore down or moved several of the cottages and demolished the hotel complex except for the south wing. In about 1902, this surviving remnant was moved on scows across Black Rock harbor to Hancock Avenue, took on a new life housing stores and apartments, and disappeared at the direction of the West End Renewal Project in 1967.[10]

Four miles southwest of New Haven in West Haven, on a rocky promontory reaching into Long Island Sound, is Savin Rock, one of Connecticut's oldest resort and amusement park communities. Formerly located there off Beach Street were two nineteenth-century hotel structures of some architectural distinction. One of New England's oldest coastal resort hostelries, the Savin Rock House (fig. 2-7), was erected in 1838, was later enlarged, and by the Civil War boasted accommodations for 200 "boarders." Considered a popular and pretentious destination for the wealthy and fashionable, this two-and-one-half-story, T-shaped wooden hotel was situated on a generous twenty-acre tract featuring a beach for bathing, a dock for boating and fishing, tree groves, and flower and "kitchen" gardens. At the rear of the hotel were large stables for the horses and carriages, used in addition to steamboats to transport guests to and from the hotel site. Protected by intersecting pitched roofs and surrounded by connected verandas, the building resembled uncomplex residential architecture, its limited decorative details including simple roof cornice and gable molding, square veranda columns with plain capitals, and entablatures between the columns. A major fire leveled much

Fig. 2-6. George Hotel, Black Rock, Bridgeport, Conn. Photograph, c. 1890. Historical Collections, Bridgeport Public Library.

of the complex in 1860, and it was promptly rebuilt, only to be totally destroyed by a second fire on 13 September 1870.[11]

Built a few blocks from the site of the Savin Rock House commencing in 1870, the Sea View House was somewhat smaller in size but of greater aesthetic merit and architectural significance. Strategically positioned on the corner of Beach and Grove streets, it first took the form (facing Beach Street) of an unostentatious three-story wooden building with stacked verandas, topped by a pitched roof with dormers. Three years later, owner and local entrepreneur George R. Kelsey, regarded as the father of the Savin Rock development, added a corner tower and wing fronting on Grove Street, thereby creating an L-shaped complex (fig. 2-8) capable of housing 75 to 100 patrons. Rivaling that gracing the Indian Harbor Hotel in Greenwich (see above), the tower assumed a similar Second Empire–style form, but with superior articulation of its assorted decorative details. The Sea View served its customer base for half a century until it was razed in 1922.[12] Although it cannot be classified as a "large" hotel (see preface), it is deserving of attention due to its important design legacy.

Fig. 2-7. "Savin Rock House, West Haven, Conn." Hotel menu engraving (19 July 1861), T. J. Stafford, Printer, New Haven, Conn. Courtesy, American Antiquarian Society.

Fig. 2-8. "Sea View House," Savin Rock, West Haven, Conn. Engraving from Thursty McQuill [Wallace Bruce], *The White and Green Mountains and Routes There* (1873 ed.), n.p. Author's collection.

Fig. 2-9. Branford Point House, Branford Point, Branford, Conn.
Photograph, n.d. Courtesy of the Branford Historical Society, Conn.

A few miles to the east of New Haven, Branford Point, Double Beach, the Thimble Islands, and Stony Creek became destinations for summer leisure and recreation commencing in the 1850s. The initiation of steamboat service from New Haven in 1855 was the principal contributing factor in encouraging their transformation to small resort communities containing several, mostly modest, hotel enterprises. Overlooking a sheltered harbor excellent for boating, fishing, and bathing, the Branford Point House (fig. 2-9) was one of the first as well as largest hotels in the region. Captain John Johnson is credited with its opening prior to 1842. Over the years, this uninspiring, elongated, wooden vernacular complex grew in stages, its guest capacity reaching 140 in 1866, 200 in 1868, and, with outbuildings, roughly 300 by 1910. George Parker and his wife, Alice, acquired the property in 1885, and in 1912 their son, Frank, bequeathed the land and buildings to the Town of Branford for use as a park. Deteriorating and no longer usable, the hotel was torn down in 1915.[13]

Also located in Branford, on a high bluff in a parklike setting above the beach at Indian Neck, was the Montowese House (fig. 2-10), put up by its developer and first owner William A. Bryan from 1866 to 1867. Easily reached by secondary roads and from the "Shore Line"

railroad route, the Montowese operated continuously under four generations of Bryan family ownership for nearly a century, recalling the saga of the Dodge family, which owned and managed the Mountain View House in New Hampshire's White Mountains from 1866 to 1979. Closed in 1963 by the Nobles, who had married into the Bryan clan, the hotel (including a summer playhouse) was seized by the town in lieu of unpaid taxes, sold at public auction, and, deteriorating and posing a fire threat, demolished for residential development in February 1965. This ignominious final chapter, however, should not diminish the stature of the Montowese as one of the earliest and most popular large-hotel enterprises on Long Island Sound, bearing the flattering title "The Queen of the Sound."

Though a highly functional three-and-one-half-story wooden vernacular structure, the Montowese attracted notice for the balanced symmetry of its main façade, with a 300-foot-long veranda running parallel to the shoreline. Protected by intersecting pitched roofs with dormers, the central, unembellished portion, dating from 1866, was flanked by nearly identical gambrel-roofed wings with dormers, the larger east wing added circa 1902 and increasing the capacity from 175 to about 225 guests. The primary public space in the east wing (fig. 2-11) was a spacious, informally furnished assembly room (fig. 2-12) with exposed ceiling rafters and was used for music, dancing, and other amusements. Supplementing the main building were the summer playhouse, stables, tennis courts, croquet grounds, and bathhouses and a pier at the beach.[14]

At Guilford, the next major town east of Branford, was one of the earliest and architecturally most distinguished resort hotels along the Connecticut coast. The initial portion of the Sachem's Head House was raised from about 1831 to 1832, "the name derived from the execution, by the celebrated [Mohegan chief] Uncas, of a captive Pequot chief, whose head he cut off, and placed in the crotch of a large oak tree here, where the skull remained for many years."[15] First conceived and owned by entrepreneur Nathaniel Griffing and others, this historic hostelry was advantageously positioned on the "Head," a promontory overlooking the Sound three miles southwest of Guilford Village. Griffing intended the hotel to be a significant destination in the successfully implemented plan to make Guilford a key link — where steamboats met stagecoaches and the railroad — on the transportation route between New York and Hartford. As a fully developed complex housing at least 400 patrons, the Sachem's Head House was the largest summer hotel between New York and Newport until its business declined as a result of the Civil War, and it was destroyed by fire on 14 June 1865. A center of summer social life for three decades, it attracted the wealthy and the professionally successful, including the Vanderbilts, Astors, Harrimans, and other prominent families from New York City and elsewhere in the United States.

Like many other coastal resort hotels of its era, the Sachem's Head House was constructed in stages over several years in response to growing guest demand. In 1831, Nathaniel Griffing purchased the former Soloman Leete residence, over the next year converted it to a small hostelry, and in 1835 added a west wing providing space for 40 guests. Under son Frederic R. Griffing's direction, expansion continued in the late 1840s when a long east wing was appended to the complex, making it five times the size of the original Leete house with a guest capacity of 250. In 1859, Horace Lee Scranton, the proprietor of the Tontine Hotel in New Haven, bought the ten-acre hotel property and in 1860 launched a program of im-

Fig. 2-10. "The Montowese House, Indian Neck, Conn." Color postcard, c. 1910. The Connecticut Historical Society Museum, Hartford, Connecticut.

Fig. 2-11. Front elevation plan, annex (east wing), Montowese House, Indian Neck, Branford, Conn. From booklet, *The Montowese, Indian Neck, Branford, Conn.* (c. 1905), n.p. The Connecticut Historical Society Museum, Hartford, Connecticut.

Fig. 2-12. "Interior Assembly Room," Montowese House, Indian Neck, Branford, Conn. From booklet, *The Montowese* (n.d.), n.p. The Whitney Library, New Haven Museum & Historical Society.

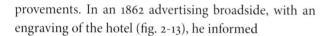

Fig. 2-13. "Sachem's Head Hotel, Guilford, Conn." Broadside wood engraving, 1862, J. W. Orr, New York City. The Connecticut Historical Society Museum, Hartford, Connecticut.

Fig. 2-14. "Fenwick Hall, Saybrook Point, Conn.," from the southeast. Engraving from *History of Middlesex County, Connecticut* (1884). The Connecticut Historical Society Museum, Hartford, Connecticut.

provements. In an 1862 advertising broadside, with an engraving of the hotel (fig. 2-13), he informed

former patrons and the public generally, that he has built on three hundred feet this spring, making seventy-four new bedrooms, new dining room forty by one hundred, new parlor forty by seventy. Every room in the house is newly furnished with new Carpets and new Cottage Furniture. The hotel is of modern construction, built on an extensive scale.

Local lumber dealer and contractor Alfred G. Hull was hired by Scranton to direct the construction project, which also included new barns for horses and carriages, a dock, a billiard room, a bowling alley, and greenhouses. The end result until its demise was an elongated wooden structure, its front elevation facing the water, consisting of six contiguous components—three four-story, low-pitched-roof, rectangular pavilions with their open gables facing forward, linked by three-story pitched-roof connectors, their long sides exhibiting three-story verandas supported by round columns with Doric capitals. An extension, similar in size and appearance to the connectors, was attached to the west end of this imposing, asymmetrical structure.[16]

The Fenwick Colony and Fenwick Hall

A stark contrast to the formal, refined, and relatively plain Sachem's Head House was Fenwick Hall (fig. 2-14), a sprawling, irregular, and magnificently articulated Stick-

style resort hotel once situated at the center of the Fenwick (New Saybrook) summer colony, Saybrook Point, Saybrook, just west of the mouth of the Connecticut River. Surrounded by water on three sides, the flat, grassy site had great appeal to the socially prominent, financially secure, and politically powerful families of central Connecticut, particularly the Hartford area. Members of these families, several of whom were important business and civic leaders, formed the New Saybrook Company and purchased the peninsula in 1870 with plans to create a special, upscale summertime seaside retreat. The chief financial backer of the project was the Charter Oak Life Insurance Company, which also was a partial owner of the Valley Railroad, opened in 1871 and strategically connecting Hartford with Saybrook Point the same year that Fenwick Hall was completed and opened. Although the hotel enterprise achieved only modest success initially, numerous private cottages were built, and in 1885 Fenwick residents established a borough government to regulate use of community property. Two years later, the Charter Oak Life Insurance Company went into bankruptcy, and in 1889 Fenwick Hall came under the ownership of hotel proprietor and New York City politician Edward D. Stokes. In July 1894, following several years of closure and a tax dispute with the town, the hotel was auctioned to Hartford insurance executive, Fenwick resident, and former Connecticut governor Morgan G. Buckley. For the remainder of its existence, it was used by Fenwick cottage owners as a social and recreational center, and a place to house friends and associates. A continuing financial burden, while under demolition it was lost to a dramatic fire on 18 May 1917, never to be rebuilt.[17]

The credit for the design of Fenwick Hall falls to Hartford architect S. W. Lincoln, whose career and other work is otherwise undocumented in published sources. The 1884 Beers & Company *History of Middlesex County, Connecticut*, recognized, nonetheless, the attributes of Lincoln's work at the Fenwick colony:

S. W. Lincoln . . . evinced a thorough knowledge of the wants and comforts of seaside guests. On every floor [see fig. 2-15], extending the entire length of the building, is a hall twelve feet wide, on the south side of which is the grand saloon, 45 by 31 feet, besides drawing room and parlors on the same [first] floor. On the north and east side of the building, looking out upon the sea, is the dining room, 44 by 80 feet. The sleeping rooms [see fig. 2-16] are all large and well ventilated, and arranged in suites of two, four and six rooms connecting, provided especially for the accommodation of families. By the peculiar architectural construction of the building, a cool sea breeze is in nearly every room in the house. The ascent to the rooms is by broad open staircase. . . . A broad [two-story] verandah [for promenaders] extends along the entire length of the east, south, and west sides of the building, 454 feet long by 16 feet wide.[18]

Containing 110 rooms with a capacity of 200 people, Fenwick Hall featured "pure water in set bowls in many of the rooms," was initially lighted by gas and then electricity, and possessed a telegraph office, a steam laundry, and a broad range of recreational facilities typical of large coastal resort hotels of the era. For fire safety purposes and to avoid cooking odors, the kitchen was located in a separate but adjunct structure built of brick.[19]

Four stories high in the central, rectangular section, flanked by three-story wings, Fenwick Hall possessed a conventional L-shaped floor plan, with double-loaded corridors on each floor. At the end of each wing was a pavilion tower topped by a steep-pitched, truncated, pyramidal roof with iron cresting, broken by pitched-roof dormers and triangular ventilators. Typical of the most eclectic interpretations of the Stick style, the entire wood-frame and clapboard structure was painted in contrasting colors, the exterior surface expressing the interior fabric the building. Decorative embellishment was applied to the wall surfaces, notably the upper wall

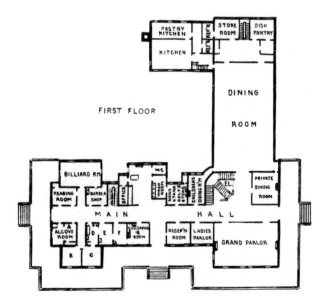

Fig. 2-15. First floor, Fenwick Hall, Saybrook Point, Conn. Fenwick Hall promotional brochure (c. 1902). The Connecticut Historical Society Museum, Hartford, Connecticut.

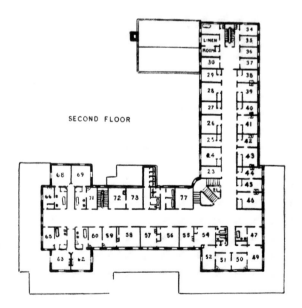

Fig. 2-16. Second floor, Fenwick Hall, Saybrook Point, Conn. Fenwick Hall promotional brochure (c. 1902). The Connecticut Historical Society Museum, Hartford, Connecticut.

Fig. 2-17. "Pequot House, New London, Conn.," from the east. Engraving from *Pleasant Days in Pleasant Places* (1886), p. 24. Maine Historic Preservation Commission.

PEQUOT HOUSE, NEW LONDON, CONN.
(Lighted with Pratt's Patent Prepared Gasolene.)

angle brackets supporting flared roof planes, the gable trusses, and the thin, wooden veranda roof and balcony supports. Along the New England shoreline, only the Hotel Nantasket at Hull and the Sea View House at Oak Bluffs, Martha's Vineyard, both Stick-style hotels in Massachusetts (see chapter 4), rivaled Fenwick Hall in quality and flamboyance of design.

Hotels of the Thames River Estuary

The Thames River estuary, with New London on the west bank and Groton on the east, empties into Long Island Sound directly opposite the west end of Fishers Island and the Gateway, connecting the Sound with the open waters of the Atlantic Ocean. Given its natural advantages and its easy accessibility from major population centers, this area became highly desirable for resort development beginning in the mid-1800s. A major impetus, as it was for other eastern Connecticut coastal communities, was the expansion of steamship service along the shoreline and the opening of the Shore Line and the New London, Providence and Stonington railroads and the New London Northern Railroad, which ran from New London north into Massachusetts.

With the historic name of General Neck, more com-

monly known as the Pequot Colony, the southern portion of the city of New London achieved prominence as a socially prestigious, scenically attractive, and architecturally distinguished summer resort community between the early 1850s and 1920. In large part responsible for the establishment of this fashionable center were two area businessmen, Perry Douglass and John Bishop, who made a major purchase of farmland there and commenced real estate development in 1852. Among his many talents, Bishop (1811–92) achieved recognition as a building contractor as well as designer, though he had received no formal training as an architect, and many of his buildings survive today in New London and environs. From 1852 to 1853, Bishop supervised the construction of the Pequot House (which in all likelihood he had designed), a substantial three-and-one-half-story, wood-frame, vernacular hotel structure (fig. 2-17), with rooftop observatory, at the corner of Glenwood and Pequot avenues, with one thousand feet of prime shore frontage at the mouth of the Thames River. The hotel formally opened in June 1853, and came under the ownership and administration of the newly formed Pequot Hotel Corporation the following year. Well-to-do families from New York, Washington, Boston, and other eastern population centers traveled by steamboat and train to this scenic location on the Sound. With Henry Scudder Crocker as manager, during the fifties and sixties the Pequot was enlarged, and several rental cottages were added until the total capacity peaked at over 500 by the early 1880s.

Under Crocker's management and assumption of ownership by 1863, the hotel struggled financially. The colony, however, continued to grow with the addition of more cottages and other buildings in a variety of whimsical Victorian eclectic styles (Gothic Revival, Second Empire, Italianate, etc.). Around 1875, the Pequot House assumed a quite awkward appearance as the result of the addition of a five-story rectangular wing with an extended veranda, multistory side porch, and mansard roof, its flat, sloping surfaces pierced by dormers. Hotel outbuildings included carriage houses and stables behind the primary structure, several of which are still surviving. In 1894, the newly formed Pequot Casino Association built a substantial Shingle-style casino nearby, later to undergo drastic transformation in response to four major fires. During the nineties, the hotel underwent further expansion by the addition of an upper story under a raised roof and highly ornamental, multistage

towers in the center and northeast corner of the main façade. On 7 May 1908, under undetermined and suspicious circumstances, the Pequot House was completely destroyed by fire (fig. 2-18), depriving the Connecticut shoreline of one of its larger and better-known summer hostelries. In the immediate ensuing years, the Pequot Colony lost favor as a socially exclusive, luxurious resort, and in the 1920s and 1930s the former Pequot Hotel Corporation holdings were divided and sold. After World War II, however, the district became the prime residential neighborhood that it is today.[20]

On the opposite side of the Thames estuary (often referred to as New London harbor), in the extreme southwest section of Groton, is Ocean Point, long recognized for "the advantages of strong sea-air, fine sea and sunset views, excellent bathing facilities, and all the appurtenances for fishing and seaside amusements."[21] By 1871, the members of the Harbor View Association had erected thirty-two cottages there. Simultaneously, from 1871 to 1872, Roswell S. Edgecomb, working with contractor C. Maxon & Company, initiated the construction of the Edgecomb House, a massive five-story, wood-frame, Second Empire–style hotel structure with a

Fig. 2-18. Fire at the Pequot House, New London, Conn., 7 May 1908. Photograph. (Note: original photograph was printed in reverse.) The Connecticut Historical Society Museum, Hartford, Connecticut.

Fig. 2-19. Fort Griswold House (Edgecomb House), Eastern Point, New London [Groton], Conn. Photograph, c. 1900. Courtesy of Mystic Seaport, Photography Collection, Mystic, Conn., #1983.57.181.

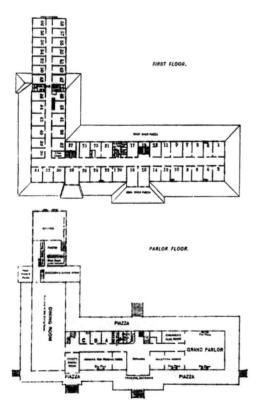

FIRST FLOOR.

PARLOR FLOOR.

Fig. 2-20. *(left)* Parlor floor and first floor plans, Fort Griswold House (Edgecomb House), Eastern Point, New London [Groton], Conn. Fort Griswold House brochure (1886). The Connecticut Historical Society Museum, Hartford, Connecticut.

two-tiered wraparound veranda on three sides and a flat mansard roof accented by corbeled brick chimneys and dormers. At the center of a perfectly symmetrical front façade was a square six-story tower protected by a tall mansard roof with iron cresting and double dormers. An 1872 New England regional guidebook excerpt underscores the benefits of this important addition to the main hotel-building block:

. . . from the top of the tower, the eye takes in a vast sweep of the ocean and adjacent islands. In full view at evening are the governmental lights at New London, Fisher's Island Sound, Montauk, Gardiner's Island, Plum Island, Bartlett's Reef, Gull Island, etc., and from the broad varandah . . . we have a rich variety of scenery and the most exhilarating sea breezes.[22]

Altogether, the Edgecomb, along with and under the same management as the much smaller Ocean House (1846) nearby, had sleeping space for more than 200 guests. The 1872 guidebook offers additional useful observations about the hotel:

The halls are wide and airy, the sleeping rooms are large, each one is well ventilated and lighted with gas, and the arrangements of the entire house have been made with a view to the greatest comfort and convenience of guests. In front of the house is a lawn extending to the beach, affording ample room for croquet and other out door exercises.

In its original form, the Edgecomb operated as a financially successful vacation center for over a decade.[23]

From 1885 to 1886, under the guidance of new owners A. P. and J. D. Sturtevant of Norwich, Connecticut, the Edgecomb House, with the new name of "Fort Griswold House" (fig. 2-19), underwent major, transforming renovation and expansion. The principal structure, facing on the mouth of the Thames, received an addition of the same style and massing at the southwest end, increasing the frontage to just over 200 feet. A smaller tower, imitating the form and decorative features of the main tower, was placed on the front façade of the addition, and the veranda, built around the entire structure, was increased in length to 580 feet. The ell of the L-shaped floor plan (fig. 2-20) was extended to the rear by the construction of a five-story brick addition, containing a portion of the enlarged dining room, private and children's dining rooms, and kitchens, with single rooms

Fig. 2-21. "The Griswold, Eastern Point," New London [Groton], Conn. Photograph from *Views of New London* (New London, Conn.: E. A. Bardol & Company, 1908). Courtesy of the New London County Historical Society, New London, Conn.

on the floors above. Committed to modern technology, the hotel ownership actively promoted the presence of Otis elevators, "hygienic" drainage, piped water systems, water hoses to fight fire on each floor, and steam heaters supplementing traditional fireplaces. As a result of the building project, the number of bedrooms was increased to 175 (300 total capacity), with every room, as advertised, commanding a view of either the Sound or the Thames estuary. The owners, like their competition in the hospitality industry, sought to achieve the highest in resort hotel standards.[24]

In 1904, railroad executive and philanthropist Morton F. Plant, the wealthy and influential owner of a summer estate, Branford House, at nearby Avery Point, purchased the popular but outmoded Fort Griswold House. Recognizing the scenic and functional advantages as well as the additional business potential of the property, Plant had the venerable hotel torn down, and from 1905 to 1906 replaced it with the much larger and more elegant Griswold Hotel (fig. 2-21). Amazingly, the demolition and new construction projects were finished in just 225 days. Opening with great celebration and fanfare in June 1906, the Griswold was, by all definitions, a true "grand" resort hotel, one of the most ambitious ever conceived and erected in the entire New England region. As a work of architecture, the Griswold was comparable in scale and visual quality to the former Poland Spring House

Fig. 2-22. "The New Hotel Griswold As It Will Look When Completed," Eastern Point, New London [Groton], Conn. Drawing by architect, Robert W. Gibson, *The Architectural Record* 19, no. 5 (May 1906): 344. Courtesy of the University of Delaware Library.

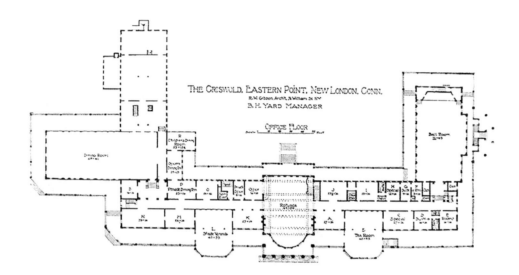

Fig. 2-23. Office floor, the Griswold, Eastern Point, New London [Groton], Conn. Plan by Robert W. Gibson, *The Architectural Record* 19, no. 5 (May 1906): 354. Courtesy of the University of Delaware Library.

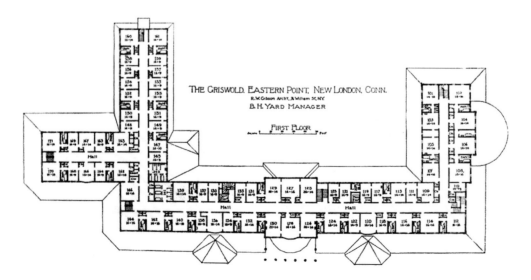

Fig. 2-24. First floor, the Griswold, Eastern Point, New London [Groton], Conn. Plan by Robert W. Gibson, *The Architectural Record* 19, no. 5 (May 1906): 356. Courtesy of the University of Delaware Library.

at South Poland, Maine (see chapter 8), and the Mount Washington Hotel, built about the same time from 1901 to 1906 and still operating at Bretton Woods in New Hampshire's White Mountains.[25]

As architect for his new hotel venture, Plant selected Robert W. Gibson (1854–1927), a leading New York City designer who had previously prepared plans for Branford House (see above). The partnership of Maquire and Penniman of Providence, Rhode Island, was hired as building contractor. A naturalized American citizen of English birth, Gibson carried on a large and successful practice for many years, planning and completing numerous commercial and public structures (including hotels) in New York City, and country houses and other building types in New York State and New England. Fortunately, in the May 1906 issue, the professional periodical *The Architectural Record* published an exhaustive article about Gibson and the project, along with a conjectural front elevation perspective drawing of the hotel (fig. 2-22) and a set of floor plans (see examples, figs. 2-23 and 2-24). Although the completed Griswold assumed a larger form, with slight variations in decorative detail, these illustrations are of inestimable documentary value in helping to chart the history of pre–World War I American resort-hotel design.[26]

The monumental wooden complex, with its symmetrical front façade and open quadrangle configuration, displayed many distinctive features of the Neoclassical style—closed pediments with plain and dentil molding, round Doric-capital columns adorning sweeping verandas, and round Corinthian-capital columns supporting two-story rectangular and semicircular entrance porches. The massive, rambling structure, initially four stories in height, lacked, however, the cohesiveness and simple, pure formality of well-executed, well-proportioned, primarily residential Neoclassical buildings. Not surprisingly, business aspirations somewhat compromised the virtues of successfully executed architectural styling with the addition of a south-side wing from 1906 to 1907, an annex from 1909 to 1910, and a new top story to the entire structure from 1916 to 1917. At its optimal size, the Griswold possessed 400 rooms of all types, with a capacity of at least 500 guests.[27]

The architect and his associates gave the most careful thought to the layout of the interior floor plans of the

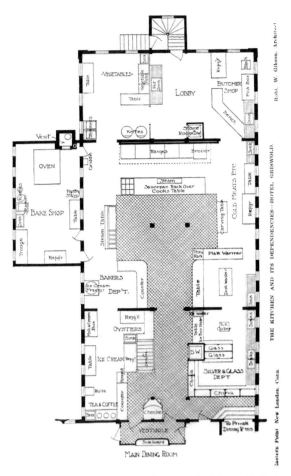

Fig. 2-25. The kitchen and its dependencies—Hotel Griswold, Eastern Point, New London [Groton], Conn. Plan by Robert W. Gibson, *The Architectural Record* 19, no. 5 (May 1906): 359. Courtesy of the University of Delaware Library.

Griswold. Particularly impressive was the arrangement of the office or main floor (see fig. 2-23), with double-loaded corridors servicing the central block, the northwest wing, and the two ells. At the middle of the building, opening out to the primary entrance porch and free of columns, was the rotunda, a grand entrance hall, seventy by forty feet, with the main stairway and outer walls primarily of glass panes. A great dining room, forty-two by one hundred feet, was placed in the northwest wing, with casement windows encouraging panoramic views and exposure to sea breezes. The kitchen and associated rooms (fig. 2-25) occupied the connecting north ell. Situated in the south ell was a ballroom, forty-eight by ninety feet, and positioned above a basement containing a café, billiard room, playroom, and shops. The central block

Fig. 2-26. Lounge, Hotel Griswold, Eastern Point, New London [Groton], Conn. Booklet, *The Griswold, New London, Conn.* (New York: F. W. Robinson, [c. 1909]), p. 11. The Connecticut Historical Society Museum, Hartford, Connecticut.

housed a variety of smaller spaces, among them the reception area; offices; private, staff, and children's dining rooms; parlors; reception rooms; a telegraph, telephone, and news room; a tearoom with veranda; a "shade" veranda; and a lounge (fig. 2-26). The entire main floor was "finished with white pillars, columns, and cornices in the Colonial style of simple, dignified effect, encouraging the luxury of quiet rather than that of ostentation." Provided with steam heating, direct water flow, telephones, and electrical lighting, the elevator-accessed floors above contained stacked bathrooms, a variety of bedrooms and multiroom suites, the most desirable located on the corners of the central block, northwest wing, and ells. Small adjacent buildings included a laundry, staff dormitory, powerhouse, and boiler house. The entire grounds were meticulously planned, with trees, gardens, terraces, stone walls, fountains, statuary, paths, and approach roads. The hotel and surrounding land drew praise as "a complex machine . . . an achievement in its own class, . . . a demonstration of the splendid organization of American business."[28]

The Griswold Hotel persevered well into the twentieth century, attracting traditional summer visitors, conventions, yachting groups, wedding parties, and spectators for the Yale-Harvard rowing regatta, held each June farther up the Thames River. After Morton Plant's death in 1918, the hotel property passed to a series of owners including John McEntee, the Griswold Hotel Corporation (headed by Robert Farley), John H. Livingston, Jr.,

and a syndicate of New York businessmen (1933), John G. Venetos (1933), the Menlip Corporation of New York (1945), and Milton O. Slosberg (1956). Slosberg, dealing with the debilitating double impact of the Great Depression and World War II, repeatedly renovated the structure and conducted extensive marketing, exerting every effort to make the hospitality landmark a financial success. Ultimately, Slosberg closed the hotel in September 1967, auctioned the contents in June 1968, and in the following October sold the property to the well-known pharmaceutical firm Charles Pfizer and Company, for a bargain price of $395,000. In 1969, the Barnum Lumber Company of Bridgeport completed the lengthy demolition of the complex until only a vacant, grassy waterfront knoll remained. Some years later, Pfizer conveyed a portion of the tract to the adjacent Shennecossett Municipal Golf Course (Groton) and preserved the remainder as undeveloped, open space overlooking the Thames estuary and the Sound. It continues to offer the same picturesque views as the Griswold did for sixty-three years when it was actively promoted as "the ideal summer resort hotel."[29]

Fishers Island

Although it is within the boundaries of New York State, Fishers Island has been an integral part of the Connecticut shoreline and summer resort life there for a century and a half. Running nearly parallel with and only a few miles off the coast from Groton to Mystic, this narrow, nine-mile-long landmass has transitioned over time to an insular, self-contained community of cottages and estates owned by affluent families, primarily from the urban centers of the Northeast. In the late 1800s and early 1900s, the island was occupied, however, by less ambitious summer residences, an active U.S. military base (Fort Wright), and three substantial wood-frame resort hotels—the Munnatawket Hotel, originally the Lyles Beach Hotel; the Mansion House and Cottages; and the Mononotto Inn. These hostelries were all located on the island's west end, close by boat access from New London and other Connecticut coastal communities. The hotels have disappeared, but the older cottages and portions of the military base remain, supplementing the country club (Fishers Island Club) and the larger, more

Fig. 2-27. Mansion House, Fishers Island, Long Island Sound, N.Y.
Postcard, n.d. Courtesy of Sandy and George Esser, New York City and Fishers
Island, N.Y.

recent residential properties located primarily on the
east end.[30]

The major developers of Fishers Island, the Ferguson
family, owned and operated both the Munnatawket
Hotel (Lyles Beach Hotel) and the Mansion House and
Cottages during the years prior to World War I. Raised
circa 1882, the Lyles Beach was bought in 1891 by brothers Edmund M. and Walter Ferguson, who rebuilt it and
renamed it the "Munnatawket," the Native American
name for Fishers Island. The smallest of the island's major hotels in guest capacity (up to 150), this late Victorian
eclectic edifice was partially demolished and reconfigured as a more modest structure in 1905, was expanded
to nearly its original size in 1912, and, in a deteriorating
state, was finally torn down circa 1926.[31]

The Fergusons purchased the Mansion House (fig.
2-27), to become the largest of the island's hotels, in 1889,
opening it for business in 1892. At first an enlarged summer residence, it grew in several stages over many years,
achieving its full-blown form in the late 1910s. Though
not situated directly on the shorefront, this elongated

complex, an unadorned composite of the Second Empire, Shingle, and Colonial Revival styles, occupied a
grassy, tree-shaded site, surrounded by, ultimately, over
thirty rental cottages. At its peak, the Mansion House
had space for about 200 overnight visitors, with well over
100 additional spaces available in the cottages. Suffering
from the impact of the Depression on summer tourism,
the hotel closed in 1941 and, with the exception of its
oldest portion (originally the Winthrop family home),
which still survives, was demolished just after World
War II.[32]

Financed and built by Maria Bodine Hoppes and
members of her family from Bethlehem, Pennsylvania,
the Mononotto Inn (fig. 2-28) was the most distinguished
architecturally of the island's three major hotels. Planned
by a yet unidentified architect, erected from 1892 to 1893,
and enlarged in the next year, it remained in business
until the 1930s, when it was closed and subsequently
razed circa 1939. With a capacity of 175 after 1900, the
Mononotto, impressively set on a high bluff at water's
edge, was an outstanding example of the Shingle style,

Fig. 2-28. Mononotto Inn, Fishers Island, Long Island Sound, N.Y.
Postcard, n.d. Courtesy of Sandy and George Esser, New York City and Fishers
Island, N.Y.

rivaling if not surpassing many other resort hotels of its design mode and period along the New England coast. Possessing an elongated, crescent-shaped floor plan, this three-story structure was marked by its double-hipped roof, accented with an assortment of dormers, and its typically expansive veranda encircling much of the building mass.[33] It is fitting that this consideration of Connecticut's limited but superlative coastal resort-hotel architecture concludes with a building meeting high design standards and conveying rich images of seaside summer vacation life.

RHODE ISLAND

Narragansett Bay, Watch Hill, and Block Island

ALTHOUGH RHODE ISLAND is just forty-eight miles long and thirty-seven miles wide, ranking as the smallest of the nation's fifty states, it has had a rich, diverse, and widely recognized architectural history. Represented in the surviving building legacy of the state is one of the most significant collections of architecture that can be seen and appreciated anywhere in the country. As a consequence, over the years Rhode Island architecture has been meticulously studied, resulting in the publication of numerous illustrated books and articles, some general and others limited in scope, treating specific styles, building types, architects' repertoires, or communities, notably Providence and Newport. Those who have researched and written about Rhode Island buildings include such distinguished architectural historians as Henry-Russell Hitchcock, Antoinette F. Downing, Vincent J. Scully, Jr., and William H. Jordy. In addition, for each of the state's thirty-nine cities and towns, the Rhode Island Historical Preservation and Heritage Commission in Providence has maintained archives and published over time a voluminous collection of historical introductions and inventories constituting an invaluable, in fact essential, documentary resource for understanding Rhode Island's architectural heritage.

Approximately 14 percent of Rhode Island's surface area is occupied by Narragansett Bay, regarded by many as the state's "single most defining feature."[1] Since its inception, much of the state's history, as well as economy and culture, has been oriented toward and conditioned by the irregular mainland and island shorelines of the bay and its centers of population. Altogether the coast of Rhode Island, including Narragansett Bay, East Bay, the southern townships, and Block Island and other islands, is an astounding four hundred miles in length. Consisting of bluffs, rocky cliffs, and broad, sandy beaches, this coast has provided generous opportunities for resort development since the early nineteenth century. Not surprisingly, the hospitality industry, centering on resort hotels, has established deep roots in the state, largely at Newport, Warwick, Jamestown, Narragansett Pier, Watch Hill, and Block Island. The pre-1950 hotels themselves, however, have all but disappeared, with the exception of surviving examples on Block Island. Despite the intense interest in and publication about Rhode Island architecture, these buildings, many of outstanding design integrity, have been subjects of far less examination than they deserve. As such they command our retrospective attention today.[2]

Newport and Its Defined Resort Hotel Era

Long termed "America's First Resort," Newport occupies a highly advantageous location at the southwest corner of Aquidneck Island on Narragansett Bay, approximately five miles from the open ocean. Its economic and social development, however, has been far from consistent, dramatically influenced by the course of events in American national and New England regional history. A medium-size, magnet tourist destination and summer community today, Newport enjoyed the distinction of being the fifth-largest city in the United States, with a population of more than nine thousand, in the years immediately preceding the American Revolution. With its easy sea access, the city had become a major center for international commerce and related business enterprise during the colonial era, as well as the capital of the Rhode Island colony. In the same period, as early as the 1720s, it also became home to a small but burgeoning resort industry, contributing markedly to the origins of hospitality tourism in America. Benefiting from its mild climate, Newport was a fashionable center of leisure and enlightenment, with particular appeal as a summer haven for the wealthy from the South and the islands of the West Indies.

This first period of prosperity, however, ended with the beginning of the Revolutionary War and British occupation of Newport in December 1776. The effects of the war devastated the city's economy, including the

Fig. 3-1. "Belle Vue House," Newport, R.I. Engraving from *Hand-Book of Newport* (1852), p. 157. Courtesy, The Winterthur Library Printed Book and Periodical Collection.

resort industry. This depressed condition persisted well into the nineteenth century as a result of the passage in 1807 of the Embargo Act, the ending of the legalized slave trade, the War of 1812, and the unsuccessful attempts in Newport to participate in New England's newly developing industrial economy. Fortuitously, in the 1820s and 1830s, the resort industry, spearheaded by local residents, reappeared, marked by the opening of two small hotels—the Francis Brinley House (later the Greek Revival–style Bellevue House, enlarged in 1844) (fig. 3-1) and the Whitfield House (later renamed the Touro House). Southern visitors, many of whom had never entirely departed, gravitated to Newport in greater numbers. As the resort business regenerated and guest accommodations became harder to secure, it became clear that the city needed at least one large hotel to meet new tourism demands and further reawaken the pre-Revolution tourism economy.[3]

The construction and opening of the first Ocean House (Bellevue Avenue and East Bowery Street) from 1843 to 1844, and the Atlantic House (Bellevue Avenue and Pelham Street) from 1844 to 1845, represented a major response to the pressures of revived tourism. These were two of the earliest large resort hotels to grace the coastline of New England. Built by William T. Potter at an unprecedented cost of $22,000, enlarged in fall 1844, and positioned on a rise with views of the harbor and ocean, the first Ocean House (fig. 3-2), in all its simple, pure Greek Revival splendor, stood four stories tall and initially accommodated over 200 persons. Covered by a flat roof pierced by chimneys and topped by a central lantern, this cube-shaped building featured level cornices and, on its symmetrical façade, a two-story portico with square Doric pillars. In their widely acclaimed book, *The Architectural Heritage of Newport, Rhode Island*, Antoinette Downing and Vincent Scully properly regarded the first Ocean House, one of the last of Newport's Greek Revival buildings, to be a final vestige of the classical tradition—"a simple wooden box with applied classical detail, painted a uniform light color and expressive of the Greek Revival tendency toward the abstract elegance of geometrical shapes rather than the expression of space, structure, or materials." Short-lived, it was destroyed in a sensational fire on 5 August 1845, to be replaced during the next year by a much larger second Ocean House (see

Fig. 3-2. "Ocean House. Newport. Rhode Island." Lithograph, c. 1844, G. A. W. Endicott, N.Y. Courtesy of The Newport Historical Society, R.I.

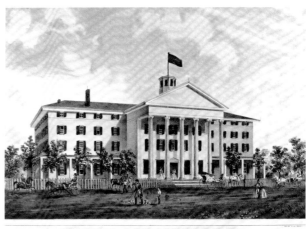

Fig. 3-3. "Atlantic House, Newport R.I." Lithograph, c. 1845, G. A. W. Endicott, N.Y. Courtesy of The Newport Historical Society, R.I.

below) embodying the contrasting stylistic motifs and forms of the mid-Victorian era in America.[4]

The other of Newport's outstanding Greek Revival hotels was the Atlantic House (fig. 3-3), also a shining example of the city's return to prominence as a resort center. William T. Potter, also associated with the Ocean House (see above), was the primary developer. The Atlantic House remained open until 1877, when it was partially demolished and portions relocated, to be replaced by a private residence. Configured like many earlier college buildings in New England, it consisted of a central pitched-roof pavilion flanked by identical four-story hipped-roof wings. The primary, eye-catching feature of this white-painted, 250-guest establishment was its beautifully proportioned pavilion portico that comprised a plain, closed gable pediment, a plain entablature, and a tall six-column Ionic portico. Anticipating the great verandas of the post–Civil War resort hotels, one-story porches extended along the wings from the portico, and around the corners along the north and south end walls. As Downing and Scully articulate, like the first Ocean House, the Atlantic House stood "as a symbol of both past and future," representing "the end of the long eighteenth-century tradition, continued and unified," but also "the product of a new point of view, born out of knowledge of the historic past."[5]

The most ambitious resort-hotel building project in Newport in the nineteenth century was the construction

of the second Ocean House (fig. 3-4) on the same site as its ill-fated predecessor. Financed and subsequently managed by John G. Weaver and family members, this high-profile "grand" summer hostelry was completed in less than one year during 1845 and 1846 at a cost of $62,000. Serving as designer was Russell Warren (1792–1860), a Rhode Island native who had developed an architectural and engineering practice in Bristol and who, during his career, compiled an extensive list of commissions in Providence, southeastern Massachusetts, and other locations, including Newport. The hotel received a major sixty-room addition in 1848 and underwent renovations

Fig. 3-4. "Ocean House," Newport, R.I. Lithograph, T. Sinclair, Philadelphia, from [John Collins], *The City and Scenery of Newport, Rhode Island* (1857). Courtesy, The Winterthur Library Printed Book and Periodical Collection.

Fig. 3-5. "Grand Veranda of the Ocean House, Newport," R.I. Photograph, c. 1890. Courtesy of The Newport Historical Society, R.I.

in 1873, the latter under the direction of local builder Dudley Newton. At its full-blown size, the second Ocean House had a listed capacity of 400 to 600 guests, the figures varying in period travel guides. These frequent, widely distributed publications consistently extolled its virtues as the finest hotel at "Saratoga by the Sea."[6] The 1882 Taintor guide, *American Seaside Resorts*, contains a passage in the Newport section that cites the hotel's most positive features:

The principal hotel is the [second] Ocean House, which stands nearest the ocean beach. From its rooms and cupola some of the most extensive views of the ocean and harbor can be obtained. Block Island, thirty miles to the southwest, and several smaller islands in Narragansett Bay, are visible in clear weather. The hotel is nicely furnished, and affords ample space upon its wide piazzas [fig. 3-5] for pleasant promenades. A fine band of music is usually employed for the season, and the . . . hops and balls are reckoned among the most brilliant entertainments of our American summer resorts.

The second Ocean House was an imaginative expression of Gothic Revival architecture, but as Downing and Scully correctly point out, unlike the Greek Revival first Ocean House, it was "less strictly stylistic," and the design less traditional and more innovative. In the newer, grandiose 250-foot-long building (fig. 3-6), interior space needs resulted in steep-pitched roofs on the main block and wings, punctured by the octagonal cupola and steep-pitched dormers. The full, picturesque potential of wood-frame construction was creatively realized in the light, fragile-appearing two- and three-story verandas with their ornate diagonal bracing and balustrades. Exuding a "mixture of rationalism and romanticism," the building demonstrated flexibility in design, both exterior articulation and interior layout, with the optimal use of its naturalistic building materials. From all indications, the second Ocean House was an aesthetic as well as functional success.[7]

Newport's tourist boom, which had reached its peak during the 1850s, subsided during the years following the Civil War, resulting in the decline of the local resort-hotel business. The major reason for this was the development of the exclusive, upscale "cottage" community accessed by Bellevue and Ocean avenues. This "privatization" of space transformed the character of the city as a seaside resort and the nature of the tourist trade, to the extent that it remained. Gradually, hotels such as the Atlantic, Bellevue, and Fillmore were closed until, by the 1890s, the second Ocean House was the sole survivor. It responded to the city's transformation with minimal change until it became "a Newport anachronism." Regarded as "a landmark and a reminiscence," it was destroyed in a spectacular fire on 9 September 1898.[8] Karl Baedeker's 1904 guide, *The United States*, contains the terse citation

Fig. 3-6. Ocean House, Bellevue Avenue, Newport, R.I. Photograph, c. 1890. Courtesy of The Newport Historical Society, R.I.

"Ocean House, burned down in 1898 and not yet rebuilt." It never was.[9]

The North Bay: Rocky Point and Oakland Beach

After the Civil War, as Newport transitioned to an exclusive "cottage" community and the resort hotel industry declined there, shoreline towns on the west and east sides of Narragansett Bay entered the tourism market. While on the west side Jamestown and Narragansett Pier became the primary centers of tourism development (see below), there were other, secondary centers featuring resort hotel enterprises. Of these, Warwick, on a pronounced, rockbound promontory twelve miles south of Providence, most conspicuously stands out, with its earliest, less elite tourism activity concentrated largely at Rocky Point and Oakland Beach.[10]

For a century and a half, Rocky Point, with one of New England's most popular amusement parks, has been the major, predominantly summer, attraction along Warwick's thirty-mile coastline. Reaching its greatest

popularity before World War I, it attracted visitors from all over the United States. It entered its heyday with the construction and opening of the Rocky Point Hotel (fig. 3-7) during the 1860s. This hostelry and its siting are succinctly described in a celebratory manner by J. R. Cole

Fig. 3-7. Rocky Point Hotel, Rocky Point, Warwick, R.I., c. 1875, photographed by Alden, Providence, R.I. Courtesy of Mystic Seaport, Photography Collection, Mystic, Conn., #1981.120.4.

in his *History of Washington and Kent Counties, Rhode Island* (1889):

A conspicuous object as one nears the massive rocks which line the shore of the Point, is the Rocky Point Hotel, an imposing structure, three stories in height, very commodious, with a splendid prospect from its windows and of sufficient capacity to accommodate 300 boarders. It is a first class house in construction and appointments.

Behind the hotel on a slight rise was one of its most appealing offerings—a tall, octagonal observation tower from which commanding views of the bay and islands could be obtained. Also present on one hundred acres nearby were a farm for food supplies, groves and grottoes accessed by walking paths, bowling alleys, billiard rooms, pistol galleries, bathhouses, and other outbuildings. Architecturally, the wooden hotel complex, created in stages, consisted of two major, linked components, one distinctly Second Empire in style with a hipped-on-mansard roof, and the other of late Italianate inspiration possessing two-story verandas and a pitched roof with paired cornice brackets and hooded dormers similar to those adorning the National Hotel (1888, etc.) (see below) on Block Island. Like most of its hotel contemporaries, the Rocky Point succumbed to fire, in this instance a massive conflagration during the off season on 16 March 1883 that received extensive newspaper coverage. In addition to the hotel, the dining hall, a boathouse, a dock, and other small buildings were lost.[11]

Fig. 3-8. "Oakland Beach Hotel, Warwick Neck, R.I." Photoengraving from Wilfred H. Munro, *Picturesque Rhode Island* (1881), n.p. Courtesy, The Winterthur Library Printed Book and Periodical Collection.

Another popular shore resort on the upper bay was Oakland Beach, located in Warwick almost two miles west of Rocky Point on Horse Neck Peninsula. Opened in 1873 by the Oakland Beach Association and accessed by railroad, the grounds contained bathing facilities, a large dining hall for serving seafood, a casino, and, after 1880, Elias Hotchkiss' Oakland Beach Hotel at the tip of the peninsula overlooking the bay and a small, artificial saltwater lake used for recreation. In its first incarnation, housing 100 people, this hotel (fig. 3-8) was a fairly conventional three-and-one-half-story Second Empire structure surrounded by open, one-story verandas and topped by a hipped-on-mansard roof virtually identical to the one covering the oldest section of the Rocky Point Hotel. In the late 1800s, the hotel was doubled in size (200 capacity, with cottages) by the addition of a connected but smaller wing of the same form and proportions, and with the same stylistic elements as the first building. Simultaneously, a service ell was appended to the rear of the complex, creating a T-shaped floor plan. Fire destroyed the Oakland Beach in 1903, depriving Warwick of its last large Victorian-era resort hotel.[12]

Jamestown: The Hotel Row

Located on Conanicut Island (also referred to as "Jamestown Island") in lower Narragansett Bay, the resort town of Jamestown faces due east toward the city of Newport, approximately three miles across the scenic East Passage. Despite its close proximity to the recognized summer capital of East Coast American high society, historically Jamestown has stood in sharp contrast. In his book *Buildings of Rhode Island*, William Jordy refers to "the simple, unaffected quality" of the smaller island town, epitomizing "an opposite view of summer bliss" and "different values in life." Although Jamestown had its social set, largely from Philadelphia, St. Louis, and the Midwest, "the sense of the simple agricultural past of the island persisted throughout its early period of summer colonization," with a quiet, relaxed existence the prevailing summer lifestyle. Great value was placed on rusticity and a modicum of privacy and seclusion, and, at the same time, on opportunities to participate selectively in Newport's fancier, more public summer scene. These attitudes and living patterns influenced the entire island

Fig. 3-9. Looking north past the hotels (first Thorndike, Gardner, and Bay View), Jamestown, R.I. Photograph, c. 1910. Jamestown Historical Society Collection.

and its architecture, and, as Jordy points out, created the "village quality" of the center of Jamestown.[13]

The inauguration in 1872 of steamboat ferry service from Newport transformed Jamestown's Victorian-era economic base, from agriculture and fishing largely to hospitality tourism. In much the same way as the bay coastal communities to the north, Jamestown benefited as Newport transitioned from a center of resort hotel life to a community of lavish "cottage" estates. Farming areas around Jamestown were converted to cottage sites, while the town center took on a new look and atmosphere with a small but distinguished group of large resort hotels arrayed along Narragansett Avenue, paralleling the beach in the vicinity of the East Ferry landing. These three major structures, though of varying masses and design features, constituted most of an informal row (fig. 3-9) that inspires comparison today with the usually symmetrical, more formal building rows of many pre–Civil War New England colleges and academies, and with other types of public-building architecture.[14]

For over a century, the Bay View House (fig. 3-10) occupied a conspicuous site at the north end of the row, on the north corner of Narragansett and Conanicus avenues. William H. Knowles erected the first portion of the hotel circa 1872, perfectly timed to take advantage of the new ferry links with Newport. Set back from the street corner, this two-and-one-half-story structure displayed a dormered mansard roof and porches commonly associated with the Second Empire style. Fifteen years later, in 1889, Knowles' son Adolphus incorporated this first section into a much larger, L-shaped, shingled structure (fig. 3-11) four and one-half stories tall, dominated by a dramatic, tall, cylindrical tower with four levels of porches and topped by a high, cone-shaped roof penetrated by three levels of dormers. Predominantly Queen Anne style in its overall conception, the Bay View, with bedroom space for 200 patrons, continued its marvelous, monumental presence as a hotel in Jamestown until the 1960s. In 1975, garbed in white paint with its tower truncated and its porches removed, it was converted to

Fig. 3-10. Bay View House, Jamestown, R.I. Photograph, c. 1900. Courtesy of The Newport Historical Society, R.I.

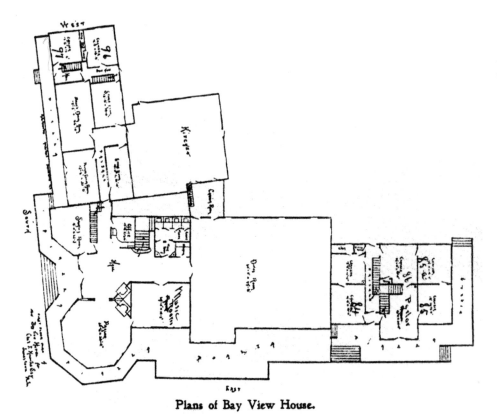

Plans of Bay View House.

Fig. 3-12. Bay View Condominiums (c. 1987–89), Jamestown, R.I. Photograph, 2004, by the author.

Fig. 3-13. Gardner House, Jamestown, R.I. Photograph, c. 1900. Jamestown Historical Society Collection.

a commercial building with offices, apartments, a restaurant, and a store. It fell to the wrecking ball in 1985, ending its long period of service.[15]

The onetime eye-catching physical presence of the Bay View House has not been lost, however. In 1989 a new, $6 million edifice titled "Jamestown Bay View Condominiums" (fig. 3-12) rose on the site from designs prepared by the firm of ADD, Inc., of Cambridge, Massachusetts. Planned to contain thirty-five living units and a restaurant above a ground-floor garage, this massive wooden-shingled, concrete, and steel structure is roughly twice the size of the former hotel. Despite this fact, it bears close resemblance to the Bay View with its similarly configured corner tower, neo-Victorian eclectic decoration, stacked porches, and shallow, wraparound first-story veranda. The condominium building is the only example of a contemporary work of architecture intended to closely simulate the look and ambience of one of the great resort hotels that once graced the New England coastline.[16]

To the south of the Bay View House, on Conanicus Avenue between Narragansett Avenue and Union Street, the Gardner House (fig. 3-13) had a commanding presence for nearly sixty years. The first two-and-one-half-story section was built from 1882 to 1883 for Mr. N. S. Littlefield and Mr. and Mrs. Stephen Gardner, from whom the name derived. Its long side facing the shoreline, the building was expanded to the north by four window bays (added to the initial section) in 1888. Another rather standard example of Second Empire–style hotel architecture, the original Gardner possessed a hipped-

on-mansard roof with belvedere, a dentiled cornice, and a one-story veranda of fragile stick construction on the main façade and side walls. Around 1892, the hotel roof was raised and an additional story inserted underneath. Several years later, about 1900, the guest capacity peaked at 300 when the main block received an addition to the rear (parallel to Union Street), resulting in an L-shaped floor plan. Likely architect-designed, this coherent, visually satisfying Shingle-style ell commanded notice for its two-story, polygonal bay windows and central gambrel-roof pavilion. In 1942, after several years of closure, the entire complex was demolished and within the next year replaced by the wartime United Services Organization center.[17]

Completed from 1889 to 1890, about the same time as the enlarged Bay View House, the Hotel Thorndike (or "Thorndyke") (fig. 3-14) occupied an equally prominent location facing the water on the south end of the row, on Conanicus Avenue between Union and Lincoln streets. The initiator of the building project was Patrick H. Horgan, a Newport real estate investor, who acquired the land at auction in April 1889. He promptly contracted with builder Nicholas Dillon, also of Newport, to construct the new hotel based on plans by architect Charles L. Bevins, the designer of other structures in Jamestown. The first phase of the project produced a rather bland two-story building, fifty by two hundred feet, which received a temporary low-pitched roof and was available for partial use in August. At the conclusion of the summer season, work continued with the addition of three more stories set under and within a main

Fig. 3-14. Hotel Thorndike, Jamestown, R.I. Photograph from *Newport, R.I.* (Portland, Maine: L. H. Nelson Co., 1907). Courtesy, The Winterthur Library Printed Book and Periodical Collection.

gambrel roof and intersecting steep-pitched roofs, their planes penetrated by single, double, and triple dormers. A dominant, one-hundred-foot-tall tower and centered block rose on the main façade during the winter of 1890, and by June the building was closed in and ready for occupancy. Strategically placed on the main façade to take full advantage of the highly touted views was a first-story veranda screening storefronts, above which, on the next two floors, were linked, recessed porches with arched apertures. Altogether there were 113 guest rooms sufficient for 250 to 300 people and enhanced with the latest in expected technology—a hydraulic elevator, telephones, steam heat, electric lights (after 1898), hot and cold baths, sanitary systems, and electric bells. For the first year, this striking shingle-sheathed building bore the names of the Horgan Hotel, the Horgan block, or the Casino, becoming the Hotel Harwarden the second year and the Thorndike in 1891.

Its various components skillfully articulated and integrated, the Hotel Thorndike merits recognition as one of the finest of coastal New England's Shingle-style resort hotels, in the same league as the Mathewson Hotel at Narragansett Pier (see below), the second Ottawa House (1888) on Cushing's Island, Casco Bay, and the Passaconaway Inn (1893) at York Cliffs, both in Maine (see chapters 7 and 8). To borrow Vincent Scully's apropos phrasing, they were "mountains of shingles," each achieving "a dynamic architectural form" and, characteristic of their style, "a monumentality of inspired impermanence." Viewed from Newport and the bay, the architectural panorama formed by the Bay View, Gardner, and the Thorndike was temporarily broken on 5 October 1912 when the Thorndike was completely lost to a disastrous fire, the largest in Jamestown's history. In 1912 and 1913, a replacement hotel, the "new" Thorndike, was erected at the same location as the old, but it failed to draw the

Fig. 3-15. Narragansett Pier, R.I., from Steamboat Pier. Photograph, 1883. North Kingston Free Library, Lawrence Collection.

same high praise for its architecture. Comparable in scale to its predecessor, the second Thorndike, with its plain, flat walls and stacked rows of porches, resembled an exaggerated version of a stark, mid-twentieth-century motel. Known as the "Tin Palace" because of the presence of interior tin ceilings and walls, this uninspiring structure, like so many a victim of the Great Depression, was torn down in the autumn of 1938, ironically just one week before the great hurricane of that year devastated the Rhode Island coastline.[18]

Narragansett Pier: The "City of Hotels"

Narragansett Pier occupies a prime seaside location overlooking Rhode Island Sound at the western entrance of Narragansett Bay, approximately ten miles southwest of Newport and four miles northeast of Point Judith. Blessed with the natural advantages of the state's most expansive, crescent-shaped beach, as well as picturesque cliffs, sand dunes, and highlands, the Pier evolved from a small, low-profile community to a renowned coastal resort, its late nineteenth-century hospitality industry one of the largest and busiest in New England, rivaled only by Old Orchard Beach and Bar Harbor, Maine. From

humble beginnings in the 1780s, when the first wharf was built (to which the town owes its name) to serve the backland agricultural economy, Narragansett Pier became the locus of varied commercial and mercantile interests, by the 1850s including steam and planing mills. Paralleling this development were the first signs of tourism when, in the 1840s, people from other areas of Rhode Island began traveling to the Pier to take advantage of the superlative beach bathing (still water or surf). As there were no public accommodations at the time, these first visitors boarded at the homes of local farmers, in quiet, unsophisticated but attractive settings.[19]

During the 1850s, the local economic and social structures underwent dramatic change, and the Pier became, like Jamestown, a low-key competitor with Newport, drawing wealthy society types and men of stature. In 1856, the town's first hotel, the Narragansett House, was built, signaling the beginnings of the Pier's rapid transformation to a predominantly tourism-based economy. Between 1866 and 1871, on the heels of the Civil War, ten new hotels, with guest capacities eventually ranging from 150 to 250, appeared, primarily along Ocean Avenue fronting on the beach (fig. 3-15) and on the side streets. Included in this august but unpretentious group

Fig. 3-16. "Atlantic House, Abijah Browning, Esq., Prop., Narragansett Pier, R.I." Lithograph from *History of the State of Rhode Island* (Philadelphia: Hoag, Wade & Company, 1878), op. p. 296. Courtesy, The Winterthur Library Printed Book and Periodical Collection.

Fig. 3-17. Metatoxet House, Narragansett Pier, R.I. Photograph from *Views of Narragansett Pier* (Providence, R.I.: Tibbetts & Preston, 1884), p. 13. North Kingston Free Library, Lawrence Collection.

were the near twin Atlantic (1866–67) (fig. 3-16) and Atwood (1866–67; later, The Breakers) houses; the Metatoxet House (1866–67; later, the Beachwood Hotel) (fig. 3-17); the Revere House (1868); the Mathewson (1868), the first portion of the Pier's most architecturally noteworthy hotel complex (see below); the Delavan House (1869); the Ocean House (1869–70); the Maxson House (1870; later, the Massasoit Hotel); the Continental Hotel (c. 1870–71; later, the Hotel De La Plage) (fig. 3-18); and

the Mount Hope House (1871; later, the Hotel Berwick) (fig. 3-19), the largest of the group, taking upward of 300 guests after it assumed its fully developed form in the late 1880s. A similarly configured hotel was the Tower Hill House and Cottages (c. 1870–71) (fig. 3-20), until it closed in 1892, situated at Narragansett Heights, three miles west of the Pier but with magnificent, sweeping views of the sound and bay from its spectacular site, 200 feet above sea level.[20]

Fig. 3-18. Continental Hotel, Narragansett Pier, R.I. Photograph, c. 1875. Albumen photograph, Unknown, RHi X3 7812, Graphics Collection: PF Narragansett–Narragansett Pier. Courtesy the Rhode Island Historical Society.

Fig. 3-19. "Mount Hope House, Hon. W. G. Caswell, Prop., Narragansett Pier, R.I." Lithograph from *History of the State of Rhode Island* (Philadelphia: Hoag, Wade & Company, 1878), op. p. 296. Courtesy, The Winterthur Library Printed Book and Periodical Collection.

Fig. 3-20. Tower Hill House, Narragansett Heights, R.I. Advertisement engraving, *A Guide to Narragansett Bay* (1878). Courtesy, The Winterthur Library Printed Book and Periodical Collection.

Architecturally, the collective hotels were strikingly similar in building mass and detail. Each consisted primarily of a long, rectangular main block of wooden materials that ranged in height from two and one-half to four stories. Some possessed wings and ells, and a few fronts, such as those of the Mount Hope and Tower Hill houses, featured monumental, square central towers with roof caps, creating an almost ecclesiastical air. Others, like the Continental, displayed gabled central pavilions in lieu of towers. Most of these structures were covered by mansard roofs accented by dormers, and all had first-level verandas running along the main façade and side walls. The horizontal plans were less uniform, the wings and ells producing T-, L-, or U-shaped floor schemes. As is so accurately articulated in a 1991 Rhode Island Historical Preservation Commission report, the "combination of similarity and dissimilarity must have created a picturesque townscape with an underlying unity." The loss of these and more recent hotels (see below) to fire, and obsolescence and demolition, has left a huge hole, literally as well as figuratively, in the history and physical environment of Narragansett Pier.[21]

The opening of the Narragansett Pier Railroad spur in 1876 greatly improved transportation access to the Pier, thus further stimulating resort hotel development there. During the 1880s and 1890s, four large complexes joined the growing list of local summer hostelries. The first of these was the Rockingham Hotel, erected from 1882 to 1883 by J. G. Burns, and for the initial five years

of its existence known as "Hotel McSparren." It was situated off Ocean Road at the north end of the hotel district, overlooking the beach next to McKim, Mead and White's famed Casino and Towers, which achieved final form about the same time, between 1883 and 1886. In 1888, Burns substantially enlarged the original structure seaward, renaming it "The Rockingham" (fig. 3-21). Offering space for 200 boarders, this symmetrical, five-story, T-plan structure with older mansard-roof ell seemed anchored to the land by virtue of its square front façade tower with its highly embellished, truncated, pyramidal roof cover. In the early 1890s, the Rockingham (fig. 3-22) achieved its full-blown, 500-capacity form

Fig. 3-21. "The Rockingham, Narragansett Pier," R.I. Engraving from Robert Grieve, *The New England Coast* (1892), p. 39. Maine Historic Preservation Commission.

Fig. 3-22. The Casino and Rockingham Hotel, Narragansett Pier, R.I. Photograph, c. 1895. Courtesy of the Westerly Public Library, R.I.

Fig. 3-23. Fire at the Rockingham Hotel, Narragansett Pier, R.I. Photograph, 12 September 1900. Courtesy of The Newport Historical Society, R.I.

when the front block was totally rebuilt in the Colonial Revival vein, distinguished by a multistage central roof tower, a steep-hipped roof with cross-gable and assorted dormers, and a well-articulated bracketed cornice. Tragically, on 12 September 1900, a fire started on the top floor and destroyed the hotel (fig. 3-23) but also adjacent buildings, including the Casino, leaving only the stone masonry Towers to remind us today of what once was.[22]

Though a far more subdued architectural statement than the Rockingham, the Gladstone Hotel (fig. 3-24) also merits our attention. Run in conjunction with the much smaller Columbus Hotel (c. 1879; 100 capacity), the first portion of the Gladstone was financed by George C. Robinson in 1887. A second stage was added

Fig. 3-24. Gladstone Hotel, Narragansett Pier, R.I. Photograph, c. 1889. Albumen photograph, Detroit Photographic Co., RHi X3 7858, Graphics Collection: Scrapbook Collection—Narragansett. Courtesy the Rhode Island Historical Society.

during the 1890s, creating space for 350 to 400 guests. The two stages, in fact, resulted from the combination and enlargement of two older hotels, the Delavan, which was moved, and the Elmwood, located on the Gladstone site. A massive, L-shaped Colonial Revival structure, the Gladstone was protected by a gambrel roof with dormers, and on the ground floor was encircled by the customary veranda, used by guests for respite, particularly fashionable promenading. The overall building form, with its shingled wall surfaces, fit well into the surrounding environment—four acres of tree-shaded, manicured lawns proximate to the beach and the waters of the bay. The Gladstone was a vital player in the Narragansett Pier hotel economy until 1920, when it was unceremoniously torn down.[23]

Without question, the most significant architecturally of the Pier's numerous hotels was the Mathewson, the original component of which was raised in 1868 by owner S. W. Mathewson, also a mineral water producer, on an Ocean Avenue plot near the later site of the Rockingham Hotel. Like the other local hotels (see above) erected soon after the Civil War, this mansard-roof building (fig. 3-25), augmented by an expansive, L-shaped rear extension circa 1875, possessed many of the characteristics associated with the then highly popular Second Empire style. This first incarnation of the Mathewson, though, would not be long-lasting.

During the 1880s, the Shingle style made its initial impression at Narragansett Pier and environs, most emphatically in the Casino and Towers (see above) and several seasonal cottages. The first hotel to express rec-

Fig. 3-25. The Mathewson Hotel, Narragansett Pier, R.I. Photograph, June 1883. North Kingston Free Library, Lawrence Collection.

ognizable qualities of this style was the quaint Greene's Inn (fig. 3-26), designed by Boston architect William G. Preston (1844–1910) (see chapter 8) in 1887 and located at the south end of Ocean Avenue until it burned in 1978. Following this was the Mathewson, to which was added (1895–96) a monumental, L-shaped front block from plans by New York City architect C. P. H. Gilbert. A front elevation perspective drawing (fig. 3-27) was reproduced in the promotional booklet *The Woods, Lakes, Sea-Shore and Mountains* (Portland, Maine: G. W. Morris) in 1896, followed by a full-page photograph in the 26 February 1898 issue of *American Architect and Building News*. Old and new construction were combined to create a final U-shaped floor plan enclosing a large, open rear court with gardens.

The "new" Mathewson Hotel, with rooms for 500 visitors, was clearly deserving of the attention it attracted. As William Jordy and Christopher Monkhouse observe in their 1982 book, *Buildings on Paper: Rhode Island Architectural Drawings, 1825–1945*, the enlarged and recast structure (fig. 3-28) was inspired, in part, by the prior designs for Greene's Inn and the Casino and Towers, characterized by the flexible use of forms and decorative elements. On the other hand, as Gilbert planned the Mathewson about a decade later, "increasing academicism made design in general a matter of symmetry and historical correctness." This was reflected in the hotel's nearly perfect, balanced front façade symmetry and various design details drawn from the tradition of American Colonial-era architecture. Particularly worthy of notice was the double-gambrel-roof central pavilion surmounted by a polygonal belvedere with concave roof caps, as well as the matching polygonal corner towers with similarly shaped flared caps and bands of windows with their broken-scroll pediments and round arches with keystones. A masterpiece in wood fabrication, the Mathewson exhibited an extraordinary collection of Colonial-inspired details, giving it special status among Shingle-style New England coastal resort hotels of the same period. Nonetheless, its architectural excellence

Fig. 3-26. "Greene's Inn," Narragansett Pier, R.I., William G. Preston, Architect, 1887. Drawings from *American Architect and Building News* 23 (28 January 1888). Courtesy of the University of Delaware Library.

Fig. 3-27. *(below)* "The Mathewson, Narragansett Pier, R.I." Front elevation perspective drawing, C. P. N. Gilbert, Architect, New York, c. 1895, from *The Woods, Lakes, Sea-Shore, and Mountains* (1896). Author's collection.

Fig. 3-28. The Mathewson Hotel, Narragansett Pier, R.I. Construction photograph (c. 1896) from the northeast by Davidson, Narragansett Pier. North Kingston Free Library, Lawrence Collection.

did not guarantee its long-term preservation, and, bowing to the depressing effects of the World War I era on the tourism economy, it was demolished in 1918.[24]

In the same Shingle-style "grand" resort-hotel tradition as the Mathewson was the Imperial Hotel (fig. 3-29), completed from 1897 to 1898 under the direction of Walter A. Nye. Nye had acquired the Columbus Hotel (see above) in 1893, had it enlarged, and then moved it to a new location where it formed a portion of the new complex. Accommodating over 250 patrons, the Imperial was not as large as the Mathewson but gave the impression of greater height owing to the presence of an extra story in the central front façade gable. Many of the same shapes and motifs present in the older building, how-

ever, were visible in the corner towers, gables, dormers, and veranda of its successor. Considered in its prime to be the Pier's most luxurious guest establishment, appealing to an upper-class clientele, it survived the war era, succumbing to a much publicized fire in September 1923. The loss of the Imperial was followed by the further decline of Narragansett Pier's resort-hotel industry, until the last of the proud old wooden structures passed into history after World War II.[25]

Watch Hill and the Ocean House: A Lost Survivor

Like Jamestown and Narragansett Pier, Watch Hill developed primarily as a summer resort of hotels, with

Fig. 3-29. "The Imperial Hotel. Narragansett Pier, R.I." Colored postcard (c. 1900), Rhode Island News Company, Providence. North Kingston Free Library, Lawrence Collection.

Fig. 3-30. Plimpton House and annex, Watch Hill, R.I. Engraving from Robert Grieve, *Picturesque Narragansett* (c. 1889), p. 187. Maine Historic Preservation Commission.

private, secluded cottage life significant but secondary until the decline of the hotels commenced in the late nineteenth century. Rhode Island's primary mainland Atlantic Ocean resort community, Watch Hill is situated in the town of Westerly at the extreme southwest corner of the state, on a triangular neck of land bounded on the south by Block Island Sound and on the northwest by Little Narragansett Bay and the Pawcatuck River. The principal local topographical features fostering resort development were the long, continuous, slightly curving, sandy beaches and the gently rolling terrain, with knolls, depressions, and small ponds. At the center, "The Hill" provided excellent scenic view sites for all categories of architecture, the ocean being the most compelling environmental and recreational attraction.

At first sparsely settled with an agrarian economic base, Watch Hill Peninsula gradually transitioned to a summer colony following the patterns common to most New England seaside resorts (see chapter 1). Local resort development began in the 1830s when large landowner and lighthouse keeper Jonathan Nash opened his home to boarders and then erected a small hotel, the first Watch Hill House, circa 1835 at a commanding location atop "The Hill." The Dickens Inn, a modest guesthouse, was the next hostelry to be built, in 1840. Nash's son, Nathan, launched the Narragansett House from 1844 to 1845, while at the same time another son, Winslow, constructed and opened the Bay View House. A decade then passed before the building of the Atlantic House (see fig. 3-35) by the partnership of Dickens and Taylor from 1855 to 1856. With initial rooming space for 150 visitors, this compact, T-shaped Italianate structure was Watch Hill's first significant resort hotel, rivaling its larger, more recent competitors until, renamed "Colonial House," it was lost in the great conflagration of 1916 (see below).[26]

Chronologically, the next Watch Hill hotel of reasonable size was the Plimpton (also "Plympton") House, erected in 1865 by Andrew S. Plimpton, the former manager of the Dixon House in downtown Westerly. Of simpler, more austere design than the Atlantic, the four-story, L-shaped-plan Plimpton (fig. 3-30) consisted of joined flat-roofed rectangular box masses, very utilitarian in form and devoid of any obvious embellishment. Present on the main façade and south end walls were three- and two-story verandas, positioned to take advantage of the views of the hotel dock and Little Narragansett Bay. Though a less than distinguished architectural statement, the hotel provided benefits to its guests in the central, double-loaded corridors and narrow building blocks affording excellent natural light and ventilation. On the first floor, large public spaces—an entrance rotunda, music room, dining room, smoking rooms, and ladies' parlor—provided essential places for social gathering. By the end of the century, the Plimpton's capacity reached 350, the main building supplemented by adjacent annexes, including the former Dickens Inn, and Bay View and Narragansett houses (see above). Facing competition and declining patronage, the original hotel and annexes, except the Narragansett, were torn down in 1906.[27]

The only one of Watch Hill's large resort hotels to survive beyond the great 1916 fire was the Ocean House (fig.

Fig. 3-31. Southwest view, Ocean House, Watch Hill, R.I. Photograph, 2004, by the author.

3-31), located on the southeast side of "The Hill" on Bluff Avenue overlooking Block Island Sound. In recent years, this truly "grand" hotel was the focus of a lengthy historic preservation debate and renovation planning, but finally it was deemed structurally unsound and was demolished by the current property owners, Bluff Avenue LLC, in late 2005 and early 2006. Fortunately, many exterior and interior fragments and decorative elements were saved, to be incorporated into a larger, flexible re-creation (with new north wing) of the original complex that will be erected in the near future on the thirteen-acre site, with a reopening of the estimated $70 million edifice tentatively scheduled for summer 2008. Conforming to modern building and safety codes, this near replica will be based on photogrammatic architectural drawings prepared by Centerbrook Architects and Planners of Connecticut. In the spirit of the original, the new hotel will include guest rooms and suites, a spa, a lobby area, enclosed porches, a dining room, banquet and meeting rooms, a fitness center and pool, other public spaces, condominium units, and a lower parking garage. This enlightened, ambitious project will help preserve the spirit and recollections, if not the entire fabric, of one of New England's last surviving nineteenth-century resort hotels.[28]

But, what of the beginnings and evolution of this newsworthy former center of hospitality? The initial portion was erected from 1867 to 1868 by George M. Nash, another son of Jonathan Nash, the original owner and proprietor of the first Watch Hill House (see above). Additions were made circa 1885. The resulting L-shaped section consisted of two three-and-one-half-story mansard-roof wings with modillioned cornices, set at right angles to a five-and-one-half-story tower with corner pilasters, a modillioned cornice, and a tall, steep, hipped roof pierced by hipped double dormers. Two-story verandas of delicate, wooden construction surrounded most of the building mass. Appended to the southeast circa 1903, and rising above the hillside on high basements, were two massive, plain, parallel ells, each five stories high with low-pitched roofs (fig. 3-32). With these expansions, the capacity peaked at around 300.

Fig. 3-32. Southeast view, Ocean House, Watch Hill, R.I. Photograph, 2004, by the author.

Fig. 3-33. Southwest veranda, c. 1905, Ocean House, Watch Hill, R.I. Photograph, 2004, by the author.

At the outer end of each ell were second-level recessed, glazed, wraparound porches. Likely also dating from about 1903 were a Colonial Revival veranda with round columns (fig. 3-33) on the southwest side and northeast end, and a two-story semicircular front entrance porch supported by graceful Ionic columns. On its raised site, this great wooden ark, with its abundant classical details, was a dominant presence in Watch Hill's architectural repertoire for almost 140 years. In its reinvigorated form, it should reassume that role in future years.[29]

In 1869, under the direction of Daniel F. Larkin & Co., the Larkin House (fig. 3-34) rose on a near perfect site at the south end of the village near the principal bathing beach, steamboat docks, and Lighthouse Point. Without question, in its fully developed form it was the grandest of Watch Hill's large hotels, accommodating upward of 400 guests. As initially constructed, the Larkin took the shape of the older Atlantic House (see above), its four-story main block perfectly symmetrical, displaying a concave mansard roof with dormers, a one-story

Fig. 3-34. Larkin House, Watch Hill, R.I., 1889. Courtesy of Mystic Seaport, Photography Collection, Mystic, Conn., #1985.112.3.

wraparound veranda, and a central gable-roof pavilion crowned by an octagonal cupola. The structure remained unchanged until about 1896, when the ownership added one hundred feet to the south end, including stacked verandas and a matching second pavilion with cupola, resulting in a dominant, almost perfectly balanced architectural composition. With business clearly thriving, during the following year an ell was added to the north end containing an enlarged music and dance hall, dining room, and a kitchen and other service rooms. In their size, appointments, and special features, bedrooms were not overlooked, as evidenced in an 1887 promotional booklet for the hotel:

The rooms are large, with high ceilings, airy and well furnished, good woolen carpets, spring beds, and hair mattresses. The house is lighted with gas throughout, has electric bells and clothes-presses in every sleeping-room, and many of the rooms are *en suite*. Telegraph office in the main hall.

Over nine hundred feet of verandas encircled the entire complex, demonstrating the importance placed on sitting, public socializing, conspicuous appearance, and

moderate exercise by promenading. From east to west, guests could enjoy sweeping views over water, including Point Judith and Weekapaug, Block Island, Montauk Point and Long Island, Fishers and Little Gull islands, and the Connecticut shore. The Larkin House, like many similar contemporary hotel structures along the New England seaboard, successfully combined such public connection with nature and the surrounding environment, with the more insular, inside world of the hotel catering to the many needs of its clientele. It did this until 1906, when it was bought by members of the Griscom family, who demolished it and built their summer vacation home on the site.[30]

Watch Hill's last large resort hotel was the New Watch Hill House (fig. 3-35), the result of a major expansion of Jonathan Nash's first Watch Hill House (see above) completed from 1877 to 1878. This replacement structure was positioned on the foundations of its predecessor and attached to the ell of the older building, which was then twice relocated and used as an annex. Set on the highest elevation of "The Hill," the New Watch Hill House possessed quite conventional massing, comparable to

Fig. 3-35. New Watch Hill House (with Atlantic House to the left), Watch Hill, R.I., c. 1889. Courtesy of Mystic Seaport, Photography Collection, Mystic, Conn., #1985.112.2.

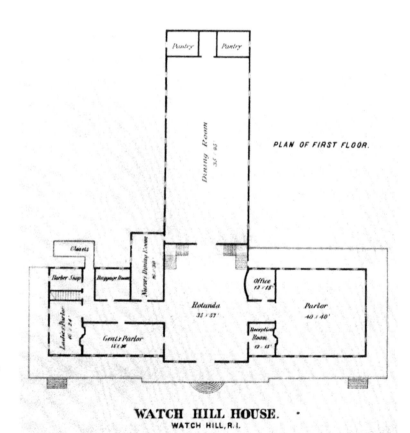

PLAN OF FIRST FLOOR.

Pantry

Pantry

Dining Room
35 x 95'

Closets

Barber Shop

Baggage Room

Nurses' Dining Room
16 x 30'

Office
12 x 15'

Ladies' Parlor
16 x 24'

Gents Parlor
18 x 30'

Rotunda
35 x 57'

Reception Room
12 x 15'

Parlor
40 x 40'

WATCH HILL HOUSE.
WATCH HILL, R.I.

Fig. 3-36. "Plan of First Floor," Watch Hill House, Watch Hill, R.I. From booklet, *Watch Hill House, Watch Hill, R.I.* (c. 1885). Courtesy of Historic New England.

that of the Larkin House and hotels at Narragansett Pier and Block Island during the same period. The 160-foot main front section of the T-shaped complex (fig. 3-36) was symmetrical with four-story, flat-mansard-roof wings attached to a central six-story block, protected by a tall, heavy mansard roof cap pierced by two levels of dormers. Typical of the time and the building type, a long, wide, one-story veranda encircled the entire front section, offering almost 360-degree vistas. Promoted as Watch Hill's largest hotel (it was in fact eclipsed by the Larkin House), the New Watch Hill House boasted 165 rooms, with a total capacity, including annexes, upward of 400 guests by 1900. Along with the Atlantic (Colonial) House (see above), it was totally destroyed by fire on 19 October 1916, never to be reconstructed.[31]

As a consequence, of Watch Hill's large resort hotels, only the Ocean House remained, to survive another ninety years until its recent demolition and planned reconstruction (see above). Prior to 1900, the town had become a prime destination resort, consisting of little else but the hotels; since then, economic and social change, coupled with pure fate, have resulted in its transformation to a largely upscale summer cottage community. Such a transformation mirrors that of numerous other ocean (as well as mountain and lake) vacation centers throughout New England.

Block Island

Block Island, with its curious eleven-square-mile pork chop shape, is located twelve miles from the southern Rhode Island shoreline in the Atlantic Ocean, about half way between Newport and Montauk Point on the eastern end of Long Island. Constituting the town of New Shoreham, it has long been accessed by boat from Point Judith, New London, Long Island, and other seaside locations in the immediate region. Until the mid–nineteenth century, Block Island was a relatively unpopulated, sleepy agrarian and fishing community, lacking a natural harbor and docking facilities like nearby Fishers Island, Nantucket, and Martha's Vineyard. The island's character, however, was dramatically changed when, in the years from 1870 to 1876, led by entrepreneur and state representative Nicholas Ball, funds were appropriated by the U.S. Congress to construct a breakwater and Gov-

ernment Harbor, along with two new lighthouses and other navigational aids, on the east side. The immediate effect was the creation of a new commercial center, today referred to as "Old Harbor," at the new point of ocean access, featuring shops, boardinghouses, hotels, and other buildings, as well as summer houses in the general vicinity. With the establishment of the harbor, Block Island entered a new era in its history, its economy predicated on summer hospitality tourism. Offering a mild-climate, low-key vacation experience, it was to become one of New England's major coastal resorts, challenging Rhode Island's other resort centers.

With closer connections to the mainland, Block Island gradually saw the introduction of new, more sophisticated, stylized architecture, supplementing the older vernacular tradition. This was evident in all building types but particularly in the impressive array of rectangular-block, mansard-roofed Second Empire hotels with their cupolas and verandas that amassed at Old Harbor. The several remaining examples comprise by far the largest and most diverse collection of surviving early resort-hotel structures left on the New England seaboard today. As a result of federal tax incentives for historic preservation, several of these have been restored since the late 1970s. The first hotel opened on Block Island in 1842, followed by the Spring House (see below) on Spring Street ten years later. Among other extant medium- to large-size hotel buildings at Old Harbor are the Surf Hotel (1873, etc.) (fig. 3-37); the front block of the

Fig. 3-37. The National Hotel (*left*) and the Surf Hotel (Cottage) (*right*), Old Harbor, Block Island, R.I. Photograph, 2005, by the author.

Fig. 3-38. Hotel Manisses, Old Harbor, Block Island, R.I. Photograph, 2005, by the author.

Fig. 3-39. "The Spring House, Block Island, R.I." Engraving from Samuel T. Livermore, *Block Island* (1886 ed.), n.p. The Connecticut Historical Society Museum, Hartford, Connecticut.

Fig. 3-40. The Spring House, Old Harbor, Block Island, R.I. Photograph, 2005, by the author.

Hotel Manisses (United States Hotel) (1876) (fig. 3-38), lacking its 1883 ell; and, with its "sunbonnet" dormers, the New National Hotel (1888; burned, 1902; rebuilt, c. 1903) (see fig. 3-37).[32]

The Spring House and two other large hotels, the Ocean View and the Hygeia, both gone, merit close scrutiny. Erected in 1852 and considerably expanded in 1877 and 1898, the Spring House (fig. 3-39), along with its annex, constitutes the oldest, largest, and best-preserved surviving hotel complex on Block Island, as well as the entire Rhode Island coast. Capable of housing 250 boarders at its peak, it enjoyed great popularity, in large part because of its raised site looking out on the Atlantic and because of the health-enhancing mineral springs on the property. Three stories in height under a bellcast or concave mansard roof with central mansard-roof cupola, the T-shaped main building (fig. 3-40) was second only to the Ocean View House (see below) in size. A one-story, bracketed veranda extended along the north front façade, east side wall, and east wall of a long, pitched-roof ell. Set at right angles to this structure is the three-story annex, its most unusual design feature the ogee dormer gables in the bellcast mansard roof.[33]

Once dominating the harbor from its elevated site, the Ocean View House, the largest resort establishment in the island's history, no longer stands, having been lost to fire in 1966. The hotel had auspicious beginnings,

however. The first portion, erected by Nicholas Ball as steamboat service commenced in 1873, opened the following year, as described in the 9 June 1874 edition of the *Providence Evening Bulletin*:

Last Saturday evening, May 30, the Ocean View Hotel was illuminated with gas, from cellar to cupola, the new gas works and fixtures having just been completed. Three years ago such a sight was not even dreamed of by the quiet fishers of this little island, yet here we have, right on Block Island, a large, commodious, first-class hotel, located upon its eastern bluffs, only 250 feet off the breaking surf of the broad, blue Atlantic; surrounded by broad cool piazzas [verandas], and smooth, grassy lawns; finished with large, high sleeping apartments, parlors, halls, billiard-room and barbershop; well supplied with water, and every room lighted with gas, in fact a first-class hotel in all its appointments.

With its numerous assets, the Ocean View quickly established an esteemed reputation in New England's increasingly competitive resort-hotel industry.

As was customary with most substantial, high-capacity hotels of the period, the Ocean View developed in stages over several years in response to customer demand. Initially a conventional, Second Empire-style, four-story block with hipped-on-mansard roof and central cupola, it received matching wings and an ell within three years of its opening (fig. 3-41). By 1883, after several

Fig. 3-41. "Ocean View Hotel, Block Island. Hon. Nicholas Ball, Prop." Lithograph from *History of the State of Rhode Island* (Philadelphia: Hoag, Wade & Co., 1878), op. p. 192. Courtesy, The Winterthur Library Printed Book and Periodical Collection.

Fig. 3-42. Ocean View Hotel and Cottages, Old Harbor, Block Island,
R.I. Photograph, c. 1875. Albumen photograph, Unknown, RHi X3 7813,
Graphics Collection: PF–Block Island. Courtesy the Rhode Island Historical
Society.

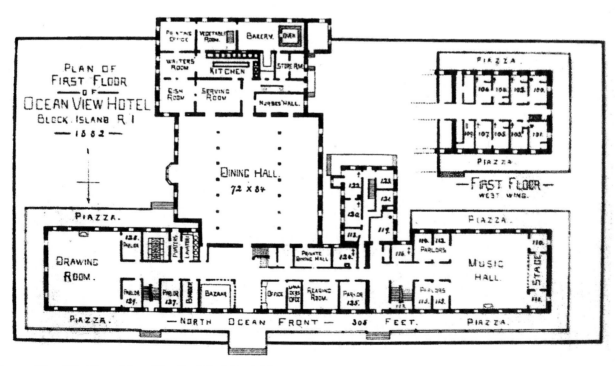

Fig. 3-43. "Plan of First Floor of Ocean View Hotel, Block Island, R.I.,
1882." From Samuel T. Livermore, *Block Island Guide* (1882 ed.), n.p. The
Connecticut Historical Society Museum, Hartford, Connecticut.

Fig. 3-44. "The Hygeia," Block Island, R.I. Photograph from viewbook,
Block Island: Hotels, Residences (1900). Author's collection.

completed construction projects, its wings had been further extended, producing an asymmetrical front façade
of over 350 feet (fig. 3-42) and interior space for over 500
guests. A fragile-appearing wooden bridge linked the
northwest end of the hotel to an adjacent annex of compatible design, for most its existence known as the "Ocean
View Cottage" and then the "Shamrock Inn." Overall,
this bridge, combined with the wraparound veranda of
the hotel, resulted in a remarkable 1,500-foot strip for
promenading and other social activities. The first floor
(fig. 3-43) of the fully mature complex, as was typical,
contained the large primary as well as secondary public
rooms and service areas, while the bedrooms and bathrooms, modest and functional, were concentrated on the
floors above. Touted as "the palace hotel of Block Island,"
the Ocean View, with its ample facilities and diverse offerings, was the summer home of the elite. Among its
most distinguished visitors were President U. S. Grant,
members of the U.S. Congress, ambassadors, governors,
U.S. Supreme Court justices, business leaders, and the
independent well-to-do.[34]

The third of Block Island's large nineteenth-century

resort hotels, the Hygeia (fig. 3-44), was a stylistic depar-
ture from the Second Empire structures of Old Harbor,
and was located less than a mile to the northwest at
New Harbor on a knoll between two small lakes, with
extensive ocean views. Named for the Greek goddess
of health, this hotel was built by Dr. Charles H. Hadley,
who served as resident physician, and was promoted as
a haven for those seeking a healthy and comfortable vacation lifestyle. Hotel literature underscored the restful,
health-enhancing environment, excellent opportunities
for nearby surf bathing and boating, inside showers, and
large, airy rooms with open fireplaces, washbowls, and
running springwater. Special efforts were made by the
management to attract families of business and professional men, those recovering from illness, and invalids
seeking "to combine recuperation and recreation" in
"remarkable purity of atmosphere." While other hotels of
the same time along the New England coast offered many
of the same benefits to their patrons, the Hygeia, with its
emphasis on good health conditions, was regarded as a
particular standout.

The oldest portion of the Hygeia Hotel, later to become the central block of an enlarged complex, dated from 1885 to 1886 and, given its modest scale, resembled a wooden, Stick-style summer cottage more than it did typically Second Empire–style hotel architecture of the time. Most certainly architect-designed, this picturesque three-story, T-shaped building, its front façade of balanced symmetry, expressed lightness and strong verticality in its square central tower; steep-pitched-roof, central pavilion, and flanking gables; tall, narrow windows; and thin porch-support columns. In 1899, the Hygeia assumed a more obvious hotel look, made possible by the addition of matching gambrel-roof wings, increasing the capacity, including an annex and cottages, to approximately 300 persons. As a consequence of this building project, the main hotel complex was transformed, becoming predominantly horizontal in form, enhanced by long, encircling, one-story verandas. The Hygeia's service as a hotel ended in 1916 when it burned to the ground.[35]

The hotel trade on Block Island, like that at Jamestown, Narragansett Pier, and Watch Hill, continued to prosper during the first part of the twentieth century but began to show signs of decline during the World War I years. The downward trend continued during the 1920s as social and vacation patterns significantly changed, and accelerated during the Depression and World War II. Since the 1970s, however, Block Island has experienced a renaissance, entailing further expansion of the summer homes community and a revitalization of the hotel industry. In recent years, the local economy, again based primarily on hospitality tourism, has prospered, and this, coupled with federal tax incentives (see above), has resulted in the restoration and reactivation of older hotel structures of architectural and historic value. These serve as material reminders of the indelible summer resort legacy of Block Island, as well as Newport and the other communities along Narragansett Bay and the southern Rhode Island shoreline.[36]

MASSACHUSETTS

The South Shore, Cape Cod, and the Islands

COMPRISING WELL OVER five hundred miles of the Massachusetts coastline south and southeast of Boston, the South Shore, Cape Cod, Martha's Vineyard, and other islands became significant centers of summer resort development commencing in the early decades of the nineteenth century. While the principal component of such development, hospitality tourism, ultimately became a major economic enterprise in the entire region, large resort hotels, despite the presence of highly desirable and usable shoreline, were fewer and less concentrated than they were in Rhode Island and along Boston's North Shore (see chapters 3 and 5). Factors inhibiting their origins and proliferation were distance from major population centers, except for the area just southeast of Boston, and the relatively late development of efficient public transportation links. As a consequence, the most ambitious hotel structures were situated on the seaboard near Boston from Hull to Plymouth and, with the exception of Nantucket and Martha's Vineyard, were in much less evidence farther removed from the city on Cape Cod and the southern coast of Massachusetts between Westport and Buzzards Bay.

Although the region possessed no distinctive "grand" examples of resort hotel architecture like those of Rhode Island and the North Shore, it did boast an extremely impressive group of buildings exhibiting Victorian eclectic stylistic combinations, as well as specific architectural styles such as Second Empire, Stick, Queen Anne, Shingle, and Colonial Revival. The latter design idiom was represented all along the area coastline, while earlier styles were in particular evidence at Hull and Nantasket Beach, and Martha's Vineyard. Virtually all of the region's large, pre–World War II coastal resort hotels have succumbed to burning or demolition, but two survivors — the Chatham Bars Inn at Chatham, Cape Cod, and the Harbor View Hotel at Edgartown, Martha's Vineyard — have continued to represent traditional hospitality tourism entrepreneurship, attracting notice for their venerable, unmistakable Colonial Revival styling and ambience.

Hull and Nantasket Beach

Nine miles southeast of Boston, at the end of a long, hooked peninsula separating Massachusetts Bay from Hingham Bay, is the town of Hull, one of Massachusetts' oldest and most popular "sea-bathing" and entertainment resort communities. Its most notable physical asset is scenic Nantasket Beach, over four miles in length on the ocean side of the peninsula, and

Fig. 4-1. "The Oregon House, Hull," Mass. Photolithograph from Moses F. Sweetser, *King's Handbook of Boston Harbor* (1882), p. 30B. Courtesy, The Winterthur Library Printed Book and Periodical Collection.

Fig. 4-2. "Rockland House, Nantasket Beach," Hull, Mass. Lithograph by the New England Lith. Co., Boston, from sheet music, "Rockland Echoes Waltzes" by J. S. Knight, published by G. D. Russell & Company, Boston, 1870. Author's collection.

traditionally referred to as "the Coney Island of Boston" and "one of the finest ocean shores on the United States coast." Accessed by the South Shore Railroad as early as the 1850s, and later by the Nantasket Beach Railroad, the beach became recognized for its expansive, sandy shore, flashing surf, headlands and highlands, offshore islands, nearby lighthouses, its ship life on the water, and its almost unbroken line of restaurants, boardinghouses, and hotels varying in sizes and pretensions. Catering to people of "moderate means," Nantasket Beach, encouraged by the arrival of steamboat service in 1869, became a center of hospitality and recreational entrepreneurship that has continued into the modern era.[1]

The oldest of the large hotels was the Oregon House, its earliest portion built in 1848 on a hillside in Hull at the corner to Highland and Nastasket avenues overlooking the north end of the beach. Constructed with wood timbers recycled from the Castle Island military barracks, the three-and-one-half-story hostelry (fig. 4-1) was marked by its steep gambrel roof, dormers with finials, and, central to the front of the building, a square stair tower crowned by a concave mansard roof cap with finial. Enlarged and modified several times during its history, the Oregon compiled a lengthy record of service lasting to 1926, when it was demolished.[2]

Hull's next major hotel enterprise was the Rockland House (fig. 4-2), established in 1854 by Colonel Nehemiah Ripley, who operated it for nearly forty years. Situated at the end of the beach near Nantasket Pier on a rise overlooking the former Paragon Park, this imposing, Second Empire–style guest facility grew from a 60-foot-façade structure with forty rooms to a 275-foot-façade structure, surrounded by verandas, with nearly two hundred rooms accommodating over 300 overnight visitors. In the 1882 *King's Handbook of Boston Harbor* (p. 56), Moses F. Sweetser observed that the Rockland "was successful from the start" and "was a result of re-modellings and improvements of so many years, [so that] the hotel is now one of the best and most commodious on the coast, with all the modern necessities of aqueduct water, gas, steam-heat, richly furnished parlors, billiard rooms, music rooms, etc." Like other large resort hotels of its size and quality, in addition to billiards it offered its guests golf, tennis, basketball, roulette wheels, and dice tables. A mecca for wealthy and high-profile patrons, the

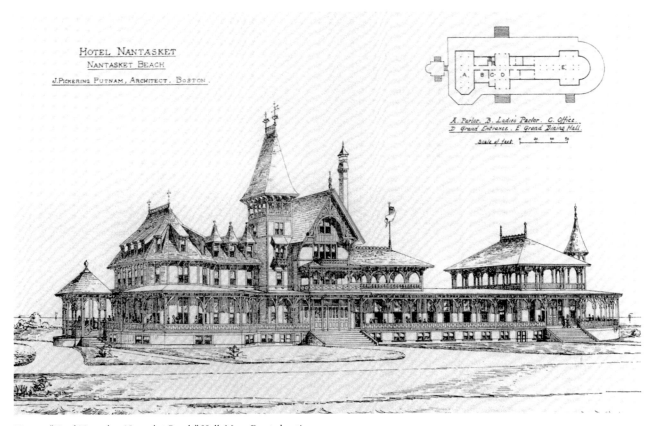

Fig. 4-3. "Hotel Nantasket, Nantasket Beach," Hull, Mass. Front elevation perspective drawing by J. Pickering Putnam, Boston, from *American Architect and Building News* 6, no. 196 (27 September 1879). Courtesy of the University of Delaware Library.

Rockland entertained many famous guests, including President Grover Cleveland and New York governor and presidential candidate Al Smith. Last owned by Patrick Bowen, the massive hotel edifice was destroyed during a snowstorm by a major fire on 4 February 1916.[3]

Designed by the noted Boston architect J. Pickering Putnam, the Hotel Nantasket (fig. 4-3) at Nantasket Beach, in its original 1879 form, was one of the most outstanding Stick-style resort hotels on the New England seaboard, in stylistic quality rivaled only by the Sea View House and Mattakeeset Lodge on Martha's Vineyard (see below). Often referred to as the "Aladdin's Palace" of the area because of the presence of its central tower, gables, dormers, support brackets, roof finials, balconies, and porches, this remarkable, fragile-appearing, irregularly shaped structure was located at the center point of the beach near the railroad station and steamboat landing. With space for 150 to 200 patrons at its maximum size (fig. 1-5), the hotel promoted the facts that all its rooms

possessed outside views and that its wide single- and double-tier verandas, totaling one thousand feet in length, completely enveloped the building. As much a pavilion as it was a hotel, the Nantasket hosted numerous band concerts and was popular for its metropolitan dining hall with its galaxy of electric lights. Associated with the hostelry were bowling alleys, a billiard room, a shooting gallery, bathhouses, and the Rockland Café, physically linked by an extension of the verandas in 1899. After being closed and boarded up for many years, the hotel and the café were torn down in 1955 and replaced by an automobile parking lot for tourists visiting the beach. Still present on the site is the arcade-like structure once connecting the Nantasket and the café and today used for band concerts.[4]

Erected in 1880 on the salt flats at Windmill Point at the site of Hull's first summer hostelry, the Mansion House (c. 1848), the Hotel Pemberton (fig. 4-4) was an exemplary example of Queen Anne–style architecture.

Fig. 4-4. "The Hotel Pemberton, Windmill Point, Hull," Mass. Photolithograph from Moses S. Sweetser, *King's Handbook of Boston Harbor* (1882), p. 30A. Courtesy, The Winterthur Library Printed Book and Periodical Collection.

It was designed by the well-known Portland, Maine, architect John Calvin Stevens (1855–1940), the planner of other New England resort hotels (see chapters 7 and 8), and built by the firm of William McKenzie & Company. Catering to an affluent clientele, the Pemberton was praised in the *Hingham Journal and South Shore Advertiser* as "a model of sea-side architecture — refreshing to the eye, cool, light and airy" and "one of the most perfect buildings of its kind." This commission was considered to be Stevens' most significant design work during his brief stay in Boston, and his only known work constructed while he was there.

In *King's Handbook of Boston Harbor* (1882), Moses F. Sweetser offered a compelling description of this luxurious bastion of summer hospitality:

[The Hotel Pemberton] is in that quaint and somewhat *outré* form of architecture for which good Queen Anne has been held responsible, with towers, gables, balconies, piazzas [verandas], and other picturesque adjuncts, and a coloring of olive and gold. . . . There are a hundred rooms, with wide and airy halls and parlors, rich furniture and carpets, elevators, wine-vaults, gas works and lights, vast kitchens, billiard-tables,

and a bar of generous proportions. The first and second stories are carpeted with Brussels, and furnished in black walnut; the third and fourth stories have ash furniture and ingrain carpets. There are broad piazzas around the three lower stories. In front of the house is a band-stand, where the best military music is given; and the scene is very brilliant at evening, when a score of electric lights are flashing through the darkness, and crowds of people promenade in the vicinity. The steamboat-pier and railway-station are in front of the house.

A victim of declining business fortunes over many years, the Pemberton sat closed and boarded up for several decades until it was removed in 1956 to make way for the newly constructed Hull High School.[5]

Hull's last major summer resort hotel, another superb specimen of Queen Anne design, was the Atlantic House (fig, 4-5), formerly located atop Atlantic Hill overlooking the south end of Nantasket Beach. The major portion of the complex was put up in 1877 by first owner John L. Damon, and was later enlarged and managed by his son, J. Linfield Damon. As initially conceived, this widely renowned four-story hostelry was perfectly symmetrical, its central and flanking end tower sections protected by

Fig. 4-5. "Atlantic House, Nantasket Beach, Mass." Postcard view, c. 1920.
Courtesy of the Hull Historical Society.

striking steep-pitched, concave hipped roofs. Set aloft, wide verandas possessed commanding views of the beach and ocean, and a stairway connected the hotel to private bathhouses at the water's edge. In its fully developed form, the Atlantic, expanded by the addition of wings at both ends, contained about 175 sleeping rooms and was supplemented by a small compound of cottages, together accommodating at least 300 overnight guests. Public spaces included several dining rooms, a huge ballroom, game rooms, and lounges. Suffering the same fate as most of Hull's other distinguished resort hotels, the Atlantic burned to the ground on 7 January 1927 during a blizzard. The Atlantic Hill Condominiums occupy a substantial portion of the site today.[6]

Hingham, Cohasset, and Scituate

Close by the Hull peninsula on the northern segment of the South Shore are three towns — Hingham, Cohasset,

and Scituate — each of which contributed to the region's resort-hotel legacy. The historic community of Hingham may rightfully lay claim to two coastal hotels worthy of mention, the Rose Standish House and the Old Colony House. The earliest of these, the Old Colony House, was located on Neck Gate Hill (later Old Colony Hill) off Summer Street, a short distance from the Hingham Harbor steamboat landing. Built by the Boston and Hingham Steamboat Company and opened for the 1832 summer season, this traditional three-story, ninety-room wooden structure with central Greek Revival cupola later passed to private ownership, and after varying fortunes over many years it was leveled by fire on 7 October 1872. Plans for a much larger Queen Anne–style, Tudoresque successor were published (fig. 4-6) by the Boston architectural partnership of Bradlee (Nathaniel J., 1829–88) & Winslow (Walter T., 1843–1909) in the 30 April 1881 issue of *American Architect and Building News*, but newspaper and local history sources contain no references to

Fig. 4-6. "Old Colony House, Hingham, Mass." Front elevation perspective drawing by Bradlee & Winslow, Architects, Boston, from *American Architect and Building News* 9, no. 279 (30 April 1881). Courtesy of the University of Delaware Library.

a second Old Colony House. It appears, regrettably, that this aesthetically striking, well-proportioned, and nicely integrated design was never implemented.

Hingham's other shore hotel, the 150-capacity Rose Standish House (c. 1871) (fig. 4-7), was situated at the Melville Garden entertainment district near Downer Landing on Hingham Harbor. Distinguished by its gambrel roofs and gables, dormers, and delicately crafted entrance porch and veranda, this late Victorian eclectic

Fig. 4-7. Rose Standish House, Hingham, Mass. Engraving from the *New Columbian Railroad Atlas and Pictorial Album of American Industry* (New York: George H. Adams and Sons, 1884). Author's collection.

edifice, developed in stages, featured a rich combination of elements but lacked design coherence. In many respects, it possessed an overgrown residential character typical of many small- and medium-size hotel buildings of its era. Catering to families, the hotel contained a playroom and gym for children, a large dining room, a laundry, game rooms, and the "Vue de L'Eau Café" on the nearby wharf. Upon the conclusion of summer 1896, the Melville Garden resort was closed by the managing Trustees of Downer Estates, and most of its buildings, including the Rose Standish House, were summarily demolished.[7]

Twenty-one miles down the coast from Boston and accessed as early as the 1850s by railroad is the town of Cohasset, lauded in Bachelder's guidebooks for its "moody sea" and "cliffy rocks . . . with a broken sea-margin." Catering initially to waterfowl hunters and fishermen and then to vacationers, there was the Black Rock House, three versions of which were located at North Cohasset on Jerusalem Road near the end of Black Rock Beach. The initial hostelry, likely a derivative of a small residence, was built in 1757. After 1800 this modest inn

Fig. 4-8. Black Rock House, North Cohasset, Mass. Photograph, c. 1960.
Courtesy of the Cohasset Historical Society.

was incorporated into a larger structure, which in its last years was owned and managed by Sarah R. Smith. In 1903, she had it dismantled and portions relocated to improve the water views for summer residents who had erected cottages nearby. Committed to hospitality tourism, Miss Smith then financed and directed the construction of the third Black Rock House in 1904 on a pinnacle of rocks just west of the beach. Within a few years she had the hotel enlarged to lodge up to 200 patrons. The end product was a hotel edifice like no other on the New England coastline—a monumental late Shingle-style wooden complex (fig. 4-8), its tall, variously configured towers and asymmetrical massing simulating the appearance of a great medieval European castle. A conspicuous landmark and true visual delight, the Black Rock struggled to remain solvent after World War II, was finally closed down except for its "Ship's Bar" lounge, and fell to the wrecking ball in 1968.[8]

At Scituate, the next coastal town southeast of Cohasset, there were two substantial resort-hotel structures that at one time played an active role in the hospitality industry of the South Shore. The oldest of these, dating from about 1880, was the Hotel Humarock (fig. 4-9), a great, L-shaped wooden ark that once had a dominant presence at Humarock Beach, near the railroad station at Sea View, slightly north over the Marshfield town line

Fig. 4-9. Hotel Humarock, Humarock Beach, Scituate, Mass. Photograph, c. 1897. Courtesy of Scituate Historical Society.

Fig. 4-10. The Cliff Hotel, Minot Beach, North Scituate, Mass. Postcard photograph, c. 1925. Courtesy of Scituate Historical Society.

about thirty miles from Boston. Although it possessed a unifying four-story corner section with a low pyramidal roof and central cupola, this rather awkward edifice was a bland expression of hotel architecture of the time, resembling a highly functional industrial complex. With space for 250 overnight patrons, the Humarock adopted the latest in modern technology with gas lights, electric bells, telegraph service, steam heat, and bedrooms furnished with oak sets, springs, and hair mattresses. Coincidental with the accelerating decline of traditional New England resort hotels, the Humarock was in business for just two decades, going up in flames on 26 June 1901.

Scituate's other large seaboard hostelry was the Cliff Hotel (fig. 4-10) which had a long life span from its origins (1898–99) until it was destroyed by a much-publicized fire on 22–23 May 1974, one day before it was scheduled to open for the summer season. With accommodations for 250 guests at its maximum size, this rambling wood-frame, shingle-clad, L-shaped Colonial Revival structure was located at Minot Beach in the north district of the town. Surrounded by cottages, some of which were associated with the hotel enterprise, the Cliff, like so many of its counterparts, grew in stages over many years. Despite this fact, the hotel had a cohesive, homogeneous appearance, enhanced by its uniform wall surfaces, closed gables, encircling veranda, and truncated dormers. Regarded by many as one of the South Shore's most exclusive vacation havens, the Cliff attracted numerous public figures during its existence, particularly well-known radio, television, theater, and motion picture personalities.[9]

Marshfield

At Marshfield, the age of resort hotels commenced in the 1860s, principally at the coastal village of Brant Rock. The early tourism economy there was largely fostered by the extension of the Duxbury and Cohasset Railroad to Marshfield in 1871 and the subsequent creation of stagecoach connections from the town to the outer shoreline. The first of Brant Rock's many hostelries was Pioneer Cottage (later Atlantic House), erected in 1861. This was followed by the 1868 construction and opening of the Churchill Hotel (fig. 4-11) on Ocean Avenue (Street), named for Captain George Churchill, its originator, first owner, and proprietor. Like so many of its contemporary hotels, the Churchill grew in stages, reaching its completed 250-guest form by the early nineties. Commencing as a three-story, rectangular Second Empire structure with a hipped-on-mansard roof, by virtue of expansion it became a predominantly Queen Anne edifice, a square corner tower with pyramidal roof cap its most visually attractive component. A great conflagration ended the Churchill's period of service to vacationers in 1909.

Positioned farther south on Ocean Avenue was the Colonial Revival–style Peace Haven Hotel (fig. 4-12), by far the largest of Brant Rock's many pre–World War I guest establishments, with outbuildings capable of housing up to 300 people during its prime years. Built in 1909 by its first owner, E. S. Freeman, it fell on hard times during the Depression years and was demolished by Arthur Macker of Marshfield in the early 1940s. An impressively large, amply shingled, three-and-one-half-story L-floor-plan structure of no particular architectural distinction, it possessed a surrounding veranda and hipped roof with truncated dormers, common elements of coastal resort hotels of the period. The Peace Haven was supplemented by the Peace Haven Hotel Annex, which still stands to the north of the hotel site.[10]

Plymouth: Heritage and Vacation Tourism Destination

As the site of the first permanent settlement in New England, Plymouth, some thirty-seven miles from Boston, is more widely acclaimed for its historical associations than its offerings as a summer resort destination. Yet owing

Fig. 4-11. Churchill Hotel, Brant Rock Village, Marshfield, Mass. Photograph, c. 1900. Courtesy of Historical Research Associates, Marshfield Hills, MA.

Fig. 4-12. Peace Haven Hotel, Brant Rock Village, Marshfield, Mass.
Photograph, c. 1925. Courtesy of Historical Research Associates, Marshfield
Hills, MA.

Fig. 4-13. Hotel Pilgrim (Clifford House), Plymouth, Mass. Photograph before renovations, c. 1890. Pilgrim Hall Museum, Plymouth, MA.

to its attractive shoreline and interior ponds, hills, and woodlands, it became a desirable and accessible place of vacation sojourn well before the Civil War. The first vacation hotel in Plymouth was the diminutive Samoset House, built by the Old Colony Railroad from 1845 to 1846 as a tourism investment. Situated with a water view near the town center at Court and Samoset streets, this

nicely articulated 100-guest structure, marked by its late Greek Revival columns and other elements, met public lodging needs for almost a century, falling victim to fire on 29 April 1939.

Plymouth's first large resort hotel, said to do "full honor to the quaint old town," was the Clifford House (fig. 4-13), raised in 1857 on high land overlooking Plymouth Beach and Warren's Cove in the south district of the town. A quite conventional rectangular block, four-story Second Empire structure, it was protected by the customary hipped-on-mansard roof with dormers and encircled by a one-story veranda of light timber construction. First owned by Reuben Leach and Obediah King, the hotel failed to become a popular tourist destination during its first three decades and changed hands several times. In 1891, it was purchased by the Brockton and Plymouth Street Railway Company and renamed "Hotel Pilgrim." In 1903, the hotel was sold again, and under the direction of its new manager, A. J. Davis, was enlarged and recast in the Colonial Revival style (fig. 4-14) to accommodate 150 to 200 patrons. Most conspicuous of its many classical features were its flat Doric corner and wall pilasters,

Fig. 4-14. Hotel Pilgrim, Plymouth, Mass. Photograph, c. 1940. Pilgrim Hall Museum, Plymouth, MA.

cornice dentil molding, and monumental porte cochere with its imposing round Doric support columns set on cubical bases. Facing declining patronage and changing visitor habits, the Hotel Pilgrim ownership made every effort to add amenities including golf course access, formal gardens, a swimming pool, a new dining room, and an automobile parking garage. Finally, in the mid-1950s, the hotel was closed, was soon after demolished, and the site, after remaining vacant for several years, became occupied by condominiums.[11]

The largest and most recent of Plymouth's seaside resort hostelries was the Mayflower Hotel (fig. 4-15), which opened in June 1917 not far from the Hotel Pilgrim on Point Road at Manomet Point, with sweeping vistas across Cap Cod Bay. This ambitious 170-room (including outbuildings) Colonial Revival–style structure was designed by Boston architect J. Williams Beal (1855–1919), head of the firm of J. Williams Beal & Sons, whose most important commissions were several other buildings in Plymouth County and numerous residences throughout the New England states. The David Irving Company of nearby Brockton served as contractors. A front elevation perspective drawing (fig. 4-16), published in the 26 January 1917 issue of the *Old Colony Memorial* newspaper, illustrates a low, 260-foot-long three-story gambrel-roof edifice, highlighted by its expansive shed-roof dormers, paired front gambrel bays, and extended veranda with balustrades. The first owner was the Keith Hotel Company (Elijah A. Keith, president), followed by members of the Boston Dooley family, who retained title until 1945. The hotel was subsequently owned by a succession of partnerships and corporations until it was partially gutted by an early morning fire on 12 April 1973. The Mayflower was further victimized by the fire curse, and after efforts to reconstruct the facility failed, it was demolished in 1975 and replaced by condominiums.[12]

Marion and the Southern Coast

Pre–World War II resort-hotel development was minimal along the southern coast of Massachusetts facing Buzzards Bay, with several modest-size structures constructed at Mattapoisett, Wareham, Westport, Dartmouth, and Marion. Following the tradition of the much smaller Marion House (1860) in the latter town was the

Fig. 4-15. Mayflower Hotel, Plymouth, Mass. Photograph, c. 1920. Pilgrim Hall Museum, Plymouth, MA.

A NEW HOTEL FOR PLYMOUTH

Fig. 4-16. "The Mayflower Inn, Manomet Point, Plymouth, Massachusetts." Front elevation perspective drawing by J. Williams Beal, Architect, Boston, from the *Old Colony Memorial*, 26 January 1917, p. 1. Courtesy of the Plymouth Public Library, Mass.

Fig. 4-17. The Sippican Hotel, Marion, Mass. Photograph from *DeLuxe Hotels of New England* (1915), p. 29. Author's collection.

Fig. 4-18. "Vineyard Sound Hotel, Falmouth, Mass." Colored postcard view, c. 1925. Courtesy of the Falmouth Historical Society.

Sippican Hotel, the only substantial summer lodging complex to be built in the district before 1940. Positioned on Water Street looking out on Sippican Harbor, the Sippican originated in 1864 as the small Bay View House, a three-story Second Empire–style enlargement of a farmhouse converted to hotel use by Joe Snow Luce, the first manager. In 1895, a plain, pitched-roof wing was added, followed in 1900 by a four-story Colonial Revival wing, set at right angles to the main axis of the complex, creating a T-shaped floor plan (fig. 4-17). Covered by a hipped roof with truncated dormers, the wing was fitted out with balconies and a square corner tower resembling that of the Churchill Hotel in Marshfield (see above). Situated across Water Street, just north of the hotel, was the Sippican Casino, a visual pleasure with its two-tiered verandas and broad, hipped roof with cupola and flagpole. After a succession of owners and declining business fortunes, the Sippican was torn down circa 1927.[13]

Cape Cod: From Bourne to Chatham

For complex reasons relating to location, local preferences, declining industry, reduced population, and other economic alternatives, Cape Cod, lagging behind other New England coastal regions, did not commence development as a major center of tourism until the last quarter of the nineteenth century. National guidebooks of the era paid scant attention to Cape Cod's assets and in some instances published unflattering commentary. Since that time, however, the Cape has become one of the principal leisure-time vacation centers on the nation's East Coast. The initial signs of change entailed the appearance of

small hotel and cottage communities sustained by affluent summer visitors along the east side of Buzzards Bay and on the southern seaboard of the Cape overlooking Nantucket Sound. As Dona Brown accurately points out in her 1995 book, *Inventing New England*, "these resorts were basically spin-offs of the [older] Martha's Vineyard and Nantucket trade [see below], built along the railroad route from Boston to the islands" (p. 203). Despite the slow growth of tourism on Cape Cod, by 1900 there were over half a dozen large resort hotels conducting business between Bourne and Chatham, supplementing those that were still operating on the islands. As architectural creations, these rambling, asymmetrical structures were highly conspicuous embodiments of the Shingle or Colonial Revival styles, sometimes in fruitful, aesthetically gratifying combination.

Two large hotel edifices, formerly located at Falmouth, satisfy the criteria (see preface) for inclusion in this study. The oldest of these was the Pickwick House, located on the Falmouth Heights beachfront at Grand and Worcester Park avenues. Responsible for its origins as a boarding establishment was C. L. Hobson, one of a group of Worcester, Massachusetts, businessmen who participated in the development of Falmouth Heights. Erected in 1880, the initial portion of the structure consisted of two understated Stick-style building components, their gable ends facing the ocean, connected by a one-story covered walkway. Around 1900, the property passed to George L. Giddings, was renamed the Vineyard Sound Hotel, and was transformed into an L-shaped Shingle-style structure (fig. 4-18) accommodating as many as 200 guests, punctuated by a four-story octagonal corner tower with arched viewing apertures in its upper level. In 1943, the aging hostelry was acquired by Captain John R. Peterson, renamed the Park Street Hotel, and transformed into a motel by building around the old structure and demolishing the remnants. Subsequently, the property changed ownership again and at last glance was operating as the Park Beach Motel.

The largest of Cape Cod's early resort hotels, located at Hamblin Point on Buzzards Bay, Sippewissett, was built as the Sippewissett Hotel on former farmland from 1899 to 1900 by Boston music publisher John C. Haynes. Costing nearly $67,000, the entire property included a golf course, a pier, a horse stable, bathhouses, tennis courts, a casino for dances and games, bowling alleys, and an electric generator. In 1902, a four-story addition covered by a flat roof was appended to the south side, thereby increasing the guest capacity to 250 and including a large dining room. In its fully mature form, the Sippewissett (figs. 4-19 and 4-20) successfully expressed many familiar elements of the Colonial Revival style

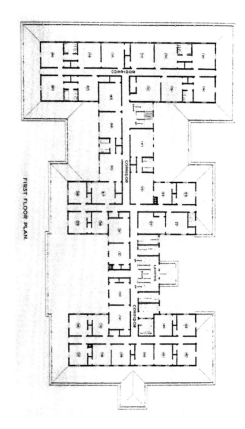

Fig. 4-20. "First Floor Plan," Sippewissett Hotel, Falmouth, Cape Cod, Mass. From booklet, *The Sippewissett, Falmouth, Mass.* (n.d.). Courtesy of the Falmouth Historical Society.

Fig. 4-19. Sippewissett (Cape Codder) Hotel, Falmouth, Cape Cod, Mass. Photograph after the 1902 addition. Courtesy of the Falmouth Historical Society.

THE NOBSCUSSETT HOUSE
DENNIS MASS

Fig. 4-21. "The Nobscussett House, Dennis, Mass." Lithograph from Simeon L. Dejo, *History of Barnstable County, Massachusetts* (1890), op. p. 155. New Hampshire Historical Society.

including intersecting gambrel roofs, shed-roof dormers, twin octagonal cupolas with concave, bellcast roof caps, and long, sweeping verandas with classical column supports and balustrades. In 1917, the Sippewissett Club, Inc., bought the complex, and for a time it was operated as the Cleveland Hotel, the Falmouth Arms, and, under the ownership of Charles Dooley, as the Mayflower Hotel to match the Dooley guest establishment of the same name in Plymouth (see above). Finally, in 1939 Captain John R. and Shirley Peterson acquired the property and successfully ran the hotel as the Cape Codder for an amazing forty-one years. In 1980, they sold out to Hotels of Distinction, a Boston-based corporation, which in 1985 passed the hotel complex to International Developers, Inc., which razed the building three years later to make way for condominiums titled "Cape Cod Residences."

Farther out on Cape Cod at Dennis was the Nobscussett House (fig. 4-21), the only large resort hotel on the north coastline before World War I. The story of its origins is particularly compelling. In 1872, business investors had the modest-size Minot House in Cohasset moved across Cape Cod Bay and relocated in Dennis under the new name of Cape Cod Bay House on a bluff at modern-day Bay View Beach. This modest, migrant

building became the basis of an expanded structure reflecting the impact of several current styles, with a four-and-one-half-story end block section encircled by two-story verandas and topped by a balustraded roof platform with tall flagpole. The end section was designed by Boston architect Samuel D. Kelley (1848–1938), the planner of other hotels, and constructed by the firm of John Hinkley & Son of East Barnstable.

Opened in 1873, the Bay House was sold to Charles Humphrey of Weymouth in 1876, who subsequently transferred ownership title to Charles and Francis Tobey in 1875. It was the Tobeys who carried out the expansion. Retitled "Nobscussett House," with a guest capacity of 200, the property comprised over two hundred acres of land on which were the hotel, three cottages, horse stables, a nine-hole golf course, a billiards room, bowling alleys, and a long pier with pavilion extending out into Cape Cod Bay. Attracting a large clientele from Boston, Hartford, Indianapolis, and especially Chicago, the Nobscussett proved a successful business venture for much of its history, until the 1920s, when long-term patronage decreased because of the summer cottage phenomenon and mobility provided by automobile travel (see chapter 8). The onset of the Depression dealt the final blow, and the hotel was closed in 1930. Soon thereafter, it was dismantled, the cottages were sold to private families, and the land was subdivided for house lots.

Another of Cape Cod's sprawling Colonial Revival–style resort-hotel complexes was the Hotel Belmont (fig. 4-22), located on Nantucket Sound at West Harwich. At the time of its dedication and opening by first owner Benjamin Johnson on 4 July 1894, it was a single three-and-one-half-story, gambrel-roof, rectangular structure with a low wing and ell, and one-story veranda. Within a few years, after at least two expansions, it consisted of two principal, connected units as the result of an aesthetically less pleasing, bulky pitched-roof addition and smaller attachment on the east end. Known as "The Aristocrat of the Cape," the Belmont ultimately incorporated overnight accommodations for 200 to 225 guests (including four adjacent cottages), bathrooms with hot and cold running water, electric bells, and the Cape's first stock market ticker tape machine, and offered bathing, boating, fishing, bowling, and horse riding recreational options. Further modified and enlarged, with numerous window bays and dormers, it remained open throughout the 1969 season, suffered a major fire in 1974, underwent demolition in 1977, and was replaced by a modern condominium complex by the Green Company with the sentimental name of "The Belmont."[14]

Chatham

Situated at the point of the elbow where Cape Cod bends northward toward Provincetown is the town of Chatham, which became a major summer resort community after the arrival of the railroad from Harwich in 1887. During the ensuing years before the end of World War I, several resort hotels were constructed at Chatham, three of which were substantial complexes of considerable architectural merit. The first of these was the short-lived Hotel Chatham (fig. 4-23), funded primarily by Boston department store magnate Eben Jordan and local Eldredge family investors, and constructed at Eastward Point on Pleasant Bay from 1889 to 1890 after plans generated by Boston architect Franz Edward Zerrahn. A

Fig. 4-22. Hotel Belmont, West Harwich, Cape Cod, Mass. Photograph from *DeLuxe Hotels of New England* (1915), p. 39. Author's collection.

Fig. 4-23. Hotel Chatham, Chatham, Cape Cod, Mass. Photograph,
c. 1890. Courtesy, The Chatham (MA) Historical Society.

massive three-story Shingle-style edifice exuding a sense of luxury and ostentatiousness, the Chatham assuredly impressed onlookers with its round central tower with conical roof, steep-pitched, intersecting gambrel roof planes, and delicately fabricated porte cochere, extensive verandas, and porches. From published designs, we know that the hostelry contained over seventy rooms accommodating upward of 150 people, a lounge, a main dining room, separate dining areas for small groups, parlors, and a billiards room and other game rooms, all heated by steam and illuminated with electricity. A victim of overly ambitious planning, a remote location, and difficult economic times caused by the financial Panic of 1893, the Chatham was closed after just four summer seasons, and sat idle and deteriorating for many years before its razing in about 1910.

More realistically conceived as a business venture — and a contrasting, low-stated, more typical specimen of coastal resort-hotel architecture — was the Mattaquason, its initial portion funded and built by Marcellus Eldredge in 1898. After leasing the property for a few years,

Frederick Wilkey of Chatham purchased it outright in 1907, and enlarged the hotel and added cottages until he could house 200 guests. The fully articulated, T-shaped complex (fig. 4-24) possessed an unmistakable Colonial Revival–style aura, its gambrel-roof front central section and veranda with classical detailing comprising a well-integrated work of architecture. In 1943, after Wilkey's death, the Mattaquason Hotel was leased to the Waves of the U.S. Navy and then passed to Wilkey's daughter, Dorothy Wilkey Frey. She and her husband, Milton, ran the operation until 1956, when it was finally closed, later demolished, and the land subdivided for a residential community under the name "Mattaquason Point Associates."

In contrast to the Hotel Chatham and the Mattaquason, the elegant Chatham Bars Inn, erected from 1913 to 1914 (fig. 4-25), has continued to thrive to this day at its advantageous, raised location at Pleasant Bay on Shore Road (formerly Ocean Boulevard). Cape Cod native and Boston developer Charles A. Hardy headed the syndicate behind the real estate purchase and construction

Fig. 4-24. "Hotel Mattaquason, Chatham, Mass." Colored postcard view, c. 1905. Courtesy, The Chatham (MA) Historical Society.

Fig. 4-25. Chatham Bars Inn, Chatham, Cape Cod, Mass. Construction photograph, 1917. Courtesy, The Chatham (MA) Historical Society.

of the main hotel and outbuildings. Responsible for the design of the Chatham Bars (figs. 4-26 and 4-27) was architect Henry Bailey Alden (d. 1939) of Boston, known for his office and residential buildings in and around the city. Unusual for its crescent-shaped building mass, this venerable Colonial Revival hostelry is crowned by dominant, steep-pitched, intersecting gambrel roofs with double rows of dormers like those of the Colonial Arms at Gloucester, Massachusetts (see chapter 5). Exterior brick chimney stacks frame the building at each end, and the entire façade is fronted by a veranda supported by square brick piers. While the hotel interior possessed generous public spaces, it initially contained just forty sleeping rooms, its advertised 250 guest capacity made possible by the presence of over twenty-five nearby cottages of varying size and similar contemporary styling. The Chatham Bars was operated by the Hardy family trust until 1933 and since then has been owned by E. R. McMullen, then William Langelier and Alan Green, and today the Great American Insurance Company. In 1994, the hotel was designated as one of the Historic Hotels of America, having "faithfully maintained . . . [its] historic integrity, architecture and ambience" as determined by the National Trust for Historic Preservation. It is the last surviving "grande dame" of Cape Cod's small but superlative collection of large pre–World War I seacoast resort hotels.[15]

Fig. 4-26. Chatham Bars Inn, Chatham, Cape Cod, Mass. Photograph, 2007, by the author.

Fig. 4-27. Lounge, Chatham Bars Inn, Chatham, Cape Cod, Mass. Postcard view, c. 1920. Courtesy, The Chatham (MA) Historical Society.

Nantucket

The removed location, cool climate, ample beaches, scenic beauty, historic atmosphere, and recreational potential of the islands south of Cape Cod have made them renowned among American seacoast summer resort centers for over a century and a half. Approximately twenty-five miles south of Cape Cod and twenty miles east of Martha's Vineyard is the irregularly shaped, flat, virtually treeless island of Nantucket, about sixteen miles long and three to four miles wide. In the past one of the major whaling centers of the world, as well as the locus of extensive farming and fishing activity, this quaint, picturesque area was struck by a disastrous fire in the town of Nantucket in 1846, followed by the rapid decline of the whaling industry and a long period of economic stagnation. Beginning in the 1880s, however, aided by improved steamboat access and America's growing infatuation with the summer vacation experience, Nantucket underwent a rapid and total economic revival as a highly popular and successful summer cottage and hotel center. Though the hotel industry there has suffered decline and transformation, and all early, large-building examples are gone, the island has retained its great appeal, particularly to the more affluent business and professional families

of the Northeast who have built or adapted vacation or second residences there.[16]

The earliest large hostelry on the island, accommodating up to 200 guests in full-blown form, was the Hotel Nantucket (fig. 4-28), set on the beach near the lighthouse at Brant Point. The project to create the Nantucket originated with the Boston architect George F. Hammond (1855–c. 1938), who had purchased several large house lots on the beach and had two buildings, the Friends meetinghouse and a dwelling, moved from the town to the site in 1883. The meetinghouse became the central pavilion and the residence the west end of the evolving complex, connected over the following year by four-story wings to create a lengthy, nearly symmetrical edifice. Lending architectural character to the structure were two open cupolas with contrasting roof caps, an array of pitched, truncated, and shed-roof dormers, and wall balconies of light construction. A narrow veranda extended along the entire two-hundred-foot front façade, and, a most unusual practice for the time, the name of the hotel was set on the roof ridgepole in six-foot letters, and was repeated in the upper portion of the central part of the veranda. In the main, central section of the complex were a dining room, office, grand parlor, barber's shop, and baggage and toilet room, while

Fig. 4-28. "The Nantucket, Nantucket, Mass." Engraving from Robert Grieve, *The New England Coast and Its Famous Resorts* (1892 ed.), p. 89. Maine Historic Preservation Commission.

Fig. 4-29. Sea Cliff Inn, Nantucket Island, Mass. Photograph, c. 1910.
Courtesy of the Nantucket Historical Association, P10015.

the ell contained the kitchen, boiler room, and steam pump room. In the wings were bedrooms for upward of 200 overnight patrons. Behind the main block was a detached structure housing a billiard and bowling room, salon, and the help's quarters. In 1886, the east wing was moved to the rear of the hotel and a new, three-story addition appeared in its place. After its final summer of 1904, the Hotel Nantucket, its best days long passed, was dismantled, the main, central portions relocated, and other portions razed.

Nantucket's leading hotel for eighty years was the Sea Cliff Inn (fig. 4-29), once located on Cliff Road (formerly North Street) on a rise looking out on Nantucket Sound and the Great Harbor. The Sea Cliff achieved its fully realized form as a result of two major building projects. Commissioned and managed by Charlotte W. Pettee, the initial section of the hotel, based on plans drafted by architect Robert A. Slade, was framed in Maine and raised in 1887 by local builder Charles H. Robinson. Considered the first local hotel in the Queen Anne vernacular, it displayed both shingled and clapboarded wall surfaces, several dormer types on its complex roofs, tall chimney shafts, and elaborate crestings. Appended to this struc-

ture was an early nineteenth-century dwelling converted to a pavilion with a new door and window hoods and a gambrel-roof gable on the third story, all intended to blend the old building with the new. While the pavilion housed a kitchen and lodging for the employees, the hotel contained the customary dining room, office, parlor, and stair hall accessed by a main entrance and veranda, with some forty guest rooms above.

From 1892 to 1893, under the direction of E. T. Carpenter of Foxboro, Massachusetts, a new, much larger Queen Anne–style building was constructed and connected to the original Sea Cliff Inn by a twenty-five-foot covered walkway. To facilitate ocean bathing, the owners built a lengthy boardwalk from the new hotel to the beach so that guests would not have to make their way through the sand dunes. Set on a high basement story, the ponderous, awkward-appearing four-story structure clearly contained ample, functional interior spaces, as described by Clay Lancaster in his 1979 book, *Nantucket in the Nineteenth Century*:

Ascending from the foyer was an imperial staircase, with a huge parlor at the south end and several reception rooms to the north. In the basement was a billiard room (under the great parlor) and an assembly hall with a stage and seating capacity for three hundred (under the rear wing). Above were seventy-five guest rooms. At the summit of the stair tower terminating the wing was a sun parlor opening to the flat sun deck. . . . At the completion of the new building the entire complex was equipped with electricity.

This great, sprawling 250-guest establishment passed to the Nantucket Company in 1902, to Clifford Folger and W. D. Carpenter in 1907, and to subsequent owners, the last being Shelburne Associates in 1965, which ran the hotel until its demolition in 1972.

Nantucket's third large resort hotel, the Beach House (fig. 4-30), was constructed by Sea View contractor Charles H. Robinson for G. H. Brinton at the village of Siasconset on the island's east shore from 1900 to 1901. The most ambitious of Siasconset's several lodging establishments, Brinton's new hostelry was an irregularly shaped, late Shingle-style building, which Lancaster described as "having a four-story polygonal pavilion attached to a summer cottage with a square section beyond a third story within a gambrel roof." The hotel was a financial success in its first few years, and in the spring of 1906 the original cottage was supplanted by an addition "equal in size to the mansard section," increasing the overnight capacity to between 150 and 200. Acquired by Mrs. Miriam Barbara Buckley in 1935, the Beach House was sold to Siasconset Beach House, Inc., in 1947, was operated for the next decade, and was finally closed and razed in 1957. The hotel tract is now occupied

Fig. 4-30. The Beach House, Siasconset, Nantucket Island, Mass. Photograph, c. 1930. Courtesy of the Nantucket Historical Association, P12517.

by summer houses, a pattern repeated consistently along the New England seaside as resort hotels have met their respective fates over the past century.[17]

Martha's Vineyard

Like Nantucket, the island of Martha's Vineyard just to the west underwent an economic and social metamorphosis in the middle of the nineteenth century. Also a major whaling center in the early part of the century, the Vineyard was closely identified with its principal port, Edgartown, which was dedicated almost exclusively to this ocean industry. By the 1840s, however, circumstances had changed markedly, and whaling activity, faced with growing worldwide competition, severely declined. The loss of most of the whaling fleet during the Civil War proved to be the final blow. Like Nantucket, the Vineyard then suffered through a lengthy period of depression during the 1860s and 1870s, followed by economic revival founded on new forms of entrepreneurship. Leading the way was the religious camp-meeting movement centered at Wesleyan Grove on the north shore, about ten miles across Vineyard Sound from the south coast of Cape Cod. This established the basis for the cottage phenomenon and summer vacation tourism on the island, which assumed concrete form in the 1867 establishment of the Oak Bluffs Land and Wharf Company and the creation of a new resort community, Oak Bluffs, on land adjacent to Wesleyan Grove. Combining business, religion, and leisure-time pleasure for a largely middle-class clientele, Oak Bluffs joined with Wesleyan Grove and another nearby investor project, Vineyard Highlands, to form what promoters termed "Cottage City." As Dona Brown has correctly observed in her 1995 book, *Inventing New England*, Cottage City became the prototype for other New England coastal resorts with their plethora of summer cottages and hotels. Of Cottage City's three components, Oak Bluffs became the primary locus of hotel development and the principal hotel center on Martha's Vineyard.[18]

The landmark centerpiece of the development plan for Oak Bluffs was the Sea View House (Hotel) (frontispiece and fig. 4-31), situated directly on the shoreline slightly south of the wharf servicing steamboats traveling between the Vineyard and Woods Hole, Cape Cod. Raised by the Oak Bluffs Company at a cost of $102,000 from 1871 to 1872 to accommodate 250 to 300 guests, this visually magnificent, distinctively Stick-style structure was arguably the finest example of its design mode on the New England seaboard. Four and one-half stories high and topped by a truncated gambrel roof with dormers and two cupolas, the 225-foot-long main building façade was framed by two contrasting towers crowned by steep-pitched roofs with finials and displaying roof surfaces with colored bands and pitched-roof, crested dormers. On the north end of the hotel was a lightly fabricated gateway structure, which spanned the road leading to the wharf. In all its aesthetic splendor, the Sea View was a forceful, representative architectural embodiment of the vacation experience of late Victorian America.

John Bachelder's national guidebook, *Popular Resorts and How to Reach Them* (1876 ed.) contains a valuable, unusually comprehensive description of the Sea View's well-equipped, lavish interior:

From the wharf, the entrance is made through an ornamental gate-house, which is devoted to offices. In the tower at the right is the baggage-room, with a general railway ticket-office over it. At the left is the wharfinger's office, over which is the office of the Oak Bluffs Company. The basement of the hotel is approached by a private entrance from the wharf, by which baggage and stores are taken, and, by steam elevator, raised to any part of the house.

Wide passage-ways extend through the basement, cutting each other at right angles. At the left of the entrance, opening to the sea, are the barber's shop, bath-rooms, and billiard-hall, beyond which is the engineer's and boiler room, etc. On the right are store-rooms, ice-house, chill-room, laundry, bakery, and servants' rooms. The house and promenades are lighted by Walworth's solar gas generator. . . .

The Sea View House is approached by a broad flight of stairs, leading to a capacious veranda at the east end, twenty-six feet in width. This is an important architectural feature of the house. It is three stories high, giving beauty to the structure, and comfort and pleasure to the guests. . . . The ladies' reception-room is at the right of the entrance, with hat and coat and wash rooms, and stairway beyond. On the left is the gentlemen's reception-room, elevator, and office. Opposite the main entrance, the doors open to the dining-hall, which occupies the entire width of the building. . . . The private din-

Fig. 4-31. "Oak Bluffs Galop [Sea View House — Oak Bluffs — Martha's Vineyard.]" Sheet music illustration by J. H. Bufford's Lith., Boston, 1872. Courtesy, American Antiquarian Society.

ing-rooms are beyond. Broad stairways and the elevator lead to the stories above.

The public parlor, on the second floor, is pleasantly located across the southern end of the building, commanding . . . an extended view in three directions. On either side of the passage are private parlors and sleeping-rooms; and the two stories above are similarly arranged, with walks the entire length, affording excellent ventilation. Balconies lead from every story. A tank of two thousand gallons capacity, placed under the roof, supplies the water for the house.

The peak of the south tower has three fine sleeping rooms. The north tower has two, with a passage-way leading to the look-out room above, from the four windows of which a most extensive marine and landscape view can be had.

It has been observed that the Sea View House was both a colossus and a fantasy, its great mass and exuberant features influencing the entire character of the Oak Bluffs community. Its destruction by a massive conflagration on 24 and 25 September 1892 deprived Oak Bluffs of its

Fig. 4-32. Highland House, Vineyard Highlands, Martha's Vineyard, Mass., stereo view, c. 1880, R. G. Shute, Edgartown, Mass. Courtesy of Mystic Seaport, Photography Collection, Mystic, Conn., #1984.121.3.

life symbol, and Martha's Vineyard of its largest nineteenth-century resort hostelry.[19]

Cottage City's other substantial resort hotel, the Highland House (fig. 4-32), was somewhat smaller than the Sea View House, and of a very different type of architectural expression. Erected circa 1872 by the Vineyard Grove Company at Vineyard Highlands near Oak Bluffs, this new hospitality enterprise was intended to be an economic rival to the Sea View, which in fact never occurred. Yet it was an imposing structure of Second Empire–style inspiration, built in two stages, with a composite appearance like so many other resort hotels of its style and era. Of its many strongly stated features, that drawing the greatest notice was its four-story front

central tower capped by a truncated, pyramidal roof and open observation cupola with balustrade, paired open-arch apertures, and finial. Also striking were the color-banded hipped-on-mansard roof with dormers, the arched second-story window openings, and the two-tiered front veranda turned slightly around the side walls and connecting with an octagonal, three-level open porch at the east corner. With bedroom space for upward of 150 patrons, the Highland House attracted numerous beach worshippers during its existence. In close proximity to the hotel were about two hundred bathhouses allowing great numbers of people to indulge in sun and sea bathing each summer day. When the Highland House burned down in the fall of 1893, there was conclusive evidence that the fire had been set by an arsonist who had also plundered the empty hotel. At the time, it was owned by John D. Flint, Clofus L. Gonyon, and Augustus G. Wesley, the owner and manager of the smaller and still surviving Wesley House at Oak Bluffs.[20]

Continuing the late nineteenth-century practice of organized coastal resort development, there were other attempts to follow the example of Oak Bluffs on Martha's Vineyard. One of these was Katama on Katama Bay south of Edgartown, where in 1872 speculative investors, under the name of the Katama Land Company, launched plans for a new cottage community with hotel, serviced by a steamboat wharf. In that year, based on drawings prepared by architect S. F. Pratt of Boston, construction began on the hotel, Mattakeset Lodge (fig. 4-33), just as the Sea View House at Oak Bluffs (see above) was preparing to open. Completed in spring 1873 after some delays, the new structure was positioned just a few feet from the water's edge and spanned the approach to the wharf. Of the same Stick-styling and form as the larger Sea View, the Mattakeset, with its ostentatious ornamentation, set a similar tone, encouraging the pursuit of pleasure, relaxation, and leisure-time pursuits. At the north end of the 125-foot front façade was an octagonal tower topped by a spire roof with steep-pitched-roof dormers and a tall flagstaff. At the south end was a rectangular two-and-one-half-story block topped by a steep-pitched, hipped roof pierced by dormers, with iron cresting on the ridgepole. Between the end sections was the center portion, two stories high, topped by an open walkway later converted to third-story bedroom

Fig. 4-33. "Mattakeset Lodge, Katama, Martha's Vineyard," Mass. Engraving from John Bachelder, *Popular Resorts, Routes to Reach Them* (1873), p. 70. Author's collection.

space. Balconies of light wood construction were present at some of the north tower windows and in the second story of the central portion above the gateway to the wharf. The north tower contained a dining room, office, kitchen, billiard room, and guest rooms, while the south block was devoted to the land company office and guest rooms. A ballroom, promenade, and additional guest rooms occupied the central section. All told, there was sleeping space for a maximum of 150 visitors, including hotel-owned cottages. The Mattakeset Lodge, after over three decades of operation, was closed after the 1905 season, stood idle and deteriorating for many years, and was finally torn down.[21]

The burgeoning tourism economy of the historic community of Edgartown gained additional momentum in 1890 when three investors, led by local physician-druggist Dr. Thomas J. Walker, purchased former pastureland on Starbuck's Bluff at the end of North Water Street overlooking the outer harbor, the harbor lighthouse, and Chappaquiddick Island. At this desirable location, under the direction of architect Charles A. Cummings (1833–1906) of the Boston firm of Cummings and Sears, the first (southern) portion of the new Harbor View Hotel was erected in time for the 1891 summer season. Three and one-half stories tall with a hipped roof, this rather austere, functional wooden structure possessed roof dormers and a wraparound veranda on the front end facing the harbor. A two-story ell extended to the rear. Operated by managers J. W. Drew and then William D. Carpenter, the hostelry weathered trying economic conditions in the early 1890s and, upon the improvement of the national economic climate, was doubled in size (fig. 4-34) by new owner Frank A. Douglas in the late 1890s to house up to 150 patrons. Set to the north of the original building, the new addition was of similar scale and detailing with a hipped roof, shed-roof dormers, stacked bay windows, and a surrounding veranda with square support posts. Since World War II, the original Colonial Revival hotel has been the beneficiary of new, freestanding housing units in 1967, cottage additions, and sweeping renovations and improvements by the owning First Winthrop Corporation from 1989 to 1990, and since by subsequent owners, the latest in 2006 and 2007. The resulting changes, both exterior and interior, have included the replacement or restoration

Fig. 4-34. Harbor View Hotel, Edgartown, Martha's Vineyard, Mass. Photograph, 2007, by the author.

of older architectural elements and the addition of new architectural features (gazebo, porte cochere, bay windows, roof turrets, etc.) that enhance the late Victorian elegance of the venerable complex. In its restored, operating state, today's Harbor View Hotel has been returned to its original grandeur with state-of-the-art amenities. It provides the current generation with insights into the architecture and summer leisure life of American seaside hospitality tourism in its early decades, and endures as a representative survivor of the early resort-hotel industry of Boston's South Shore, Cape Cod, and the islands.[22]

MASSACHUSETTS

The North Shore

ALTHOUGH IT IS ONLY a fraction of the length of the Massachusetts coastline southeast of Boston, and possesses a smaller percentage of beach frontage, the North Shore from Boston to the New Hampshire border saw at least as much if not more widespread large resort-hotel development between 1820 and 1950. Irregular in shape, highlighted by the Nahant, Marblehead, and Cape Ann peninsulas, it combines attractive, rocky ledge with sandy beach coastal features over a distance of some seventy miles, including several small offshore islands. Encouraged by close proximity to Boston and easy access by sea and land, resort communities, including their places of public accommodation, appeared at desirable locations between Chelsea and Cape Ann prior to World War I, the primary growth phase fostered by the opening of the Eastern Railroad (later the Boston & Maine) during the 1870s. With the exception of limited, modest-size hotel development at Salisbury Beach, there were no large pre–World War I coastal hostelries of note north of Cape Ann, due to the predominance of low marshlands, less accessibility to population centers, competing land uses, residential ownership, and protectionist sentiment.

The primary concentrations of large hotels on the North Shore were at Revere Beach, Swampscott, Marblehead, Magnolia, Gloucester, and Rockport, with isolated examples elsewhere. Comprising a rich array of specific architectural styles and eclectic stylistic combinations, this collection of sprawling, substantial building complexes included four "grand" specimens of New England coastal resort-hotel architecture, surely the most impressive grouping among the seaboard regions treated in this book. Few other grand hotel examples, whether in New England or elsewhere in the United States, could rival the Oceanside and the Magnolia at Magnolia, the New Ocean House at Swampscott, and the Colonial Arms at Gloucester (see below) for advantageous siting, overwhelming size, prolific design detail, and luxurious ambience. Alas, unlike the shorelines of Rhode Island, southeastern Massachusetts, New Hampshire, and southern Maine, no large pre-1950 resort hotels, including the four grand standouts, have remained intact on Boston's North Shore. Given this reality, we must turn to visual images, printed materials, and unpublished sources to gain an understanding and appreciation of the region's hospitality tourism industry and its quite astounding architectural legacy.

Revere Beach and Point of Pines

The east side of the town of Revere (set off from Chelsea Township in 1871) consists of Revere (formerly Chelsea) Beach, a long stretch of sandy shore that fronts on Massachusetts Bay between Winthrop and Lynn. Easily accessible by steamboat, ferry, and railroad by the late 1870s, Revere Beach quickly became a popular summer resort, described in *Appletons' . . . American Summer Resorts* (1876 ed.) as frequented primarily by "the less well-to-do classes of Boston" for short weekend and holiday stays, sea bathing, and promenading. Occupied by cottages, entertainment facilities, and mostly small hotels, the principal areas of visitation were Crescent Beach, Oak Island, and Point of Pines. It is the latter tourism destination that merits particular scrutiny as the former location of one of the largest and most active late Victorian resort hotels along the New England seaboard.

Situated at the north end of Revere Beach, just below the Saugus River estuary, the Point of Pines is a mile-long promontory initially recognized for its sand and pitch pine tree growth. Prior to the opening of the Boston, Revere Beach and Lynn Railroad in 1875, the only hotel there of any consequence was the small-scale Ocean House, which originated as the Robinson Crusoe House circa 1834 and ultimately burned in 1884 as the Hotel Goodwood. The renaming of the Ocean House occurred in 1881 when owners Amos Tarlton and Lewis B. West sold out to the newly formed Chelsea Beach Company, which also acquired two hundred acres of prime adjacent land. In the spring of that year, the company owners commenced the construction of what would soon be-

come the dominant hotel building at Point of Pines and all of Revere Beach, housing over 400 overnight guests.

In the 1888 edition of their guidebook, *The North Shore of Massachusetts Bay*, Benjamin Hill and Winfield Nevins included a graphic description of the great new hospitality and entertainment enterprise at Point of Pines:

The principal feature of this beautiful spot is the magnificent Hotel Pines [fig. 5-1], a wonderful structure, both in design and detail. Light, airy, breezy, shady and healthful; an imposing and elegant edifice which forms a most striking landmark from almost any point near or distant view. It is 300 feet long by 100 in width, and five stories high. . . . It is of Queen Anne [and Stick composite] style of architecture, and fitted up for the comfort and convenience of guests in the best manner, and with all the modern appliances of comfort, and luxury. The entire first story is encircled by magnificent verandas, thirty-two feet wide, which are reached by broad flights of steps from both sides, at each end affording ample room for promenading. From the front side ocean views can be enjoyed, while from the rear a wide stretch of inland scenery bordering on the Pines and Saugus rivers meets the eye. . . . On the lower floor of the Hotel Pines, besides office, etc., there are two large dining halls, 50 by 126 feet, each capable of seating one thousand persons at a time, so that at this hotel alone there is a capacity of feeding many thousands of visitors during the day.

Less exclusive and reclusive than most of the large hotels on the New England seaboard, the Hotel Pines—like certain of the hostelries at Nantasket Beach, Hull, Massachusetts (see chapter 4), and Old Orchard Beach, Maine (see chapter 7)—was a major focal point of entertain-

Fig. 5-1. "Beach View at the Point of Pines," Hotel Pines, Revere, Mass. Lithograph, Forbes Litho. Co., c. 1890. Courtesy, The Winterthur Library Printed Book and Periodical Collection.

ment and other activities for large numbers of people. Early in the hotel's history, the property accommodated a steamboat wharf, railroad terminus, racetrack, and bandstand, along with walkway arches illuminated by gaslights, later interspersed with new electric lights. In addition to the verandas, seating for events and simple relaxation was made available on shaded lawns and nearby in tents, pagodas, pavilions, and groves. Complementing the customary bathing, boating, and fishing activities were numerous contained spectacles and musical and theatrical events drawing thousands to the very public hotel grounds each summer. While it prospered for many years, hosting Theodore Roosevelt during his 1912 presidential campaign, the Hotel Pines encountered declining patronage characteristic of the broader New England resort-hotel industry in the immediate years prior to World War I. In August 1913, it was closed by its owners, Lancaster and Mills, the final blow being Revere's decision to become a no-liquor-licenses town. Demolition occurred a year later, and the land was sold for house lots.[1]

Nahant: A Resort Forerunner

Other than Newport (see chapter 3), Nahant is the only other New England seacoast resort/residential community to have achieved national exposure and recognition prior to 1850. It is advantageously situated on a bold, rocky ledge promontory about twelve miles northeast of Boston that is connected to the mainland at Lynn by a narrow, two-mile-long, sandy isthmus. Initially, in the early 1700s, Nahant was utilized primarily for sheepherding, but its healthful, cool climate, salt air, sea breezes, and scenic terrain and viewpoints soon attracted numerous recreationists, naturalists, pleasure seekers, fishermen, invalids, and convalescents for brief visits from the Boston region, the North Shore, and beyond. By the end of the century, there were three houses on the promontory, each of which took boarders, this number doubling by 1810. By 1815, Nahant had established a reputation as a burgeoning summer resort, and residential construction rapidly increased over the subsequent decade. Rev. William Bentley's diaries indicate that the first specialized hotel or "house of entertainment" was a small building erected on the western head circa 1801, burned circa 1803,

and was rebuilt and reopened. Later historians, such as Fred A. Wilson, have reached differing conclusions as to when the first real resort hotel, however modest, appeared on the peninsula.

It took the vision and commitment of Colonel Thomas Handasyd Perkins, a wealthy merchant and longtime visitor from Boston, to galvanize support for a major resort-hotel venture at Nahant. Soon after purchasing land and building a summer cottage circa 1818, Perkins launched plans for a large, pioneering hostelry, to become the first large example of its building type in New England and one of the earliest along the entire Atlantic seaboard. In June 1821, seizing an opportunity to realize his goal, Perkins joined with William Payne, and they purchased the east end of the peninsula, known as East Point and Ram Pasture, from Nehemiah and Daniel Breed for $1,800. Over the next year, Perkins and Payne solicited investment capital through the sale of shares to a group of subscribers, ultimately numbering around 125. Construction proceeded apace, and the new hotel was opened for business in June 1823.

In its initial form, the Nahant Hotel (also called "Nahant House") (fig. 5-2) possessed a two-story rectangular stone-masonry core entirely surrounded by two-tiered wooden verandas and capped by an expansive, hipped roof set on an early version of a concave mansard roof. Enclosing two additional stories, the roof surfaces were

Fig. 5-2. "Nahant Hotel," Nahant, Mass. Engraving from promotional broadside (1 May 1825) by Annin & Smith and J. R. Penniman. Courtesy, The Winterthur Library Printed Book and Periodical Collection.

Fig. 5-3. "Nahant House" from "Nahant Polka" sheet music cover (Boston: Oliver Ditson, 1854). J. H. Bufford's Lith. Courtesy of Peabody Essex Museum.

pierced by dormers and tall brick chimneys, and surmounted by a cupola (referred to as a "belvidere" in early hotel literature) topped by a metal weather vane. This striking vernacular hotel structure was said to contain seventy chambers, mostly sleeping rooms augmented by hot- and cold-water baths, a foyer, a substantial dining room, private parlors, bowling alleys, and billiard rooms in the cupola.

Despite its many positive features and amenities, the Nahant Hotel was not an immediate financial success, and in 1825 the original directors rearranged the ownership, with Perkins and Edward H. Robbins, Jr., as the principal shareholders. A period of business upswing was ended by the commercial depression of 1829, and the property reverted to Perkins. From 1831 to 1832, the structure was substantially enlarged by the addition of a new, highly functional three-story east wing including a hundred additional rooms and a spacious dining hall intended to cater to short-term Boston-area visitors. Curiously configured, the wing inspired much critical

commentary, its ungainly rectangular-box form with double, shed-monitor roof conjuring up images of contemporary textile mills in the industrial centers of Rhode Island and the nearby Merrimack River Valley. Though lacking in design appeal, it occupied a unique place in the New England hotel architecture of the time.

The Perkins period of ownership lasted to 1842, when he sold the hotel to Phineas Drew, who directed a successful operation for the next eleven years, transferring title to two Lynn-based entrepreneurs, F. S. Newhall and D. C. Baker, in 1853 for the sum of $40,000. Anticipating an increase in patronage as Nahant's reputation as a resort continued to grow, the new owners, working with proprietor Paran Stevens, funded the addition of two huge wings from 1853 to 1854, increasing the guest capacity to approximately 600, a remarkable figure for the time. Described by Alonzo Lewis in *The Picture of Nahant* (1855), the expanded edifice (fig. 5-3),

which includes the old stone building, is two hundred and eighty-four feet in length, eighty feet in breadth, and five stories in height. . . . It is fitted with all modern hotel improvements, provided with bathing apartments for hot and cold, salt and fresh water baths, lighted with gas, warmed by steam, and is so located that every window commands an unobstructed ocean view. This immense establishment is furnished throughout in a style which will compare favorably with the best first class houses in the Atlantic cities, and is open . . . from the middle of June till October.

Credited with the design of the enlarged and remodeled hotel is the versatile, productive, and widely recognized Boston architect Gridley J. F. Bryant (1816–99), the planner of numerous Boston-area public, commercial, and ecclesiastical buildings during his lengthy professional career. Never able to achieve consistently profitable operation, and facing a national economic downturn and Nahant's decline as a prominent public summer resort, the great hotel fell on hard times in the late fifties, was largely closed and deserted, and, under suspicious circumstances, fell victim to a disastrous conflagration on 11–12 September 1861 that leveled the complex within three hours. The ruins, most notably the stone core of the original building, continued to stand for many years as a reminder of Nahant's preeminence as an early American seaside resort community.[2]

Fig. 5-4. Eastern façade of the Lincoln House, Swampscott, Mass. Photograph, c. 1895. Photo courtesy of the Swampscott Public Library.

Swampscott and the New Ocean House

Just above the Nahant peninsula and Lynn, roughly fourteen miles northeast of Boston on Nahant Bay, is the town of Swampscott, which like Nahant was very much affected by the more affluent citizens of Boston and environs starting in the mid–nineteenth century. Initially a fishing community, Swampscott also became a fashionable watering place starting in the 1860s, accessed by horse carriage roads, ocean routes, and then the Eastern Railroad from Boston. Possessing high bluffs, rock ledges, and a long, flat, sandy beach, said to be one of New England's finest, the town contained numerous elaborate summer residences and, by 1875, several places of guest accommodation including three resort hotels of consequence—the Ocean House and the Lincoln House, near the town center, and the Hotel Preston, farther north toward Marblehead at Phillips Beach.[3]

In late 1864, the same year the first Ocean House burned down (see below), Stephen H. Wardwell commenced the building of the initial portion of the Lincoln House at the western end of Fishing Point (also known as Lincoln Point), commanding superb ocean views in three directions. Completed by the summer of 1865, this imposing structure entered a period of fifty years of Wardwell family ownership, Stephen W. and Robert B. Wardwell, the sons of the founder, succeeding their father as owner-managers. Named in honor of President Abraham Lincoln, the new hostelry at first was an unassuming three-story wood-frame building with a flat roof accommodating 75 people. Actively patronized from the onset, the Lincoln was remodeled and enlarged circa 1870, including an additional story covered by a flat, concave mansard roof. Further expansion from 1894 to 1895 increased the capacity, including cottages, to 200 guests, resulting in a two-section edifice (figs. 5-4 and 5-5) en-

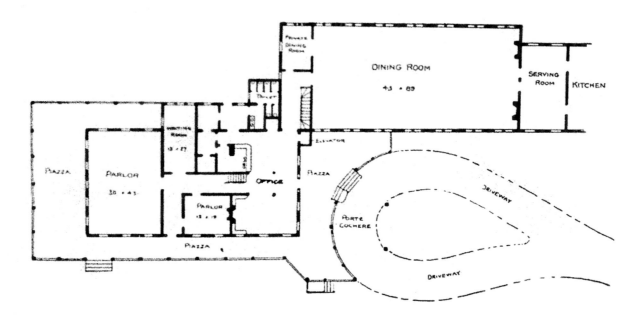

FIRST FLOOR PLAN

Fig. 5-5. "First Floor Plan," Lincoln House. From booklet, *The Lincoln House, Swampscott, Mass.* (c. 1895). Courtesy of Peabody Essex Museum.

Fig. 5-6. "The New Office," Lincoln House. Photograph from booklet, *The Lincoln House, Swampscott, Mass.* (c. 1895). Courtesy of Peabody Essex Museum.

circled by verandas and capped in entirety by the circa 1870 mansard roof form, surmounted by square cupolas and, at the center of the building mass, by a tall, square tower of Queen Anne–style, "Florentine" pretensions. Promoted in hotel literature of the day were a spacious new dining room, mechanical elevator, and remodeled office (fig. 5-6), "handsome in finish, cool, secluded, delightful as a retreat." Passing to brothers Charles H. and Roy F. Bergengren of Lynn around 1915, the Lincoln became outmoded, its fortunes declined during the World War I years, and it was razed during the summer of 1918 to be replaced by privately owned cottages.[4]

Named for its originator, Andrew Preston, the owner of the United Fruit Company, the Hotel Preston (fig. 5-7) was erected in 1872 at Beach Bluff, a commanding location on Atlantic Avenue overlooking Phillips Beach just below the Swampscott-Marblehead boundary. With distant views of Nantasket, Boston Harbor, and Nahant to the south, and Marblehead to the north, this elongated, three-story wooden structure successfully combined

Fig. 5-7. The Hotel Preston, Beach Bluff, Swampscott, Mass. Photograph, c. 1925. Photo courtesy of the Swampscott Public Library.

shapes and elements of both the Second Empire and Queen Anne idioms. Most in evidence along its asymmetrical front façade were the stately, off-center porte cochere screening the main entrance; the off-center main segment covered by a steep-pitched, truncated, hipped roof; the wide, lengthy veranda; and, five window bays, each rising above the flat mansard roof and crowned by octagonal roof caps. The horizontality of the building mass, accented by the veranda, was nicely countered by the vertical lines of the main segment and the bays. In about 1905 the Preston received a major addition containing sixty-five rooms and perpetuating the look of its older Victorian eclecticism. Including three contiguous cottages, the hotel reached a maximum capacity of 300 guests, remained in business for several decades, and was demolished in the mid-1940s.[5]

The story of Swampscott's sumptuous, monumental grand hotel, the new Ocean House, begins with two similarly named predecessors. The first Ocean House dates from 1835, when Boston restaurant owner William Fenno purchased nineteen acres of land on Phillips (later

Galloupe's) Point and erected a small hostelry, the first summer hotel, excluding the Nahant peninsula, on the North Shore mainland coast. Little is known about this early establishment, except that the Fenno family leased it to other operators for many years and it was destroyed by fire in 1864. That same year, Stephen H. Wardwell's brother, E. N., bought the Beach House (formerly the Awawan), which he moved from a site on Phillips Point to Whale Beach, renaming it the Ocean House. R. W. Carter of Boston bought the hotel from H. F. Pitman of Marblehead in 1881, but, suffering the fate of its namesake, it fell victim to fire on 6 September 1882.

Not to be deterred, Carter promptly rebuilt the hotel from 1883 to 1884 as the New Ocean House, with bedroom space for 250 patrons. In 1895, the mansard-roof hostelry (fig. 5-8), displaying many of the same basic features of the Hotel Preston (see above), changed hands, and in 1902, following a damaging fire, was sold to Allen Ainsile and Edward Grabow. In subsequent years, the new owners invested the staggering sum of $100,000 in interior improvements, including an elevator, call bells

Fig. 5-8. "Ocean House, Swampscott, Mass." Lithograph from *New England's Summer and America's Leading Winter Resorts* (1897), n.p. Author's collection.

Fig. 5-9. New Ocean House, Swampscott, Mass. Letterhead lithograph, c. 1902. Courtesy of Peabody Essex Museum.

Fig. 5-10. "Impressive Façade of the New Ocean House, Swampscott, Massachusetts, Since its Recent Additions and Improvements." Photograph from *The North Shore Reminder* 7, no. 1 (14 July 1908). Courtesy of Peabody Essex Museum.

Fig. 5-11. "The Foyer," New Ocean House, Swampscott, Mass. Photograph from *The North Shore Reminder* 6, no. 3 (13 July 1907): 13. Courtesy of Peabody Essex Museum.

and telephones, and substantial additions to both ends of the complex (fig. 5-9), creatively blending Queen Anne, Shingle, and Colonial Revival–style features. Visually, the full building composition was unified and bound by identically scaled five-story gambrel-roof wings at opposite ends, each displaying similar window configurations and embellishment. In 1904, the New Ocean House underwent further rebuilding and expansion. The total capacity was raised to 350 by modifications to the long central section (fig. 5-10), resulting in augmented bedroom space in the now flat-roofed upper story, and square, twin towers with open cupolas and pyramidal roof caps framing the main entrance and porte cochere at ground level. The ground floor of the hotel contained the customary cavernous public spaces for socializing, leisure-time pursuits, and dining (fig. 5-11). The last major expansion project at the Puritan Road facility was carried out in 1917 by the construction at the east end of the freestanding, fire-resistant seven-story Puritan Hall (see fig. 1-7), raising the number of guest sleeping spaces to between 550 and 600.

In its fully developed form, the New Ocean House achieved the height of New England resort-hotel elegance and luxury, as expressed in the embellishment of both the exterior architectural elements and the largely classical revival décor of its interior spaces and their furnishings. A favorite destination for people from all areas of the United States as well as abroad, it hosted those on personal or group visits as well as those attending

professional and business conferences. Over the years, the management organized concerts, plays, dances, vaudeville, and a wide range of athletic and recreational activities centering on tennis, golf, horseback riding, boating, fishing, and sea bathing. High-profile, celebrated personalities were frequent visitors and included social types, political leaders, entertainers, writers, diplomats, and international figures. Sadly, the life and times of the New Ocean House came to a catastrophic end on 9 May 1969, when the massive complex (excluding Puritan Hall), then owned by Dr. George I. Rohrbough, was leveled by fire, never to be rebuilt. New England thus lost one of its largest wooden hotel structures, eclipsed in size only by the Poland Spring House in Maine and the Mount Washington Hotel and Wentworth Hotel in New Hampshire (see chapter 6).[6]

Marblehead, Beverly, and Manchester

From the mid–nineteenth century to the World War I era, there was a limited large resort-hotel presence along the central North Shore between Swampscott and Gloucester. This was in large part due to the emphasis on other economic activities, single-season and year-round residential development, and the less suitable qualities of certain segments of the shoreline. The region's most populated community, Salem, possessed relatively modest hotel enterprises, while Beverly and Manchester each boasted one large hostelry, and smaller inns and boardinghouses. The old maritime commerce town of Marblehead, on the other hand, became the primary focal point of hospitality tourism on the central North Shore, benefiting from its fine, protected harbor and its location on a rugged, rocky peninsula exposed to health-enhancing, cool sea breezes and salt air, most notably on picturesque Marblehead Neck.

Connected to the mainland by a long, narrow bar or isthmus, the Neck, essentially an island some eighteen miles from Boston, traditionally has accommodated much of the summer recreation and vacation life in Marblehead. The largest and most distinguished architecturally of the Neck's several late Victorian hostelries was the fashionable Nanepashemet Hotel, built from 1881 to 1882 by Robert C. Bridge from plans prepared by Boston architects M. P. Clark and Ion Lewis. An architectural drawing (fig. 5-12) of the Nanepashemet, published in the July 1882 issue of the *American Architect and Building News*, depicts a skillfully articulated, asymmetrical four-and-one-half-story Shingle-style structure marked by an expansive, composite gambrel roof with

Fig. 5-13. Rockmere Inn from Crocker Point, Marblehead, Mass. Postcard photograph, 1906. Courtesy of Peabody Essex Museum.

dormers, a wraparound veranda, and an off-center tower with rounded roof cap and flagpole. With rooms for 150 boarders, it was set on a bluff with several neighboring cottages, offering unobstructed ocean views to its patrons. The Nanepashemet conducted business until 1914, when it was sold to Paul Brackett, renamed the Ocean

Fig. 5-14. "Part of the Foyer, Rock-mere Inn," Marblehead, Mass. Photograph from booklet, *Rock-mere Inn, Marblehead* (c. 1907). Courtesy of Peabody Essex Museum.

Manor, and totally destroyed by an untimely fire on 21 October of the same year.[7]

Situated for sixty-five years at Skinner's Head on the opposite side of the harbor on the main Marblehead peninsula was the Rockmere Inn (also known as the Rock-mere and the Rockmere Hotel) (fig. 5-13), by far the largest and most prominent summer hostelry in town and one of the most superlative examples of Colonial Revival resort-hotel architecture on the Massachusetts seaboard. Most impressive among its many stylized features were the large pitched and gambrel roof gables and the two-story front entrance portico supported by Doric columns. Opened in 1901 and enlarged in 1905 by its initial owner, Gilbert Brackett, to house over 200 guests, it provided many magnificent vistas and quality amenities, as described by Samuel Roads, Jr., in *A Guide to Marblehead* (c. 1902):

The new Rockmere Inn . . . is situated within one hundred feet of the water on high land, commanding a fine view of the North Shore. Directly in front of the broad and spacious verandas a grand panorama of all yachting, the club houses, the numerous lighthouses and the ancient fortress. Well-kept grounds surround and slope gradually to the water. Tennis courts on Rockmere Point afford a charming, cool spot for this game. Salt-water bathing, boating and sailing. The Rockmere Inn is modern in every way, with large assembly halls and living rooms [fig. 5-14]. Spacious dining-room seating one hundred and fifty, opens on three sides. Call bells and electric lights in all rooms and excellent service. The rooms are planned in pleasant suites, each arranged to command a view of the water and yachting.

Fig. 5-15. The Gun Deck, Fo'cas'le, Rockmere Inn, Marblehead, Mass. Postcard photograph, c. 1930. Courtesy of The Marblehead Museum & Historical Society.

After 1929, the year that it was premiered, the hotel was particularly known for the Fo'cas'le, an appended two-story classical-revival dining and dancing restaurant with basic wooden furniture and maritime trappings (fig. 5-15). The Rockmere retained its original name, with variations, until 1937, when it was retitled "Hotel Marble-head," only to complete its lengthy period of service as "Hotel Rockmere" in 1963. Unused and boarded up, it sat idle for two years, and in the spring of 1965 was torn down and replaced by the Glover's Landing residential complex.[8]

Once located on Lowell (Cotta or "Cat") Island, a mile from Marblehead in outer Salem Harbor, the Low-ell Island House (fig. 5-16), constructed by the Salem Steamboat Company from 1851 to 1852, was one of the first major resort hotels in the North Shore region, ac-commodating up to 250 people at its maximum size. Par-ticularly popular with the residents of Lowell and other Merrimack Valley textile centers, the hotel was regularly accessed by steamboat from both Salem and Marblehead

during the summer season. A bland, vernacular wooden building of little aesthetic character, the hotel possessed a T-shaped floor plan and was two-and-one-half stories high under pitched, dormered, intersecting roofs with a central cupola. The rear ell appears to have been added to the original rectangular block during the early 1850s. After just six years of operation, the Salem Steamboat Company sold the Lowell Island House to Gorham L. Pollard of Lowell, who kept it open, with varying suc-cess, until 1869, when it, along with the entire island, was purchased by Andrew L. Johnson of Boston. After several more years of financial insecurity, the property changed hands several times until it was ultimately bought by

Fig. 5-16. Lowell Island House, Lowell (Cat) Island, Salem Harbor, Mass. Photograph, n.d. Courtesy of Peabody Essex Museum.

"THE QUEEN."

Fig. 5-17. "The Queen," Beverly, Mass. Photoengraving from Benjamin D. Hill and Winfield S. Nevins, *The North Shore of Massachusetts Bay* (1891 ed.), p. 51. Courtesy of the University of Delaware Library.

occupied by residential buildings, including the large country estates of Beverly Farms, after the Civil War. The town's sole Victorian-era resort hotel, the Queen (fig. 5-17), was put up from 1888 to 1889 by Israel LeFavour at a Lothrop Street seaside site where Independence Park is located today. A rambling, three- to four-and-one-half-story wooden edifice, it was 177 feet long with extensive verandas on three sides. Emphatically Queen Anne in style, this building undoubtedly impressed onlookers with its varied roof forms and its square and octagonal towers with their steep-pitched roof caps. Erected at the then extravagant cost of about $107,000, including furnishings, the Queen, capable of housing 150 people, lasted only three seasons before it was obliterated by a massive fire, believed to have been set by an arsonist, on 24 November 1891.[10]

Seven miles northeast of Beverly, Manchester (also known as Manchester-by-the-Sea) fared considerably better as its only early resort hotel of substance, the Hotel Masconomo (Masconomo House) remained open to patrons for over half a century. Surrounded by extravagant summer residences and overlooking the renowned "Singing Beach," the Masconomo had its origins in 1867 when actor Junius Brutus Booth, Jr., and his actress wife, Agnes Perry, bought land on Beach Street and built a house there known as "Booth Cottage." In 1877, Booth made the decision to enlarge the house and convert it to a hotel (fig. 5-18), and contracted with builders Phillips and Killan to carry out the ambitious project. Opened in

Samuel J. Rindge of Marblehead in 1878 for a mere $4,500. A well-known philanthropist, Rindge presented the island and its buildings to St. Margaret's (Episcopal) Home of Boston, which established the Children's Island Sanitarium for the care of young people. In 1900, the succeeding Children's Island Sanitarium Association, formed to manage the facility, deemed the hotel "no longer safe," and it was demolished soon thereafter, having served as an excellent example of resort hotel adaptive reuse.[9]

Slightly northward, across the Danvers River from Salem, is the town of Beverly, historically a shoe-manufacturing center whose desirable shoreline became

Fig. 5-18. "Masconomo, Manchester By The Sea," Mass. Photograph from *North and South Shore Views*, Forbes Company, 188?. Courtesy, American Antiquarian Society.

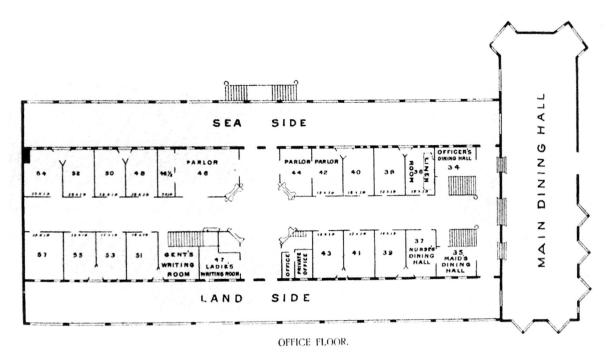

Fig. 5-19. "Office Floor," Hotel Masconomo, Manchester, Mass. Plan from booklet, *The Masconomo, Manchester-by-the-Sea* (1906). Courtesy of Peabody Essex Museum.

June 1878, the Masconomo, named for a former Indian chief, was touted as a "model of hotel architecture," accommodating upward of 300 people in its fully developed form. A sprawling complex, 275 feet long and low to the ground, the two-and-one-half-story edifice echoed in a more subdued manner the Second Empire–style qualities of the attached Booth Cottage. Its most pronounced feature was the ample octagonal observatory, strategically positioned off center on the truncated, pitched roof and embraced by four tall brick chimneys servicing four mammoth fireplaces in the grand octagonal hall below (fig. 5-19). Advertised as a haven for the rich and the famous, the Masconomo, enlarged in 1887, was supplemented on the property by other buildings including a bandstand, guest cottages, and two other structures containing a pool room, bowling alleys, a dance hall, and living quarters for the hired help. After Junius Booth's death in 1883, Agnes Booth married John B. Schoeffel, and they ran the enterprise with success until her death in 1910. Schoeffel purchased the property outright at public auction in 1911, and it changed hands again before its nearly complete destruction by fire in 1919. Most

of what remained was demolished a year later, though greatly altered portions of Booth Cottage and the hotel still survive today on the site.[11]

Magnolia: Resort Hotel Mecca

Just over the Manchester line in the western section of Gloucester is the major portion of the village of Magnolia at Magnolia Point, long one of the North Shore's most important hospitality tourism destinations with a rich resort-hotel architectural heritage. Originally a fishing and farming settlement, Magnolia had its beginnings as a summer resort center in the early 1870s with the construction of the first summer cottages there, along with the first hotel, the Crescent Beach, later the Blynman. The section known as the "Point" had been purchased by Daniel W. Fuller of Swampscott in 1867, and he ultimately built cottages for sale and rental, and sold lots to others for private residences. In 1877, halfway out on the Point on rising ground, Fuller erected what would soon become one of the village's three large resort hotels. Blessed by immediate success, the Hesperus

Fig. 5-20. "The Hesperus, Magnolia, Mass." Carte-de-visite, 1908. The Magnolia Historical Society.

House (fig. 5-20) was doubled in size two years later to accommodate, along with cottages, roughly 100 guests. The two two-and-one-half-story wings, one of Second Empire and the other of Queen Anne inspiration, stood some seventy feet apart and were connected by a covered walkway, at the center of which was an eye-catching Chinese pagoda with a porte cochere. Sold by the Fuller family to Mrs. Orra Paige in 1884, within the next year a substantial three-and-one-half-story central section, with traces of Shingle-style influence, was raised, set back behind the pagoda and covered walkway. The noted Gloucester contractor John W. Day has been credited with the building of this addition, and possibly was responsible for the two earlier wings. Achieving a maximum capacity of over 300 people, the Hesperus was bought by the Magnolia Hotel Corporation in 1912, operated as an annex of the Oceanside Hotel (see below), and concluded its long service tenure after World War II as the North Shore Inn under new ownership. Outmoded and no longer appealing to prospective patrons, it was closed in the early 1950s, leveled by controlled burning and demolition, and the property (on Hesperus Avenue) converted to residential use.[12]

Magnolia Point's other two large resort hostelries, the Oceanside and the Magnolia, with their incredible mass-ing and striking array of Queen Anne–style elements, deservedly rank among the nation's most impressive Victorian-era grand hotels. The oldest of these, the Oceanside, had its beginnings in 1876 when Daniel Fuller sold a piece of property (abutting the Hesperus tract on Hesperus Street) to Mr. and Mrs. James Perkins. Within a year, Mr. Perkins had a four-story, Second Empire, hipped-on-mansard-roof building (fig. 5-21) erected, half to be used as a family residence and half as a summer boardinghouse, Perkins House, which formally opened in 1877. In 1879, the property passed to George A. Upton, who

Fig. 5-21. The Oceanside (early state), Magnolia, Mass. Photograph, c. 1880. The Magnolia Historical Society.

Fig. 5-22. The Oceanside, Magnolia, Mass. Photograph, c. 1905. The Magnolia Historical Society.

endowed it with the new name of "Hotel Oceanside" and in the 1880s launched a multistage expansion over several years, taking the enterprise from near obscurity to national prominence. Local builder John W. Day, contractor for other Gloucester resort hotels, worked with Upton on the various phases of the complex. By 1908, when he sold out for over $500,000, Upton presided over a huge, sprawling, six-story, ark-like complex containing six hundred rooms, ten adjacent cottages, staff dormitories, a cavernous 150-by-45-foot dining room with chandeliers, over eight hundred feet of two-level verandas, and a casino noted for its black ceiling fitted out with starlike electric globes. Most notable on the exterior (fig. 5-22) and emblematic of the Queen Anne idiom were the rounded corner towers with their various-shaped roof caps, and the multiple, stacked porches and window bays, intended to provide optimal ocean views and exposure to cool, moist, health-enhancing seacoast air. Despite the proliferation of varied design features, highlighted by the contrasting roof shapes, the structure achieved aesthetic unity, indeed a tribute to its yet unidentified architect(s).

Arguably New England's largest-capacity resort ho-

tel in its prime years, the Oceanside, in addition to its sleeping quarters, offered its customers opulent interior public spaces, formal gardens, clay and grass tennis courts, and a nearby beach pavilion for relaxation, visual contemplation, and water-related activities. Known for its "classy" appeal to national and international leaders of business, politics, culture, and society, the hotel was considered in the same select category as the Royal Poinciana in Florida, the Poland Spring in Maine, and the Mount Washington Hotel and the Balsams in New Hampshire's White Mountains. During the 1920s, the Oceanside was owned by the famed Abbot Hotels company, owners of hotels in Florida, North Carolina, Massachusetts, and the White Mountains, including the renowned Profile House in Franconia Notch, lost in a devastating fire in 1923. In 1931, George C. Krewson, Jr., a New Jersey resident who had never owned or operated a hotel before, acquired the Oceanside and, remarkable for the Depression years, further expanded the clientele and created "a royal palace of elegance" during his tenure. In 1946, Krewson sold the great hostelry and outbuildings to the Oceanside Hotel Corporation, which presided over its decline, perpetuated by changing lifestyles and expanding transportation options. On 11 December 1958, the ultimate tragedy struck, and the once 750-capacity Oceanside Hotel was totally destroyed in one of the most spectacular fires ever observed on the North Shore. For a while thoughts circulated about a possible replacement, but today the former site is occupied by a multiunit apartment building, a condominium complex, and three single-family homes.[13]

Despite its unusually fine Queen Anne design, the smaller but still grand Magnolia Hotel (commonly referred to as the "New Magnolia") has received much less attention than the Oceanside in the literature published to date treating Magnolia, Gloucester, and the North Shore. Similarly configured and adorned, and equally pretentious, the Magnolia (fig. 5-23) was erected by Rev. Frank Sprague on Lexington Avenue, proximate to both the Oceanside and the Hesperus on the highest ground on the Point. Greeted with much fanfare, the new hostelry, with its characteristic hipped-on-mansard, dormered roof, dominant corner towers, balconies, and enveloping two-tiered veranda, is described in typically promotional but informative language in the 1891 edition of *The North Shore of Massachusetts Bay* by Benjamin Hill and Winfield Nevins:

The Magnolia. . . . Six stories high . . . the views from its piazzas and windows are superb. The skill with which a house of 160 rooms is so planned that nearly every one looks out over the water, although several hundred feet from the shore, is something which astonishes the ordinary mortal. In the Magnolia

Fig. 5-23. "The Magnolia, Magnolia, Mass." Lithograph from *New England's Summer and America's Leading Winter Resorts* (1897). Author's collection.

there are only two rooms on a floor (and those on the north side of the house) from which the ocean may not be viewed without raising the window. The hotel has a frontage of 186 feet . . . and contains, with the cottage opposite, over two hundred sleeping rooms, besides office, parlors, smoking-rooms, [billiard parlors, reading and writing rooms,] bath-rooms, [hot and cold running water,] and other rooms of convenience. . . . The interior decoration of the rooms is beautiful in many cases, all being papered and carpeted or covered with handsome rugs. The house is lighted by electricity from cellar to attic and heated with steam on every floor; while an elevator affords a luxury which no other hotel on the shore can boast. Parlors, dining-room and many rooms for guests have fire-places, some of which are indeed works of art. The great dining-hall will seat 300 persons at one time and is lighted by eighty incandescent lights. There is also a nurse's dining-room accommodating fifty persons. The fire-escape is unique . . . , being a series of handsome balconies connected by easy and safe stairways. A telephone and post-office are located in the house.

Clearly, guest services were predicated on convenience, attractiveness, the most modern technology, and the magical, irresistible features and effects of the sea, the primary rationale behind the origins of the resort hotel industry on the New England coast.

Achieving a maximum capacity (with cottages) of 300 people, the Magnolia maintained its original size and form with only a few modifications, mostly cosmetic, for its all too brief history. Among several upgrades were a new 250-foot-long bathing pavilion opened for the 1903 season, "the most complete and attractive . . . on the coast," and, in 1904, a spacious sun parlor for dancing and other entertainment. The Magnolia burned down in 1907 and, according to Karl Baedeker's well-known guidebook, *The United States . . .* (1909 ed.), was scheduled to be rebuilt. Likely because of continually rising operational and contracting costs, coupled with the increasing volatility of the resort hotel business, this never happened.[14]

Gloucester on Cape Ann

Occupying the major portion of Cape Ann is the nationally renowned fishing and tourism city of Gloucester, its rugged, scenic southern coastline extending from Magnolia Point to Gloucester Harbor, Eastern Point, Bass Rocks, and Cape Hedge. Thirty-one miles from Boston, initially on the Eastern and then the Boston & Maine railroads, this venerable community, including Magnolia Point (see above), became the North Shore's most significant summer resort center in the mid to late nineteenth century, boasting numerous single-season residences and the largest concentration of resort hotels between Boston and the southern coastline of Maine. Although the majority of these hostelries were modest boardinghouses, inns, and small hotels, the city possessed at various times half a dozen large hotels of contrasting architectural styles and aesthetic/functional merit, each accommodating 200 or more guests.[15]

Gloucester's first conspicuous, bona fide resort hotel, discussed in depth by architectural historian James O'Gorman in his book *This Other Gloucester* (1976), was the Pavilion Hotel (later the "Surfside"), erected west of the center of the city between April and June 1849. Located on Western Avenue at Crescent Beach overlooking the busy harbor, the Pavilion was conceived and funded by Gloucester native Sidney Mason, and was constructed by the contracting team of White and Winchester. Responsible for the design, modified in the final version of the building, was the obscure architect S. Charles Bugbee, first based in Boston and later in San Francisco. Documenting Bugbee's association with the project, along with newspaper sources, are preliminary elevation and floor plans, fortunately preserved in the archives of Gloucester's Cape Ann Historical Museum.

Drawings, photographs, and published illustrations (fig. 5-24) show a nicely proportioned two-and-one-half-story, pitched-roof, wooden structure surrounded by a two-level veranda seemingly of early Stick-style inspiration. An 1849 article in the *Boston Evening Transcript* underscored the "spacious and airy" sleeping apartments, drawing and dining rooms, healthy atmosphere, breathtaking harbor views, and bathing and bowling activities. In its 5 September 1849 issue, the *Gloucester Telegraph* made the bold claim that the Pavilion was "the first specimen of architectural good taste ever seen here." As finally executed, the pace-setting hostelry departed from the Bugbee designs, with a split central dormer, a larger, simplified cupola, and a light-construction (as

Fig. 5-24. Pavilion Hotel, Crescent Beach, Gloucester, Mass. Etching, c. 1875. CAPE ANN HISTORICAL ASSOCIATION, Gloucester, Massachusetts.

opposed to bracketed) lower veranda, the latter contributing to the southern plantation, houselike openness of the building. With guest space for 150 persons, this landmark structure, with later small additions, survived the ups and downs of the hospitality industry until 7 October 1914, when fire "made a grand illumination through fog and mist," ending its lengthy period of service.[16]

East Gloucester's sole early large resort-hotel complex was the Hawthorne Inn, originated on Wonson's Point in 1891 by the enterprising hotel developer George O. Stacy, and later to become a massive, multibuilding establishment taking 450 to 500 or more guests in twenty-four separate units, most newly built or converted cottages. The primary component was a central Shingle-style edifice (fig. 5-25), with its proliferation of verandas, porches, and angled window bays, to which were attached the less auspicious Manse and south wing containing bedrooms and public spaces. The prolific Gloucester contractor John W. Day, builder of other local hotels, was associated with the primary building projects. The individual structures possessed names recalling the life and writings of Nathaniel Hawthorne, Stacy's favorite author and the hotel's namesake—Seven Gables, Province House, Orchard Cottage, Wayside, Peabody, Endicott, Felton, Cherryfield, and Blythedale. In 1930, after Stacy's death, the ownership of the Hawthorne Inn and Cottages transferred to Thomas White. Eight years later, on 10 February 1938, the hotel was visited by a devastating fire, believed to have been intentionally set and leading to the

Fig. 5-25. The main building and wings, Hawthorne Inn and Cottages, East Gloucester, Mass. Photograph, Eben Parsons, 1913. CAPE ANN HISTORICAL ASSOCIATION, Gloucester, Massachusetts.

arrest of those held responsible. The business never fully recovered, though the hotel remained open until after World War II.[17]

At Bass Rocks, on Gloucester's "back shore" at the base of Eastern Point on the east side of Cape Ann, there were once three substantial hospitality enterprises that justifi-

Fig. 5-26. "Bass Rock House," Gloucester, Mass. Engraving from Benjamin D. Hill and Winfield S. Nevins, *The North Shore of Massachusetts Bay* (1881 ed.), p. 63. Courtesy of Peabody Essex Museum.

ably merit attention in this study. The oldest of these was the Bass Rock House, its two contiguous, connected, Second Empire–influenced buildings (fig. 5-26) opened in 1879 by Mrs. E. G. Brown as an enlarged version of a former, more modest resort known as Whitings. Around 1880, two stories and a broad veranda were added, and the dining room was substantially enlarged, all in response to immediate business success largely driven by the beauty and offerings of nearby Little Good Harbor Beach. Continually expanded and upgraded, the Bass Rock's capacity, with cottages and outbuildings, peaked at 250, but the core complex was lost to fire in 1896.[18]

That same year, George O. Stacy expanded his hotel interests beyond the Hawthorne Inn (see above) and, partnering with Edward P. Parsons and local contractor John W. Day, built what would become the 300-capacity (including a large annex, casino, and five cottages) Hotel Moorland off Atlantic Road near the site of the smaller Pebbly Beach Hotel, which had previously burned in 1884. The main building (fig. 5-27), raised in two stages, was an imposing L-shaped, four-and-one-half-story, hybrid Queen Anne/Shingle–style edifice, with the required first-level verandas and a gambrel roof broken by single and double shed-roof dormers. Seemingly anchoring the building to the ground was an octagonal corner tower, common to many hotels of the era, with a steep-pitched roof cap and finial. The guest annex, known as Moorland Hall, was of a scale and proportions similar to the main hotel, and possessed comparable stacked balconies for pleasant ocean viewing, some with connecting stairways. Outlasting most large resort hotels of its time and region, the Moorland offered guest services well beyond World War II. In 1958, the same year as Magnolia's grand Oceanside Hotel, it was destroyed by fire.[19]

Near Good Harbor Beach at Bass Rocks, the Hotel Thorwald was put up in 1899 by builder and first owner Eli Jackman. Like the Moorland, the physical plant (fig. 5-28) consisted of a multipurpose main structure and a substantial annex connected by a covered walkway and devoted primarily to guest sleeping quarters. The annex, in all likelihood, was erected at a later date. Of the two buildings, the four-story, hipped-roof main hotel, while defying stylistic classification, was by far the most interesting aesthetically. Its symmetrical front façade featured square corner towers with pyramidal roofs, and, above the main entrance, a somewhat taller, square tower was topped by an open cupola with balustrade and pyramidal roof cap and displayed a fine Palladian window at the fourth-floor level. In business for half a century, the 200–250 capacity Thorwald met the all too familiar fate of its wooden hotel contemporaries when it burned on 5 March 1965, after which the remnants were removed. The annex also was lost to fire just six weeks later.[20]

In his well-received book *Boston's Gold Coast: The North Shore, 1890–1929* (1981), the prolific author Joseph Garland asserted that "the Colonial Arms was the greatest, grandest hotel, winter or summer, ever conceived in a single stroke north of Boston." He was absolutely correct by any standards of measure! Erected from 1903 to 1904 (fig. 5-29) on Eastern Point between Gloucester Harbor and Niles Pond, it was the brainchild of George O. Stacy and was by far the biggest hotel development project undertaken by one of New England's most successful and best-known hotel men. Stacy's initial conception was a massive new edifice, three and one-half sto-

Fig. 5-27. "Hotel Moorland, Gloucester, Mass." Colored postcard, c. 1930. Courtesy of Kenneth Nickerson, Rockport, Mass.

Fig. 5-28. "Bass Rocks, Mass. The Thorwald Hotel." Colored postcard, c. 1930. Courtesy of Kenneth Nickerson, Rockport, Mass.

ries in an angular, crescent shape, possessing 175 rooms, including a dining room with harbor and inland vistas, supplemented by guest cottages, a horse stable, an automobile garage, a steamboat wharf, and, at Niles Beach, a casino, teahouse, and bathing pavilion. When the Colonial Arms opened on 25 June 1904, however, the room total had been increased to about 300 accommodating upward of 400 overnight guests, and the height raised to four and one-half to five stories. Unquestionably, Stacy was well rewarded for his $230,00 land and physical plant investment, coupled with the fact that the hotel was completely filled with appreciative patrons during the brief four-year period it was open for business.

Fig. 5-29. The Colonial Arms under construction with work crew, Eastern Point, Gloucester, Mass. Photograph, 1904. Courtesy of the great-grandaughters of John Warner Day, building contractor.

Built under the direction of Gloucester contractor John W. Day (under the firm name John W. Day & Sons) from plans by architect W. C. Hazlett of New York City, the Colonial Arms (fig. 5-30) was an awe-inspiring expression of the then highly popular Colonial Revival style, its various forms and decorative features successfully interrelated and amalgamated to create a powerful, cohesive architectural statement of wood materials. With approximate dimensions of 360 by 60 feet, the full structure, shaped in conformance with the harbor shoreline, gave the impression of near perfect symmetry despite the presence of a flat-roofed east-side service wing containing employee living quarters and a kitchen, laundry, and storeroom. Protecting the building were a succession of gambrel roofs over the central section and the wings, enclosed by cross-gable extensions framing the major portion of the complex. The roof surfaces were studded with an almost overwhelming collection of some seventy-five single and double dormers with pitched roof covers, breaking both gambrel roof planes. Surrounding the full structure were balustraded veran-

das, double-tiered on the harbor façade. Serving as the primary visual and functional focal point was the central section and its inland-facing main entrance shielded by an imposing portico with four Ionic columns and a full, dentiled architrave rising up three stories, flanked by stacked balconies and accessed at ground level by a delicate, balustraded, one-story porte cochere. For some unexplained reason, perhaps purely aesthetic, a duplicate of this entrance portico was appended to the west wing end wall. Crowning the entire complex on the center section was a small, balustraded observatory, above which rose a tall flagpole, appropriately mimicking a sailing-ship mast.

Entering the Colonial Arms through the main doorway, visitors would have first encountered the spacious, beautifully furnished grand lobby (foyer) extending through the building and offering panoramic views of the always active harbor. The main and private dining rooms and grill, with bowed front overlooking the harbor, were situated in the east wing, while the ballroom was located in the west wing. In addition, the first floor contained a

Fig. 5-30. The Colonial Arms, Eastern Point, Gloucester, Mass. Photograph, c. 1905, Detroit Photographic Company, Henry G. Peabody, Photographer. From the Collections of The Henry Ford.

"morning" room, a newsstand, "toilet parlors," a music parlor, administrative offices, and game and reception rooms. On the floors above, reached by elevator, were guest rooms and suites, some with private baths and others with adjacent shared baths, and all with telephones, electric lights, and steam heat. Stacy, the contractor, and the architect made every effort to ensure fire prevention and protection through the use of noncombustible building materials, the inclusion of two brick firewalls dividing the building into three separate units, and the installation of metal hallway doors intended to act as fire barriers.

George Stacy's original intention had been to own and operate his newest and most ambitious hotel venture independently, but the need for additional capital neces-

sitated the formation of a corporation and the involvement of other parties. After the first season of operation, in 1905 he signed a five-year lease with H. W. Priest and Company, said to generate $15,000 a year, to manage the business, but the lease terms were never completely fulfilled as fate intervened. In the early evening of New Year's Day, 1908, it was reported that fire had commenced in the far end of the west wing and was raging uncontrollably, fanned by unfortunately high winds. The entire complex, despite the enlightened fire-protection features (see above) and the best efforts of local firefighters, was consumed by a spectacular, history-making conflagration. Three and one-half hours after the fire was discovered and the alarm sounded, the remnants of the blazing inferno collapsed, and one of the nation's grandest resort

Fig. 5-31. Turk's Head Inn, Rockport, Mass. Photograph, n.d. CAPE ANN HISTORICAL ASSOCIATION, Gloucester, Massachusetts.

hotels was left a smoking, smoldering ruin. As the hotel was well insured, Stacy talked about rebuilding, and a year later it was reported that he and other potential investors were considering replacing the Colonial Arms with a substantial "Venetian" hotel of fireproof design and materials on the original site, to be supplemented by a colony of cottages. With hopes of a grand opening for the 1911 season, the project, for unexplained reasons, was never carried out, leaving indelible memories of the short-lived but unforgettable Colonial Revival icon.[21]

Rockport and the Turk's Head Inn

Formerly part of Gloucester, about four miles northeast of Gloucester Harbor on the eastern tip of Cape Ann, is the town of Rockport with its two historic coastal villages at Sandy Beach and nearby Pigeon Cove (also known as Ocean View). During the latter part of the nineteenth century, the town owed its commercial prosperity to granite quarrying, textile manufacturing, fishing, and its growing popularity as a summer resort. The primary concentration of resort hotels, albeit modest-sized buildings, was at Pigeon Cove, and included three high-visibility but no longer extant hostelries — the second Pigeon Cove House (c. 1871), the Ocean View House (1871), and the Linwood Hotel (1877). Located in the same village was the first Pigeon Cove House (c. 1860), moved to Green Street and Cathedral Avenue in 1871, later renovated and enlarged, and operated as the Hotel Edward, and subsequently as the Ralph Waldo Emerson Inn to this very day. Another hotel of note at Straitsmouth Point (Gap Head) in Rockport was the former Straitsmouth Inn, a plain, rectangular block of

100-guest capacity that was put up by founder Ella S. Wilkenson from 1906 to 1907 and burned to the ground on 31 December 1958.[22]

Despite its prominence as a summer vacation community, Rockport possessed only one pre–World II large resort hotel satisfying the specifications for inclusion in this study. Once situated at Land's End on South Street, with ocean views to Thatcher's and Milk islands, was the Turk's Head Inn (fig. 5-31), the initial portion erected from 1889 to 1990 by builder J. M. Wetherill of Rockport based on plans by architect H. M. Stephenson of Boston. Impressively sited on a 150-foot elevation, this rambling, E-shaped Colonial Revival structure possessed a seaboard frontage of two hundred feet and wraparound verandas over three hundred feet in length. Providing vertical sight lines to what was otherwise a flat, horizontal edifice were tall brick chimneys and an octagonal tower with spire roof cap. The main entrance opened into a large hall with a massive fireplace of Rockport granite, accessing parlors, a music room, a spacious, L-shaped dining room, and other public spaces. Over the years, the Turk's Head suffered a number of fires, and its central and southeast wings were rebuilt, the latter in 1905 by then owner C. B. Martin. With a peak capacity of 200, the hotel, uncharacteristic of the regional hospitality tourism industry, remained in operation for eighty years before it was closed down, partially destroyed by fire, and the remains removed in 1970 to make way for the present Turk's Head Motor Inn. The original inn was the last survivor of Cape Ann's distinguished collection of large resort hotels originating prior to 1950, and a representative example of the last phase of the Gilded Age hotel era along Boston's North Shore.[23]

NEW HAMPSHIRE

The Beaches, New Castle, and the Isles of Shoals

O F   T H E   F I V E   S E A S I D E New England states, New Hampshire possesses the smallest coastline, approximately eighteen miles in length extending from Seabrook to New Castle and the entrance to Portsmouth Harbor. Also an integral part of this region's coastal life, economy, and history are the Isles of Shoals, just nine miles out to sea from the harbor, and split between New Hampshire and Maine. Commencing in the early nineteenth century, resort communities developed along New Hampshire's ample beaches and distinctive promontories, supplementing those simultaneously appearing in the White Mountains and other interior regions of the state. Most notable were those at Hampton, Rye, and New Castle, the latter closely identified with the Wentworth Hotel (Wentworth-By-The Sea), one of America's most historic and renowned ocean resort establishments. While the Wentworth is deserving of primary attention as a superb, partially extant specimen of Victorian grand resort-hotel architecture, there are other, smaller New Hampshire examples, only one surviving on Star Island, that also merit close scrutiny. Though a collection of modest size and pretense, these hotel structures, reflecting several contrasting style modes and spanning nearly a century, constitute an important segment of New England's coastal resort hotel legacy.

Great Boar's Head and the Hampton Beaches

The Hampton shoreline, its beaches extending north and south of the Great Boar's Head (commonly referred to as "Boar's Head"), was initially home to a thriving fishing industry in the late 1800s and early 1900s. As this economic enterprise grew, and increasing numbers of people frequented the area, private residences were built, some becoming boardinghouses and small inns, thereby laying the basis of the subsequent tourism economy. The first bona fide hotel, one of the first seaboard hotels north of Boston, was erected at Boar's Head in 1819 and opened the following year by Abraham Marston, Jr., and Amos Towle, III. The construction of this modest, early Greek Revival hostelry, known primarily as the Winnicumet House, helped to establish Hampton as one of the New England region's earliest summer resort centers. The town's first substantive hotel operation was soon to follow.[1]

Around 1824 or 1825, local businessman David Nudd and others formed a company, acquired a small inn owned by Jerry Lamprey, and erected a second area hotel, the Hampton Beach, on the summit of the sixty-foot Boar's Head promontory, projecting a quarter of a mile from

Fig. 6-1. Boar's Head Hotel, Hampton, N.H. Stereo #398, n.d., Davis Brothers, Portsmouth, N.H. New Hampshire Historical Society.

Fig. 6-2. First Ocean House, Hampton Beach, N.H. Stereo, n.d., W. H. Hobbs, Exeter, N.H. New Hampshire Historical Society.

the mainland into the sea. Raised under the direction of contractor Ebenezer Leavitt, the hotel, later known as the Boar's Head, was opened to boarders in 1826. In about 1841, a substantial ell was added, creating a four-story, L-shaped vernacular complex (fig. 6-1), which, when later enlarged, was capable of accommodating at least 150 guests. In 1866, the property passed from Nudd's heirs to Colonel Stebbins H. Dumas, who further enlarged and "improved" the hotel in the Second Empire style, characterized by its flat, dormered mansard roof, central observation cupola, and encircling verandas. Remaining in this form, it was lost to a disastrous fire on 23 October 1893. While it existed, however, it commanded from its windows and veranda a broad view of the ocean, the Isles of Shoals, and the coast from Portsmouth to Cape Ann, Massachusetts. Extensively marketed in published literature, the hotel promoted its scenic location, healthful sea breezes, quality cuisine, beach bathing, livery stable, fishing, bowling, billiards, promenading, and other social and recreational activities.[2]

The first Ocean House (fig. 6-2), built in 1844, was one of the largest coastal hotels of its era in New England and the largest in the entire history of Hampton Beach. Set back from the shore, about one-half mile southeast of Boar's Head, this substantial, precedent-setting wooden

hostelry was financed and constructed by Stacy Nudd, the oldest son of David. At first of modest proportions, it was enlarged several times in response to increased patronage, eventually reaching four stories, with space for 250 overnight patrons. Though quite plain in appearance and lacking in stylistic décor, it possessed an impressive collection of linked, pitched-roof gables and the customary enveloping veranda with post support brackets and an upper balustrade. The last major expansion took place in 1866 under the ownership of Philip Yeaton and Company of Lawrence, Massachusetts. Following the all too common pattern, the Ocean House, its stables, three cottages, and two smaller adjacent hotels, the Atlantic and the Sea View, were leveled by fire on 6 May 1885. The legacy of the Ocean House as appealing to a broad spectrum of society helped to mold the character of Hampton Beach as a popular leisure-time center.[3]

Rye Beach: The Farragut and Its Contemporaries

Contiguous to and north of Hampton Beach is Rye Beach, consisting of two segments—the upper shore and the lower shore, formerly known as Jenness Beach. Historically, Rye Beach has been broadly regarded as the New Hampshire coast's most fashionable summer resort community, featuring substantial and, in some instances, luxurious seasonal cottages and several sizable hotels, entirely gone since the demolition of the second Farragut House in 1975 (see below). As consistently observed in travel guides over the years, it is, however, the beachfront, famous "for its hardness, smoothness, gentle slope and splendid drive of several miles," that has been and will continue to be the focal point of visitor attention and activity.[4]

In the 1840s, urban residents from the Northeast and Midwest began to migrate each summer season to the coast areas of New Jersey, Long Island, and New England in pursuit of romantic scenery, and the healthful and restorative qualities of fresh air and the seaside experience. A beneficiary of this phenomenon, Rye assumed its role as a signature summer destination with the opening of the first Ocean House circa 1847 or 1848 and the Atlantic House (see below) circa 1848. As initially conceived, the first Ocean House was a comparatively small building, erected under the direction of local resident Jonathan Rollins Jenness and then taken over and enlarged by his brother, Job Jenness, the following year. Initial business success continued, and by the mid-1850s the hotel was able to house over 300 guest clients, providing competition for its time with the other large hotels on the New England coast. As depicted in a circa 1855 lithograph (fig. 6-3) by John H. Bufford (after H. Harnden), the first Ocean House was a formidable three-and-one-

half-story, T-shaped edifice with Italian Revival gable and roof overhang brackets and veranda stickwork. This interesting architectural landmark experienced a sad and unexpected demise when it burned to the ground on 22 June 1862 in the middle of the Civil War.[5]

Immediately afterward, Job Jenness, who had maintained ownership of the hotel since 1848, commenced planning for its replacement. Designed by the noted Newburyport, Massachusetts, architect Rufus Sargent, the second Ocean House, its opening delayed by wartime labor shortage, was built between 1863 and 1865. Although it never received the hexagonal towers and arched-roof dormers depicted in preopening guidebook and advertising brochure engravings (fig. 6-4), this was compensated for by the replacement of the planned central cupola by a stunning, ornate, octagonal Italianate observatory displaying beautifully articulated paired, arched apertures with screening and a surrounding balustrade. The inevitable, stock-in-trade veranda or piazza surrounded the full two-story, symmetrical wooden complex.[6]

The 1873 edition of John B. Bachelder's *Popular Resorts* contains a valuable and quite enthralling description of the interior of the second Ocean House:

This Hotel has 250 feet front, is 100 feet deep. . . . The rotunda in the centre is fifty feet square, lighted by octagonal windows, from the right of which are four private parlors, barber's room,

Fig. 6-3. "Ocean House, Rye Beach, N.H., Job Jenness, Proprietor." Lithograph, c. 1855, by John H. Bufford, Lith., Boston, after H. Harnden, del. New Hampshire Historical Society.

Fig. 6-4. Second Ocean House, Rye Beach, N.H. Engraving from John B. Bachelder, *Popular Resorts, Routes to Reach Them* (1873), p. 45. Author's collection.

and an immense dining-hall, seating 400 people, and children's dining-room, seating 50. . . . Also, carving, crockery, glassware room, and pantries. From the left are four private parlors, office, gentlemen's reading-room, and the splendidly furnished ladies' parlor. The entire building is finished in black walnut, butternut, chestnut and cherry. In the rear of the rotunda are spacious stairways leading to all parts of the Hotel. From a fine observatory . . . the views of land and ocean scenery cannot be excelled.

On the second, third and fourth stories are the sleeping rooms—admirably arranged in suites for families, or can be used singly if desired—lighted by windows seven feet long, of which there are over three hundred in the building. Each room has a ventilator over the door.[7]

Claimed to be "the most substantial, comfortable, and best seaside resort in the country,"[8] this distinguished hotel succumbed to fire on 4 April 1873, never to be rebuilt.[9]

Most directly associated with Rye Beach's resort hotel history is the name "Farragut House," of which there were two Victorian-era representations. The first, initially known as Philbrick's Hotel, was erected from 1864 to 1865 by hospitality entrepreneur John Colby Philbrick and was intended to compete with Jenness' second Ocean House (see above). After a visit by Admiral David G. Farragut in the mid-sixties, the hotel was subsequently known as Farragut House. Three and one-half stories tall, the initial vernacular version of the hotel

Fig. 6-5. The first Farragut House, Rye Beach, N.H. Photograph, c. 1880. Courtesy Rye Historical Society.

(fig. 6-5) was protected by a truncated, pitched roof with central cupola and was surrounded by a veranda of two stories, its roof supported by thin, rounded posts. Operated under the same management as the adjacent Atlantic House, and supplemented by an annex and small cottages, the first Farragut, expanded in the 1870s, advertised an overnight capacity of 250 to 300 persons. The town's tourism-based economy, therefore, suffered a major blow when fire reduced the hotel to ashes on 18 April 1882, sparing the Atlantic (razed in 1975) for future generations of summer visitors.[10]

Recognizing the continuing business potential of hospitality tourism, the Philbrick family promptly committed to the immediate rebuilding of the hotel on the same site. The second Farragut House opened to an appreciative public for the 1883 summer season. Responsible for the drafting of the plans and supervision of construction was Samuel J. F. Thayer (1842–93), a Boston-based architect of considerable professional standing who was particularly active in the designing of public buildings in various New England cities and academic structures at Dartmouth College. Thayer's front elevation perspective drawing (fig. 6-6) for the new edifice was published in the *American Architect and Building News* in February 1883. Forcefully displaying the qualities of the Queen Anne style, then so popular in American resort-hotel architecture, the new Farragut quickly gained recognition as one of the most current and innovative architectural statements among New England's growing collection of coastal resort hotels. The primary functional and visual features of the asymmetrical, moderate V-plan structure were its front entrance porch with square central block, gazebo, and paired cylindrical towers with conical roofs; pitched-roof gables and shed-roof dormers; lengthy front veranda with narrow, bracketed posts and decorative trusses; recessed porches; varied wooden wall surface treatment; and monumental northeast octagonal corner tower, with complementary embellishment (figs. 6-7 and 6-8).[11]

Advertising itself as the "Gem of the North Shore," the second Farragut possessed many advantageous attributes, as described aggressively in numerous travel guides, such as Frank Rollins' *The Tourists' Guide-Book to the State of New Hampshire* (1902):

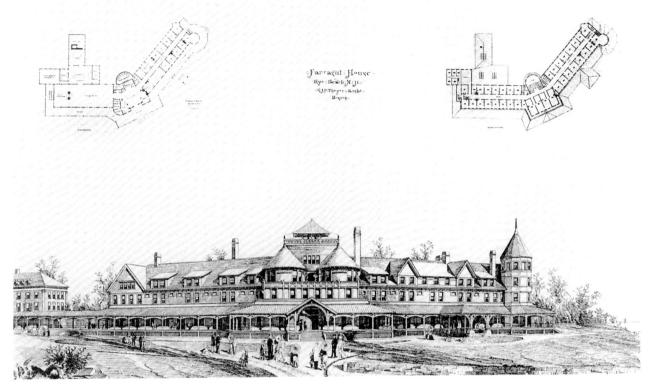

Fig. 6-6. "Farragut House, Rye Beach, N.H." Front elevation perspective drawing by Samuel J. F. Thayer, Architect. From *American Architect and*

Building News 13, no. 374 (24 February 1883). Courtesy of the University of Delaware Library.

Fig. 6-8. The Farragut House, Rye Beach, N.H. Photograph, 1973, by the author.

Fig. 6-7. *(left)* Tower, northeast corner, Farragut House, Rye Beach, N.H. Photograph, n.d. Courtesy Rye Historical Society.

Fig. 6-9. The Sea View Hotel, Rye Beach, N.H. Photograph, c. 1890. Courtesy Rye Historical Society.

Is beautifully situated facing the water, directly on the beach, surrounded by a fine lawn and many beautiful shade trees which affords ample and well protected lawn tennis courts. The house is furnished with all the modern conveniences to be found in first-class hotels, and has long enjoyed an enviable reputation, combining as it does such a variety of attractions in grand ocean views, the ever-tumbling surf, and shores fringed with evergreen; . . . variety of foliage, beautiful shaded walks, and . . . some of the finest views in the whole country. . . . Connected with the house is a fine music hall and casino, billiard and reading-rooms, Western Union telegraph, long distance telephone . . . fine facilities for bathing. The bathing houses are the best and most thoroughly equipped of any on the coast. Hot salt water baths . . . pleasant excursions with our tallyho coach and other turnouts, which are supplied from the stable.[12]

Blessed with these and other positive qualities, the 200-capacity hotel, avoiding the all too common curse of fire, persevered until after World War II, finally closing in 1974 because of the obsolescence of its physical plant and declining patronage. The Farragut was torn down in 1975 and was promptly replaced by another hotel building, which never opened and was demolished in 2003. Today, the site, with its manicured grassy lawn, is vacant.[13]

The last of Rye Beach's large resort hotels deserving mention is the Sea View Hotel (fig. 6-9), constructed from 1868 to 1869 by regional public official and hotel

manager George G. Lougee. Located half a mile inland, with the only sea views from its cupola, this elongated, three-story, rectangular wooden block, blending an assortment of Second Empire and Stick-style elements, was a highly functional, more restrained architectural statement than the second Farragut House. Among its most compelling features were a two-level veranda enveloping the structure, an angled rear ell, an interior dance floor mounted on rubber blocks, and a fourth-story observatory room with central cupola. Accommodating between 175 and 200 patrons after a circa 1870 enlargement, the Sea View remained in business for a relatively long period until it was demolished in 1917, a victim of wear and tear and the dampening effects of World War I on the national economy.[14]

The Wentworth Hotel: Grand Survivor and Replica

Magnificently set on the ledge rock ridge of southern New Castle Island, with panoramic vistas of Little Harbor and the open sea, the Wentworth Hotel (commonly referred as "Wentworth-By-The-Sea" since 1923) has long been recognized for both its history and its architecture as one of America's most significant coastal grand-resort hotels. As a fine specimen of late nineteenth-century Second Empire design, its surviving central section has no equal anywhere along the country's eastern seaboard. The extensive and episodic history of the Wentworth, in certain respects, has been a mirror reflection of evolving American life and social, cultural, economic, and military/diplomatic facets of our national past. Since the early 1980s, the Wentworth and its uncertain future have been a major regional and national news story as the property has changed hands several times, large portions of the pre–World War I complex have fallen to the wrecking ball, and various plans have been put forth for its redevelopment. Finally, in the late 1990s, the unceasing efforts of a coalition of preservationists, community activists, and the nonprofit Friends of the Wentworth group achieved success in saving the hotel for future generations. In 1999, Ocean Properties, Ltd., a Portsmouth-based company, purchased the property for $2.45 million and instituted a massive $20 million restoration, renovation, and expansion project, successfully completed by the end of spring 2003. Reopened

Fig. 6-10. The Wentworth Hotel, New Castle, N.H. Panorama engraving from brochure, c. 1880. New Hampshire Historical Society.

that June, visually recalling the first hotel with nearly 170 guest rooms and suites, it is operating under a franchise contract as the Wentworth By The Sea Marriot Hotel and Spa, its appearance and ambience recalling the early years of its Gilded Age splendor. Fortunately, for those of us interested today, the full saga of the hotel has been comprehensively chronicled, establishing a sound foundation for tracing the eventful development of this important architectural landmark since its origins.[15]

The progressive building history of the Wentworth, named for the local Wentworth family, begins in the early 1870s when Massachusetts investor Daniel Chase, the owner of the ten- to fifteen-acre site, and Charles E. Campbell, the former owner and first proprietor, collaborated on the construction of the initial portion of the complex. Erected from 1873 to 1874 as the new bridge from Rye to the island was being contemplated, this building, ultimately to cost $50,000 including furnishings, was the product of Erastus G. Mansfield of Somerville, Massachusetts, a relative of Chase, who served as both architect and contractor. A modest-sized, symmetrical, three-story, flat-roof, L-shaped wooden structure, this first vernacular incarnation was topped by a rectangular observation cupola and possessed a one-story veranda, typical of the period, on the front (south) and side walls. Experiencing financial success from the outset, the hotel was enlarged from 1875 to 1876 by the addition of an ell on the east side of the rear (north) wall facing the millpond and Portsmouth. In this first-stage form it was

capable of accommodating approximately 170 overnight guests.[16]

In 1879, the Wentworth, after an unstable period marked by ownership changes, was purchased by local brewing, railroad, and hotel magnate Frank Jones along with Frank Hilton under the name of Frank W. Hilton and Company. The leading force and financier in the new venture, Jones immediately set out to convert the Wentworth into one of the major centers of summer hospitality on the East Coast. Under his direction, the complex would undergo four distinct expansion phases, dramatically altering its exterior and interior appearance and, correspondingly, its entire architectural character. Arguably, the most significant makeover in the hotel's long history took place from 1879 to 1880 and entailed a roughly $100,000 expenditure for extensive additions incorporating the original structure and employing large supplies of prefabricated lumber, the individual components used interchangeably. Harvested and systematically labeled in Waterville, Maine, by contractors Foster & Dutton, the new framing members were transported to New Castle by ship. As a result of the transforming renovations (fig. 6-10), the length of the hotel was increased by 100 feet, reaching a total of 160 feet. This created a series of window bays, anchored by a tall, square central tower and framed by identical corner towers, each with unmistakable Second Empire roof caps pierced by dormers and topped by balustrades and fluttering banners. Simultaneously, Jones and his contractors enlarged the 140-foot ell and added a fourth story to the main building, covered by a red-colored hipped-on-mansard roof. A new veranda was fabricated and ran along the main façade and end walls of the complex, exhibiting square posts, triangular brackets, and gingerbread detailing on the eaves. A separate carriage house also rose on the property. On the hotel interior, exhaustively described in an 1880 issue of *Granite Monthly* magazine, the 1874 lobby and entrance were retained; a parlor and ballroom were added to the west, and a dining room and additional office space to the east. Interior spaces, arranged in an L-shaped floor plan (fig. 6-11), were finished either in ash or maple wood, walls and ceilings were frescoed in the Eastlake style, and guest room walls were plastered, with most spaces furnished with black walnut Queen Anne–style furniture. The initial exterior color of the ex-

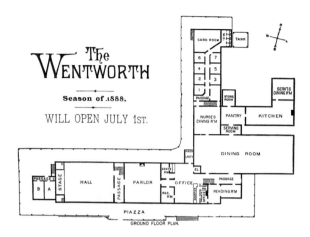

Fig. 6-11. The Wentworth, New Castle, N.H. Ground floor plan incorporating 1879–80 expansion, from brochure, 1888. New Hampshire Historical Society.

Fig. 6-12. *(below)* Hotel Wentworth, New Castle, N.H. Cabinet view, c. 1883, Davis Brothers, Portsmouth, N.H. New Hampshire Historical Society.

the expanded complex is unknown, but in 1883 it was painted Nile dark green (fig. 6-12), appropriately suggesting the color of paper currency! Other guest amenities included steam-driven elevators, telegraph service, a horse stable, a floating dock, bathhouses, bowling alleys, a billiard hall, a dam-contained swimming area, flush toilets, a freshwater reservoir, and, in subsequent years, electrical lighting and telephone communications. The guests, some 300 at full capacity, expected the latest and the best, and they surely were not disappointed.[17]

In all of his many business ventures (see also chapter 8), Jones never failed to think and plan ambitiously, and the Wentworth project was no exception. In 1882, he contracted with architect Fred N. Footman, operating from Boston and nearby Dover, who created a set of plans for a massive expansion of the hotel that were to remain unexecuted. Modified many times, these plans envisioned a front façade of roughly 550 feet; verandas totaling over 1,900 feet; five towers, the central of which was to rise to 190 feet; 450 bedrooms; and spacious public spaces, including a 170-by-50-foot dining room. For many years, Footman's conjectural sketch of the proposed megacomplex hung in the reading room of Portsmouth's Rockingham Hotel, also owned by Jones.[18]

Fig. 6-13. "Hotel Wentworth, New Castle-By-The-Sea, Portsmouth, N.H."
Photoengraving from *DeLuxe Hotels of New England* (1914). Author's
collection.

Soon thereafter, from 1884 to 1885, a second, largely
Queen Anne–style addition (see fig. 6-13) was appended
to the east end of the Wentworth. To date, the identity of
the architect is not known, though an obvious possibility
is Footman, and another architect, Jesse B. Edwards of
Salem, Massachusetts, has been credited with "renovations" to the hotel at this time. Four stories high with a
hipped roof, the rectangular-shaped addition was linked
to the older main hotel block at the ground level and by
a second-floor passageway, the third and fourth floors
to be connected at a later date. The twelve-bay façade
possessed fine alternating and protruding bays, the sixth
and tenth with conical roofs. Traces of the new Colonial
Revival style were evident in the first-story Palladian
windows of each protruding bay. The main dining room
was relocated to the new wing, with sleeping rooms on
the three upper floors. It was then that the entire complex
was painted white, as it is today. A few years later, from
1888 to 1889, a one-story rotunda, with ceilings finished
in the trompe-l'oeil style, was added to the rear of the
main building at the back of the main lobby.[19]

From 1895 to 1896, a third building (fig. 6-13) known
as the Colonial Wing was constructed on a site slightly
set back and to the east of the 1884–85 addition, to which
it was joined by a second-floor enclosed bridge. It was
conceived as an economical, independent, fully functioning hotel facility that could be operated for an extended
season using only a portion of the regular Wentworth
staff. Therefore, in addition to bedrooms, it possessed its
own fourth-floor dining room and small entrance lobby.
In terms of scale, it resembled the 1884–85 structure and
featured some of the same design elements as this and
the 1879–80 main building. Attracting primary notice
was a central bow-shaped tower set just to the west of
the front façade center, with open porches commanding sea views on the upper three floors. Extending the
entire length of the façade was a one-story veranda, with
a porte cochere at the lobby entrance. The detailing was
decidedly neo-Adamesque in appearance.

In 1898, a fourth building (fig. 6-13) was attached to
the east end of the 1895–96 section. Previously employed
as an annex, this hipped-roof, four-story accretion, con-

Fig. 6-14. Wentworth-By-The-Sea, New Castle, N.H. Photograph, 1973, by the author.

Fig. 6-15. "Interior Views." Photographs from booklet, *The Wentworth, New Castle, New Hampshire* (c. 1900). New Hampshire Historical Society.

Fig. 6-16. Wentworth-By-The Sea, New Castle, N.H. Photograph, 2004, by the author.

nected by an enclosed second-floor walkway, was the last significant addition to the full 600-capacity complex, which remained basically unchanged on the exterior until recent years (fig. 6-14). As dictated by changes in taste and maintenance demands, after the turn of the century the interior (fig. 6-15) was continually subjected to alterations, particularly the public spaces, for the most part according to Colonial Revival design precepts. In this configuration, the Smiths and a successor firm operated the hotel from 1946 through 1982, when its prolonged period of closure commenced.[20]

Six years later, in 1988, the Henley Group purchased the Wentworth complex and surrounding lands with ambitious plans to redevelop the site into a high-end residential community, with the hotel reconfigured and reconstructed as a year-round conference center, the focal point of activity. The project moved rapidly forward, and within a year approximately 80 percent of the complex had been demolished, leaving only the original

1873–74 structure as a starting point for the new development. During the economic downturn of the early 1990s, the Henley vision, by necessity, was reduced in scale, and the last remnants of the Victorian-era masterpiece thus became threatened with possible demolition. Enduring subsequent property changes and unsuccessful restoration proposals, the property, aided by the Friends of the Wentworth and other supporters, underwent a highly successful and saving transformation under the leadership of Ocean Properties, Ltd. (see above). Led by TMS Architects of Portsmouth, the vintage 1873–74 Wentworth Hotel, in slightly modified exterior form (fig. 6-16), has been saved, its new east and west wings relating sympathetically to the original Second Empire design, while also conjuring up images of the lost east end additions and other components of the original complex. It is hoped that future generations will continue to enjoy the Wentworth-By-The-Sea, both grand resort survivor and modern replica, as an architectural reflection of the life of summer leisure, social interaction, and recreation in late nineteenth- and twentieth-century America.[21]

The Isles of Shoals

Within easy distance from the Wentworth-By-The-Sea, Portsmouth Harbor, and the adjacent New Hampshire and Maine coasts are the Isles of Shoals, a group of nine small, rocky islands divided between the two states. Resident author Celia Thaxter once described them as "mere heaps of tumbling granite in the wide and lonely sea." Long recognized for their pleasant remoteness, clear air, and temperate, stimulating, and health-enhancing climate, the Isles of Shoals, beginning as early as the 1840s, became a significant summer haven, attracting a broad range of visitors and never succumbing to upper-echelon society like many resort communities along the northern New England shoreline. The islands' history dates back to the early 1600s, when they were first discovered by French and English navigators, and they became a substantial community of traders and fishermen by the middle of the seventeenth century, their population peaking at about six hundred by the Revolutionary War. At the outbreak of this conflict, however, all inhabitants were ordered to leave the islands; only a few returned at the close of the war, and their numbers gradually dimin-

ished into the nineteenth century. Fortuitously, a new form of economic enterprise, hospitality tourism, would soon arise to give the islands new life and direction into the modern era.[22]

It is to Thomas B. Laighton, a former Portsmouth businessman and New Hampshire elected public official, that credit should be given for helping to resurrect the Isles of Shoals, ending their period of near obscurity. In 1834, Laighton purchased the three Maine islands of Malaga, Smuttynose, and Hog (he later changed the name to Appledore). For several years, starting in 1839, Laighton and his family moved back and forth between Appledore, where they periodically resided, and the mainland, finally settling permanently on Appledore in the mid-1840s. Initially, Laighton operated a small inn, the Mid-Ocean House, on Smuttynose but soon shifted his attention to Appledore, where, from 1847 to 1848, he and his financial partner, Levi Thaxter, constructed the first eighty-room portion of what would soon become one of the largest resort hotels of its time on the northern New England seaboard, rivaling the first Ocean House at Hampton Beach, New Hampshire (see above). The official opening occurred on 15 June 1848, and the new venture, serviced by steamboats from the mainland, experienced immediate success.

In its initial form, Appledore House (fig. 6-17) was

Fig. 6-17. Appledore House, Appledore Island, Isles of Shoals, Maine. Engraving from William C. Gage, *"The Switzerland of America"* (1879). Author's collection.

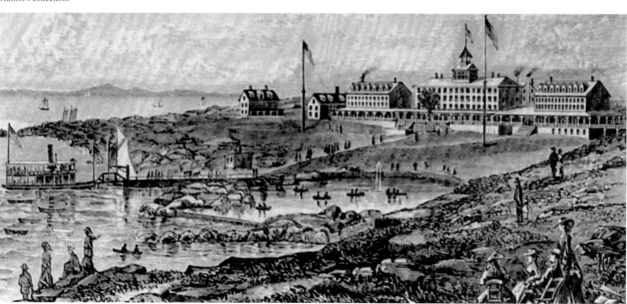

a plain four-story pitched-roof structure of the highly functional hotel variety, consisting of a seventy-foot central pavilion, two small wings, a central roof gazebo, and a wraparound veranda. The two-story wings were subsequently raised to four stories and the full building block covered by a new hipped roof. From 1861 to 1862, the hostelry received a northern addition with pitched roof and dormers, connected to the central portion of the growing complex by an extended veranda and adding forty guest rooms. From 1870 to 1871, a south wing was constructed with the clear intention of balancing the north addition, increasing the total capacity of the hotel to 500, nearly unprecedented for its time.[23] In its impressive completed state, the hotel and its many offerings were thoroughly described in travel guides of the period:

The Appledore House . . . is first-class in every particular, and fitted with modern elements of comfort. Broad piazzas [verandas], providing a covered promenade, surround the house, extending five hundred feet on the front. A fine hall for dancing has been provided, also a theatre, billiard room, bowling-alleys, etc. A regular physician will be in attendance and a band of music has been engaged for the season. The house has a perfect system of drainage, and it is lighted with gas throughout. The distance of the islands from the continent insure, during the hot months, a delightfully cool and even temperature, very grateful to the weary invalid, and to all those seeking the refreshment of the sea. . . . The fishing is the best on the coast, and good boats, with careful skippers are always to be had.[24]

For nearly three decades, the Appledore prospered, aided by adjacent cottage construction encouraged by the Laightons. By the end of the century, faced with industry competition, a consistent decline in patronage, and diminishing financial assets, a corporation formed to raise new funds, and, subsequently, the island was unsuccessfully divided into building lots for development. The unceremonious end came on 4 September 1914, when a disastrous fire destroyed the hotel and seven nearby cottages. Newspaper reports of the day recount the tragic spectacle, viewed from the Wentworth Hotel and other resort locations on the mainland coast.[25]

The Isles of Shoals' other major resort hostelry of the Victorian era was the Oceanic Hotel, two versions of

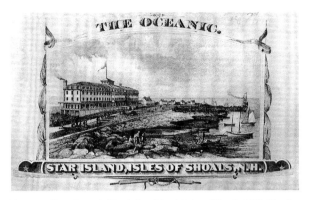

Fig. 6-18. First Oceanic Hotel, Star Island, Isles of Shoals, N.H. Hotel stationery logo, c. 1876, engraved by John R. Lowell. CAPE ANN HISTORICAL ASSOCIATION, Gloucester, Massachusetts.

which were built in the 1870s on nearby Star Island (Gosport) in New Hampshire. The developer of the first Oceanic Hotel (fig. 6-18), erected from 1872 to 1873 to compete with the Appledore, was John R. Poor of Massachusetts, a partner in the well-known spice and mustard firm of Stickney and Poor. The total cost, including a substantial new two-hundred-foot wharf, was more than $65,000, a large sum for the time. Accommodating, with connecting cottages, up to 350 patrons, a smaller number than the Appledore, the Oceanic was widely regarded as more luxurious, promoting its direct boat access, elevator service, superior plumbing, and other modern appointments. Architecturally, the full four-story, Second Empire–style complex was imposing and strikingly handsome, its square central section flanked by identical wings. The entire symmetrical edifice was protected by a hipped-on-mansard roof crowned by a square observation cupola. A veranda reaching one thousand feet encircled the entire building, providing generous space for sitting, viewing, socializing, and promenading. A shore-hotel design gem for its era, the first Oceanic was open for just two summer seasons until it was struck by lightning on 11 November 1875. There being few people available to extinguish the resulting blaze, it was completely burned to the ground in approximately one hour.[26]

Although he had incurred a substantial loss from the fire, Poor, inspired by the success of the first Oceanic, promptly committed to replace it with a less grand hotel, accommodating a similar number of guests. He would complete the entire project before selling out to

Fig. 6-19. "The Oceanic," Star Island, Isles of Shoals, N.H. Lithograph
from *Town and City Atlas of the State of New Hampshire* (1892). Author's
collection.

Fig. 6-20. The second
Oceanic Hotel (Star Island
Conference Center), Star
Island, Isles of Shoals, N.H.
Photograph, 2007, by Carolyn
K. Tolles.

Fig. 6-21. "Piazza of the
Oceanic," second Oceanic
Hotel, Star Island, Isles of
Shoals, N.H. Photograph
from booklet, *Oceanic Hotel,
Star Island, Isles of Shoals*
(1907). New Hampshire Histori-
cal Society.

Laighton Brothers & Company in 1877, which in turn conveyed the property to the Universalist Unitarian Association in the early 1900s. Built from 1875 to 1876, the new complex (fig. 6-19), still extant, is an ingenious combination of older Gosport boardinghouses that were moved from their original sites, joined together, and augmented with a new central unit, some believe using part of the original plans for the first Oceanic. As the complex may be viewed today (fig. 6-20), it possesses a four-story, mansard-roofed central section, flanked by a lower gable-roof wing and by an adjacent, attached L-shaped unit, combining mansard and gable roof forms. A broad veranda (fig. 6-21) connects all sections at the first-floor level. The central unit is believed to incorporate a building frame that had been shipped previously to Star Island before the 1875 fire for use in a new addition to the first Oceanic. Attached to the mansard-roofed section of the hotel at the west end is the former Atlantic House, dating from 1869. The semidetached east end is the onetime Gosport House, originally erected in 1871. Appended to the Gosport House section to the rear is the Caswell House, a boarding facility of an earlier vintage.

The second Oceanic Hotel never equaled the first Oceanic or the Wentworth Hotel in size, coherence, embellishment, or architectural integrity, but it enjoys the distinction of being in the small group of pre–World War II large coastal resort hotels surviving in New England. In modern times, it has taken on new uses as the Star Island Conference Center, its huge mass visible on clear days from locations along the nearby Maine and New Hampshire coastline. In a most fortunate turn of events, as a surviving pair the Wentworth and the second Oceanic continue to make bold, enlightening statements about the past hotel architecture and summer life of seaside New England resort communities.[27]

7

MAINE

From Kittery to Cape Elizabeth

IT IS HIGHLY APPROPRIATE that the state of Maine has often been characterized as a love affair between land and water, for it possesses some of the most beautiful and varied coastal scenery in all of North America. Combining dramatic rocky cliffs, ledges, and promontories with expansive sandy beaches and forested backlands, the highly irregular shoreline, including the offshore islands, extends, astoundingly, for over three thousand miles from Kittery at the mouth of the Piscataqua River to Calais at the head of the Passamaquoddy Bay. Because of its scenic attributes, and the cool climate fostered by Arctic currents off the Gulf of Maine, the Maine coast has been successfully marketed and popularized as "America's summer playground" for the past 150 years and continues to occupy a major place in the tourism economy of the Northeast. As in other coastal regions of New England, the success of the hospitality industry on the Maine seaboard is largely attributable to the access provided by the development of railroad routes beginning in the mid–nineteenth century, followed by modernized highways. Continued transportation improvements, other forms of advancing technology, and sophisticated promotion techniques have perpetuated Maine's success in the twentieth-century American tourist economy.

Lacking the predominantly rocky features, lengthy peninsulas, and islands of the Maine coast northeast of Portland, the coast to the southwest of this major civic and commercial center is generally straight and possesses extensive beach frontage. Easily accessible from major eastern population centers, the southern Maine shoreline became New England's principal seaside vacation center, rivaled primarily by Narragansett Bay and the southern Rhode Island shoreline (see chapter 3). Serving the needs of an eclectic international public was the largest of the region's resort centers, Old Orchard Beach, which rose to prominence soon after the Civil War. Other significant, more upscale communities developed at York, Kennebunkport, Kennebunk Beach, and Biddeford Pool, along with smaller but still notable centers at Kittery, Cape Neddick, Ogunquit, Wells Beach, Scarborough Beach, Prouts Neck, and Cape Elizabeth. These communities and their stylistically varied and expressive forms of resort hotel architecture will be considered beginning at the southwest end of the coastline and proceeding northeast toward Portland and Casco Bay.

Fig. 7-1. The Champernowne Hotel, Kittery Point, Maine. Photograph, c. 1900. Courtesy of the Rice Public Library, Kittery, ME.

Kittery: Gateway to the Maine Coast

When a Victorian-era vacationer traveled to Maine from the south or west, Kittery, including Kittery Point, was the first coastal town to be reached. This geographical advantage, coupled with rugged, diverse scenery, cool air, and the architecture and ambience of a historic New England village, contributed to Kittery's rejuvenation as a summer vacation destination in the 1870s and 1880s. Its earliest hotel of consequence was the Pepperrell House, a plain hipped-roof, wooden building erected by Edward Safford in 1872 for a maximum of 100 guests, and situated near the railroad depot on a rise overlooking the Piscataqua River and downtown Portsmouth. Adjacent to the Pepperrell was the Park Field Hotel, of comparable capacity, erected by Jesse E. Frisbee in 1887 and in business until 1935, when it burned.

Complementing these two hostelries in the same vicinity of Kittery was the larger Champernowne Hotel, the first portion of which was erected by Horace M. Mitchell of Kittery in 1890. After two enlargements in 1897 (fig. 7-1, with two towers) and 1912, it was able to accommodate over 200 boarders, only to be demolished in 1922, just two decades later, by new owner J. M. Howells. A three-story, pitched-roof structure with Queen Anne–style decorative details, the Champernowne was notably distinguished after 1912 by three evenly spaced, square towers with octagonal cupolas and triangular roof caps on the symmetrical front façade. The main building mass was embellished by half-timbering on the gable ends and front façade, and hand-sawn, triangular dormer and veranda column brackets. In contrast to the hotel's quite traditional look, the owners embraced the

Fig. 7-2. "The Pocahontas, Kittery Point, Me." Photoengraving from booklet, *Hotel Pocahontas*, n.d. Maine Historic Preservation Commission.

most advanced technology of the era in electric lighting and bells, plumbing, and sanitation systems, steam heat, hot and cold running water, and elevator service.[1]

Kittery's other large hotel, the Pocahontas (fig. 7-2), was erected on Pocahontas Point, Gerrish Island, at the mouth of the Piscataqua around 1890. Blessed with "rocks on one side and firm sandy beach on the other," this well-recognized resort establishment promoted its "extensive grounds, fishing and boating and bathing for the active, and illimitable ocean air and views for the tranquil." At its peak before demolition by Charles Brooks about 1920, the Pocahontas accommodated 150 people,

supplemented by several nearby cottages that increased the capacity to 250. It was the first Kittery resort hotel to go out of business, attributable primarily to the firing of guns at nearby Fort Foster, disturbing guests, shattering glass, and discouraging patronage. In its prime, however, the hotel was a fine example of gambrel-roof, Shingle-style architecture with T-shaped floor plan and a square, multistage front observation tower. From the veranda on three sides there were views across water of the Isles of Shoals, and the New Castle and Rye shorefront of New Hampshire. Like Kittery's other hotels, the Pocahontas could be reached by steam and electric railroads as well as steamboat in the late nineteenth century.[2]

York: Historic Resort Center

Six miles northeast of Kittery is the maritime community of York, one of the first areas to be settled on the Maine coast. A major shipping center early in its history, the town experienced significant economic decline during the pre–Civil War years, only to be revived, like many other New England seaside communities, by the development of summer tourism during the 1870s and 1880s. While there were earlier and much smaller hotel ventures there, the primary impetus for the development of York, particularly York Harbor, into an important resort center was the building from 1870 to 1871 of the first Marshall House (fig. 7-3), the initial and most prominent local example of a large hotel enterprise. Situated on a

Fig. 7-3. "Marshall House—Edward S. Marshall, Proprietor." Lithograph from [W. W. Clayton], *History of York County* (1880), op. p. 226. Courtesy, The Winterthur Library Printed Book and Periodical Collection.

Fig. 7-4. "The Marshall House," York Harbor, Maine. Lithograph from booklet, *The Marshall House . . .* (n.d.). Maine Historic Preservation Commission.

lofty promontory, Stage Neck, overlooking the mouth of the York River and Short Beach, this grand Second Empire–style, four-story, wooden hostelry was erected under the direction of its initial owner, Nathaniel Grant Marshall, assisted by his sons Edward S. and Samuel B., as the Marshall House Corporation. By 1900, as a result of three additions, the complex, including rental cottages, accommodated up to 400 guests. Possessing two main frontages of 170 feet each, plus wings, the hotel contained spacious parlors, a large dining room, reading rooms, dance and billiard rooms, a telephone and telegraph office, and guest quarters with suites for families. Immensely popular because of its many amenities and unusual setting, the first Marshall House was leveled by a fire of unknown origins on 26 January 1916 when it was closed and shuttered for the off season.[3]

Quickly rebounding from this disaster, the Marshall family determined to rebuild on the same York Harbor site. For their architect, they commissioned John Cal-

vin Stevens (1855–1940) of Portland, widely recognized for his public building and residential designs, and simultaneously committed to a remodeling project for the Samoset Hotel in Rockland, Maine (see chapter 8). Within six months after the fire, a massive L-shaped, blockular, four-story structure (figs. 7-4, 7-5, and 7-6) of "fireproof" red brick construction rose, capable of housing 300 patrons. A stylized pavilion served as a visual ordering point at the center of the flat roof. The firm of McDonald and Johnson acted as general contractors. A surviving front elevation drawing (fig. 7-7) portrays a more elaborate, eclectic Colonial Revival building than the end product (fig. 7-8), suggesting that the Marshalls were influenced by cost considerations or preferred a less refined, functional design. Nonetheless, after its opening in 1917, the new Marshall House quickly assumed prominence as one of the most desirable summer hotels on the New England seacoast. Operated in conjunction with the nearby Emerson House, consisting of several connected

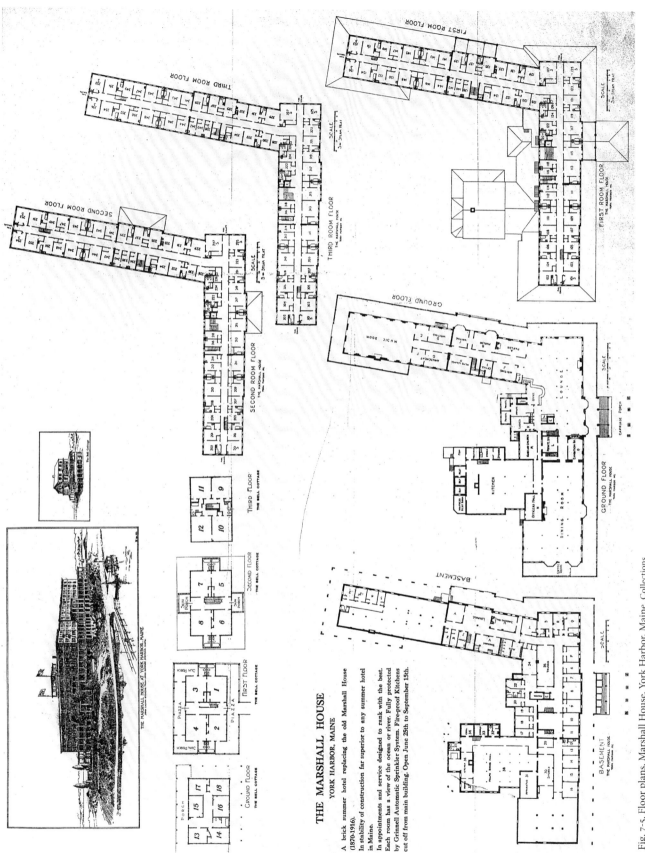

Fig. 7-5. Floor plans, Marshall House, York Harbor, Maine. Collections of Maine Historical Society, Coll. 209, OS 1-D-1.

Fig. 7-6. "The Lounge, Marshall House," York Harbor, Maine. Photograph from booklet, *The Marshall House* (n.d.). Maine Historic Preservation Commission.

cottages opened as a stopgap for the summer of 1916, the Marshall thrived as a center for social, recreational, and cultural activities. After the death of Frank D. Marshall in 1949, Edward D. Marshall managed the business for several years before selling the hotel to Pinehurst, Inc,.

of Pinehurst, North Carolina, owned by the Tufts family, formerly of New England. The second Marshall House was torn down by a new owner, Stage Neck, Inc., in 1972, and was replaced on the same site by another small but first-rank resort hotel, the Stage Neck Inn, and condominiums.[4]

Without question, the most significant architecturally of York's impressive collection of resort hotels was the elegant and alluring Passaconaway Inn (fig. 7-9) at York Cliffs (Cape Neddick). A grand resort hotel by virtually any definition, this imposing Shingle-style edifice was designed and erected (fig. 7-10) in the spring of 1893 by local architect and builder Edward B. Blaisdell for the Vermeule family syndicate of New York, known as the York Cliffs Improvement Company. Resembling a fairy-land castle rising above the sea, the Passaconaway was distinguished by its tall, gambrel-roof gables, two-story verandas, octagonal towers with conical spire roofs, central block with square cupola, and numerous double, truncated-roof dormers piercing the main roof surfaces. From its verandas and balconies there were expansive

Fig. 7-7. "The New Marshall House, York Harbor, Me." Perspective drawing by John Calvin Stevens, Portland. Old York Historical Society Collections, York, Maine.

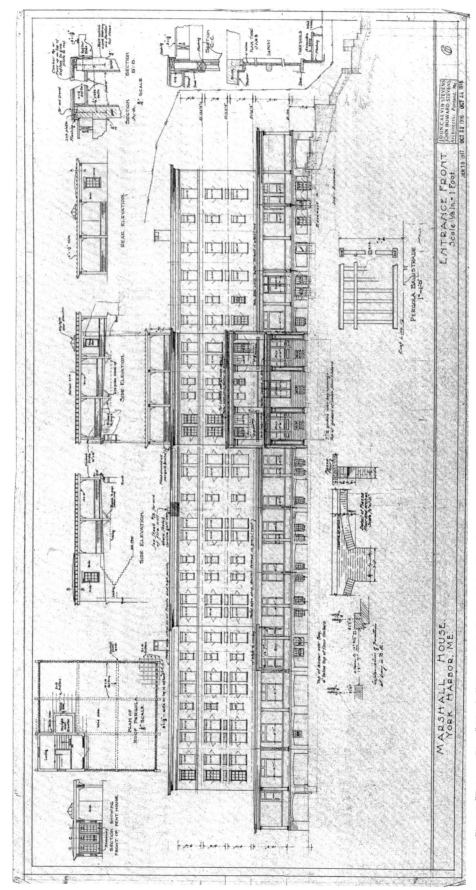

Fig. 7–8. "Entrance Front," Marshall House, York Harbor, Maine. Drawing,
1916. Collections of Maine Historical Society, Coll. 209, OS 1-D-1.

Fig. 7-9. Passaconaway Inn, York, Maine. Photograph, c. 1925. Old York Historical Society Collections, York, Maine.

Fig. 7-11. Hotel Abracca, York, Maine. Postcard, n.d. Maine Historic Preservation Commission.

ocean views extending from Cape Porpoise southward to the Isles of Shoals, which at night featured numerous lighthouse beacons. Known as "The Breakers" late in its history, the 200-capacity hotel fell victim to the Depression and, financially stressed and in disrepair, appears to have been razed in 1935, though some printed sources state 1937. This unfortunate ending represented a great

Fig. 7-10. Passaconaway Inn, York, Maine., with construction workers. Photograph, 1893, by W. N. Gough. Maine Historic Preservation Commission.

loss to New England's rich late Victorian architectural repertoire.[5]

Another superb local example of the Shingle-style vernacular was the Hotel Albracca (fig. 7-11), built and subsequently managed by Elias W. Barker around 1890 from plans also prepared by Edward W. Blaisdell (see above). Situated not far from the Passaconaway Inn at

Fig. 7-12. Ocean House, York Beach, Maine. Photograph, n.d. Old York
Historical Society Collections, York, Maine.

Fig. 7-13. Young's Hotel, York Beach, Maine. Photograph from *DeLuxe
Hotels of New England* (1914). Author's collection.

York Harbor, this smaller hostelry was enlarged in 1892 and ultimately accommodated 150 guests. Like the Passaconaway, the three-and-one-half-story Albracca was sheathed with wooden shingles, possessed a two-story encircling veranda, was protected by a gambrel roof broken by double dormers, and was capped by a central observation cupola on the roof ridge. Rivaling the Passaconaway and the Marshall House for quality of clientele and services provided guests and the York community, the Albracca burned to the ground in 1924 and was not rebuilt.[6]

While the York area boasted numerous other pre–World War II resort hotels, only a few meet the specifications for inclusion in this study, and none possessed the design character of the aforementioned structures. A standout building at York Beach, however, was the Ocean House (fig. 7-12), the earliest portion built during the 1870s as a roller rink. Enlarged circa 1888 and in subsequent stages, it ultimately housed over 250 patrons, including four cottages and annexes. A rambling, rather incoherent wooden complex with square and octagonal towers, the building was visually held together by a long front veranda facing the ocean. After it was destroyed by fire in the summer of 1986, the original Ocean House was replaced by a larger, modern, sixty-six-unit condominium residence with an asymmetrical configuration recalling its historic predecessor.[7]

At the north end of York Beach on Union Bluffs was Young's Hotel (fig. 7-13), originally Thompson House. The largest of the town's earliest hostelries, it offered space for up to 300 boarders in its large, four-story, asymmetrical building mass, with a front veranda, an offset frontal tower, and hipped roof, all common features of shoreline hotels of the period. Smaller local guest establishments such as the Idunda Springs Hotel (1885) and the Fairmount Hotel (c. 1880, etc.) were similarly configured. Erected in at least two phases commencing about 1890, Young's had a long record of service culminating in its demolition in September 1965. Promotional brochures emphasized its commanding site above the sea, its reception room, music hall, and parlor, its recreational opportunities, and its associations with the rich historical lore and venerable architecture of York and other nearby Maine communities.[8]

Ogunquit and Wells Beach

Proceeding farther northeast along the southern Maine shoreline, one next reaches Ogunquit and Wells Beach, coastal communities long committed to summer hospitality tourism, but on a smaller scale than York and the Kennebunks (see below). By far the most pronounced architectural statement of this area's resort hotels was the Island Ledge Hotel (House), the largest of three late Victorian eclectic structures (the others, the Atlantic and Ocean houses) that once stood at Wells Beach. Though it existed for just six years from its opening in 1872 until its elimination by fire in 1878, the Island Ledge (fig. 7-14) became widely known for its services and amenities, as well as its unmistakable Second Empire–style architecture. Capped by a hipped-on-mansard roof with cupola, the three-story block was enveloped by a two-story veranda and adorned with corner quoins and eaves brackets. With a one-hundred-foot long front façade, the hotel possessed two ells of the same length, with a detached kitchen, livery stable, billiard hall, bowling saloon, and boating facilities. The Island Ledge was developed and managed by Harrison Davis (Somersworth, N.H.), William A. Worster (Berwick, Maine), and Alfred Davis (Worcester, Mass.).[9]

Just to the southeast at Ogunquit, the 1889 construc-

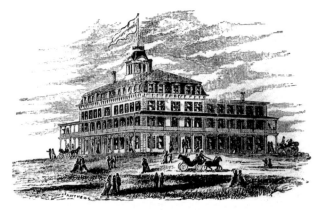

ISLAND LEDGE HOTEL.
DAVIS, WORSTER, & DAVIS, Proprietors.

Fig. 7-14. "Island Ledge Hotel," Wells Beach, Maine. Engraving from John B. Bachelder, *Popular Resorts, Routes to Reach Them* (1873 ed.), p. 47. Author's collection.

Fig. 7-15. Sparhawk Hall, Ogunquit, Maine. Photograph, n.d. The Brick Store Museum, Kennebunk, ME.

tion of the bridge leading to the beach resulted in the construction during the 1890s of numerous hotels, boardinghouses, and cottages. The two most spacious hostelries there command our attention. Displaying the most superior design integrity was Sparhawk Hall (fig. 7-15), initially built in 1897, burned on 2 October 1899, rebuilt in 1903, later expanded, and, after a long period of use, demolished in the 1960s. Distinguished by its gambrel roof and gables, and substantial square central tower, this sprawling, multiunit complex merits recognition for its emphatic Colonial Revival form and modest embellishment. Like most examples of its building type, Sparhawk Hall contained upper floors with double-loaded corridors, allowing each guest chamber natural light and outside window views. Adjacent to the 250-capacity hotel were several rental cottages, initially conceived by the first owner and proprietor, Nehemiah P. M. Jacobs.[10]

Of comparable size but of inferior aesthetic quality was the Lookout Hotel, on a rise slightly southeast of

Fig. 7-16. Lookout Hotel (Condominiums), Ogunquit, Maine. Photograph, 2006, by the author.

Sparhawk Hall. Originating as a small Second Empire building of residential size and detail (c. 1880), the Lookout received successive additions over many years until it reached its maximum size by World War II. With its linked, austere, rectangular components extended parallel to the shoreline, the hotel provided its occupants with maximum exposure to the pleasant sights, smells, and noises of the ocean surf. Long owned and operated

Fig. 7-17. Atlantis Hotel, Kennebunk Beach, Maine. Photograph, n.d. Maine Historic Preservation Commission.

by the Merrill family, the Lookout survives today largely intact, but modified as a condominium complex (fig. 7-16).[11]

Kennebunk Beach and Kennebunkport

Roughly twenty miles northeast of York are Kennebunk Beach and Kennebunkport (Cape Arundel), forming a resort community, like York, that has long been associated with exclusivity and a strong sense of the historical past. Resort development commenced there in the early 1870s with the arrival of the railroad, diversifying a local economy traditionally predicated on shipping, shipbuilding, farming, and some small manufacturing. The driving force behind this transformation was the formation in 1872 of the Boston and Kennebunkport Seashore Company, which acquired over five miles of shorefront from the fishing village of Cape Porpoise to the southwestern end of Kennebunk Beach, and subdivided the land for cottage and hotel lots.[12]

Separated from Kennebunkport to the southwest by the Kennebunk River, Kennebunk Beach, the less "social" of the two areas, has played a significant role in Maine's seacoast hospitality industry. Owen Wentworth's Granite State House, built in 1879, was the first of twelve new hotels constructed there before 1920. Originating in the 1860s as Wentworth's farmhouse, the typically vernacular Wentworth Hotel was expanded four times before 1900 to meet the growing tourism demand, and lasted until it was razed in 1982. Other hostelries of similar size (100 capacity) or smaller followed, and included the Seaside House (1884), the Sea View House (1885), the

Eagle Rock House (1886), the Grove Hill House (1887), the Ridgewood (1892), and the Sagamore Hotel (1896). The two largest hotels (at least 200 capacity) were the last to be erected at the beach.[13]

The first of these, the Atlantis (1903) (fig. 7-17), occupied a leading position among Maine's oceanside hotels until it was torn down in 1967. The last hotel to be built on Seashore Company land, it was designed and built by Lewis Killam. Conceived in the Spanish Mission Colonial Revival style, this intriguing structure, with its sandblasted walls, arched veranda support level, and other details, was quite unconventional for the region where the Shingle, Colonial Revival, and other contemporary styles were most prevalent. The rectangular block form, hipped roof with dormers, encircling veranda, and square central tower, however, repeated features present in other hotels of the time. In many respects the Atlantis closely resembled the former Rock End Hotel (see chapter 8) at Northeast Harbor, Maine, after its transformation in 1894 from a clapboarded Victorian eclectic to a Spanish Colonial Revival–style edifice.[14]

Situated at Oake's Neck, a rock promontory on the beach, the Narragansett Hotel (the Narragansett-By-The-Sea) (fig. 7-18) is the only large resort hotel there predating 1940 to have survived fire or demolition. Its advantageous location allowed guests on both the rear and front sides to enjoy views of the sea. Built by John Curtis in 1905, the first portion of the hotel displayed Colonial Revival massing and decorative details, including a cross-gable roof, closed end and side gables, corner

Fig. 7-18. Narragansett Hotel (Condominiums), Kennebunk Beach, Maine. Photograph, 2006, by the author.

Fig. 7-19. Ocean Bluff Hotel, Kennebunkport, Maine. Photograph, n.d., by J. S. Mitchell. Maine Historic Preservation Commission.

pilasters, clapboarded siding, and components of the first-story veranda. From 1928 to 1929 an addition of nearly identical size and embellishment was attached to the northwest end at a slight angle, doubling the guest capacity to approximately 200. The Narragansett was closed in 1979, sold by the Wentworth family, and converted to condominium units from 1982 to 1983 by new owner John J. Hoffman of Boston.[15]

Northeast of the Kennebunk River, not far from its mouth, is Kennebunkport, known for its old residential buildings but also its rich heritage of hotel architecture. The earliest of the large resort hotels in this community, at the high land of Cape Arundel overlooking the river mouth, was the Ocean Bluff Hotel (fig. 7-19), erected by the Seashore Company in 1873 and doubled in size in the early 1880s to house over 300 patrons. The design of this imposing, late Victorian eclectic structure has been attributed to Kennebunk native Joseph Mendum Littlefield. Consisting of linked rectangular blocks, typical of hotel architecture of the period, the Ocean Bluff was distinguished by its hipped-on-mansard, patterned roof, square cupolas with roof support brackets and finials, and multistory end bay with steep-pitched py-

ramidal roof cap. It was operated by Job Jenness & Son and the partnership of Edward C. Simpson and George A. Devnell until 30 June 1898, when it burned while a second addition was under construction. The Seashore Company decided not to rebuild.[16]

Two other major Kennebunkport hotels of the same era closely resembled the Ocean Bluff Hotel, primarily in their rectangular massing if not specific design features. Located near the Ocean Bluff, the Cliff House (fig.

Fig. 7-20. Cliff House, Kennebunkport, Maine. Photograph, n.d. Courtesy of The Kennebunkport Historical Society.

7-20) was erected in 1881 by contractor E. N. Larrabee for B. F. Eldridge, and initially was two stories covered by a mansard roof. During the eighties it was enlarged to four stories, with dimensions of one hundred by forty-five feet, about half the size of the full-blown Ocean Bluff. The hotel reached a maximum 200 capacity as a consequence of additions in 1902 and 1906. The latter building project was implemented from plans drafted by architect William E. Barry (1846–1902) of Kennebunk, who, after extensive experience working with Boston architectural firms, based his practice in his hometown designing summer cottages and other buildings. In its final form, the Cliff House exhibited elements of the Queen Anne and Colonial Revival styles, consistent with other examples of Barry's building repertoire. The hotel was leveled by fire on 23 September 1923 and was never reconstructed.[17]

Also situated at Cape Arundel and of comparable scale was the Oceanic Hotel (figs. 7-21 and 7-22), a mas-sive, wood-frame Colonial Revival structure built as the Glen House circa 1880 and enlarged in 1902. Likely architect designed, the pitched-roof Oceanic displayed a cohesive, symmetrical oceanfront façade, with a central tower and window bays in gabled pavilions and at the end corners. This establishment was later in business as the Glen Haven Hotel, became an annex of the Colony Hotel (see below), and in 1965 had its "attic" and upper two stories removed for conversion to a two-story motor inn. Unrecognizable today as a portion of the original Oceanic, it survives as the East House of the Colony Hotel.[18]

Until the construction of the Breakwater Court (see below) in 1914, the Old Fort Inn reigned supreme as the dominant summer resort hotel at Cape Arundel. Erected by contractors Allen and Tibbetts of nearby Biddeford for the Boston and Kennebunk Seashore Company and Ruel T. Norton, this striking 250-guest, Shingle-style edifice rose in two major stages from 1901 to 1902 (fig.

Fig. 7-21. Oceanic Hotel, Kennebunkport, Maine. Photograph, n.d. Maine Historic Preservation Commission.

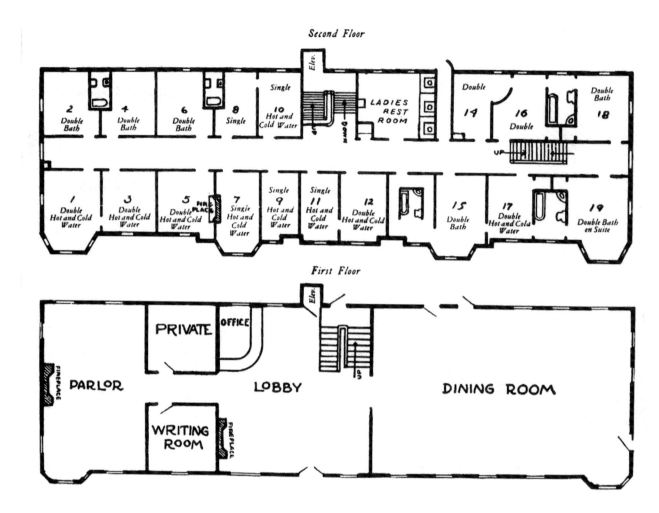

Fig. 7-22. First and second floor plans, Oceanic Hotel, Kennebunkport, Maine. From broadside, "The Oceanic and Cottages" (n.d.). Maine Historic Preservation Commission.

7-23) and 1902 to 1903 from plans provided by the architectural firm of Clark and Russell of Boston (see below). An L-shaped complex with gambrel main roof and intersecting gables, the original section and the ell were joined by a square, crenellated tower, supposedly inspired by an early nineteenth-century fort that stood nearby. A circa 1922 advertisement for the hotel emphasized modernity, service, and pleasant atmosphere:

The Inn is modern in all respects. Every room is furnished with a long-distance and local telephone which is connected with the office. There is a private bath with every suite—with almost every room. An elevator, electric light service and barber shop are among the other conveniences. The spacious lobby, music and billiard rooms are much admired, while an excellent orchestra furnishes music for daily concerts and enjoyable dances. The broad covered verandas command a fine view of both forest and sea, while the very natural curves of the roadways around the Old Fort lend a charm to the landscape suggestive of a private estate. The cuisine . . . receives the most careful attention and is maintained at the highest standards.[19]

An entrepreneurial success for most of its history, the Old Fort Inn closed after the death of its last owner, Maurice Sherman, in 1962, and was later demolished in 1967, depriving Maine of one of its most outstanding large-scale Shingle-style structures.[20]

The raised seaside site formerly occupied by the Ocean Bluff Hotel (see above) was sold in 1908 to Ruel W. Norton, who proceeded to erect Breakwater Court (figs. 7-24 and 7-25) in 1914 and manage its operations for many years afterward. Contracted as architect was the firm of Henry Paston Clark (1853–1927) and John Russell (1851–1926) of Boston, the previous designers of the nearby Old Fort Inn (see above). With family roots in Kennebunkport, Clark secured many commissions there, including cottages, public buildings, and hotels, beginning in 1878 with the Second Empire Parker House in the village. The largest project ever undertaken by Clark and Russell, this magnificent, formal, Neoclassical complex, enlarged in 1917, accommodated a maximum of 250 guests and was supplemented by cottages, an auto garage, kitchen and laundry buildings, a casino, and housing for staff members. As accurately pointed out by architectural historian Kim Lovejoy, the hotel, in all its Colonial Revival–style splendor, was likely modeled after American college and university architecture of the late 1800s. As she observes in Kevin Murphy's edited work *Colonial Revival Maine* (2004), "the dominant central projecting portico, the building's conception as a solid rectangular block of three or more stories, and its low-pitched roof and dormers are characteristic features of large forms" assumed by academic structures. Other common components are the front façade central portico, the central cupola on the roof ridge above, and the flat wall pilasters. Fortuitously, Breakwater Court, renamed the "Colony Hotel" in 1948, has survived, largely intact, to this day, and is still meeting its original purposes. Well proportioned with nicely blended and articulated details, the building ranks with the Wentworth in New Hampshire (see chapter 6) as one of New England's most outstanding functioning grand resort hotels.[21]

Biddeford Pool

The summer resort community of Biddeford Pool is situated on a peninsula fifteen miles down the Maine coast from the Kennebunks and three miles from the mouth of the Saco River within the city limits of Biddeford. Present here, and from which its name was derived, is a pool basin almost entirely encircled by land, just to the west of a lofty headland where the summer residences and hotels were first positioned. The oldest large hostelry there was the second Highland House (fig. 7-26),

Fig. 7-23. Old Fort Inn (first stage), Kennebunkport, Maine. Photograph, c. 1902. The Brick Store Museum, Kennebunk, ME.

Fig. 7-24. The Colony Hotel (Breakwater Court), south façade, Kennebunkport, Maine. Photograph, 2006, by the author.

Fig. 7-25. The Colony Hotel (Breakwater Court), north entrance façade, Kennebunkport, Maine. Photograph, 2006, by the author.

Fig. 7-26. "Highland House, . . . Biddeford Pool, Me." Engraving from J. S. Locke, *Shores of Saco Bay* (1880), op. p. 50. New Hampshire Historical Society.

Fig. 7-27. Ocean View Hotel, Biddeford Pool, Maine. Photograph, n.d. Courtesy of the McArthur Public Library, Biddeford, Maine.

Fig. 7-28. Ocean View Hotel (Marie Joseph Spiritual Center), Biddeford Pool, Maine. Photograph, 2006, by the author.

designed by architect A. E. Upham of Melrose, Massachusetts, and built for the first owner and proprietor, W. S. Starkweather, from 1879 to 1880. While of fairly conventional Second Empire/Queen Anne styling for its time, it attracted notice for its massive size, advertising 300 bed spaces in addition to spacious public rooms.[22]

Subsequently, a second large resort hotel was constructed at the Pool, which, like the Colony and Narragansett hotels (see above), is on the list of rare survivors on the New England coast. Situated on Evans Road facing the beach is the former Ocean View Hotel, raised circa 1885 for Thomas Evans and purchased in 1948 by the Presentation of Mary Congregation of Hudson, New Hampshire, to house Marie Joseph Academy, later Marie Joseph Spiritual Center. In its original four-story form (fig. 7-27), this rectangular-block wooden structure, otherwise of plain vernacular appearance, possessed a substantial two-story Stick-style veranda on all four outer walls. Sometime in the early twentieth century, the building (fig. 7-28) underwent reconstruction, as evidenced on the exterior by new shingle siding, the added multistory window bays, and a new northwest wing with corner towers capped by pyramidal roofs. It continues to serve the Catholic Church today, not dramatically altered from its many years as a center of summer hospitality.[23]

Old Orchard Beach: A Resort for All

For nearly a century and a half, Old Orchard Beach, located northeast of Biddeford about twelve miles below Portland, has enjoyed a reputation as one of the most famous and frequently visited summer watering places in the Northeast. Favoring its development as a resort center is the presence of a nine-mile sandy beach, the longest and arguably the finest on the New England coast, coupled with extensive back woodlands, ultimately containing parks and groves, cool retreats, and walking paths. As a result of its many natural attributes, along with a highly favorable location, Old Orchard became Maine's first significant summer resort, attracting excursionists as early as the late 1830s. Among the initial vacation visitors were Canadians from Montreal and other regions of Quebec for whom Old Orchard was the most direct

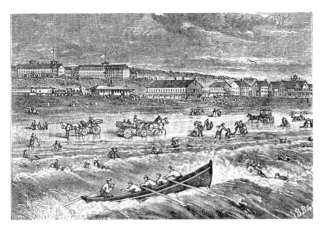

Fig. 7-29. Old Orchard Beach, Maine. Panorama from *Guide to the Sea-Shore, Mountains and Lakes* (1877), n.p. Author's collection.

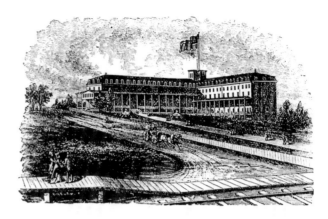

Fig. 7-30. "Ocean House, Old Orchard Beach, Me." Engraving from J. S. Locke, *Shores of Saco Bay* (1880), op. p. 36. New Hampshire Historical Society.

and convenient Atlantic coast destination. During these early years, several enterprising businesspeople, led by Ebenezer C. Staples, began accommodating guests and providing desired amenities in modest facilities. By the early 1840s, the Portsmouth, Saco and Portland Railway offered railroad transportation access to a depot just four miles away, followed in 1852 by the opening of direct rail service between Montreal and Portland, with road and water connections to Old Orchard. After the Civil War, the Boston and Maine Railroad extended its northeast coastal route to Portland, formally commencing service in early 1873. Immediately, demands for overnight accommodations increased, the local hospitality industry was launched, and hotel construction exploded, with thirty hotels in existence by the mid-1880s.[24]

As a result, Old Orchard Beach (fig. 7-29) underwent a post–Civil War transformation of dramatic proportions, becoming Maine's version of Coney Island. Ebenezer Staples' early hotel facility, erected next to his farmhouse in 1860 under the name "Old Orchard House," was able to take at least 300 boarders by 1875, the year that it was destroyed by fire. This plain, vernacular structure comprised an elongated, pitched-roof, four-story central block with ell and two cupolas set on the roof ridge. Providing business competition on an adjacent site was the first Ocean House (fig. 7-30), an immense L-shaped, wooden, Second Empire–style complex said to have accommodated between 400 and 500 guests. Believed to have possessed the largest ballroom of any New England resort hotel, the Ocean House, renamed the Imperial,

was obliterated by a huge fire on 12 September 1896 and was replaced by a much smaller building operating under the same name.[25]

Erected in 1876, also under Ebenezer Staples' direction, the second Old Orchard House was, for its time, one of the gems of New England resort hotel architecture (fig. 7-31). With bedroom space for 500 persons, it was the largest resort hotel of its era in the entire region. This landmark hostelry remained under the ownership of the Staples family until 1922, passed to new owners, and finally was razed in 1943. With a pitched-roof central pavilion, flanking wings, and hipped-roof end pavilions on its symmetrical front façade, the Old Orchard House boasted a commanding view from its piazza across open lawn to the beach and ocean. On its ground floor (fig. 7-32), the hotel contained generous public spaces in its office, music room, drawing room, and dining room (fig. 7-33). It was in all likelihood designed by a professional architect, but to date the name of this individual has escaped researchers.[26]

Presenting a distinct architectural contrast to the second Old Orchard House was the 300-capacity Seashore House (Sea-Shore Hotel) (fig. 7-34), formerly located on the beach near the railroad depot and the Old Orchard. Not surprisingly, a promotional booklet (c. 1896) described the Seashore as "one of the most perfect hostelries on the Maine coast." In many respects, this bold assertion was not inaccurate, for this early hostelry, built from 1872 to 1873 and expanded circa 1882, combined appealing late Victorian eclectic styling and modest scale

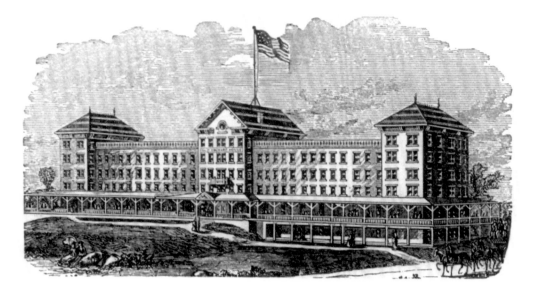

Fig. 7-31. "Old Orchard House, Old Orchard Beach, Me." Advertisement from *Saratoga Illustrated: The Visitor's Guide to Saratoga Springs* (New York: Taintor Bros., Merrill & Co., Publishers, 1880). Author's collection.

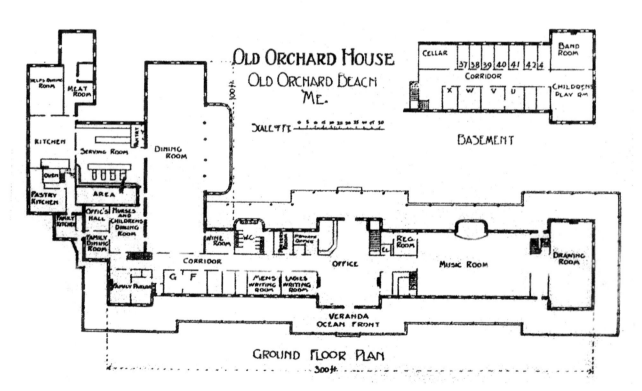

Fig. 7-32. "Ground Floor Plan," Old Orchard Beach House. From booklet, *Old Orchard Beach House, Old Orchard Beach, Maine* (1910). Maine Historic Preservation Commission.

Fig. 7-33. "Section of Main Dining Room," Old Orchard Beach House. From booklet, *Old Orchard Beach House, Old Orchard Beach, Me.* (c.1900). Maine Historic Preservation Commission.

Fig. 7-34. "Seashore House, Old Orchard Beach." Photograph from booklet, *Old Orchard Beach, Maine* (1900), p. 26. Maine Historic Preservation Commission.

with ample interior spaces and the customary veranda facing the Atlantic. The Seashore gained particular renown for its large, single-story, seventy-by-forty-foot music hall set off from but connected to the main building. Initially owned and managed by Frederick G. Staples, the hotel remained in business until its destruction, along with scores of other local hotels, in the great fire of 15 August 1907.[27]

Three other large local hotels of this period (c. 1875), each displaying Second Empire–style detailing, were the Blanchard House (fig. 7-35), Wesley G. Smith's Central House (fig. 7-36), and the Bay View Hotel (later Ocean Crest Manor), located at nearby Ferry Beach. While the Central and the Bay View were quite common expressions of their style, the L-shaped Blanchard was surmounted by a striking pitched-on-concave-mansard roof with dormers and truncated gables. Smaller Old Orchard Beach hotels of the seventies and eighties possessed many of the same basic Second Empire elements.[28]

For many, Old Orchard's standout summer hostelry was the Hotel Fiske, which occupied a prominent seaside position (fig. 7-37) at the center of the community from its opening in 1882 to its destruction in the 1907 fire. It stood on the site of the Fiske and St. Cloud houses, both lost to fire in 1881. Configured much like the second Old Orchard House, the Fiske (fig. 7-38) had the presence of a formidable ecclesiastical structure, its central tower and end pavilions topped by tall, steep-pitched roofs. Operated for its entire history by its builders, C. H. and A. H. Fiske, the hotel had sleeping space for 300 persons

Fig. 7-35. "Blanchard House, Old Orchard Beach, Me." Engraving from J. S. Locke, *Shores of Saco Bay* (1880), op. p. 9. New Hampshire Historical Society.

Fig. 7-36. Central House, Old Orchard Beach, Maine. Photograph, n.d., by J. H. DuPee. Maine Historic Preservation Commission.

Fig. 7-37. Hotel Fiske, Old Orchard Beach, Maine. Photograph, n.d., by
J. S. Towle, Lowell, Mass. Collections of Maine Historical Society, MMN 12151,
Coll. 423.

Fig. 7-38. "Hotel
Fiske, Old Orchard
Beach, Me." Broad-
side, n.d. Maine
Historic Preservation
Commission.

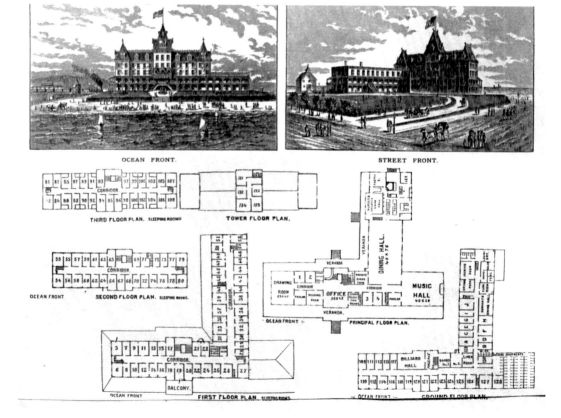

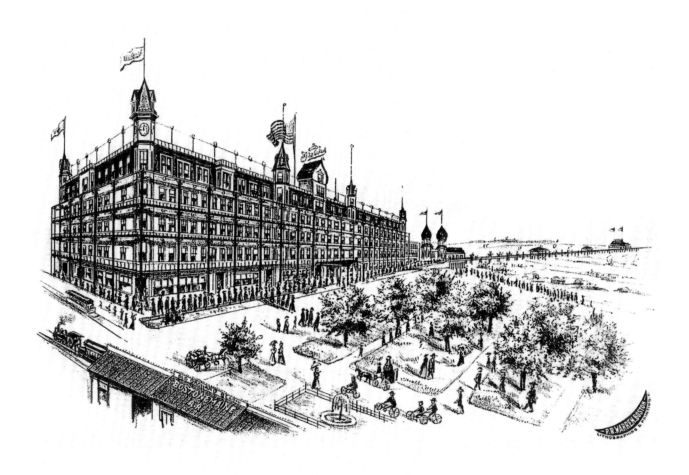

Fig. 7-39. Hotel Velvet, Old Orchard Beach, Maine. Lithograph by P. R. Warren, Boston, from booklet, *Hotel Velvet, Old Orchard Beach, Maine* (c. 1900). Maine Historic Preservation Commission.

and catered primarily to the affluent. Contemporary printed sources highlighted the hotel's spacious verandas, presenting a gala appearance with their cheerful promenaders "clad in the brightest garb of summer." Its broad central front steps led directly to the beach and its many activities, a connection enhanced at high tide when waves would break dramatically within a few feet of the front façade.[29]

Two substantial turn-of-the-century hotels, the Velvet (last known as the "Emerson") and the Alberta, also occupied prime waterfront land until they were leveled by the 1907 fire. The majestic, five-story Hotel Velvet (fig. 7-39), a superb example of "gingerbread" architecture, was erected from 1898 to 1899 by Herbert L. Hildreth, the creator of Velvet molasses candy, and greatly enlarged in

1900. This eye-catching, five-story edifice overlooked the town square and faced directly on the new steel pier for which Hildreth had supplied the land and financing in 1897. An expansion of the relocated Cleaves Hotel and the Sears Bath Houses, the Velvet was notable for its tall central and corner towers with their steep-pitched roof caps, multilevel verandas, and flat roof containing an unusual fenced, 250-foot-long promenade. The Velvet ownership claimed the latest in technology and conveniences—the first elevator at Old Orchard, the first lobby circular staircase, its own electric power plant, and ironically, as events would prove, the latest fire alarm system and fire escape access on each story level. Sleeping floor plans (fig. 7-40) were not an asset, however, possessing multiple as opposed to double-loaded corridors, limit-

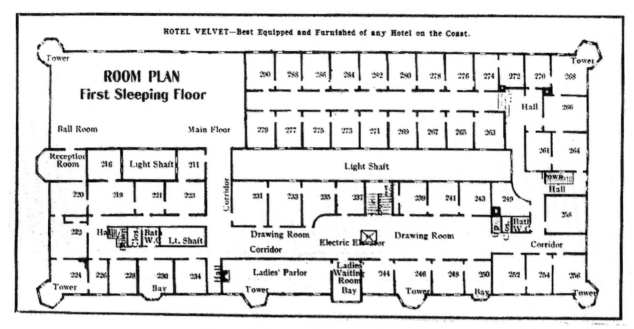

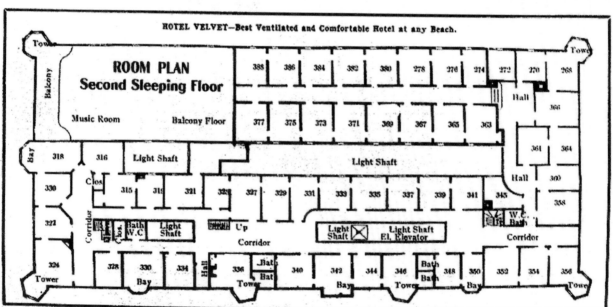

Fig. 7-40. Room plans, first and second sleeping floors, Hotel Velvet, Old Orchard Beach, Maine. From brochure, *Hotel Velvet . . .* (1902). Maine Historic Preservation Commission.

Fig. 7-41. Hotel Alberta (*left*) and Hotel Velvet (*right*), Old Orchard Beach, Maine. Photograph, 1903. Collections of Maine Historical Society, MMN 12154, Coll. 423.

ing the number of rooms with exterior window views and exposure to fresh air. A staid interpretation of the Colonial Revival, Selden W. Holt's Hotel Alberta (fig. 7-41), raised next to the Velvet site in 1898, could house 200 patrons (less than half the capacity of the Velvet) but was somewhat overwhelmed by its huge, freely embellished neighbor.[30]

Like the Sea-Shore, Fiske, Velvet, and Alberta, the Hotel Everett (fig. 7-42) was also located near Old Orchard Street, paralleling the shoreline. Built in 1884 for Mrs. Marie F. Libby, this 200-guest establishment had the longest life span of any of the large pre-1900 local hotels, surviving until 17 October 1976, when it burned. Using the time-honored name of Old Orchard House after 1946, the H-shaped Everett was marked by its Stick-style veranda and dominant roof dormers, each topped by a pronounced finial. With the passage of the Everett and the loss of other, smaller hotels during the 1970s

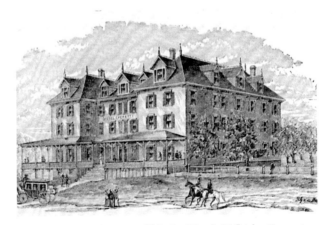

Fig. 7-42. "The Hotel Everett, Old Orchard Beach, Me." Advertisement from booklet, *The Vacation Route* (1891). Author's collection.

Fig. 7-43. The Jocelyn House, Prouts Neck, Scarborough, Maine.
Photograph, n.d. Courtesy Scarborough Historical Society.

and since, Old Orchard Beach has been deprived of the major physical evidence of its remarkable hotel heritage. The stately hotels of the past have been replaced by more modest overnight facilities, restaurants, and an amusement park, but for many Old Orchard Beach is still the locus of summer vacation life.[31]

Scarborough Beach, Prouts Neck, and Cape Elizabeth

Half a dozen miles above Old Orchard Beach, west of Cape Elizabeth, is the town of Scarborough, with two recognizable historic resort centers at Scarborough Beach and Prouts Neck. Two miles in length, the beach, known for its unobstructed ocean views and many water diversions, was home to two medium-size hotels—the Kirkwood Inn (1870s; demolished, 1920s) and the Atlantic House (c. 1850; 1855; demolished, 1987). The Atlantic, the most interesting architecturally, originated as a large, three-story, pitched-roof farmhouse, which was augmented by two mansard-roof wings in 1877 and the

1890s. The Atlantic received special recognition for its architecture and tourism role when it was listed on the National Register of Historic Places in 1979.[32]

One mile to the south of the beach, projecting into the sea, is Prouts Neck (originally Black Point), a rocky peninsula most often associated with the summer residency there of the renowned artist Winslow Homer. With a panoramic vista of Old Orchard Beach, Prouts Neck was a modest center for single-season hotel entrepreneurship. Of the two large, 200-capacity hotels once present there, the Jocelyn House (fig. 7-43) possesses the most compelling history, undergoing a sweeping physical transformation around 1898 under the direction of Portland architect John Calvin Stevens, the designer of the second Marshall House at York (see above) and a remodeling of the Samoset Hotel at Rockland (see chapter 8), both in Maine. Built in 1890 on a raised bluff for Mr. and Mrs. Frank B. Libby, the Jocelyn, in its initial, quite common form, was a four-story elongated rectangular block capped by a hipped-on-mansard roof with dormers. The

Stevens alterations enhanced the building's imposing presence, giving it a Queen Anne–style look with the addition of a front, pitched-roof wing, turrets, towers, porches, dormers, and fragile-appearing balustrades, decorated with carved support brackets. On 27 July 1909, six weeks into the tourist season, the Jocelyn fell victim to a dramatic fire, and was not replaced. Today, the site is a parking lot servicing a bathing beach.[33]

Once situated on Checkley's Point at the entrance to the Scarborough River, the Checkley House (fig. 7-44) underwent a dramatic architectural metamorphosis similar to that of the Jocelyn House. Motivated by the arrival of Boston and Maine Railroad service to Scarborough, developer Ira C. Foss opened a small mansard-roof boardinghouse, resembling the first stage of the Jocelyn, in 1873. Over many years, until his death in 1919, Foss capitalized on the financial success of the operation, making several additions and improvements to the hostelry. The original structure received an additional

story and was extended in length on both ends, the most spectacular in the Colonial Revival vein in 1895 at the tip of the rocky peninsula. John Calvin Stevens has been credited with the design of this major growth phase. Most striking visually was the two-level veranda, the lower stage with its succession of large, semicircular apertures. Of the interior ground-floor public spaces, the dining room received the most notice for its windows opening on the sea, each framing a different pictorial view. Of highest priority was the latest in technology, which by 1904 included electric lights and bells, and fire hoses on each floor. The Checkley thrived until World War II, when five years of forced coastal evacuation and blackouts badly curtailed business. In a state of disrepair, it was torn down in 1944, leaving the Black Point Inn (originally "Southgate House"), constructed in 1878 and since expanded, as a much smaller (125 capacity) but last hotel reminder of Scarborough's Victorian-era hospitality tourism legacy.[34]

Fig. 7-44. "The Checkley House from the Ocean Side," Prouts Neck, Scarborough, Maine. Photograph from booklet, *The Checkley* (n.d.). Courtesy Scarborough Historical Society.

Fig. 7-45. Cape Cottage, Cape Elizabeth, Maine. Photograph, n.d. Collections of Maine Historical Society, MMN 17391, Photographs – Cape Elizabeth.

With its near proximity to Portland, Cape Elizabeth became a popular leisure destination for residents of the city as well as visitors from other regions of Maine and the Northeast. While the town is primarily a suburb of Portland today, and was never a major resort center, it has been home to several modest resort hotels during its history, starting as early as the mid–nineteenth century. Its prime attractions were its diverse scenery, including bold, rocky shore cliffs and cool ocean breezes. Closest to the city (actually in South Portland) was the second Cliff Cottage (Cliff House), a plain but representative example of Stick-style architecture that was raised circa 1864, closed in 1910, and burned in 1914. At the south end of the cape, the farthest distance from Portland, was the Ocean House, an uninspiring three-section expression of domestic-appearing design, first opened in 1849, later expanded to accommodate 100 patrons, and entirely burned in 1892.

Just south of the Cliff Cottage, three miles from Portland, was the third Cape Cottage (fig. 7-45), built from 1850 to 1851 for Portland owner John Neal and replacing two prior hotels on the same site that had been lost to fire. Its picturesque setting was perhaps its primary attraction, as noted by William Willis in his 1859 *Guide Book for Portland and Vicinity:*

In front, outposts of the grassy knolls and hollows which surround the house, is an array of ragged cliffs and sunken ledges, about which breakers are forever toiling; and beyond is the ocean, stretching without a break to the horizon. On the left is the main entrance to Portland harbor, and every vessel of magnitude which enters or leaves the port passes in full sight. In the distance are the outer islands of Casco Bay.

The largest of Cape Elizabeth's hotels, with space for around 200 people, the Cape Cottage consisted of two connected pitched-roof ells set behind an unusual rubble-stone masonry front section, covered by a hipped-on-mansard roof and displaying broken-arch Gothic Revival window apertures on the ground-floor level. Erected in stages, this curious structure, dominated late in its history by a large tower with flat roof and balustrade, was quite atypical of its building type. After more than forty years of catering to the public, it succumbed to fire on 21 October 1894, with only ruins and ashes remaining.[35] Such was the fate of virtually all of the pre–World War II resort hotels that once graced the southern Maine coast, annunciating the fertile relationship between land and water, and contributing to the state's status as "America's summer playground."

8

MAINE

From Casco Bay to New Brunswick

IN STARK CONTRAST to the relatively straight, often sandy beach coast southwest of Portland and Casco Bay, Maine, the much longer, frequently forested shoreline extending northeast to New Brunswick contains numerous irregular and rocky peninsulas, inlets, bays, and offshore islands. Despite the lack of significant beach frontage, and the cooler climate conditioned by proximity to the Gulf of Maine, this scenically attractive and geographically diverse segment of the Maine coast has seen major summer resort development since the immediate post–Civil War years. Serviced by earlier railroad companies, the Maine Central Railroad system, ferryboats, coastal steamers, and improved roads, many shoreline communities became centers of tourism in the 1870s, 1880s, and 1890s, drawing visitors primarily from Maine and the Northeast but also from other areas of the United States, Canada, and Europe.

While the hospitality industry, with its attendant resort hotels, was most in evidence at Bar Harbor and Mount Desert Island communities, large resort-hotel development also occurred at nearby Hancock, Sorrento, and Winter Harbor, and to the southwest at Castine, Stockton Springs, Islesboro Island, Rockland, Popham Beach, Christmas Cove, Boothbay Harbor, Freeport, and the islands of Casco Bay. Proximate to the most northeasterly portion of the Maine coast, and an integral part of the regional hospitality enterprise, were the hotels of New Brunswick's southeastern coast and islands, several of which were designed by Boston architects or architectural partnerships and owned largely by American interests. In all instances, the hotels northeast of Portland were assiduously planned and strategically positioned to take full advantage of the compelling aesthetic, sensual, and climatic qualities of the seaboard region. Commencing with Casco Bay, resort communities and their distinctive hotel architecture will be treated in a northeasterly direction, concluding with Passamaquoddy Bay and southeastern New Brunswick.

The Casco Bay Islands

Linking the city of Portland with the open Atlantic is expansive Casco Bay, extending roughly twenty-five miles from Cape Elizabeth to Cape Small Point, with a width of approximately fourteen miles. It has long been recognized for its many picturesque landscape forms, including elevated rocky shoreline, headlands and peninsulas, and a large concentration of 120 islands, the most extensive group in a comparable body of water along the Atlantic coast.

Accessed from Portland by several steamboat and ferry routes since the mid–nineteenth century, these islands were initially frequented by local citizens and then underwent development, in some cases into popular summer resorts, at the instigation of both Portlanders and individuals from elsewhere on the mainland. Of principal importance in bay region hotel development were Cushing's, Peak's, Orr's, and Bailey's islands.[1]

Cushing's merits foremost attention as one of the first of the islands to become a summer resort, and the former location of the largest and architecturally most prominent hotel edifice in the Casco Bay region. In 1851, sensing the advantage of its position at the entrance of the harbor, Lemuel Cushing of Montreal, Canada, purchased the entire island. In 1853, he erected the first Ottawa House (fig. 8-1) on high ground with fine views of the city from its veranda, and of the open ocean from its central, octagonal cupola. Immediately, the new hotel became a magnet attraction to Cushing's fellow Canadian citizens. In its initial brick, vernacular form, it was of quite conventional design, the cupola crowning a pitched roof with truncated, pitched-roof dormers, and the façade broken by a central gable-roof projection and crossed by an enveloping first-story veranda. Originally accommodating 150 patrons, the Ottawa House was enlarged in the early 1880s by the addition of two identical flat-roofed, three-story wings, raising the full capacity to about 250. Social and recreational facilities were located

nearby in a detached building. About the same time, the island's potential as a summer resort haven was advanced when the land was configured into cottage lots, carriage roads, walkways, and paths under the direction of the distinguished landscape architect Frederick Law Olmstead of New York City. Unfortunately, progress was temporarily retarded when the first Ottawa House was destroyed by fire in 1886.[2]

Erected during the spring of 1888, the second Ottawa House (fig. 8-2) offered accommodations for 300 guests and was broadly acknowledged as "a hotel without a peer among summer resort hostelries."[3] Occupying the compelling site of its predecessor, this substantial Shingle-style structure was built under the aegis of the Cushing Island Company, consisting of Cushing family members and other New York investors. The promotional booklet *Portland and the Scenic Gems of Casco Bay* (1896) provides a complimentary and useful summation of the primary features of the new vacation retreat:

The house is built on a generous scale, has wide piazzas, a spacious and airy dining-hall, and ample drawing-room, with an open fire-place at each extremity, and parlors provided with a similar luxury; broad stairways, while the rooms—which are so arranged that any number of them may be combined in a single suite—are light, well-ventilated, handsomely furnished, and supplied with incandescent lights and electric bells. Several desirable cottages have been erected, where rooms can be secured, with table and board at the hotel.

Two of the cottages (1885–87) were designed by John Calvin Stevens (see above), the drawings for which are contained in archives of the Maine Historical Society.[4]

The stylistic equal of the Hotel Thorndike and the Mathewson Hotel in Rhode Island (see chapter 3) and the Passaconaway Inn at York Cliffs (see chapter 7), the second Ottawa House was designed by New York City architect Clarence Luce. A front elevation perspective drawing (fig. 8-3), published in the 23 July 1887 issue of *Building* magazine, depicts a building nearly identical to the final realized form, with the alternative name "Hotel Cushing's Island." Among the many attributes of the Shingle style in evidence are the long, low-pitched, intersecting roofs, offset octagonal and round towers, multistory bay windows, rubble stone foundations and round-arched main entrance, recessed porches and

Ottawa House, Cushing's Island.

Fig. 8-1. First Ottawa House, Cushing's Island, Casco Bay, Maine. Engraving from Edward H. Elwell, *Portland and Vicinity* (1876), p. 91. Courtesy of the University of Delaware Library.

Fig. 8-2. Ottawa House, Cushing's Island, Casco Bay, Maine. Photograph,
n.d. Collections of Maine Historical Society, MMN 17392, Photographs – Portland – Islands.

Fig. 8-3. "Hotel Cushing's Island, Maine." Front elevation perspective
drawing by Clarence Luce, Architect, New York City, from *Building* 8,
no. 4 (23 July 1887). Anne and Jerome Fisher Fine Arts Library, University of
Pennsylvania Library.

Fig. 8-4. "Granite Spring Hotel and Casino, Long Island, Portland Harbor, Me." Photograph from *The Island & Shore Gems of Beautiful Casco Bay, Portland, Maine* (Portland: Casco Bay Steamboat Company, 1895). Maine Historic Preservation Commission.

veranda, and side-wall shingle sheathing broken by patterned panels and half-timbering. The elimination of this superlative edifice by fire in 1917 represented another major loss to Maine's declining inventory of historic hotel architecture.[5]

While the two versions of the Ottawa House represent the epitome of large-hotel development in Casco Bay, there were other examples that serve as informative reference points. One of these was the 200-capacity Granite Spring Hotel and Casino (fig. 8-4) on Long Island, erected circa 1880 and displaying characteristic qualities of the Second Empire style, notably the patterned

hipped-on-mansard roofs. Another was the Peak's Island House (c. 1895) (fig. 8-5) on Peak's Island, like the Granite Spring a great multistory wooden ark of Second Empire inspiration, along with associated structures capable of housing well over 250 guests during its peak years. Three other Casco Bay hotels, smaller in size but worthy of mention, are the Stick-style Hotel Waldo (1867, c. 1880, etc.) on Little Chebeague Island and the late Italianate Hamilton Hotel (c. 1880) and the surviving Chebeague Inn (1925), both on Great Chebeague Island.[6]

Casco Castle: An Architectural Curiosity

A highly picturesque Norman stone tower rises solemnly above the village and harbor of South Freeport, Maine, twelve mile northeast of Portland. This landmark structure is all that remains of the idiosyncratic and alluring Casco Castle (fig. 8-6), a 100-capacity, three-story wooden resort hotel and entertainment facility built for $35,000 from 1902 to 1903 and burned on 7 September 1914. While its modest size would seemingly preclude its inclusion under the editorial guidelines advanced for this book, this structure, because of its unique style characteristics, occupies a special place in Maine's coastal resort-hotel history. Erected under the direction of Amos F. Gerald, a prominent Fairfield promoter and capitalist, and the Portland and Brunswick Street Railroad Com-

Fig. 8-5. Peak's Island House, Peak's Island, Casco Bay, Maine. Photograph, c. 1900. Collections of Maine Historical Society, MMN 17394, Photographs – Portland – Peaks Island.

Fig. 8-6. Casco Castle, South Freeport, Maine. Photograph, c. 1900. From the Collections of Freeport Historical Society, Freeport, Maine.

pany, the building was conceived to resemble a medieval Spanish castle, and did so with great effectiveness. A coastal showpiece, it possessed a moat and suspension drawbridge, castellated round and square corner towers, and oftentimes flags and banners flying above its turrets and battlements. Raised by Freeport contractor Benjamin Franklin Dunning, it was planned by Lewiston architect William Robinson Miller (1866–1929), known for his often flamboyant designs in a variety of styles of Maine residential, commercial, ecclesiastical, and public buildings. Included in his repertoire were two other equally outstanding hotels, the Gerald (1899–1900) at Fairfield and the Great Northern (1900) at Millinocket, Maine.

Unlike the vast majority of the state's shoreline hostelries, Casco Castle was a major social and activity center as well as a hotel, easily accessed by road, trolley line,

and ocean steamboat routes. Present on the interior were a ground-floor dining room, one of the largest on the Maine coast; a spacious ballroom, parlors, and a smoking room on the second floor; sleeping rooms on the second and third floors; and a kitchen, storerooms, and a bowling alley in the basement. Available to visitors was a wide selection of entertainment, athletic, and culinary options, including dances, musical performances, community sings, moonlight sails, picnicking, garden tours, motorboat rides, swimming, baseball, tennis, a zoo display with buffalo, and a restaurant specializing in seafood. Despite such a varied program, the Castle fell on hard times during its final years, the victim of changing automobile travel patterns, vacation preferences, and lifestyle habits. It ceased operations just prior to the terminal fire.[7]

Fig. 8-7. "Ocean View House and 'Annex,' Popham Beach, Maine."
Engraving from W. B. Lapham, *Popham Beach as a Summer Resort . . .*
(1888), n.p. Maine Historic Preservation Commission.

The Boothbay Harbor Region

Generously defined, the Boothbay Harbor region extends approximately fifteen miles to the northeast from the Small Point and Popham Beach peninsula to Pemaquid Point. One of Maine's most popular summer resort destinations, this district includes a variety of mainland and island waterfront communities, attractive to residents and vacation visitors because of their scenic beauty, easy ocean access, and temperate, health-enhancing climate. As in other coastal areas of the state, hotel and summer cottage development was initially stimulated by greatly improved transportation links in the late 1800s, in this instance railroad lines from Portland to Bath, for a time

the closest terminus to the southwest until the shore route was extended to Rockland.[8]

Four miles long and crescent in shape, Popham Beach in the town of Phippsburg occupies a prime location at the head of the Kennebec River. The first summer recreation center of consequence above Casco Bay and Freeport, it has traditionally been linked with American military history as the site of Fort St. George, Fort Popham, and Fort Baldwin at Hunnewell's Point. The principal hotel here was the Ocean View House (fig. 8-7), later titled the "Rockledge," perched on Seymore Bluff, an impressive promontory overlooking the beach with broad views across Sagadohoc (Merrymeeting) Bay. Financed by a stock company formed by in-state, Boston, and New York investors, the first portion of the Ocean View was constructed circa 1881. Of Second Empire inspiration, it was typical of wooden resort hotels of its style and era — rectangular in form, surrounded on three sides by a first-story, stick-construction veranda, and capped by a hipped-on-mansard roof with dormers and a central cupola. Experiencing immediate business success, the complex was enlarged by the addition of similarly styled three-story wooden annexes from 1887 to 1888 and 1894 to 1895, reaching a peak capacity of more than 225 before it burned to the ground in April 1915. In its final multisection, asymmetrical configuration, the Ocean View (Rockledge) assumed a form sharply contrasting with the primarily single-unit hotel structures once so common along the Maine coastline.[9]

Fig. 8-8. Oake Grove Hotel, Boothbay Harbor, Maine. Cover illustration from brochure, *Oake Grove Hotel, Boothbay Harbor, Me.* (c. 1905). Maine Historic Preservation Commission.

Like the Ocean View at Popham Beach, the Oake Grove Hotel (fig. 8-8) at West Boothbay Harbor evolved randomly in sections over time, seemingly without overarching plan. The largest of the Boothbay Harbor area's summer hostelries, advertising space for 250 guests after 1920, it substantially exceeded in size the Menawarmet (1889; burned, spring 1913) on the east shore of the harbor, as well as the harbor island hotels (see below). Situated near Boothbay Harbor Village on an oak-tree-shrouded point on the west side of the harbor, the Oake Grove occupied a highly advantageous site with commanding vistas across water to the islands. The first relatively small portion of the complex was raised circa 1893 or 1894 by the Reed family, whose members served as owners and proprietors for most of its history. Substantial four-story additions were attached to this initial core in 1897 and, more recently, the last in 1922. Dominating the L-shaped, vernacular complex was a five-story octagonal tower with square pyramidal roof serving as a central ordering point for the two angled, connected wings with their varied roof shapes. Passing from Reed family ownership in the final years, the Oake Grove was demolished in late 1964 and early 1965, and was replaced by condominiums.[10]

Once located on Mouse Island, adjacent to Southport Island, the Samoset House, along with its adjacent Rosewood (Stone) Cottage and outbuildings, was a major Boothbay Harbor hostelry with bedroom space for 200 clients during its heyday. Its history dates back to 1875, when Mouse Island was purchased by a group of twelve Skowhegan, Maine, citizens with the intention of building a profitable resort hotel. The resulting edifice (fig. 8-9) was erected in a single stage in 1877, assuming a rectangular, pitched-roof form — with roof dormers, a central cupola, and first-floor verandas — commonly associated with the hotel building type at the time. Early publicity touted "billiards, bowling and boating," along with croquet, lawn tennis, bathhouses, a dance hall, excellent "marine views," and "an abundance of pure air and pure water." After businessman Keyes H. Richards acquired the island and the Samoset in 1907, he made significant improvements by funding a new addition and tapping the town's water system through an ingenious submerged pipe on the harbor bottom. The water supply, however, was insufficient to save the hotel when it caught

Fig. 8-9. Samoset House, Mouse Island, Boothbay Harbor, Maine. Broadside engraving, c. 1881. Maine Historic Preservation Commission.

fire in mid-August 1913, and it was destroyed before a large group of stunned vacationing spectators.[11]

About two miles south of Boothbay Harbor Village, just to the east of Southport Island, is Squirrel Island, home to a major concentration of summer cottages and other buildings including, for eighty years, a substantial wood-frame resort hotel. The formal development of the summer community dates from 1870, when Professor Oren B. Cheney of Bates College, several Bates professors, and other Lewiston residents purchased the island and established the Squirrel Island Association, which is still in existence today. Constructed in entirety from 1894 to 1895, the Hotel Eastern replaced the first hostelry on the island, the modest-size Chase House, which had burned in 1893. During the latter part of the opening season, at the request of island cottagers, the name was changed to "Squirrel Inn," which the hotel retained for the remainder of its history until it succumbed to fire on 28 September 1962. Operated under the management of Keyes Richards (see above) during its first years, this three-and-one-half-story structure (fig. 8-10) possessed an L-shaped floor plan including the customary public function spaces and guest rooms, along with adjacent cottages capable of housing between 175 and 200 people. Of low-key Colonial Revival–style pretensions, the Squirrel Inn displayed a perfectly balanced front façade with gable-roof bays on either side, truncated, pitched-

Fig. 8-10. "Squirrel Inn — Keyes H. Richards, Prop." Photograph from Francis B. Greene, *History of Boothbay, Southport and Boothbay Harbor, 1623–1905* (1906). New Hampshire Historical Society.

roof dormers, and a rather commonplace first-story wraparound veranda.[12]

Slightly northeast of Boothbay Harbor and Ocean Point, on the southern tip of Rutherford Island, is Christmas Cove, a small, self-contained coastal village, its older buildings above its tiny, charming harbor a reflection of its early years as a fishing and lobstering mecca. Like numerous other Maine seaboard communities in the late nineteenth century, it was largely transformed into a single-season vacation community, evident by the dominating presence of numerous summer cottages and places of public accommodation. By far the largest of the hotels were the three Holly Inns, afflicted by a history of conflagrations on the same raised site overlooking the isthmus between the harbor and John's Bay to the east. Owned and managed by Albert T. Thorpe, the first (1902–3) was a plain, three-story building with forty rooms, which was leveled by fire in 1907. Of greater size, with ninety bedrooms, the second (c. 1908), a Colonial

Revival complex also owned by the Thorpes, was a local focal point of summer hospitality until it burned on 10 August 1923. The third (1924) (fig. 8-11), along with its annex, Rutherford House, housed roughly 200 clients and lasted until 12 September 1940, when it too went up in flames. Erected by Hiram Bisbee of nearby Pemaquid Point, this building, the largest of the Holly Inns, was a highly functional long, rectangular, factory-like structure of minimal aesthetic appeal, but for the rows of four-window shed-roof dormers extending along each side of the pitched roof planes. Nevertheless, in this form, it represented a unique contribution to the resort hotel legacy of the Boothbay Harbor region.[13]

The Samoset and Penobscot Bay

For over a hundred miles from the Boothbay Harbor region north to Mount Desert Island, resort hotel development, with only a few exceptions, was not extensive during the years predating World War II. On this stretch of coast, four hotel structures (located at Rockland/Rockport, Islesboro Island, Stockton Springs, and Castine) do, however, merit close scrutiny. By far the most ambitiously conceived and most notable in this group, and the premier resort on Maine's entire coastline, was the grand Samoset Hotel at Rockland Breakwater, in the same league as the nationally renowned Poland Spring House at South Poland and the Mount Kineo House on Moosehead Lake, both in Maine, and the Mount Washington Hotel and the Balsams in New Hampshire's White Mountains.

The Samoset originated as the sprawling and luxuri-

Fig. 8-11. "Holly Inn," with Rutherford House (*right*), Christmas Cove, Maine. Photograph from booklet, *Holly Inn, Christmas Cove, Maine* (n.d.). Maine Historic Preservation Commission.

Fig. 8-12. "Bay Point Hotel, Rockland Breakwater, Rockland, Me."
Lithograph from *The Woods, Lakes, Sea-Shore and Mountains* (1896),
p. 81. Author's collection.

ous Bay Point Hotel, erected from 1888 to 1889 at a cost of $40,000 under the leadership of entrepreneur Francis Cobb, II. It was beautifully set on Jameson Point facing the breakwater on Penobscot Bay with the interior Camden Hills as backdrop scenery. Providing start-up financing for the land and structure was a syndicate, including Cobb and family members, of sixty investors and stockholders, many from out of state. A ceremonious formal opening on 4 July 1889, attended by well-known Maine political leaders and other dignitaries, commanded broad New England regional attention and auspiciously launched the ambitious hospitality venture. W. H. Glover and Company of Rockland served as contractor for the new complex, its work based on plans generated by George M. Coombs of the Lewiston, Maine, architectural firm of Coombs & Gill. The end product was a three-and-one-half-story L-shaped structure, illustrated in an 1896 lithograph (fig. 8-12) depicting the original

building with an extension made to the west side during the early nineties, and an extension to the north that was purely fictional and not completed until later years (see below). A prominent feature of the Bay Point, as well as other large resort hotels such as Poland Springs, was the central tower at the angle of the L plan, its vertical lines nicely contrasting with the predominantly horizontal lines of the full complex.[14]

In 1902, the syndicate sold the Bay Point to the Ricker family (Hiram Ricker & Sons), the owners of the Poland Spring House, and it was renamed the Samoset, a symbol of welcome, after the area's Pemaquid Native American chief who was among the first to greet the *Mayflower* Pilgrims after their 1620 landing. Immediately, as the Ricker Hotel Company, the new owners committed themselves to a multiyear stylistic makeover and expansion of the complex reminiscent of the transformation they had orchestrated a few years before for the Poland Spring

Fig. 8-13. "Samoset Hotel, Rockland, Me." Photograph by Nathaniel L. Stebbins, c. 1910. Courtesy of Historic New England. (Negative #47397-A.)

House. In 1902, at a cost of $125,000, the company, from plans by architect Forest Walker, reconfigured the former Bay Point, adding a wing to the north and replacing the original central tower with a taller, more substantial structure combining elements of the late Queen Anne and Colonial Revival styles (fig. 8-13). At the same time, the interior was greatly altered by the enlargement of first-floor public rooms and the refitting of guestrooms, a process that was to continue in subsequent years (see figs. 8-14, 8-15, and 8-16). Guest capacity was increased from approximately 150 to 200, where it would remain for four years.[15]

Motivated by growing customer demand and generated profits, the Ricker Hotel Company continued to expand the Samoset Hotel. From 1905 to 1906, a new 46-by-145-foot addition was made to the north wing, guest capacity was increased to 300, and public spaces were newly created or further enlarged. These included an office, banquet hall, and dining, billiard, and children's

rooms, all fitted with large plate glass windows and the latest in heating, plumbing, and lighting technology. Particularly striking visually were the step gable parapets flanking a half-octagonal window bay, topped with an octagonal cupola with rounded cap, spire, and weather vane. Around 1915, adjacent to the hotel golf course, a new outbuilding, the Jameson Hotel, was raised to house the growing number of guest automobile chauffeurs. Soon after, from 1916 to 1917, additional interior and exterior "improvements" were made to the main complex, including a new, classical porte cochere and veranda on the south front. Portland's John Calvin Stevens, with prior experience in hotel design, along with his son, John Howard Stevens, served as architects for this project (see chapter 7). Only a few additional changes, relatively minor, were made after this date.[16]

In the early 1920s, the Ricker Hotel Company sold the Samoset property to the Maine Central Railroad, which held title to 1940, making numerous cosmetic

Fig. 8-14. Office, Samoset Hotel, Rockland, Maine. Photograph from booklet, *The SamOset By the Sea* (1914). Maine Historic Preservation Commission.

Fig. 8-15. Dining room, Samoset Hotel, Rockland, Maine. Photograph from booklet, *The SamOset By the Sea* (1914). Maine Historic Preservation Commission.

as well as functional improvements, both inside and outside, during its period of ownership. In that year, the Samoset was conveyed to Adriel Bird of Rockland and William A. Dow of Boston, who retained ownership for four years before selling out to the Hotel Corporation of America, whose president, A. M. Sonnabend, took title in 1945. Finally, with both vacation and convention business steadily declining and the physical plant outmoded, the Samoset completed its final summer season in 1969, the contents were auctioned, and the deteriorating hotel, outbuildings, and grounds passed to Samoset Associates on 1 October 1972. Just a few days later, on the unlucky date of Friday, 13 October, fire ravaged the Samoset, the massive edifice was reduced to smoldering ruins in a few hours, and New England lost another of its noted summer resort hotels. The cause of the suspicious, peculiarly timed blaze was never determined. Not to be denied, the new owners constructed a new, much smaller hotel building under the aegis of the Treadway-Samoset Resort and opened it to the public in September 1974. Today, under different ownership, the property persists as a major year-round resort and conference center, with the hotel the centerpiece, along with townhouses, condominiums, and recreational/athletic venues.[17]

In Penobscot Bay, fifteen miles down the coast from Rockland, is Islesboro (Islesborough) Island, the one-time location of two versions of the upscale Islesboro Inn. Fortunately for us today, the record of their history has been thoroughly researched. Both were well-

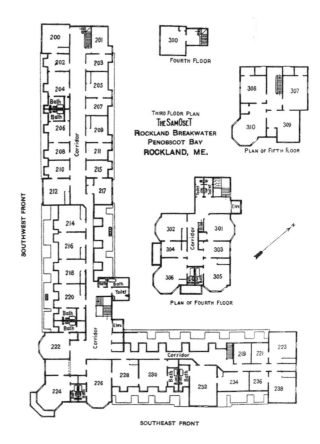

Fig. 8-16. "Third Floor Plan, The Samoset, Rockland Breakwater, Penobscot Bay, Rockland, Me." From booklet, *The SamOset* (1902). Maine Historic Preservation Commission.

Fig. 8-17. "Islesborough Inn — Westerly View," Islesboro Island, Penobscot Bay, Maine. Photograph from John P. Farrow, *History of Islesborough, Maine* (1893), op. p. 310. Maine Historic Preservation Commission.

articulated examples of their respective styles, imposing in appearance but considerably smaller in scale than the Samoset Hotel. Financed by the Islesboro Land and Improvement Company of Philadelphia, the first Islesboro (Islesborough) Inn (fig. 8-17) was constructed from 1889 to 1890 by Bangor, Maine, contractor Charles B. Brown from plans drawn by architect Edmund M. Wheelwright (1854–1912) of the well-known Boston firm of Wheelwright and Haven. Wheelwright is primarily remembered for his City Architect and other public building commissions in Boston but also for his summer cottage design work in Maine. Impressively situated on a sharp bluff overlooking Dark Harbor, the first Islesboro, displaying English Tudor Revival and Shingle-style features on its multisection exterior, received broad notice for its excellent design, combining diverse building materials. The 4 July 1890 issue of the *Mount Desert Herald* contained this provocative description of the exterior, as possessing a

graceful and unique roof outline of large gables with connecting roof broken by dormers. The faces of the gables are of

stucco work with wooden cross bars in the old English fashion. The low part of the building is stone with broad verandas and porches, the roofs of which are carried on massive stone pillars.

Servicing the two floors of sleeping rooms above, the first floor (fig. 8-18) included a lobby ("Mall") accessing parlors, a smoking room, and the dining room and kitchen facilities, along with a music room, billiard room, and barber shop later added in 1890 (see below).

Following the tradition of numerous Maine coastal resort hotels, the first Islesboro Inn proved a highly successful enterprise during its opening season, so much so that the ownership again contracted with Edmund Wheelwright to design a new forty-by-sixty-foot wing. This was finished in time for the 1891 season by contractors W. H. Glover and Company of Rockland (see above). Customer demand further increased, and another addition was completed in 1891. It appears, however, that the next major expansion was not realized until 1899, when the Glover Company appended a two-story, eighty-foot wing to the existing complex. In 1912, having purchased

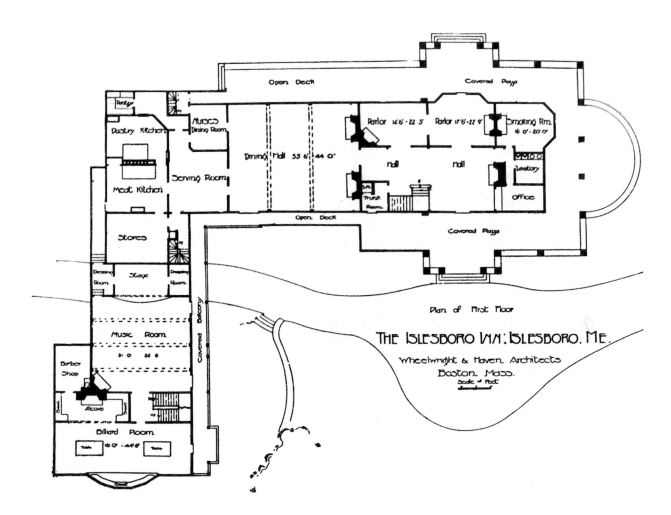

Fig. 8-18. "First Floor Plan — Islesboro Inn," Islesboro Island, Penobscot Bay, Maine. From John P. Farrow, *History of Islesborough, Maine* (1893), op. p. 310. Maine Historic Preservation Commission.

the hotel two years before, Dr. Samuel G. Dixon of Philadelphia and Dark Harbor hired the Philadelphia architectural partnership of Evans (Edmund C.), Warren & Register to plan another addition. Erected by local contractor William H. Hatch in 1913, it included an enlarged function room and thirty new guest rooms, increasing the total capacity to over 300 guests. Sadly, the marvelous structure, its stylistic components so effectively related to its environment, was totally flattened by fire on 30 September 1915.[18]

A year later, Dr. Dixon sold the property to the newly formed Islesboro Inn Company, which raised $150,000 to build a replacement hotel on the same site reusing the original foundations. After reviewing plans from Edmund C. Evans (1878–1934) (see above) as well as Fred L. Savage (see below) of Bar Harbor, the company opted for the Evans designs, and the new building was erected from 1916 to 1917 by the Bangor and Old Town, Maine, construction firm of George H. Wilbur and Son. Low and L-shaped like its predecessor, the second Islesboro Inn (fig. 8-19), with a smaller capacity of around 200, creatively incorporated a variety of Colonial Revival elements. Most striking to the eye were the well-integrated main, gable, and dormer roof forms, and the forceful horizontal lines conveyed by the white-shingled building mass and the attached verandas. After a downturn

Fig. 8-19. Second Islesboro Inn, Islesboro Island, Penobscot Bay, Maine. Photograph, n.d. Islesboro Historical Society.

in patronage caused by World War I, summer visitation improved in 1919, and the company approved the construction of a stylistically compatible addition, designed by Evans and put up by Otto Nelson, a Bangor contractor, in the first half of 1920. Closed to the public between 1930 and 1932, and again during World War II, the inn was unable to regain its prewar business momentum and terminated operations in 1951. It was demolished four years later.[19]

Farther down the coast to the northeast, where the Penobscot River meets the Bay, is Stockton Springs, the location of the former Wassaumkeag Hotel (fig. 8-20) on Fort Point. It had its origins in 1871, when Captain Charles Sanford and Hugh Bass, both of Bangor, formed a joint-stock company, raised a sum of $85,000, and commissioned Joseph W. Thompson (1822–91), a Stockton Springs resident, as architect and builder. Utilizing a great wooden frame, moved down the river from Bangor, Thompson successfully oversaw construction, completed in time for the 1871 summer season but for a few final refinements. Planned

in the Second Empire style, so common among hotel buildings of the time on the New England coast, the Wassaumkeag consisted of a three-story, rectangular block capped by a hipped-on-mansard roof broken by chimneys and a series of dormers, and topped by a balustraded promenading deck. Centered on the front façade was a fragile-appearing, two-level veranda partially enveloping a large, square, four-story tower, recessed into the building mass and itself capped by a steep-pitched, truncated mansard roof penetrated by Palladian dormer windows. Chronicled by photographs of the day, this standout edifice made an indelible impression when viewed from the sea. Following the all too familiar litany, the Wassaumkeag fell victim to fire on 7 June 1898 as it was being readied for its twenty-seventh summer season.[20]

On the east side of Penobscot Bay at the end of a long peninsula is Castine, the onetime location of the last historic resort hotel of consequence until one reaches Mount Desert Island farther to the northeast. Facing eastward on Perkins Street on a slope overlooking the harbor and the steamboat dock was the 200-guest Acadian Hotel (fig. 8-21), like so many hostelries of its era the product of multistage construction. The earliest or central portion of the structure evolved from the Cobb family house, a colonial-era building purchased by E. P. Walker of nearby Vinalhaven Island in 1875 and converted to a small inn. At the instigation of Walker family members and others who had acquired shares of the owning company, nearly identical matching wings were added to the south in 1884 and to the north around 1904 or 1905. This created a lengthy, almost perfectly balanced three-unit front façade of highly stark, functional, almost contemporary appearance that was set in sharp contrast to the ornate, Stick-style bandstand in front. Avoiding the fire curse, all too common to the summer hospitality industry, the Acadian persevered until it was torn down in 1943.[21]

Bar Harbor and Mount Desert Island

Mount Desert Island, identified by its principal town, Bar Harbor (officially called "Eden" until 1918), has long been regarded as one of America's major summer resort retreats, a social and recreational paradise commanding national as well as international attention. Traditionally referred to as a small "Switzerland afloat," the island is located about 110 miles northeast of Portland, just off the coast of Maine. Irregular in shape and roughly ten by sixteen miles in surface area, the island is characterized by its bracing climate and a diversity of beautiful scenery, enhanced by its many hills and mountains, interior lakes, and rocky shoreline penetrated by inlets, bays, and Somes Sound, which nearly divides it into two segments. Much of the island is occupied by Acadia National Park, first established as Lafayette National Park in 1919, and the first national park east of the Mississippi River. In the popular mind, Mount Desert often conjures up images of the fancy, privileged summer life as the location of the summer residences of some of the country's wealthiest and best-known families—Rockefellers, Vanderbilts, Morgans, Pulitzers, and others. In fact, the treasured features of the island, first accessed by mainland railroad and ferry connections in the 1870s, have attracted an eclectic influx of summer visitors, first prompting the rapid development of boardinghouses and hotels and

Fig. 8-20. Wassaumkeag Hotel, Fort Point, Stockton Springs, Maine. Photograph, c. 1880. Maine Historic Preservation Commission.

Fig. 8-21. "The Acadian, Castine, Maine." Booklet cover lithograph, 1905. Maine Historic Preservation Commission.

subsequently the proliferation of seasonal cottages, all contributing to a rich regional architectural heritage.[22]

Sheltered from harsh weather elements, Bar Harbor (fig. 8-22) occupies sloping land on Frenchman's Bay on the northeastern shore of Mount Desert Island, opposite the Porcupine Islands. For many over past decades, this removed oceanside retreat has represented the epitome of the American summer resort experience. As early as the mid-1860s, Bar Harbor began to attract vacation boarders, and the first, albeit small hotels as well as single-season cottages began to appear. The work of artists as well as published scientific writings greatly helped to popularize the area. In 1868, a wharf was completed, and the first steamers brought the initial flow of summer visitors to the town and the island. The earliest hotel to later grow to significant size was the Rodick House, the first stage put up in 1866 by David Rodick, Jr., facing Main Street, between what would later become Rodick Place and Cottage Street. The construction of this and

Fig. 8-22. Bar Harbor from Bar Island, Frenchman's Bay, Maine. Photograph, c. 1890. Courtesy of Peabody Essex Museum.

other small hotels in the sixties commenced the hotel phase in Bar Harbor's history, to reach its height during the mid-1880s, when there were over fifteen hotels, each taking 100 or more guests. These were located, most with partial or no sea views, on the streets or outskirts of the town, resulting in a variety of building forms influenced by the degree of ocean exposure and the position and size of the building site. Some were multiple-block structures more characteristic of urban environments, while others were imaginatively conceived to relate effectively to the ocean waters and the rolling, sylvan topography of the island.[23]

Responding to the late nineteenth-century tourism boom, the Rodick's owners progressively expanded their hotel so that by 1890, with bedroom space for 700 people, it had become the largest coastal resort hotel in New England. In 1870 and 1875, Rodick and his sons increased the size of the establishment, recast in the Second Empire style, so that it accommodated 275 people. The complex achieved its fully developed form (fig. 8-23) from 1881 to 1882 under the supervision of local architect and builder John E. Clark, who coordinated the construction of a massive addition at the northern end of the original Main Street section. The ultimate result was a huge, ponderous-looking, six-story wooden edifice, seemingly anchored to the ground by its octagonal corner tower and paired square towers on the main façade. For a distance of five hundred feet, a twenty-five-foot-wide veranda ran along the front and one of the side walls of the hotel. Blessed with cavernous interior public spaces, the Rodick became a nationally prominent social center, rivaling the great hotels of Saratoga Springs, New York, the New Jersey shore, and other locations. The office was traditionally known as the "fish pond," its name derived from young men and women congregating there searching for the ideal mate! Prosperous for the balance of Bar

Fig. 8-23. The Rodick Hotel, Bar Harbor, Mount Desert Island, Maine. Photoelectric engraving from [W. B. Lapham], *Bar Harbor and Mount Desert Island* (1886), advertisement, p. 47. Maine Historic Preservation Commission.

Fig. 8-24. "Newport House and Cottages," Bar Harbor, Mount Desert Island, Maine. Photograph from W. H. Sherman, *A Souvenir of Bar Harbor* (1896). Maine Historic Preservation Commission.

Harbor's hotel era, the Rodick fell on hard times during the 1890s, persisted for a few more years, was closed in 1902, and fell to the wrecking ball in 1906.[24]

The other large Bar Harbor hotel dating from the sixties was the Newport Hotel (House) and Cottages (fig. 8-24), the initial Second Empire–style portion built circa 1869 on a site slightly south of present-day Agamont Park, overlooking the waterfront on Newport Avenue. Enlarged at least twice during the 1880s to take upward of 200 patrons, it possessed a historic ambience, but, like certain of its contemporaries elsewhere, lacked architectural cohesiveness, its three major sections seemingly linked solely by a wraparound, Stick-style veranda. The Newport's capacity was increased in 1905 when Martin Roberts acquired the smaller Marlborough House as an annex, originally designed by John E. Clark (see above) and located on Main Street near the Rodick House. Surviving longer than most of its competitors, the hotel was torn down in 1928.[25]

During the 1870s, hotel development reached its peak at Bar Harbor. In the first half of the decade, three major hotel operations commenced, later to be expanded in response to the favorable local economy. The first of these was the St. Sauveur Hotel (later the Bellevue), once present in a residential section on Mount Desert Street, not far from the center of town. Its initial incarnation dates from 1870 and was designed by the prolific John

E. Clark for owner Fred A. Alley. Supplemented by an annex in 1881, it was badly damaged by fire the next year, was rebuilt in 1882, and embarked on a long period of business operation, ending with its demolition in 1945. Difficult to categorize in terms of style, the L-shaped St. Sauveur (fig. 8-25) displayed features of the Queen Anne, the Shingle, and the Stick, especially the latter in its three towers and veranda.[26]

Situated between Hancock and Atlantic avenues until it was torn down in 1949 was the Louisburg Hotel (fig.

Fig. 8-25. St. Sauveur Hotel, Bar Harbor, Mount Desert Island, Maine. Photograph from W. H. Sherman, *A Souvenir of Bar Harbor* (1896). Maine Historic Preservation Commission.

Fig. 8-26. Louisburg Hotel, Bar Harbor, Mount Desert Island, Maine. Lithograph from *New England's Summer and America's Leading Winter Resorts* (1897). Author's collection.

8-26), its initial portion raised from 1873 to 1874 as the second Atlantic House. Acquired by Mrs. M. A. Balch of Boston in 1887, it was renamed after Louisburg Square there in recognition of its predominantly Boston Brahmin clientele. Subsequently, it received two major additions—the first in 1888 based on plans prepared by the Boston architectural firm of Andrews, Jacques & Ran-

toul, and the second in 1889 designed by local architect Fred L. Savage (see above). The end result was a spacious, rambling, L-shaped structure similar in form to several other Bar Harbor hotels of the period and like many, highly functional with sparse decorative detail. After 1921, the hotel operated under the name "Lorraine" while it was owned by the Lafayette Hotel Corporation.[27]

Located at Main and Mount Desert streets, not far from the Rodick House on the site of the present-day town common, the 350-room Grand Central Hotel (fig. 8-27), characteristic of its building type, evolved from a much smaller predecessor, the Bay View House, erected circa 1868. The major portion of this huge, visually dominating complex was created around 1875 when the partnership of Hamor and Young, owners of the Bay View, purchased the adjacent Harbor House and joined and refurbished the two structures. Successful over the next two decades, the Grand Central was remodeled in 1893 and then fell victim to declining business fortunes and was sold to the town by its final owner, Johnson Livingston, in 1899. Promptly demolished, it was remembered long afterward for its massive scale and Stick-style components, principally the corner tower, likely inspired by the similar tower adorning the Rodick.[28]

Bar Harbor's finest example of late Victorian hotel

Fig. 8-27. Grand Central Hotel, Bar Harbor, Mount Desert Island, Maine. Photograph, c. 1895. Courtesy of the Bar Harbor Historical Society, Maine.

Fig. 8-28. "West End • Hotel • Bar Harbor • Mt. Desert • Me. Bruce Price • Archt. N.Y." Front elevation perspective drawing from *American Architect and Building News* 5 (25 January 1879). Anne and Jerome Fisher Fine Arts Library, University of Pennsylvania Library.

architecture was the West End Hotel, which once stood at West and Cottage streets. Erected by first owner O. M. Shaw in two principal stages to house roughly 400 guests, it has been closely and productively studied by architectural historians Vincent J. Scully, Jr., and Roger G. Reed in recognition of its many fine Stick- and Shingle-style-inspired qualities. Originating as a modest-size, mansard-roof hotel, Heywood House, around 1870, it was substantially enlarged and recast stylistically from 1878 to 1879 from plans submitted by Bruce Price (1845–1903), at the time a noted New York City–based architect, frequent summer visitor to Bar Harbor, and subsequent designer of summer cottages there. Limited by the small size of the urban lot, Price created a

highly effective interplay of verticality, emphasized by the tall-massing, off-center front tower, chimneys, and veranda posts, and horizontality accentuated by the deep roof overhangs and the expansive two-story veranda attached to two sides of the structure. In examining Price's 1879 *American Architect and Building News* rendering (fig. 8-28), one is immediately impressed by the picturesque, sheltering forms of the high-pitched, hipped roofs broken by dormers of varying shapes, and the eaves and their heavy, curved brackets. Scully appropriately characterized the building as "a great [shingle and clapboarded] barn, rough, boisterous and warm in its colors"—Indian red, olive green, and brown, often used in cottage architecture of the same era. Like most

Fig. 8-29. "Malvern Hotel, Kebo Street," Bar Harbor, Mount Desert
Island, Maine. Photograph from W. H. Sherman, *A Souvenir of Bar
Harbor* (1896). Maine Historic Preservation Commission.

of the town's other resort hotels, the West End was adversely affected by changing guest preferences and travel
patterns in the nineties, and was razed in January 1900.
Consequently, Bar Harbor lost a rough, appealing gem
of exterior natural materials, supplemented after 1890 by
interior "Moresque" decoration about which, hopefully,
we will learn more in the future.[29]

Despite the gradually declining prospects for local
resort-hotel enterprise, two additional large buildings
joined the Bar Harbor group. The first was the Malvern
Hotel (fig. 8-29) on Kebo Street, built from 1880 to 1881
by DeGrasse Fox and eventually supplemented by eleven
handsome cottages for the benefit of over 200 boarders.
Renovated in 1909, with a new annex in 1915 by local architect Fred L. Savage (see above), it was the only one of
the town's large early hostelries to conduct business after
World War II, and was finally leveled in the devastating
1947 fire that destroyed one-third of the cottages and

many other buildings on Mount Desert Island. Modeled
on a T-shape plan, the Malvern, like the Newport House
(see above), comprised three major sections, each, however, possessing similar, unifying Shingle-style forms
and decorative elements. These were evident in their
intersecting roofs, varied dormers, patterned gables,
wall sheathing, and two-level veranda. Fully developed,
the Malvern represented an interesting contrast to the
somewhat smaller-capacity Hotel Porcupine, later the
Florence (1887; burned, 1918), a Main Street, five-story
rectangular block with Shingle-style features and a
strong sense of verticality represented by its stacked window bays, bay roof caps, steep-pitched roof planes, and
tall, corbeled brick chimneys. As such, these two hotels
represented an impressive conclusion to Bar Harbor's
opulent Victorian hotel era.[30]

Three other coastal communities on Mount Desert
Island, smaller and more subdued than Bar Harbor,

Fig. 8-30. The Island House, Southwest Harbor, Mount Desert Island,
Maine. Photograph, c. 1886. Photographer unknown - SWHPL Number 5222 -
from The Southwest Harbor Public Library Photographic Collection.

saw significant resort hotel and cottage development
in the late nineteenth century. Included in this trio are
Northeast Harbor, Seal Harbor, and Southwest Harbor,
the latter where the island's first summer colony took
root. The launching of Southwest Harbor as a center
of vacation life occurred during the 1850s, in large part
because of its close proximity to picturesque attractions,
and the initiative of Deacon Henry H. Clark, who built
the first substantial wharf there, opening the village to
regular steamboat service from Portland. Clark also
acquired one of the town's first hotels, later to become
the 225-capacity Island House. Other, smaller hotels
then joined the group—the mansard-roof Ocean House
(c. 1850; demolished, 1940s); the Shingle-style second
Stanley House (1885–86; burned, March 1927); and,
with low-key, Stick-style features, the extant Claremont
Hotel (1884–85), a rare specimen of early New England
resort-hotel architecture maintained in an excellent state

of preservation and listed on the National Register of
Historic Places. Consistent with the subject definition
for this book, however, it is the four-story Island House
(fig. 8-30) that is most worthy of notice, highlighted by
its intriguing Second Empire embellishment. Built circa
1850 on Clark's Point, it was enlarged several times, including major modifications in 1882 and 1885, and was
closed in 1900 and ultimately demolished. Of particular
visual appeal were the multicolored horizontal strips of
clapboarding and shingles on the side walls and mansard roof planes of the main rectangular block, and the
corner tower with its elaborate roof cap surmounted by
a balustrade.[31]

Located to the east of Southwest Harbor across the
wide mouth of Somes Sound is Northeast Harbor, where
the summer resort business commenced comparatively
late during the 1880s, supplementing the older fishing
and farming economy. During a four-year span, hotels

Fig. 8-31. The second Asticou Inn, Northeast Harbor, Mount Desert Island, Maine. Photograph, 2006, by the author.

appeared, highlighted by the Kimball House and the Rock End Hotel (see below). Also present there were the much smaller Clifton House (1885–86; demolished, 1939), a Shingle-style structure designed by John E. Clark of Bar Harbor (see above), and the first version of the Asticou Inn (1883; destroyed by fire, 17 September 1900), built from plans by Fred L. Savage (see above), the son of the owner, Augustus C. Savage. Soon afterward, from 1900 to 1901, the second Asticou (fig. 8-31) rose, also de-signed by Fred Savage, and has survived and remained in business to this day. The last of Northeast Harbor's pre–World War I hotels, it is a well-maintained, nicely proportioned, quite stunning example of Shingle-style architecture with sleeping space for about 100 guests.

The initial section of the Rock End Hotel, first titled "Revere House," was built from 1883 to 1884 by Augustus C. Savage's son, Herman L., on a shoreline bluff over-looking Somes Sound and the ocean. Asymmetrical in form, the three-story, hipped-roof, wood-frame structure undoubtedly impressed onlookers with its

encircling veranda and tower, covered by a roof cap with balustrades. In 1894, likely influenced by the architecture of Florida hotels where he had been a manager, Herman Savage, with his brother Fred as architect, totally recast the Rock End (fig. 8-32) in the Spanish Revival style. Though seemingly out of context on the northern shore of New England, it proved to be an aesthetic success with its stuccoed walls, round-arched porch apertures, and open, off-center, and lower corner towers, both with hipped roofs. In 1909, Herman Savage turned to his brother again to design a blockular four-story, stucco-walled addition on the end facing the shoreline, thereby increasing the bedroom capacity, including nearby cot-tages, to about 200, with a dining room that could seat 300. Members of the Savage family continued to operate the hotel until it partially burned the first week of March 1942, never to be reconstructed.

Northeast Harbor's other large hotel, the Kimball House (fig. 8-33), was erected under the leadership of Daniel Kimball and his son, Loren, from 1886 to 1887 and remained a family enterprise until 1966. It was then sold to the Asti-Kim Corporation, which oversaw its closing and demolition in the same year, the land divided as lots for cottages. Designed by the productive local architect John E. Clark (see above), this substantial, eye-catching Queen Anne–style edifice, later to undergo a Colonial Revival makeover, featured a five-story octagonal corner tower, numerous pitched-roof double dormers, and an enveloping one-story veranda and upper porches of light wood construction. Catering to the affluent, the Kimball was one of the island's most popular summer guest establishments in its prime years, and its loss was painful for many island residents and visitors.

Situated on a snug little cove almost three miles to

the east of Northeast Harbor, Seal Harbor entered the summer hospitality business in the late 1860s, reaching a peak with the opening of the Seaside Hotel circa 1875 by the local Clement family, and the smaller Glen Cove House in 1883. In his 1888 Mount Desert Island guidebook, Moses F. Sweetser characterized the early Seaside, the beneficiary of several small expansions, as "a picturesque group of buildings of various epochs." A major project was implemented in 1891 when Amos and James Clement hired architect and builder John E. Clark (see above) to realize their fondest hopes. During that year, Clark transformed the facility into a considerably larger resort hotel (fig. 8-34) under the new name of Seaside Inn, to provide overnight quarters for 175 to 200 custom-

Fig. 8-32. Rock End Hotel, Northeast Harbor, Mount Desert Island, Maine. Photograph, c. 1910, by I. T. Moore. Northeast Harbor Library.

Fig. 8-33. Kimball House, Northeast Harbor, Mount Desert Island, Maine. Photograph, c. 1890. Collections of Maine Historical Society, MMN 17393, Photographs – Northeast Harbor.

Fig. 8-34. The Seaside Inn, Seal Harbor, Mount Desert Island, Maine. Photograph, c. 1910, by I. T. Moore. Northeast Harbor Library.

ers. After the original residence and boardinghouse were moved back, the 1882 annex, with its matching corner towers, was amalgamated into the new, three-and-one-half-story structure with a long front veranda. In its final statement, the Seaside, anchored by a 100-foot-tall, octagonal corner tower, was a marvelously coherent, L-shaped Queen Anne edifice, indeed a tribute to Clark and his versatile talents, and one of the best examples of its style in the contemporary hotel architecture of the New England region. Last owned by the Rockefeller family, and one of Mount Desert Island's last early hotel survivors, it was torn down in 1964, leaving an open field where it had stood for so long.[32]

Fig. 8-35. "The Bluffs, Mt. Desert Ferry, Me." Engraving, Philadelphia, c. 1890. Maine Historic Preservation Commission.

The Frenchman's Bay Communities

Opposite Bar Harbor, on the east side of Frenchman's Bay, are several smaller towns, each with their summer colonies and recollections of past resort-hotel entrepreneurship and architecture. At the north end of the bay, at the tip of Hancock Point in the town of Hancock, is Mount Desert Ferry, a community that was once the principal port for steamboat ferry access between the mainland railroad and Bar Harbor. Of its several late nineteenth-century hotels, the Bluffs (fig. 8-35) was the largest and most impressive, occupying a flattering, raised site, along with its several cottages, overlooking the main wharf and the ocean waters. Bangor engineer and contractor Francis H. Clergue, the builder of the Summit House on Green (now Cadillac) Mountain on Mount Desert Island, erected this monumental Queen Anne–style structure around 1885 from designs rendered by a yet unidentified architect. Representing the epitome of its idiom, the Bluffs was a skillfully articulated, shingle-clad composition, possessing a coordinated array of gable and dormer roof shapes, a surrounding stick-construction veranda, balconies, and a unifying end-wall octagonal tower with open observation deck, the tower a common feature of many Maine coastal hotels of that time. In its final years, the hotel suffered declining patronage, in part because of its proximity to the Maine Central Railroad station, and it suspended operations and was taken down in 1915 by new owner Frank Moore of Ellsworth, Maine.[33]

On the next peninsula to the east is Sorrento, which was once the site of the Hotel Sorrento (fig. 8-36), de-

scribed in promotional literature as "charmingly located upon an eminence, its broad piazzas commanding a magnificent view of the surrounding country, with a beautiful bay in front and the broad Atlantic in the distance." The largest of the community's many pre-1900 hotels, it was financed and built circa 1889 by a group of businessmen, organized as the Frenchman's Bay and Mount Desert Land and Water Company, whose principal motivator and funder was the highly successful entrepreneur Frank Jones of Portsmouth, New Hampshire, the owner of the Wentworth Hotel (see chapter 6). Jones became involved as a summer resident of Sorrento, recognized the summer resort potential of the area, and joined the company, ultimately in a controlling role, to realize local hotel as

Fig. 8-36. "Hotel Sorrento," Sorrento, Maine. Engraving from booklet, *A Summer at Sorrento* (Boston: Collins Press, c. 1893), n.p. Maine Historic Preservation Commission.

well as cottage development. As built, the Sorrento was a substantial, functional building with room for nearly 300 overnight guests at its height, including a large adjacent annex and cottage. Among Maine's rich collection of resort hotels, it enjoyed unique architectural status for its quite incredulous verandas and multitiered porches arrayed across the front façade with its two matching, pitched-roof pavilions. Experiencing the fate of so many of its contemporaries, the Sorrento, including the annex, burned on 27 June 1906 and was not replaced.[34]

Farther down Frenchman's Bay toward Schoodic Point is Winter Harbor, the location of one of New England's most creative and carefully planned summer resort developments. Inspired by the earlier, rapid growth of nearby Bar Harbor, a group of investors from cities of the Northeast incorporated as the Gouldsboro Land Improvement Company in 1889 and acquired a beautifully situated five-thousand-acre tract of land on the rocky promontory of Grindstone Neck overlooking the waters of the bay. That summer, the group issued a prospectus that outlined their plans for "a natural park," including roads, walkways, cottages, a clubhouse, and other buildings, all centered on a resort hotel. To implement the total scheme, the company contracted with Nathan Franklin Barrett (1845–1919), a prominent New York City landscape architect, and several building architects,

the primary being Philadelphia's Lindley Johnson (1854–1937) who would execute twenty commissions, most of them cottages, in the early 1890s for the new summer colony. The largest structure that Johnson designed on the Neck was the Grindstone Inn, for which he drew on his extensive background as a planner of several earlier hotels on the Atlantic coast. Raised from 1890 to 1891 by contractor P. H. Stratton of Ellsworth, Maine, the first incarnation of the Grindstone was a modest, two-story, U-shaped, fifty-room establishment at the center of the cottage colony, described in an 1891 company prospectus as "thoroughly modern, well built [partly of granite], completely finished, and peculiarly adapted to afford desirable summer residence to those who wish good hotel accommodations at moderate rates." Though it exhibited some features from current style vocabularies, it was indeed "modern" in appearance, its plain, front façade framed by square, raised sections on each end. The Grindstone remained in this form until about 1899, when the owners, again from Johnson's plans, enlarged the facility (fig. 8-37), adhering to the original design concepts. Additional buildings for a laundry and staff dormitory followed in 1902 and 1903. Fire ended the Grindstone's long period of service in 1956. With the loss of this and other pre–World War II hotels on the east side of Frenchman's Bay, Maine was deprived of all its large, early coastal resort-hotel inventory north of Portland.[35]

Fig. 8-37. Grindstone Inn, Winter Harbor, Maine. Photograph from booklet, *The Grindstone Inn* (c. 1910). Maine Historic Preservation Commission.

New Brunswick Hotels and the Boston Association

For over 150 miles to the northeast, from the Mount Desert Island region to the north end of Passamaquoddy Bay, there was no substantial early resort-hotel development in the United States. Offshore Canadian islands and the nearby St. Andrew's peninsula, all within the province of New Brunswick, were, however, an exception to this pattern, and therefore are deserving of attention in this study. Though not officially part of New England, southwestern coastal New Brunswick summer communities, in addition to their primarily Canadian clientele, did attract many American visitors and possessed several hotels structures financed with Boston capital and designed by Boston architects or architectural partnerships.

Dating from 1881 to 1883 and no longer extant, three modest-size but architecturally noteworthy hotels were

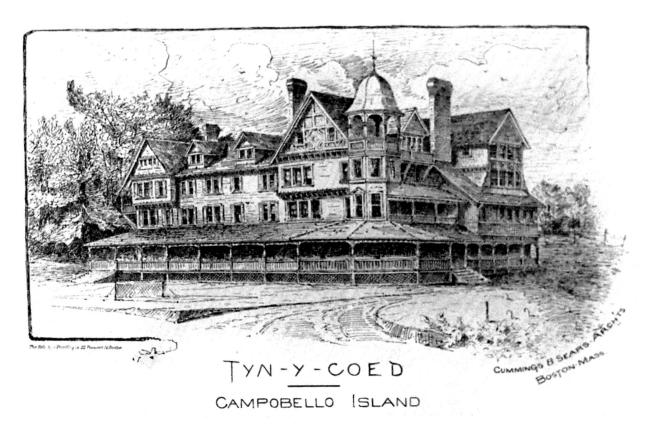

Fig. 8-38. "Tyn-y-Coed, Campobello Island, New Brunswick." Front elevation perspective drawing from booklet, *Campobello Island* (1881). Maine Historic Preservation Commission.

built by the Campobello Company on Campobello Island — the Owen, from plans by William G. Preston (1844–1910); and the Tyn-y-Maes and the adjacent Tyn-y-Coed, from designs by the firm of Charles A. Cummings (1833–1906) and Willard T. Sears (1837–1920). Of these the Queen Anne–style Tyn-y-Coed (fig. 8-38), with its characteristic corner tower, was the largest (approximately 150 capacity) and, arguably, the most sophisticated and successful architectural composition.

The most widely recognized and distinguished of the southwest New Brunswick resort-hotel group was the first wooden version of the Algonquin Hotel erected at St. Andrews from 1888 to 1889 by the St. Andrews Land Company, controlled and financed by American businessmen, largely from Boston. Set on a hill overlooking the town and both sides of the peninsula, this great hostelry, in its initial form (fig. 8-39), was designed by the firm of Rand & Taylor of which Bertrand E. Taylor, known for his hospital and school work, had the highest

professional profile. From many published illustrations, we know that the finished structure was striking, the Shingle-style-inspired front façade dominated by a central observation tower, steep gambrel roofs interrupted by three gables and dormers, and a 340-foot wraparound veranda leading to a "music pagoda" at the southeast corner. In 1894, the ownership added a visually compatible west wing to the building from plans by Henry N. Nourse of Boston. After passing through a period of financial uncertainty, in early 1903 the Algonquin was sold by the Land Company to the Canadian Pacific Railroad, thereby ending the Boston-centered ownership connection. By 1907, the hotel had been further expanded to house over 200 patrons, followed by new concrete wings added from 1909 to 1910 and in 1912, and new entertainment and sporting facilities in 1913, planned and built by Canadian architects and contractors. The Boston architectural connection was severed on 11 April 1914 when the entire older, wooden central portion of the hotel

THE ALGONQUIN HOTEL.

ST ANDREWS
NEW BRUNSWICK.

Rand & Taylor
Architects.
Boston.

Second Floor Plan.

First Floor Plan.

Fig. 8-39. "The Algonquin Hotel, St. Andrews, New Brunswick." Front elevation perspective drawing from *American Architect and Building News* 26 (14 December 1889). Anne and Jerome Fisher Fine Arts Library, University of Pennsylvania Library.

succumbed to fire and was quickly replaced by a new, modern Tudoresque central section in time for a June 1915 reopening. Though further enlarged and modernized since, the Algonquin has retained most of its circa 1915 appearance and continues its active role as one of the preeminent grand resort hotels on the Canadian and American eastern continental seaboard. In its prefire Shingle-style garb, however, it proudly expressed the best qualities of greater New England's accomplishment in coastal resort-hotel architecture.[36]

* * *

The gradual transformation of the hospitality industry, with the associated loss of its early hotel architecture along and adjacent to the northeast coast of Maine, reflects similar patterns of change on the entire New England seaboard. Since the late nineteenth century until the years following World War II, the regional industry underwent a prolonged and agonizing decline, with surviving examples of pre-1950 hotel architecture reduced to fewer than ten buildings or complexes, most of them significantly altered over time. This process of decline, coupled with change, occurred for many of the same reasons that it did at other resort areas of the Northeast over the same time period. Simultaneously, while the industry was experiencing transformation on the New England coast, it was doing the same in New Hampshire's White Mountains, in the Adirondack and Catskill regions of New York, on the New Jersey shoreline, in the Pennsylvania Poconos, and at other, less prominent regional resort centers.

Several complicated, interrelated, and largely economic factors have affected the New England coastal resort-hotel industry, resulting in the near elimination of pre–World War II examples of hotel architecture. Since the industry first took root in the early 1800s, hotel owners and managers have consistently had to deal with the business challenges posed by single-season operation, generally between late May and early October. The extended decline of the hotels, however, was most significantly affected by sweeping changes in transportation systems and related technology. By the turn of the century, the venerable symbiotic relationship between the hotels and the railroads was starting to break down,

and railroad service was substantially reduced over the ensuing decades. The appearance and immediate popularity of the automobile about the same time quickly and adversely affected both the railroad companies and the hotels of all sizes. In that it provided greater flexibility and mobility, the automobile gradually overtook the railroads as the principal means of transportation to, as well as along, the New England shoreline. The growing use of the automobile negatively affected the business enterprise of the hotels, as people on vacation or in the process of point-to-point travel preferred briefer, less expensive, and more flexible leisure-time visits that necessitated different types of accommodation. As tourism patterns underwent dramatic change, road systems were greatly improved by expansion, and by the paving and widening of outmoded gravel routes. The result was that, subject to their individualized travel schedules, the automobile transported people more quickly and directly than the railroads. Commencing in the 1920s, the older, larger hostelries encountered new competition from small hotels and inns, cabins, camping and recreational vehicle sites, and motor courts and motels, all with lower operating costs. Overriding and accentuating these developments were cyclical declines in the national economy, the debilitating effects of the two world wars, and the Depression of the 1930s.

In addition to these factors, constantly evolving American lifestyles and individual preferences have affected the resort hotel industry of the New England seaboard. During the last three decades of the nineteenth century, individuals and families with financial resources, a high percentage of whom were former hotel clients, sought independence and privacy, choosing to travel elsewhere in the United States or abroad, or opting to build their own summer cottages in the region. It is ironical that the hotels, generally to their disadvantage, played such a major role in fostering the cottage movement, familiarizing their guests with the positive characteristics of the New England seascape and summertime living experience. The early transformation of Bar Harbor, Maine (see above), is a near-perfect example of such changing times. Since World War II, the condominium and time-share unit have become major features of this phenomenon, satisfying people's desires to become long-term stakeholders in a specific geographical location and mode of living. Through real estate ownership, family life and a retreat-like existence replaced the public, often competitive society of the hotels, providing a sense of permanency not otherwise available.

Among other factors having negative economic impact was the inauguration in 1913 of the federal income tax, which reduced individual disposable income and resulted in lower numbers of people with the monetary resources and time to engage in leisure pursuits for all or generous portions of summer seasons at resort hotels. Furthermore, as the twentieth century advanced, increasing numbers of individuals, particularly women, committed to full-time careers, thereby reducing the free time available for extended periods away from the workplace, as well as the home. Encouraged initially by the expansion of ocean liner service to foreign countries, and then by the inauguration of transoceanic airplane routes during the 1930s, numerous hotel regulars, led by the most affluent, chose to take trips to Europe or other parts of the world, leaving the hotels to seek new social connections and sources of revenue.

One of the major reasons for the near disappearance of New England's older, large coastal resort hotels may be found in the buildings themselves, their various locations, and the often hard realities of business operation. With the exception of a very small number, virtually all of the hotels were constructed almost entirely of wood, and therefore were highly vulnerable to destruction by fire, the sad fate of so many. In addition, because of their large size and oftentimes inaccessible locations, local firefighting forces frequently did not possess the personnel, equipment, and expertise to combat fire and preserve buildings for future generations. Of those few hotels that escaped the fire threat, most became obsolete and shopworn from excessive use and were torn down. A close examination of the sample group of hotels discussed in this book suggests that many might have survived longer than they did if their financiers and first owners had placed greater priority on quality materials, design, and building practices than on quick profit, characterized by "built-in" obsolescence. Certain hotel facilities became programmatically and physically unsuited to modern uses and, lacking appeal to current and future patrons, were demolished. Along the New England shoreline, there are numerous examples of hotel

structures that were abandoned, left unused for several years, and ultimately deemed out-of-date and functionally inoperable, and razed. The cost of physical plant modernization and replacement proved prohibitively high even for the very few hotel owners who were able to sustain profitable hotel enterprises during the decades following World War II.

During the twentieth century, constantly increasing costs of operation, primarily at the large resort hotels, further depressed the traditional hospitality industry as it sought strategies for long-term survival and financial success. In recent decades, the expenses of labor, maintenance, supplies, heating fuel, and utilities accelerated considerably, necessitating higher occupancy rates and resulting in price increases for lodging, food, and special services. The inevitable outcome has been the passing of operational costs on to the visitor consumers to such an extant that many enterprises literally priced themselves out of existence, leaving the summer vacation option available only to the affluent. Over time, however, even these upper-middle-class and wealthy patrons have been attracted to other forms of leisure, recreation, culture, and pleasure. Despite added revenue provided by conventions, conferences, special events, and tour groups, the potential guest market has been reduced, and competition for customers has been increased. Curiously, in many respects resort hotels have been victims of their past success and the trend toward large-scale operations.

With the near elimination of the pre-1950 large resort-hotel building type along the New England coast, we have been left with memories, images, historical accounts, and an architectural legacy perpetuated by the small number of surviving examples. Fortuitously, several of these still function as hotels, the most prominent being the Wentworth-By-The-Sea at New Castle, New Hampshire; the Spring House and Annex on Block Island, Rhode Island; the Colony Hotel at Kennebunkport, Maine; the Chatham Bars Inn at Chatham, Massachusetts; and, the Harbor View Hotel at Edgartown, Martha's Vineyard, Massachusetts. Other large, extant hotel structures have been modified in appearance and size, and have been converted to other uses. These few survivors, a critical part of New England's architectural heritage, serve as irreplaceable, invaluable documentation of a summer vacation lifestyle and leisure-time philosophy very much altered in modern times. Much of America's past vision of summer by the seaside endures in these and associated forms of rich, creatively articulated architectural expression.

Notes

CHAPTER 1. INTRODUCTION: THE AMERICAN RESORT
HOTEL AND ITS EXPRESSION ON THE
NEW ENGLAND COAST

1. Tolles, *Resort Hotels of the Adirondacks*, p. 1.

2. Limerick et al., *America's Grand Resort Hotels*, p. 12. See also Limerick's essay in Maddox, ed., *Built in U.S.A.*, pp. 144–47, and Limerick, "The Grand Resort Hotels of America."

3. Tolles, *The Grand Resort Hotels of the White Mountains*, p. 14; Tolles, *Resort Hotels of the Adirondacks*, p. 1.

4. Tolles, *Resort Hotels of the Adirondacks*, pp. 1–2.

5. Limerick et al., *America's Grand Resort Hotels*, p. 13.

6. Ibid.

7. Ibid., p. 16.

8. Tolles, *Resort Hotels of the Adirondacks*, p. 4.

9. Maddox, ed., *Built in U.S.A.*, p. 144.

10. Tolles, *The Grand Resort Hotels of the White Mountains*, p. 18.

11. Ibid, p. 19.

12. For valuable recent insights on Saratoga Springs and its hotels, see Sterngass, *First Resorts*, fourth chapter, "The Public Resorts."

13. Maury Klein, "Buy the Bay: Coastal Life in the Gilded Age," from *What a Difference a Bay Makes*, p. 111.

14. Limerick, "The Grand Resort Hotels of America," p. 92; Tolles, *The Grand Resort Hotels of the White Mountains*, p. 21.

15. See Scully, *The Shingle Style and the Stick Style* (1971 ed.).

16. In addition to the previously cited books and essays, the following sources, listed in the bibliography section, are valuable references and were consulted in the preparation of this chapter: Richard Guy Wilson, "Nineteenth Century American Resorts and Hotels," and Marie L. Ahern, "Health Restoring Resorts on the New England Coast," from Wilson, ed., *Victorian Resorts and Hotels*; McGinty, *The Palace Inns*, chapter 1, "America Invents the Hotel"; Newton, "Our Summer Resort Architecture—An American Phenomenon and Social Document," *Art Quarterly* 4, no. 4 (Autumn 1941); Aron, *Working at Play: A History of Vacations in the United States*; Lencek and Bosker, *The Beach: The History of Paradise on Earth*; and Shaffer, *See America First: Tourism and National Identity, 1880–1940*.

CHAPTER 2. CONNECTICUT: THE LONG ISLAND SOUND
SHORELINE

1. McQuill [Bruce], *The White and Green Mountains and Routes Thereto* (1872 ed.), p. 46; *Appletons' Illustrated Hand-Book of American Summer Resorts* (1876 ed.), p. 87.

2. *American Seaside Resorts* (1882 ed.), p. 71.

3. Ibid.

4. Atwan, ed., *Greenwich, An Illustrated History*, p. 101; Clark, *Greenwich*, pp. 61–65; *Appletons' Illustrated Hand-Book of American Summer Resorts* (1884 ed.), p. 89.

5. *Greenwich Times*, 18 October 1980, p. 3; Richardson, ed., *Greenwich Before 2000*, pp. 60, 66, 78; unidentified newspaper source, n.d., Greenwich (Conn.) Public Library; Hubbard, *Greenwich History*, pp. 199–200; *Homes on the Sound* (1875 ed.), p. 81; *American Seaside Resorts* (1882 ed.), p. 72. Composed of both Republicans and Democrats, the club was social as well as political, with the Democrats in the majority. Tweed and his colleagues came to Greenwich in the early 1860s, initially camping out in tents on Round Island until the club grew large enough to erect the complex on land leased from brothers Augustus I. and Nelson B. Mead.

6. *Pleasant Days in Pleasant Places*, pp. 47–48.

7. Galvin, "Riches to Rubble," *The Greenwich Review* (April 1986): 29; "The Edgewood Park Inn," *Greenwich Graphic* 20, no. 40 (n.d., 1901): 1; Clark, *Greenwich*, pp. 61–63; promotional booklet, *Edgewood Inn, Greenwich, Connecticut* (c. 1910); Richardson, ed., *Greenwich Before 2000*, p. 130; advertisement, *Red Book Interstate Automobile Guide . . . New England* (1909 ed.), p. 742.

8. Promotional booklet, *Edgewood Inn, Greenwich, Connecticut* (c. 1910), n.p.; Galvin, "Riches to Rubble, *The Greenwich Review* (April 1986); "The Edgewood Park Inn," *Greenwich Graphic* 20, no. 40 (n.d., 1901): 1.

9. Promotional booklet, *Edgewood Inn, Greenwich, Connecticut* (c. 1910), n.p.

10. Justinius, *History of Black Rock*, pp. 27–32, 36–42, 123; Jones et al., ed., *Black Rock: A Bicentennial Picture Book*, pp. 26–28; Witkowski and Williams, *Bridgeport on the Sound*, p. 96; *Bridgeport Standard*, 3 July 1876; *Bridgeport Post*, 7 January 1896; *Bridgeport Sun Post*, 25 June 1967; *Bridgeport News*, 15 December 1994, p. 8.

11. *American Seaside Resorts* (1882 ed.), p. 76; *Appletons' Illustrated Hand-Book of American Summer Resorts* (1876 ed.), p. 89; Dorman, *Savin Rock: An Illustrated History*, pp. 13–15; William K. Barr, "Savin Rock House of the 1870s," *West Haven Voice*, 9 April 1998, p. 13; Johnson, comp., *Savin Rock Remembered—1985*, n.p.; "Historic West Haven," *West Haven Town Crier*, 4 August 1960; *New Haven Register*, 25 May 1952. The Savin Rock House was initially run by A. A. Upson and S. R. Hotchkiss. Beginning in 1867, it was serviced by horse-drawn railroad cars.

12. McQuill [Bruce], *The White and Green Mountains and Routes Thereto* (1872 ed.), pp. 48–49, and (1873 ed.), n.p.; *The West Haven News*, 19 September 1991; Dorman, *Savin Rock: An Illustrated History*, pp. 26–28; Johnson, comp., *Savin Rock Remembered—1985*, n.p.

13. Hanna, *A Brief History of the Thimble Islands*, pp. 24–33, 36–37; *American Seaside Resorts* (1882 ed.), p. 77; *Appletons' Illustrated Hand-Book of American Summer Resorts* (1876 ed.), p. 89; John J. Kirby, Jr., "Hotels of the Branford Shore," 1994 calendar, New Haven (Conn.) Colony Historical Society; *Public Ledger Resort Directory* (1910), p. 82.

14. *Appletons' Illustrated Hand-Book of American Summer Resorts* (1884 ed.), p. 91; Hanna, *A Brief History of the Thimble Islands*, p. 31; promotional booklet, *The Montowese, Indian Neck, Branford, Connecticut* (c. 1905), n.p.; Tolles, *The Grand Resort Hotels of the White Mountains*, pp. 203, 207; *New Haven Register*, 23 July 1950, 6 January 1965, and 24 January 1965; *Branford Review*, 7 January 1965, 14 January 1965, 28 January 1965, 11 February 1965, 18 February 1965, 1 November 2000; *Branford Opinion*, supplement, 8 July 1899. The land on which the Montowese House stood was owned by the First Ecclesiastical Society and the Beach family, and was leased to the Bryan/Noble ownership group for ninety-nine years. Among notable guests over the years was Samuel Clemens (Mark Twain) from Hartford. The 1938 hurricane did little damage to the hotel complex but leveled over three hundred trees adorning the grounds, most of which were never replaced.

Built in 1871 from plans by New Haven architect Henry Austin, the Trowbridge cottage, also on Linden Street, served as an annex to the hotel in the twentieth century and survives today as an excellent example of wooden, Victorian, Stick-style residential design.

15. *Appletons' Illustrated Hand-Book of American Summer Resorts* (1884 ed.), p. 91.

16. *American Seaside Resorts* (1882 ed.), pp. 77–78; McQuill [Bruce], *The White and Green Mountains and Routes Thereto* (1873 ed.), n.p.; *Shore Line Times*, 4 July 1907, 6 March 1924, and 13 August 1959; broadside, "Sachem's Head Hotel, Guilford, Conn.," H. Lee Scranton, 1862, Connecticut Historical Society; Norton, *History of Sachem's Head*, pp. 24–25; Stevens, *History of Sachem's Head*, pp. 7–9; Helander, *Oxpasture to Summer Colony: The Story of Sachem's Head*, pp. 218–31; "Guilford Notes—The Sachems' Head Hotels," unpublished typescript, n.d., Guilford (Conn.) Free Library. In 1878, over ten years after the fire, John W. Barker erected the second Sachem's Head Hotel, first known as the New Barker Hotel, just to the east of the original hotel site. Modest in size (50+ capacity), this building and adjacent cottages never achieved financial success, closing in 1956. The hotel was gutted by fire in 1973 and not rebuilt.

17. *American Seaside Resorts* (1882 ed.), pp. 79–80; McQuill [Bruce], *The White and Green Mountains and Routes Thereto* (1872 ed.), pp. 50–53; *Appletons' Illustrated Hand-Book of American Summer Resorts* (1876 ed.), p. 89; *Red Book Interstate Automobile Guide . . . New England* (1909 ed.), ad, p. 456; Fenwick Historic District (Old Saybrook, Middlesex County, Conn.), National Register of Historic Places Registration Form (1994), p. 8-1; *History of Middlesex County, Connecticut* (1884), pp. 466–67; [Brainard], *Fenwick*, pp. 7–18, 26–30; Withey and Withey, *Biographical Dictionary of American Architects (Deceased)*, p. 372; Grant, *The Fenwick Story*, pp. 15–16, 18–22, 24–25; Kathleen Edgecomb, "Inside Fenwick," *The Day* (New London, Conn.), pp. D-1 and D-2. The construction of Fenwick Hall was completed under the supervision of Hartford native A. M. Hurlbut, at the time the president of the New Saybrook Company.

18. *History of Middlesex County, Connecticut* (1884), p. 466.

19. *American Seaside Resorts* (1882 ed.), Fenwick Hall advertisement; *Public Ledger Resort Directory* (1910), p. 83; [Brainard], *Fenwick*, p. 12.

20. *American Seaside Resorts* (1882 ed.), pp. 81–83; *Appletons' Hand-Book of American Summer Resorts* (1876 ed.), pp. 89–90; *Pleasant Days in Pleasant Places*, p. 25; Ruddy, *New London*, p. 70; Churchill, "The Pequot Colony," *Tidings* (September/October 1987): 14–21; Starr, *A Centennial History of the Town of New London*, pp. 88–89; New London Pequot Colony Survey, 1983–84 (New London Landmarks—Union Railroad Station Trust); Deborah Donavan, "The Gayest Watering Place, New London's Pequot Colony, 1852–1908" (Undergraduate history seminar paper, Trinity College, Hartford, Conn., 2002);

broadside, "Pequot House" (New London, 1 May 1855), Connecticut Historical Society, Hartford. Representing a variety of late nineteenth-century architectural styles, many of the original Pequot House cottages have survived and continue to form a cohesive group at the former hotel site.

21. *American Seaside Resorts* (1882 ed.), p. 83.

22. McQuill [Bruce], *The White and Green Mountains and Routes Thereto* (1872 ed.), p. 52.

23. *American Seaside Resorts* (1882 ed.), p. 83; McQuill [Bruce], *The White and Green Mountains and Routes Thereto* (1872 ed.), p. 52; *Groton (Conn.) News*, 17 December 1970; Gibbs, *The City of Groton*, p. 40; *Pleasant Days in Pleasant Places*, p. 23; Kimball et al., *Groton*, p. 47; promotional booklet, *Fort Griswold House (Eastern Point), New London, Conn.* (1888); *The Day* (New London, Conn.), 9 January 1986, p. D3; *Mystic (Conn.) Journal*, 20 April and 28 September 1871. The Ocean House was run for several years by Captain Silas Fiske and his widow after his death. Mrs. Fiske's brother, Roswell S. Edgecomb, then acquired the Ocean House property and for a brief period ran it in conjunction with the Edgecomb House.

24. Gibbs, *The City of Groton*, p. 40; *Pleasant Days in Pleasant Places*, p. 23; promotional booklet, *Fort Griswold House (Eastern Point), New London, Conn.* (1888). The new name of the hotel originated with Fort Griswold, a colonial-era fortification on a nearby hill in Groton that was the scene of a massacre in 1781 when British forces led by Benedict Arnold took the fort and burned New London and Groton.

25. *The Day*, 28 June 1906; Kimball et al., *Groton*, p. 47; Tolles, *The Grand Resort Hotels of the White Mountains*, pp. 215–21; Carol W. Kimball, "Millionaire Morton Plant . . . ," *The Day*, n.d., New London (Conn.) Landmarks. At first, Plant proposed to name the new hotel the "Shennecosset Inn" after a new golf course nearby. He then opted for a variation of the old title, hoping to attract former patrons.

26. Withey and Withey, *Biographical Dictionary of American Architects (Deceased)*, p. 232; "The Griswold — A Study in Summer Hotel Building," *The Architectural Record* 19, no. 5 (June 1906): 344–47; *National Cyclopedia of American Biography*, vol. 11, p. 324.

27. "The Griswold — A Study in Summer Resort Hotel Building," *The Architectural Record* 19, no. 5 (June 1906): 344–60; booklet, *The Griswold, New London, Conn.* (New York: F. W. Robinson, [c. 1909]); advertisement, *The Automobile Official AAA 1908 Blue Book*, vol. 2, p. 236; *The New London Evening Day*, 19 April 1945. For easier location, much of the literature treating the Griswold Hotel placed it in New London, rather than Groton, Connecticut.

28. "The Griswold — A Study in Summer Resort Hotel Building," *The Architectural Record* 19, no. 5 (June 1906): 352–60.

29. Kimball, et al., *Groton*, p. 47; Carol W. Kimball, "Millionaire Morton F. Plant . . . ," *The Day*, n.d., New London (Conn.) Landmarks; *The New London Evening Day*, 19 April 1945; *The Day*, 8 March 1969; Towne, "Good Bye to the Grand Old Griswold Hotel," *Yankee* 33, no. 4 (April 1969): 66–73, 136–37; "Last Hurrah for The Griswold," *The Day*, 14 August 1997, p. B7.

30. Ferguson, *Fishers Island, N.Y., 1614–1925*, pp. 70–73; Baedeker, ed., *The United States* (1909 ed.), p. 242; *American Seaside Resorts* (1882 ed.), pp. 84–85; *New England: A Handbook for Travellers* (1885 ed.), p. 71; *The Narragansett Blue Book* (1900), p. 92; exhibition labels, Henry L. Ferguson Museum, Fishers Island, N.Y.; *New York Times*, 2 July 1911, p. 7.

31. Exhibition labels and illustration scans, Henry L. Ferguson Museum, Fishers Island, N.Y.; *New York Times*, 26 May 1895; booklet, *The Munnatawket Hotel, Mansion House and Cottages, Fisher's Island, N.Y.* (c. 1895). The Winthrop family members were the sole owners of Fishers Island until it was acquired by Robert R. Fox in 1863. After his death, it was owned by his relatives until purchased by the Fergusons in 1889.

32. Exhibition labels and illustration scans, Henry L. Ferguson Museum, Fishers Island, N.Y.; *New York Times*, 26 May 1895; booklet, *Fisher's Island, the Mansion House and Cottages* (c. 1910); booklet, *The Mansion House and Cottages at Fishers Island* (c. 1920); booklet, *Fishers Island — Mansion House and Cottages* (c. 1933); booklet, *Mansion House and Cottages, Fishers Island, New York* (c. 1935); *New York Times*, 14 July 1918, p. 45.

33. Exhibition labels and illustration scans, Henry L. Ferguson Museum, Fishers Island, N.Y.; *The Narragansett Blue Book* (1900), p. 92; e-mail, 7 February 1906, from Pierce Rafferty, director, Henry L. Ferguson Museum, Fishers Island, N.Y.

CHAPTER 3. RHODE ISLAND: NARRAGANSETT BAY, WATCH HILL, AND BLOCK ISLAND

1. Jordy, *Buildings of Rhode Island*, p. 4.

2. Ibid., pp. xxiv, 3–4; *Tour Book — Connecticut, Massachusetts and Rhode Island* (Heathrow, Fla.: AAA Publishing, 2002), pp. 196–98.

3. Sterngass, *First Resorts*, pp. 40–46; Grosvener, *Newport*, pp. 62–64; Williamson, *The American Hotel*, pp. 237–38; Panaggio, *Portrait of Newport*, p. 90; Robinson, *Coastal New England*, pp. 168, 170–72; McQuill [Bruce], *The White and Green Mountains and Routes Thereto* (1872 ed.), pp. 54–55;

Turner, "Newport, 1800–1850," *Newport Daily News*, 24 and 25 March 1897, p. 9; McQuill [Bruce], *From New York to the Summer Resorts of New England* (1880), pp. 10–11; *Stork's 1700 Mile Summer Tours* (1879), pp. 9–12; Sweetser, *Book of Summer Resorts* (1868), pp. 12–14; *Springs, Water-Falls, Sea-Bathing Resorts, and Mountain Scenery* (1855), pp. 58–59; Bachelder, *Popular Resorts and How to Reach Them* (1875 ed.), p. 104.

4. Downing and Scully, *The Architectural Heritage of Newport, Rhode Island*, pp. 120–21, 131–32; Sterngass, *First Resorts*, pp. 46–47; Hunter, "A Decade of Newport," *Bulletin of the Newport Historical Society* 53 (April 1925): 20; "The Grist Mill," *Newport Daily News*, 27 October 1942; *Newport Mercury*, 12 October and 14 June, 1884.

5. Downing and Scully, *The Architectural Heritage of Newport, Rhode Island*, pp. 120–21, 131; Sterngass, *First Resorts*, pp. 46, 183–84; *Newport Mercury*, 12 October 1884. From 1861 to 1865, after the bombardment of Fort Sumter, the national government relocated the United States Naval Academy from its vulnerable site in Annapolis, Maryland, to Newport, where it was based at the hotel.

Another outstanding though lower-capacity hotel in the Greek Revival style was the Stone Bridge House (1848; burned 1865) at Tiverton on the Sekonnet River on Rhode Island's east coast.

6. Downing and Scully, *The Architectural Heritage of Newport, Rhode Island*, pp. 131–32; Sterngass, *First Resorts*, pp. 46, 48–49; Turner, "Newport, 1800–1850," *Newport Daily News*, 24 and 25 March 1897, p. 9; Withey and Withey, *Biographical Dictionary of American Architects (Deceased)*, pp. 635–36; *New England: A Handbook for Travellers* (1885 ed.), p. 40; McQuill [Bruce], *From New York to the Summer Resorts of New England* (1880), p. 12; *Newport Mercury*, 27 May 1848 and 15 April 1873; *Appletons' General Guide to the United States and Canada* (1886 ed.), p. 82.

7. *American Seaside Resorts* (1882 ed.), Newport section; Downing and Scully, *The Architectural Heritage of Newport, Rhode Island*, pp. 131–32; Sterngass, *First Resorts*, p. 46.

8. Sterngass, *First Resorts*, p. 219; "The Grist Mill," *Newport Daily News*, 27 October 1942; Moulton, comp., *Newport and the Resorts of Narragansett Bay*, pp. 54–55.

9. Baedeker, ed., *The United States* (1904 ed.), p. 89. Subsequently, there was no large hotel in Newport until the opening of the Viking Hotel on Bellevue Avenue in 1926. An impressive, brick, Georgian Revival structure, the Viking accommodates well over 300 guests. In the strictest terms, however, it does not meet the definition of a large summer coastal resort hotel developed for this book; hence, it is not discussed in detail or illustrated. Other hotels in Newport's history—Bate-

man House, Fillmore House, Seaview House, Perry House, Hotel Aquidneck, United States Hotel, Cliff House—are not included for the same reason.

A large courtyard hotel project was planned for Newport by James Gordon Bennett, the developer of the Newport Casino (1879–81). Architect Whitney Warren (1864–1943) prepared plans for Bennett in 1893, but the project was never realized (Jordy and Monkhouse, *Buildings on Paper*, pp. 199–200).

10. Sterngass, *First Resorts*, pp. 214–15; Grieve, *Picturesque Narragansett* (2nd ed., c. 1889), p. 122.

11. D'Amato, *Warwick: A City at the Crossroads*, pp. 88–89; Grieve, *Picturesque Narragansett* (2nd ed., c. 1889), p. 128; Belcher, "Old Rocky Point," *Rhode Island History* 7, no. 1 (January 1948): 34–35; *Warwick, Rhode Island: Statewide Historical Preservation Report K-W-1* (1981); *American Seaside Resorts* (1882 ed.), p. 60; Sweetser, *Book of Summer Resorts* (1868), p. 15; *New England: A Handbook for Travellers* (1885 ed.), p. 65a; J. R. Cole, *History of Washington and Kent Counties, Rhode Island: A Guide to Narragansett Bay* (1889), p. 40; Wyatt, *Rocky Point*, pp. 37–38; Moulton, comp., *Newport and the Resorts of Narragansett Bay*, pp. 73–74.

12. D'Amato, *Warwick: A City at the Crossroads*, pp. 90, 106; booklet, *Oakland Beach Hotel on Beautiful Narragansett Bay* (1902); Munro, *Picturesque Rhode Island*, advertisement; *New England: A Handbook for Travellers* (1885 ed.), p. 67; Grieve, *Picturesque Narragansett* (2nd ed., c. 1889), pp. 125–26; booklet, *Oakland Beach Hotel* (c. 1900). Other communities on upper Narragansett Bay featured hotels, well publicized and often visited, but not of sufficient size to fit the definition of a "large" resort hotel developed for this book. These include, among other examples, the Cold Spring House at Wickford, the Riverside Hotel at East Providence, and the DeWolfe Inn at Bristol.

13. Jordy, *Buildings of Rhode Island*, pp. 581–82. Conanicut Island, after adjacent Aquidneck Island, is the second-largest island in Narragansett Bay, nine miles long and one to two miles in width.

14. Grieve, *Picturesque Narragansett* (2nd ed., c. 1889), pp. 136–38; *The Narragansett Blue Book* (1900), pp. 55, 92; *The Book of Rhode Island* (1930), pp. 106–107; brochure, *Jamestown, Conanicut Island, R.I.* (New York, New Haven & Hartford Railroad, 1903); Maden, *Greetings from Jamestown, Rhode Island*, p. 21; Jordy, *Buildings of Rhode Island*, pp. 581–83; Haun, "Jamestown, R.I., 1657–1961," *Yankee* 25, No. 5 (May 1961): 61–67.

15. Maden, *Greetings from Jamestown, Rhode Island*, pp. 22–23; Scully, *The Shingle Style and the Stick Style* (1st ed., 1955), p. 121; *Historic and Architectural Resources of Jamestown, Rhode*

Island, p. 43; Buttrick, *Jamestown*, pp. 34–35; *Newport and its Points of Interest*, p. 84; *Newport Daily News*, 28 July 1969. The tower section of the Bay View House was erected on the site of the Ellery Ferry house, which was moved to another location where it was used as an employee dormitory. In addition to the main hotel, there were four secondary buildings with accommodations for upward of 200 more guests.

16. Maden, *Greetings from Jamestown, Rhode Island*, p. 22; *Historic and Architectural Resources of Jamestown, Rhode Island*, pp. 42–43; *Providence Journal*, 10 July 1988, pp. G-1, G-2.

17. *Historic and Architectural Resources of Jamestown, Rhode Island*, p. 42; *Newport and its Points of Interest*, p. 86; Buttrick, *Jamestown*, pp. 30–31; Maden, *Greetings from Jamestown, Rhode Island*, p. 25; *The Narragansett Blue Book* (1900), p. 92.

18. Maden and Hodgkin, *Jamestown Affairs*, pp. 21–22; *Historic and Architectural Resources of Jamestown, Rhode Island*, pp. 42–44; Maden, *Greetings from Jamestown, Rhode Island*, pp. 27–32; *Newport and its Points of Interest*, p. 88; Buttrick, *Jamestown*, pp. 32–33, 36; Jordy, *Buildings of Rhode Island*, p. 583; Scully, *The Shingle Style* (1955 ed.), p. 112; *Newport Journal*, 9 August 1890; *The Standard Times* (North Kingston, R.I.), 19 January 1984. South of the hotel, Horgan had three similar "housekeeping" cottages erected in 1897 and titled them "Betty," "Nina" and "Myra" after his three daughters, or as a group, "The Three Sisters." They remain today.

The only early, wood-frame hotel of any consequence remaining in Jamestown (Conanicus Avenue and Bay View Drive) is the Bay Voyage, which originated in 1889 when a country house designed by Philadelphia architect George C. Mason, Jr. (1849–1924) was moved by barge across the bay from Middletown and converted to new uses. Enlarged in 1890 by the addition of a mansard-roofed ell to the north, the Bay Voyage at its peak had room for 75 boarders. It was converted to a combined inn and time-share facility in 1987.

19. Grieve, *The New England Coast* (1892 ed.), pp. 37–38; Jordy, *Buildings of Rhode Island*, pp. 36–37; *Historic and Architectural Resources of Narragansett, Rhode Island*, pp. 12–13; *What a Difference a Bay Makes*, pp. 111–12; *The Fall River and Newport Routes* (1884), p. 36; *Morris' Tourist Hand Book* (c. 1891), pp. 161–62; *American Seaside Resorts* (1882 ed.), pp. 65–66; *The Woods, Lakes, Sea-Shore, and Mountains*, pp. 88–89; Carroll, *Rhode Island*, vol. 2, p. 1173; Sweetser, *Book of Summer Resorts* (1868), p. 30; Moulton, comp., *Newport, and the Resorts of Narragansett Bay*, pp. 68–69.

20. *Morris' Tourist Hand Book* (c. 1891), p. 162; *Appletons' Illustrated Hand-Book of American Summer Resorts* (1884 ed.), p. 26; Watson, *Narragansett Pier as a Fashionable Watering Place and Summer Residence*, pp. 8–9, 68–71, 77; Latimer, *Narragansett-By-The-Sea*, pp. 35–54; Munro, *Picturesque Rhode Island*, p. 290; *A Guide to Narragansett Bay* (1878), pp. 48–49; Crandall, *A Sketch of Narragansett Pier*, pp. 7–8, 16–27; *The Narragansett Blue Book* (1900), p. 93; Cole, *History of Washington and Kent Counties, Rhode Island*, pp. 560–67; Grieve, *Picturesque Narragansett* (2nd ed., c. 1889), pp. 190–200; *A Sketch of Narragansett Pier* (1888); booklet, *Tower Hill Hotel and Cottages* (1887).

21. *Historic and Architectural Resources of Narragansett, Rhode Island*, pp. 12–13; Jordy, *Buildings of Rhode Island*, p. 367.

22. Grieve, *Picturesque Narragansett* (2nd ed., c. 1889), pp. 192, 197–98; *Narragansett Pier, R.I., Illustrated* (1891), n.p.; Cole, *History of Washington and Kent Counties, Rhode Island*, p. 566; Grieve, *The New England Coast* (1892 ed.), p. 39; Crandall, *A Sketch of Narragansett Pier*, p. 24; Latimer, *Narragansett-By-The-Sea*, p. 51; Jordy, *Buildings of Rhode Island*, p. 371; *Narragansett Daily Times* (R.I.), 14 September 1900.

23. Crandall, *A Sketch of Narragansett Pier*, p. 19; Cole, *History of Washington and Kent Counties, Rhode Island*, p. 566; *DeLuxe Hotels of New England* (1914), n.p.; Latimer, *Narragansett-By-The-Sea*, p. 50; *The Automobile Official 1908 Blue Book*, p. 276; *Narragansett Pier, R.I., Illustrated* (1891), n.p.

24. *American Architect and Building News* 59 (26 February 1898): 71; Jordy and Monkhouse, *Buildings on Paper*, pp. 62–63; *The Woods, Lakes, Sea-Shore, and Mountains*, pp. 90, 116; Cole, *History of Washington and Kent Counties, Rhode Island*, p. 567; *Narragansett Pier, R.I., Illustrated* (1891), n.p.; booklet, *The New Mathewson, Narragansett Pier, R.I.* (1899); booklet, *The Mathewson, Narragansett Pier, R.I.* (1903); Crandall, *A Sketch of Narragansett Pier*, p. 26; Latimer, *Narragansett-By-The-Sea*, p. 46; Withey and Withey, *Biographical Dictionary of American Architects (Deceased)*, pp. 486–87; *Providence Journal of Commerce* 4 (May 1896): 11–12.

25. Jordy and Monkhouse, *Buildings on Paper*, p. 63; Latimer, *Narragansett-By-The-Sea*, p. 54; *Providence Journal*, 7 September 1923.

26. Watch Hill Historic District, National Register of Historic Places Inventory — Nomination Form, 1981; Lang, "The Development of a Summer Resort: Watch Hill, Rhode Island," pp. 11–19; *Watch Hill, Rhode Island, and Its Attractions as a Summer Resort* (1887 ed.), pp. 11–13; *History of the State of Rhode Island* (1878), p. 337; Grieve, *Picturesque Narragansett* (2nd ed., c. 1889), pp. 185–87; Jordy, *Buildings of Rhode Island*, pp. 405–6; *A Guide to Narragansett Bay* (1878), pp. 52–53; Grieve, *The New England Coast* (1892 ed.), pp. 34–36; *New England: A Handbook for Travellers* (1885 ed.), p. 70; *Appletons' Illustrated Hand-Book of American Summer Resorts* (1876 ed.), p. 91.

27. Lang, "The Development of a Summer Resort: Watch Hill, Rhode Island," pp. 20–21; booklet, *Plimpton House, Watch Hill, R.I.* (c. 1900); Grieve, *Picturesque Narragansett* (2nd ed., c. 1889), p. 187.

28. "Reborn," *The Day* (New London, Conn.), 27 November 2005, pp. G-1, G-4; "Bidding on History," *The Day*, 27 November 2005, pp. C-1, C-2; "An Auction of Historic Proportion," *The Day*, 28 November 2005, pp. D-1, D-9; "New Ocean House being designed to blend in," *The Day*, 12 May 2006, pp. B-1, B-2; "Trying To Maintain 'A Sense Of Place,'" *The Day*, 5 December 2006, pp. A-1, A-3.

29. *History of the State of Rhode Island* (1878), p. 337; Jordy, *Buildings of Rhode Island*, pp. 407–8; State of Rhode Island and Providence Plantations Preliminary Survey Report, Town of Westerly, p. 33; Lang, "The Development of a Summer Resort: Watch Hill, Rhode Island," pp. 25–26; Watch Hill Historic District, National Register of Historic Places Inventory—Nomination Form, 1981, continuation sheet 14; Smith, *Watch Hill: By River and By Sea*, pp. 74–75; *New York Times*, 13 June 1982.

30. Grieve, *Picturesque Narragansett* (2nd ed., c. 1889), p. 186; viewbook, *Westerly, Rhode Island* (c. 1900); *A Guide to Narragansett Bay* (1878), p. 53; Utter, *Old Pictures of Westerly, Rhode Island*, pp. 50–51; *History of the State of Rhode Island* (1878), p. 337; Smith, *Watch Hill: By River and By Sea*, pp. 31, 69–70, 73; booklet, *The Larkin House, Watch Hill, R.I.* (1887), pp. 5–8; booklet, *The Larkin House, Watch Hill, R.I.* (c. 1888); Lang, "The Development of a Summer Resort: Watch Hill, R.I.," pp. 22–24; Munro, *Picturesque Rhode Island* (1881), advertisement, p. 81.

31. *History of the State of Rhode Island* (1878), p. 337; Grieve, *Picturesque Narragansett* (2nd ed., c. 1889), p. 188; Peck, *Early Land Holders of Watch Hill*, p. 25; *Hotels of New England* (1915), p. 33; booklet, *Watch Hill House, Watch Hill, R.I.* (c. 1890); booklet, *Watch Hill House* (1898); Smith, *Watch Hill: By River and By Sea*, pp. 66, 68. Although neither satisfies the guidelines for inclusion in this study, the two versions of the well-known Weekapaug Inn at Weekapaug, R.I., about eight miles east of Watch Hill, are deserving of mention. The first part of the older, Shingle-style structure was erected from 1898 to 1899, was twice enlarged from 1904 to 1905 and 1937 to 1938, and was destroyed by the great hurricane of September 1938. The second, designed in the modernistic Colonial Revival vein by architect Ralph Harrington Doane (1886–1941) of Boston in 1938, is still in use, set back from the beach across Quonochontaug Pond. The first housed up to 120 persons, and the second can accommodate roughly 100. The current hotel is listed on the National Register of Historic Places (see Buffum, *The Weekapaug Inn*, 1999).

32. Grieve, *Picturesque Narragansett* (2nd ed., c. 1889), pp. 201–4; Jordy, *Buildings of Rhode Island*, pp. 604–5; Old Harbor District, National Register of Historic Places Inventory—Nomination Form, 1974; Rhode Island Historic Preservation Commission, *Historic and Architectural Resources of Block Island, Rhode Island* (1991), pp. 6–11; *New England: A Handbook for Travellers* (1885 ed.), pp. 65b–66; *American Seaside Resorts* (1882 ed.), p. 69; Grieve, *The New England Coast* (1892 ed.), pp. 41–43; Moulton, comp., *Newport, and the Resorts of Narragansett Bay*, pp. 61–64; Tallman, *Pleasant Places in Rhode Island* (1893 ed.), p. 35.

33. Pettee, *Block Island, R.I.*, pp. 47–48; Jordy, *Buildings of Rhode Island*, pp. 609–10; D'Amato and Brown, *Block Island*, pp. 101–2; *Historic and Architectural Resources of Block Island, Rhode Island* (1991), pp. 29–30; Old Harbor District, National Register of Historic Places Inventory—Nomination Form, 1974; brochure, *Spring House, Block Island, R.I.* (1881); Livermore, *History of Block Island*, p. 211.

34. *Pleasant Days in Pleasant Places*, pp. 39–40; Old Harbor District, National Register of Historic Places Inventory—Nomination Form, 1971; Wilson, ed., *Victorian Resorts and Hotels*, p. 45; Pettee, *Block Island, R.I.*, pp. 43–47; Grieve, *The New England Coast* (1892 ed.), pp. 43–44; Livermore, *History of Block Island*, pp. 211–12; [Chase], *Newport, Block Island and Narragansett Pier*, p. 205; *History of the State of Rhode Island* (1878), p. 191; Downie, *Block Island—The Land*, pp. 21–27; booklet, *A Summer at Sea: Ocean View Hotel, The Bermuda of the North. Block Island, Rhode Island* [1899]; booklet, *Ocean View Hotel, Block Island, R.I.* (1882); *Providence Evening Bulletin*, 9 June 1874.

35. *Block Island: Hotels, Residences and Places of Interest* (1900); booklet, *Hygeia Hotel, Block Island, R.I.* (c. 1887); booklet, *Hygeia Hotel, Block Island, R.I.* (c. 1890); Wilson, ed., *Victorian Resorts and Hotels*, pp. 45–47; Downie, *Block Island—The Land*, p. 157.

36. *Historic and Architectural Resources of Block Island, Rhode Island* (1991), pp. 12–13; Jordy, *Buildings of Rhode Island*, p. 605.

CHAPTER 4. MASSACHUSETTS: THE SOUTH SHORE, CAPE COD, AND THE ISLANDS

1. *American Seaside Resorts* (1882 ed.), p. 46; Bachelder, *Popular Resorts, Routes to Reach Them* (1873), p. 62; Bachelder, *Popular Resorts and How to Reach Them* (1876 ed.), p. 99; *Tourists' Guide to Down the Harbor* (1890), pp. 14–17; Hurd, *History of Plymouth County, Massachusetts*, pp. 1189–90; *The Old Colony* (1889), pp. 22–23.

2. Committee for the Preservation of Hull's History, *Hull and Nantasket Beach* (1999), p. 29; Sweetser, *King's Handbook of Boston Harbor*, pp. 31–32.

3. Sweetser, *King's Handbook of Boston Harbor*, pp. 56–58; Arthur Hurley, "The Hotel Era," essay, Hull Public Library, Mass.; Committee for the Preservation of Hull's History, *Hull and Nantasket Beach* (1999), p. 30; Sproul, *Tourists' Guide to Nantasket Beach*, p. 19; Committee for the Preservation of Hull's History, *Then & Now: Hull and Nantasket Beach*, p. 25; Bergan, *Old Nantasket*, pp. 18–20, 22, 25. Just east of the Rockland House was the popular Villa Napoli, built as a private residence before 1890, converted to a hotel, and destroyed by a series of fires in the early 1930s.

4. Committee for the Preservation of Hull's History, *Hull and Nantasket Beach* (1999), p. 33; Sweetser, *King's Handbook of Boston Harbor*, pp. 56–60; Committee for the Preservation of Hull's History, *Then & Now: Hull and Nantasket Beach*, pp. 30–31; Committee for the Preservation of Hull's History, *Hull and Nantasket Beach* (2006), p. 17; "Hotel Nantasket, Nantasket Beach," *American Architect and Building News* 6, no. 196 (27 September 1879); Sproul, *Tourists' Guide to Nantasket Beach*, pp. 18–19; brochure, *Nantasket Hotel, Nantasket Beach, Massachusetts* (c. 1925).

5. Sweetser, *King's Handbook of Boston Harbor*, pp. 30, 30A; Withey and Withey, *Biographical Dictionary of American Architects (Deceased)*, pp. 572–73; *Hingham Journal and South Shore Advertiser*, 8 July 1881; Committee for the Preservation of Hull's History, *Hull and Nantasket Beach* (1999), pp. 27–28; Committee for the Preservation of Hull's History, *Hull and Nantasket Beach* (2006), p. 19; Committee for the Preservation of Hull's History, *Then & Now: Hull and Nantasket Beach*, p. 25; Thompson, ed., *Maine Forms of American Architecture*, pp. 187–88.

6. Sweetser, *King's Handbook of Boston Harbor*, pp. 60–61; Sproul, *Tourists' Guide to Nantasket Beach*, p. 19; Committee for the Preservation of Hull's History, *Hull and Nantasket Beach* (1999), p. 31; Committee for the Preservation of Hull's History, *Hull and Nantasket Beach* (2006), p. 21; Arthur Hurley, "The Hotel Era," essay, Hull Public Library, Mass.; Committee for the Preservation of Hull's History, *Then & Now: Hull and Nantasket Beach*, p. 26; Bergan, *Old Nantasket*, p. 22.

7. Hart, *Not All Is Changed*, pp. 165, 168, 238; *History of the Town of Hingham*, vol. 1, pp. 171–72; *American Seaside Resorts* (1882 ed.), p. 45a; *Springs, Water-Falls, Sea-Bathing Resorts, and Mountain Scenery* (1855), p. 52; Withey and Withey, *Biographical Dictionary of American Architects (Deceased)*, pp. 72–73, 666; "Old Colony House, Hingham, Mass," *American Architect and Building News* 9, no. 279 (30 April 1881); *Hingham Jour-nal and South Shore Advertiser*, 3 June 1881; Shilham, *When I Think of Hingham*, 2nd ed., pp. 16, 21; Sproul, *Tourists' Guide to Nantasket Beach*, p. 26; *Tourists' Guide to Down the Harbor* (1890), p. 27.

8. Pratt, *A Narrative History of the Town of Cohasset, Massachusetts*, vol. 2, pp. 67–68; *American Seaside Resorts* (1882 ed.), pp. 46–47; *Tourists' Guide to Down the Harbor* (1890), pp. 30–31; *Springs, Water-Falls, Sea-Bathing Resorts, and Mountain Scenery* (1855), p. 54; Bachelder, *Popular Resorts, and How to Reach Them* (1874), p. 178; booklet, *Black Rock House, North Cohasset, Massachusetts* (c. 1920); Oliver H. Howe, "Two Old-Time Cohasset Inns," unpublished essay, Cohasset Historical Society, Mass.; files, Black Rock House, Cohasset Historical Society, Mass.

9. Scituate Historical Society, *Scituate*, pp. 18, 21; *DeLuxe Hotels of New England* (1914), n.p.; brochure, *The Cliff, North Scituate Beach, Massachusetts* (c. 1930); Gale Wescott, "The Cliff Hotel Destroyed By Fire," *Scituate (Mass.) Mirror*, 30 May 1974, p. 1; *Tourists' Guide to Down the Harbor* (1890), pp. 31–32.

10. Richards, *History of Marshfield*, vol. 1, p. 205; Krusell and Bates, *Marshfield: A Town of Villages, 1640–1990*, pp. 29, 46–48, 50; Sproul, *Tourists' Guide to Nantasket Beach*, p. 75.

11. Baker, *Plymouth*, pp. 49, 52; Sproul, *Tourists' Guide to Nantasket Beach*, p. 58; e-mails, Herman Hunt (Plymouth Public Library, Mass.) to Bryant F. Tolles, Jr., 5 and 26 September 2005; "Lodging in Plymouth, 1845–1920," Web page, www.plimoth .org/plymtour2; *American Seaside Resorts* (1882 ed.), pp. 47–48; Bachelder, *Popular Resorts and How to Reach Them* (1876 ed.), pp. 99–100; *DeLuxe Hotels of New England* (1914); "Hotel Pilgrim," Web page, www.plimoth.org/plymtour2/hotelpil.htm.

12. Baker, *Plymouth*, p. 121; "The Mayflower Hotel, 1917–1975," Web page, www. plimoth.org/plymtour2/hmayf.htm; *Old Colony Memorial*, 26 January, 22 June, and 13 July 1917; Withey and Withey, *Biographical Dictionary of American Architects (Deceased)*, pp. 44–45; "Mayflower Inn had checkered history," *Old Colony Memorial*, 5 July 1973, 18 March 1982, and 22 June 1989. Elijah Keith was the owner of the adjacent Ardmore Inn (later an annex of the Mayflower Hotel) on Manomet Point, and ran the much smaller hostelry before the construction of the Mayflower.

13. *American Seaside Resorts* (1882 ed.), pp. 48–49; *Hotels of New England* (1915), n.p.; booklet, *The Sippican, Marion, Mass.* (c. 1925); Howard B. Hillar, essay, "Sippican Hotel Days" (c. 1980), Sippican Historical Society, Marion, Mass.; postcard collection, Sippican Historical Society.

14. O'Connell, *Becoming Cape Cod*, pp. ix–x, 11–26, 27–34, 35–44; Brown, *Inventing New England*, pp. 204–5; *2005 Annual Report—Cape Cod Five Cents Savings Bank*, 1–17; *American*

Seaside Resorts (1882 ed.), pp. 51–52; Bachelder, *Popular Resorts and How to Reach Them* (1876 ed.), pp. 101–2; Dyer, *Hotels & Inns of Falmouth*, pp. 41–43, 56–57; Smith, ed., *The Book of Falmouth*, pp. 222–23, 374–76; Faught, *Falmouth, Massachusetts*, pp. 117–26; Michael J. Mizell, "The Cape Codder Hotel Ages With the Century," *Falmouth (Mass.) Enterprise*, 5 August 1988, pp. 1, 3, 17–19, 24; E. Graham Ward, "New Life For Old Hotel, Perhaps Last of Its Kind," *Falmouth Enterprise*, 24 April 1981; Kay Longcope, "Cape Codder Hotel symbolizes fast-vanishing way of life," *Boston Sunday Globe*, 20 November 1988; Deyo, *History of Barnstable County, Massachusetts*, pp. 154–56; booklet, *Cape Cod Recreationland—The Nobscussett, Dennis, Mass.* (c. 1920); Withey and Withey, *Biographical Dictionary of American Architects (Deceased)*, p. 336; booklet, *The Nobscussett* (c. 1894); *Hotels of New England* (1915), p. 39; *Cape Cod Oracle*, 7 and 19 April 1983; "Cape's grand lady, Belmont, is gone," *Boston Globe*, 11 September 1977; booklet, *The Belmont, West-Harwich-By-The-Sea* (c. 1968); Charles Ullman, "The Belmont: A Revival of Grandeur," *Cape Cod Life* 3, no. 3 (Indian Summer, 1981): 76–80.

15. O'Connell, *Becoming Cape Cod*, pp. 40–41; Tim Wood, "Remembering Hotel Chatham," *The Cape Cod Chronicle*, 3 December 1998, section 2, p. 29; booklet, *Hotel Chatham, Chatham, Mass.* (c. 1892); Joshua A. Nickerson, Sr., "Hotel Chatham," *Cape Cod Business Journal* (October 1982): 14; *2005 Annual Report, Cape Cod Five Cents Savings Bank*, pp. 2, 9; *Sunday Cape Cod Times*, 12 December 1982, p. 17; Nancy Barr, "A Century of Summers," *The Cape Cod Chronicle*, 10 July 1997, pp. 28, 37; Knapton, *Chatham Since the American Revolution*, pp. 22–23; Daly, *Chatham*, p. 62; Tim Wood, "Informal Elegance: The Solution to Chatham Bars Inn Restoration," *Cape Cod Chronicle*, 15 September 1994, pp. 5, 6; Chatham Bars Inn form, Chatham Historical Commission survey, 1991; "The First Lady of Shore Road Gives Itself a Party," *The Cape Codder*, 5 July 1994, p. 10; Faye Andrashko, "Faces & Places: Room With a View," *Cape Cod Spectator*, 26 June 1996, p. 17; Eric Hartell, Jr., "Landmark seaside hotel remains a successful example of an earlier day in Chatham," *Barnstable (Mass.) Patriot*, 6 August 1982, pp. 15, 17; informational and marketing materials packet, Chatham Bars Inn, Chatham, Mass., 2005; postcard collection, Chatham Historical Society, Mass.

16. *The Old Colony; or, Pilgrim Land, Past and Present* (1889 ed.), pp. 65–72; Godfrey, *The Island of Nantucket* (1882), pp. 212–13; Sproul, *Tourists' Guide to Nantasket Beach*, pp. 54–55; *Appletons' Illustrated Hand-Book of American Summer Resorts* (1884 ed.), p. 95; McQuill [Bruce], *From New York to the Summer Resorts of New England* (1880), pp. 25–29; *Stork's Popular Summer Tours* (1881), pp. 29–31; *American Seaside Resorts* (1882 ed.), p. 55; McCalley, *Nantucket*, pp. 9–11; Brown, *Inventing New England*, pp. 105–34.

17. Grieve, *The New England Coast* (1892 ed.), p. 89; Douglas-Lithgow, *Nantucket: A History*, pp. 179–81, 187, 190–91, 201, 274–76; Lancaster, *Nantucket in the Nineteenth Century*, pp. 111–15; McCalley, *Nantucket*, pp. 11, 24–27; Withey and Withey, *Biographical Dictionary of American Architects (Deceased)*, pp. 261–62, 626–27; Lancaster, *Holiday Island*, pp. 85–136, 149–51, 202–4. Because of their stature in the history of Nantucket's resort hotel industry, it would be remiss not to mention three 150 or less capacity hotels in this section: the Point Breeze (Gordon Folger) Hotel (1890; extant); the Surfside Hotel (1883; demolished, 1899); and, the Ocean View House, Siasconset (1872; demolished, c. 1915). Had it ever been constructed, the proposed Broadview Hotel, a 250-to-300-capacity complex planned for a site on Lincoln Avenue in 1930, would have eclipsed all others as Nantucket's most ambitious resort establishment.

18. Brown, *Inventing New England*, pp. 75–104; *Appletons' Illustrated Handbook of American Summer Resorts* (1884 ed.), pp. 94–95; *Stork's 1700 Mile Summer Tours* (1879), pp. 14–16; *Stork's Popular Summer Tours* (1881), pp. 22–27; Bachelder, *Popular Resorts and How to Reach Them* (1874 ed.), pp. 166–76, and (1876 ed.), pp. 108–18; Grieve, *The New England Coast* (1892 ed.), pp. 80–85; *Tourists' Guide to Down the Harbor* (1890), pp. 65–74; McQuill [Bruce], *From New York to the Summer Resorts of New England* (1880), pp. 19–23; *The Old Colony* (1889 ed.), pp. 60–64; *New England: A Handbook for Travellers* (1873 ed.), pp. 59–60; *American Seaside Resorts* (1882 ed.), pp. 52–54.

19. Brown, *Inventing New England*, p. 102; Bachelder, *Popular Resorts and How to Reach Them* (1876 ed.), pp. 110–12; Hough, *Martha's Vineyard*, pp. 77–81, 211–14; *Appletons' General Guide to the United States and Canada* (1886), p. 146.

20. Hough, *Martha's Vineyard*, pp. 81–82, 215; Grieve, *The New England Coast* (1892 ed.), p. 83; *Stork's Popular Summer Tours* (1881), p. 25; Stoddard, *A Centennial History of Cottage City*, pp. 58, 99.

21. Sproul, *Tourists' Guide to Nantasket Beach*, pp. 47–48; *New England: A Handbook for Travellers* (1885 ed.), p. 60; Grieve, *The New England Coast* (1892 ed.), p. 85; Bachelder, *Popular Resorts and How to Reach Them* (1876 ed.), pp. 115–16; Brown, *Inventing New England*, p. 102; Hough, *Martha's Vineyard*, pp. 91–99, 263–64; booklet, *Mattakeset Lodge, Katama, M. V.*, c. 1882.

22. Virginia Poole, "Harbor View, the Grand Dame of Edgartown Hotels, Celebrates Centennial," *The Vineyard Gazette*, 27 September 1991; "Harbor View," *The Vineyard Gazette*, 27 September 1991; "The Harbor View Hotel, Now 100 Years Old," *The Dukes County Intelligencer* 32, no. 4 (May 1991): 172–75;

Railton, *The History of Martha's Vineyard*, pp. 298–302; "First Winthrop Reveals $6 Million Project To Renovate Historic Edgartown Hotels," *The Vineyard Gazette*, 8 December 1989, pp. 1, 7; "Harbor View Hotel, Edgartown, Massachusetts," *Wentworth By the Sea Project Description* (September 1993), pp. 14–15; Withey and Withey, *Biographical Dictionary of American Architects (Deceased)*, pp. 152–53.

CHAPTER 5. MASSACHUSETTS: THE NORTH SHORE

1. Garland, *Boston's North Shore*, pp. 157–63; Hill and Nevins, *The North Shore of Massachusetts Bay* (10th ed., 1888), pp. 5–9; *Hand-Book of Travel Over the Eastern & Maine Central Railroad Line*, p. 11; *Field's Hand-Book of Travel* (1873 ed.), p. 6; *Northern New England and Canada Resorts* (1884 ed.), p. 54; *Springs, Water-Falls, Sea-Bathing Resorts, and Mountain Scenery* (1855), p. 52; *Appletons' Illustrated Hand-Book of American Summer Resorts* (1876 ed.), p. 94; Bachelder, *Popular Resorts and How to Reach Them* (1875 ed.), p. 66; Grieve, *The New England Coast* (1892 ed.), p. 97; McCauley, "Revere Beach Chips," pp. 1, 2, 6b, 46b, 104, 105; Shurtleff, *The History of the Town of Revere*, pp. 340–41; Pratt, *Seven Generations*, pp. 98–99.

2. Rogers, "Resort Architecture at Nahant, 1815–1850," *Old-Time New England* 65, nos. 1–2 (Summer/Fall 1974): 13–19, 24, 26–28; Marie L. Ahearn, "Health Restoring Resorts on the New England Coast," from Wilson, ed., *Victorian Resorts and Hotels*, pp. 41–42; Williamson, *The American Hotel*, pp. 238–39; letter, Bonnie Ayers D'Orlando (assistant curator, Nahant Historical Society, Mass.) to Bryant F. Tolles, Jr., 25 May 2006; Hurd, *History of Essex County, Massachusetts*, vol. 2, pp. 417–18; *Appletons' Illustrated Hand-Book of American Summer Resorts* (1884 ed.), p. 96; *Springs, Water-Falls, Sea-Bathing Resorts, and Mountain Scenery* (1855), pp. 52–53; engraving, "Drew's Hotel, At Nahant," *Gleason's Pictorial Drawing Room Companion*, vol. 1, 30 August 1851; Mathias and Turino, *Nahant*, pp. 10, 11, 14; exhibition label by Stanley Paterson, "Nahant Hotel," Lynn (Mass.) Historical Society Museum, n.d.; Lewis, *The Picture of Nahant*, p. 27; Wilson, *Some Annals of Nahant, Massachusetts*, pp. 72–80; Paterson and Seabury, *Nahant on the Rocks*, pp. 62–69, 98, 104, 107–8, 143. The author has attempted to resolve inconsistencies (particularly dates) and errors present in secondary, narrative sources treating Nahant and the Hotel Nahant.

3. Bachelder, *Popular Resorts and How to Reach Them* (1874 ed.), p. 69; Grieve, *The New England Coast* (1892 ed.), p. 97; *Hand-Book of Travel Over the Eastern & Maine Central Railroad Line* (1875), p. 15; *Appletons' Illustrated Hand-Book of American Summer Resorts* (1876 ed.), p. 94; *New England: A Handbook for Travellers* (1885 ed.), p. 251.

4. Thompson, *Swampscott: Historical Sketches of the Town*, p. 199; Turino and Mathias, *Swampscott*, pp. 41–43; booklet, *The Lincoln House, Swampscott, Mass.* (1906); "Town Noted as Summer Resort," *Lynn (Mass.) Item*, 14 August 1909; "Lincoln House in Swampscott to be Razed," *Lynn Item*, 15 May 1918; Jean F. Reardon, "The Hotels of Swampscott," *Swampscott, Massachusetts*, n.p.

5. Thompson, *Swampscott: Historical Sketches of the Town*, pp. 198–99; Jean F. Reardon, "The Hotels of Swampscott," *Swampscott, Massachusetts*, n.p.; "Town Noted as Summer Resort," *Lynn (Mass.) Item*, 14 August 1909; *DeLuxe Hotels of New England* (1914), n.p.; booklet, *Hotel Preston, Beach Bluff, Massachusetts* (1907); booklet, *Hotel Preston, Beach Bluff, Mass.* (c. 1906); *Lynn Item*, 10 October 1977, pp. 1, 11.

6. Jean F. Reardon, "The Hotels of Swampscott," *Swampscott, Massachusetts*, n.p.; Garland, *Boston's North Shore*, p. 188; Thompson, *Swampscott: Historical Sketches of the Town*, p. 190; Turino and Mathias, *Swampscott*, pp. 48–50; *The Automobile Official AAA 1908 Blue Book*, advertisement, p. 328; *DeLuxe Hotels of New England* (1914), n.p.; booklet, *The New Ocean House, Swampscott* (c. 1910); booklet, *The New Ocean House, Swampscott, Massachusetts* (1911); "A Famous North Shore Hostelry," *The North Shore Reminder* 6, no. 4 (20 July 1907); "An Exclusive North Shore Hotel," *The North Shore Reminder* 6, no. 10 (13 August 1907); *A Handbook of New England* (1916), p. 808; Arrington, *Municipal History of Essex County in Massachusetts*, vol. 1, p. 296; *Daily Evening Item* (Lynn, Mass.), 9 May 1969; *Boston Evening Globe*, 9 May 1969; *Daily Evening Item*, 18 May 1970; *Boston Herald*, 9 May 1969; newspaper files, Lynn (Mass.) Public Library.

7. Sigler, "The Resorts of Marblehead," *Marblehead: A Quarterly Magazine* 1, no. 2 (Summer 1980): 25–27, 66; Hill and Nevins, *The North Shore* (1885 ed.), pp. 6–7, and (1893 ed.), pp. 38–39; *Appletons' Hand-Book of American Summer Resorts* (1884 ed.), pp. 97–98; Grieve, *The New England Coast* (1892 ed.), p. 97; Webber and Nevins, *Old Naumkeag*, pp. 270–71; Roads, Jr., *A Guide to Marblehead* (c. 1883 ed.), p. 69; "The Nanepashemet . . . ," design rendering, *American Architect and Building News* 12 (15 July 1882); Wright, *Marblehead*, vol. 2, p. 88; Harry Wilkinson, "Memory Lane," *Marblehead Messenger*, 24 October 1974; Withey and Withey, *Biographical Dictionary of American Architects (Deceased)*, p. 371.

8. Sigler, "The Resorts of Marblehead," *Marblehead: A Quarterly Magazine* 1, no. 2 (Summer 1980): 25–26; Harry Wilkinson, "Memory Lane," *Marblehead Messenger*, 6 November 1974; Wright, *Marblehead*, vol. 1, pp. 80, 83, 120, and vol. 2,

pp. 42–43; booklet, *Rock-mere Inn, Marblehead* (1907); "Razing Famed Landmark in Marblehead," *The Salem (Mass.) Evening News*, 11 March 1965; Roads, Jr., *A Guide to Marblehead* (c. 1902 ed.), p. 66. Another Colonial Revival–inspired but much smaller hotel in Marblehead of the same general period was the New Fountain House (Harbor Inn), erected adjacent to Crocker Park from 1905 to 1906 and razed in 1951.

9. *Hand-Book of Travel Over the Eastern & Maine Central Railroad Line* (1875), p. 17; Hill and Nevins, *The North Shore* (1879 ed.), pp. 71–72; Waite, *Guide Book for the Eastern Coast of New England* (1871), p. 102; Searle, "History of Catta Island off Marblehead," *Essex Institute Historical Collections* 83, no. 4 (October 1947): 342–50; Hercher, "Cat Island," *Marblehead Magazine* 2, no. 2 (1981): 32–34.

10. "The Queen of Ward Two," unpublished essay, Beverly (Mass.) Historical Society; Hill and Nevins, *The North Shore* (1891 ed.), pp. 50–52; *Appletons' Illustrated Hand-Book of American Summer Resorts* (1884 ed.), p. 98; Stephen P. Hall, "The death of city's Queen crowns arsonist's reign," *The Evening News* (Salem, Mass.), 23 October 2000, p. A7.

11. *American Seaside Resorts* (1882 ed.), pp. 41–41A; *Appletons' Illustrated Hand-Book of American Summer Resorts* (1884 ed.), p. 98; Hill and Nevins, *The North Shore* (1883 ed.), pp. 30–32; Floyd, *"Manchester-by-the-Sea,"* pp. 160–61; Garland, *Boston's North Shore*, pp. 270–71; Garland, *Boston's Gold Coast*, pp. 40–41; Youngman, *Summer Echoes from the 19th Century: Manchester-by-the-Sea*, pp. 72–73; Abbott, *Jeffrey's Creek*, pp. 32–33; booklet, *The Masconomo . . . Manchester-By-The-Sea, Mass.* (1899); booklet, *The Masconomo, Manchester-by-the-Sea* (1906).

12. *New England: A Handbook for Travellers* (1885 ed.), p. 245; Garland, *Boston's Gold Coast*, p. 41; Garland, *Boston's North Shore*, p. 302; Hill and Nevins, *The North Shore* (1880 ed.), p. 60; Cutter, *Genealogical and Personal Memoirs*, vol. 1, p. 143; Hart, *Magnolia Once Kettle Cove*, pp. 24–27; Foster, *The Story of Kettle Cove*, pp. 23–25; *Magnolia Souvenir*, pp. 22–24.

13. Unpublished essay, "Oceanside Hotel," Magnolia (Mass.) Historical Society; Garland, *The Gloucester Guide*, p. 8; Barbara Taorina, "Oceanside memories still burn brightly," *Gloucester (Mass.) Daily Times*, 9 November 1998, pp. A1, A9; Hill and Nevins, *The North Shore* (1883 ed.), p. 37, (1886 ed.), p. 38, and (1891 ed.), p. 53; Garland, *Boston's Gold Coast*, pp. 41–42, 47, 50–51; booklet, *The Oceanside and Cottages* (1927); unpublished essay, "George Krewson, Jr.," Magnolia Historical Society; Cutter, *Genealogical and Personal Memoirs*, vol. 1, p. 143; Hart, *Magnolia Once Kettle Cove*, pp. 27–31; *Gloucester Daily Times*, 7 October 1999.

14. Hill and Nevins, *The North Shore* (1891 ed.), pp. 61–63;

Hart, *Magnolia Once Kettle Cove*, p. 32; Foster, *The Story of Kettle Cove*, p. 20; *New England's Summer and America's Leading Winter Resorts* (1897), n.p.; booklet, *New Magnolia, Magnolia, Mass.* (1903); booklet, *The New Magnolia, Magnolia, Mass.* (c. 1905); Baedeker, ed., *The United States* (1909 ed.), p. 283.

15. Baedeker, ed., *The United States* (1904 ed.), p. 124, and (1909 ed.), p. 283; *New England: A Handbook for Travellers* (1885 ed.), pp. 245–46; *American Seaside Resorts* (1882 ed.), p. 41A; *Appletons' Illustrated Hand-Book of American Summer Resorts* (1876 ed.), pp. 96–97; *Field's Hand-Book of Travel* (1873), p. 12; Hill and Nevins, *The North Shore* (1886 ed.), pp. 38–39.

16. O'Gorman, *This Other Gloucester*, pp. 33–37; Thompson, *Cape Ann in Stereo Views*, pp. 94, 96–97; *American Seaside Resorts* (1882 ed.), advertisement, n.p.; *Gloucester (Mass.) Telegraph*, 31 March 1849, p. 2; *Boston Daily Evening Transcript*, 25 June 1849; *Boston Daily Evening Transcript*, 29 June 1849; *Gloucester Telegraph*, 5 September 1849, p. 2; *Gloucester Daily Telegraph*, 17 October 1914; *Red Book Interstate Automobile Guide . . . New England* (1909 ed.), advertisement, p. 112.

17. Babson, *History of the Town of Gloucester, Cape Ann*, p. xxvi; "Summer Hotels Have Interesting History," *Gloucester (Mass.) Daily Times*, 24 August 1949; Garland, *Eastern Point*, p. 172; Garland, *Boston's Gold Coast*, p. 51; Thompson, *Cape Ann in Stereo Views*, p. 109; *Gloucester Daily Times*, 11, 12, and 14 February 1938; *Gloucester Daily Times*, 27 November 1954; Hawthorne Inn buildings inventory, Cape Ann Historical Association, Gloucester, Mass.; Cutter, *Genealogical and Personal Memoirs*, vol. 1, p. 143.

18. Leaflet, "Bass Rock House, Little Good Harbor Beach, Gloucester, Mass." (c. 1879); Hill and Nevins, *The North Shore* (1879 ed.), n.p. and advertisement (1881 ed.), pp. 62–63, (1882 ed.), p. 57, and (1883 ed.), pp. 42–43; "Summer Hotels Have Interesting History," *Gloucester (Mass.) Daily Times*, 24 August 1949.

19. Garland, *Boston's Gold Coast*, p. 54; Thompson, *Cape Ann in Stereo Views*, p. 107; *DeLuxe Hotels of New England* (1914), n.p.; "Summer Hotels Have Interesting History," *Gloucester (Mass.) Daily Times*, 24 August 1949; *Community News* (East Gloucester, Mass.), 11 August 1937, p. 2; Cutter, *Genealogical and Personal Memoirs*, vol. 1, p. 143; Ray, *Gloucester, Massachusetts, Historical Time-Line, 1000–1999*, p. 237; booklet, *The Moorland and Cottages, Bass Rocks, Gloucester, Massachusetts* (c. 1920); *Summer Hotel Guide, Gloucester, Massachusetts* (c. 1910), n.p.

20. Thompson, *Cape Ann in Stereo Views*, p. 108; *Community News* (East Gloucester, Mass.), 11 August 1937, p. 3; "Summer Hotels Have Interesting History," *Gloucester (Mass.) Daily Times*, 24 August 1949; *Summer Hotel Guide, Gloucester,*

Massachusetts (c. 1910), n.p.; Ray, *Gloucester, Massachusetts, Historical Time-Line, 1000–1999*, pp. 181, 242.

21. Garland, *Eastern Point*, pp. 224–31; Garland, *Boston's Gold Coast*, p. 55; Garland, *The Gloucester Guide*, p. 85; booklet, *The Colonial Arms, Eastern Point, Gloucester Harbor, Mass.* (1907); Babson, *History of the Town of Gloucester, Cape Ann*, p. xxvi; "Local People Pioneered in Summer Hotel Business," *Community News* (East Gloucester, Mass.), 11 August 1937, p. 2; Cutter, *Genealogical and Personal Memoirs*, vol. 1, p. 143; Ray, *Gloucester, Massachusetts, Historical Time-Line, 1000–1999*, p. 187; *Gloucester Daily Times*, 3 July 1958; e-mail, Judy Peterson to B. Tolles, 13 March 2007.

22. *Springs, Water-Falls, Sea-Bathing Resorts, and Mountain Scenery* (1855), p. 51; *Field's Hand-Book of Travel* (1873), p. 12; *American Seaside Resorts* (1882), p. 42; *Appletons' Illustrated Hand-Book of American Summer Resorts* (1884 ed.), p. 99; "The Pigeon Cove Hotel Era," essay from the Rockport National Bank Calendar (1985); Hill and Nevins, *The North Shore* (1880 ed.), pp. 80–81, and (1882 ed.), p. 62; "Ceremony Honors Inn Founder," *Gloucester (Mass.) Daily Times*, 23 August 1960, p. 2; "Emerson Inn By the Sea, Rockport, Massachusetts," 5/1/06, www.emersoninnbythesea.com.history.html; Leonard, *Pigeon Cove and Vicinity*, pp. 44–47; Swan, *Town on Sandy Bay*, pp. 261, 264, 277, 285; *Rockport As It Was*, pp. 14, 25, 30, 32, 163, 168; Martin, *A Rockport Album*, pp. 26, 27, 30.

23. Martin, *A Rockport Album*, p. 29; *DeLuxe Resort Hotels of New England* (1914), n.p.; letter, Marshall W. S. Swan to Mr. Doherty, 17 October 1989, Sandy Bay Historical Society and Museum, Rockport, Massachusetts; booklet, *Turk's Head Inn, Land's End, Rockport, Mass.* (1890); booklet, *Turk's Head Inn on the Famous North Shore* (1892), pp. 3, 4, 6; booklet, *Turk's Head Inn, Rockport, Massachusetts* (c. 1910), p. 5; flyer, "Turk's Head Inn, Rockport, Mass." (1901).

CHAPTER 6. NEW HAMPSHIRE: THE BEACHES, NEW CASTLE, AND THE ISLES OF SHOALS

1. Randall, *Hampton, A Century of Town and Beach, 1888–1988*, pp. 2–6; Varrell, *Summer-by-the-sea*, p. 37; Teschek, *Hampton and Hampton Beach*, p. 63.

2. Randall, *Hampton, A Century of Town and Beach, 1888–1988*, pp. 6–8, 29–30, 37; Dow, *History of the Town of Hampton, New Hampshire*, vol. 1, p. 504; Teschek, *Hampton and Hampton Beach*, p. 64; *Granite Monthly* 9, nos. 1–2 (1886): 75–77; Bachelder, *Popular Resorts and How to Reach Them* (1876 ed.), p. 69; *American Seaside Resorts* (1882 ed.), advertisement. Nudd also built the Granite House, a much smaller hotel at the base

of Boar's Head. It was also acquired by Dumas, renamed the New Boar's Head Hotel after the 1893 fire, and itself burned in 1908.

3. Randall, *Hampton, A Century of Town and Beach, 1888–1988*, pp. 18–19; Dow, *History of the Town of Hampton, New Hampshire*, vol. 1, p. 505; Bachelder, *Popular Resorts, How to Reach Them* (1873), p. 42; Varrell, *Summer-by-the-sea*, pp. 45–46. Amongst Hampton Beach's many small and medium-size hotels was the second Ocean House, erected in 1901 by Wallace Lovell and demolished in 1976 (see Aykroyd and Moore, *Hampton and Hampton Beach*, pp. 40, 77, 78).

4. Gage, *"The Switzerland of America." A Popular Guide Book to the Scenery of New Hampshire* (1879 ed.), p. 103.

5. Parsons, *History of the Town of Rye*, pp. 117–18; Varrell, *Rye on the Rocks*, pp. 48–49, 52, 54.

6. Varrell, *Rye and Rye Beach*, n.p.; Varrell, *Summer-by-the-sea*, p. 76; Parsons, *History of the Town of Rye*, p. 119; Waite, *Guide Book for the Eastern Coast of New England* (1871), p. 124.

7. Bachelder, *Popular Resorts, How to Reach Them* (1873), p. 45.

8. Ibid., p. 46.

9. Varrell, *Summer-by-the-sea*, p. 77; Parsons, *History of the Town of Rye*, p. 119; Varrell, *Rye on the Rocks*, pp. 70–71; *Hand-Book of Travel Over the Eastern and Maine Central R.R. Line* (1875), p. 29.

10. Parsons, *History of the Town of Rye*, p. 117; Gage, *"The Switzerland of America." A Popular Guide Book to the Scenery of New Hampshire* (1879 ed.), p. 103; Varrell, *Rye on the Rocks*, pp. 59, 76; *Hand-Book of Travel Over the Eastern and Maine Central R.R. Line* (1875), p. 29; Varrell, *Summer-by-the-sea*, pp. 81–84.

11. Parsons, *History of the Town of Rye*, p. 117; Varrell, *Rye on the Rocks*, pp. 76–78; Withey and Withey, *Biographical Dictionary of American Architects (Deceased)*, pp. 593–94; "Farragut House, Rye Beach, N.H.," *American Architect and Building News* 13, no. 374 (24 February 1883); Lane, "Gems of the New Hampshire Shore," *Granite Monthly* 19, no. 1 (July 1895): 17–18.

12. Rollins, *The Tourists' Guide-Book to the State of New Hampshire* (2nd ed., 1902), p. 59.

13. Karabatsos, *Rye and Rye Beach*, p. 48; *The Lowell (Mass.) Sun*, 26 June 1973; *Hampton (N.H.) Union*, 16 January 1985, pp. 1, 16.

14. Karabatsos, *Rye and Rye Beach*, p. 57; Parsons, *History of the Town of Rye*, pp. 119–120; Varrell, *Summer-by-the-sea*, pp. 78–79; Waite, *Guide Book for the Eastern Coast of New England* (1871), pp. 124–25. While under construction, a violent windstorm flattened the wooden structure, but it was rebuilt

soon thereafter, and by the summer of 1970 it was a thriving hospitality enterprise.

Two other local but smaller-capacity resort hotels associated with Rye summer resort history are the Sagamore at Odiorne's Point and the Ocean Wave House (also the Harrington) at North (Sandy) Beach, the latter in business until it burned in 1960.

15. *Historic Hotels of America* (2005 ed.), p. 129; Rachel Adams, "Star of the Sea," *Preservation* (March/April 2003): 28. For a current, general history of the Wentworth, consulted often in the preparation of this section, see J. Dennis Robinson, *Wentworth By The Sea: The Life and Times of a Grand Hotel* (Portsmouth, N.H.: Peter E. Randall Publisher, 2004). Much of the hotel's history has also been recorded in Ray Brighton's unpublished manuscript, "The Wentworth-By-The-Sea: One of the Grand Hotels" (1987) in the collections of the Portsmouth (N.H.) Athenaeum.

16. *Portsmouth Journal*, 27 June 1874; "Hotel History," Wentworth-by-the-Sea Collection, Portsmouth Athenaeum; Robinson, *Wentworth By The Sea*, pp. xx, 41–43, 46–50; "New Castle and the Piscataqua," *Granite Monthly* 13, nos. 3 and 4 (March/April 1890): 74–75.

17. Brighton, *Frank Jones: King of the Alemakers*, pp. 157–58; Varrell, *Summer-by-the-sea*, pp. 60–62; Robinson, *Wentworth By The Sea*, pp. 55–58, 61–73; "Hotel History," Wentworth-by-the-Sea Collection, Portsmouth Athenaeum; Wentworth by the Sea Time Line (10/1/98), New Hampshire Division of Historical Resources, Concord, p. 1; "New Castle," *Granite Monthly* 3, no. 10 (July 1880): 446–48.

18. Brighton, *Frank Jones: King of the Alemakers*, pp. 158, 163; Wentworth by the Sea Time Line (10/1/98), New Hampshire Division of Historical Resources, Concord, p. 2; letter, Richard M. Candee to James L. Garvin, 25 June 1988, New Hampshire Division of Historical Resources files, Concord.

19. Wentworth by the Sea Time Line (10/1/98), New Hampshire Division of Historical Resources, Concord, p. 2; Robinson, *Wentworth By the Sea*, p. 91.

20. Wentworth by the Sea Time Line (10/1/98), New Hampshire Division of Historical Resources, Concord, pp. 2–3; Richard M. Candee, The Wentworth Hotel Chronology (1992), New Hampshire Division of Historical Resources files, Concord; Brighton, *Frank Jones: King of Alemakers*, p. 164. After 1900, the only major exterior changes to the Wentworth were the redesign of the veranda, the replacement of the porte cochere with a Colonial Revival substitute, and, between 1918 and 1920, the addition of new window apertures.

In 1905, the major event in the Wentworth's history occurred when the hotel hosted a historic international conference resulting in the signing of the Portsmouth Treaty ending the Russo-Japanese War.

21. *Wentworth By The Sea Project Description* (1993), presented by the Friends of the Wentworth and Prepared by Tsoi/Kobus & Associates, Architects (September 2003); Robinson, *Wentworth By The Sea*, pp. 193–212. An intriguing structure adjacent to the hotel was "The Ship" (1922), an entertainment pavilion with nearby swimming pool that was based on an elliptical plan resembling the hull of a sea vessel. It was demolished in 2001 by Ocean Properties and was replaced by a cluster of long-stay residences.

For general information on the Wentworth as it existed in 2000, see the Determination of Eligibility form, New Hampshire Division of Historical Resources files.

22. "Isles of Shoals," National Register of Historic Places Inventory — Nomination Form (c. 1979), New Hampshire Division of Historical Resources; Marie L. Ahearn, "Health Restoring Resorts on the New England Coast," in Wilson, ed., *Victorian Resorts and Hotels*, pp. 42–43; Bachelder, *Popular Resorts and How to Reach Them* (1876 ed.), p. 69; *Boston and Maine Central Summer Resorts* (1891), pp. 76–77; Babcock, ed., *Our American Resorts* (1883 ed.), p. 150.

23. Whittaker, *Land of Lost Content*, pp. 103, 107–8; Laighton, *Ninety Years at the Isles of Shoals*, pp. 20–21, 23, 24–25; Varrell, *Rye on the Rocks*, p. 126; Bardwell, *The Isles of Shoals: A Visual History*, pp. 49, 55, 56; *Hand-Book of Travel Over the Eastern & Maine Central Railroad Line* (1875), advertisement, p. 60; Neagle, "Appledore — Maine's House of Entertainment," *Down East* 9, no. 7 (July 1963): 34; *A Stern and Lovely Scene*, pp. 42–46, 48, 50; *New England: A Handbook for Travelers* (1873 ed.), p. 265.

24. Gage, "The Switzerland of America." *A Popular Guide Book to the Scenery of New Hampshire* (1879 ed.), p. 105.

25. *A Stern and Lovely Scene*, pp. 65–66; Rutledge, *The Isles of Shoals in Lore and Legend*, pp. 140–42.

26. Bigelow, *Brief History of the Isles of Shoals*, pp. 62–65; Whittaker, *Land of Lost Content*, p. 119; *New England: A Handbook for Travelers* (1873 ed.), p. 265; Bardwell, *The Isles of Shoals: A Visual History*, p. 79; Varrell, *Summer by-the-sea*, pp. 100–101; *Hand-Book of Travel Over the Eastern & Maine Central Railroad Line* (1875), pp. 32–34; Randall and Burke, eds., *Gosport Remembered*, pp. 94–95.

27. Varrell, *Rye on the Rocks*, pp. 129–30; Bardwell, *The Isles of Shoals: A Visual History*, p. 79; Whittaker, *Land of Lost Content*, pp. 119–20; Wentworth Hotel Determination of Eligibility Form (September 2000), New Hampshire Division of Histori-

cal Resources, Concord; Gage, "The Switzerland of America." A Popular Guide Book to the Scenery of New Hampshire (1879 ed.), pp. 107–8.

CHAPTER 7. MAINE: FROM KITTERY TO CAPE ELIZABETH

1. The Great Vacation Route (1891), pp. 62–63; Boston & Maine and Maine Central Summer Resorts (1891), p. 78; Bachelder, Popular Resorts and How to Reach Them (1875 ed.), p. 70; booklet, The Champernowne (c. 1915); Sprague's Journal of Maine History 10, no. 4 (1922): 193; Bardwell, Old Kittery, p. 68; Coast Pilot (York County, Maine), week of 11–17 September 1985, pp. 3–4. The Champernowne was used by the U.S. Navy to house sailors during World War I.

2. Boston & Maine and Maine Central Summer Resorts (1891), p. 78; The Great Vacation Route (1891), p. 62; Arti-Facts (Kittery Historical Society, Maine) 3, no. 5 (February 1994): 1–5; booklet, From Kittery Point to Casco Bay (c. 1900); booklet, The Pocahontas, Gerrish Island, Kittery Point, Maine (c. 1900).

3. The Great Vacation Route (1891), p. 63; Field's Hand-Book of Travel (1873 ed.), p. 19; Boston & Maine and Maine Central Summer Resorts (1891), pp. 78–79; Grieve, The New England Coast (1892 ed.), p. 100; Moody, Handbook History of the Town of York, p. 176; Bardwell, A History of York Harbor, pp. 63–64; Viele, The Origins of Modern York, p. 6; Spiller, 350 Years as York, p. 30; Hepburn, Great Resorts of North America, p. 25; The Old York Transcript, 28 January 1916; booklet, Marshall House and Cottages, York Harbor, Maine (c. 1925).

4. Hepburn, Great Resorts of North America, pp. 25–26; Withey and Withey, Biographical Dictionary of American Architects (Deceased), pp. 572–73; Thompson, ed., Maine Forms of American Architecture, p. 207; Spiller, 350 Years as York, pp. 30–31, 397–400; Bardwell, A History of York Harbor, pp. 64–65; Rolde, York is Living History, p. 58; York County Coast Star, 25 August 1971; booklet, The Marshall House, York Harbor, Maine (c. 1925).

5. Veile, The Origins of Modern York, p. 64; Spiller, 350 Years as York, pp. 39–40; Bardwell, Old York Beach, pp. 129–37; Ellen M. Ward, "Ninety-Day Wonder," Down East 47, no. 2 (September 2000): 66; booklet, Passaconaway Inn, York Cliffs, Maine (c. 1910); booklet, York Cliffs, Coast of Maine (1893); booklet, The Breakers, York Cliffs, Maine (c. 1930); The Old York Transcript, 14 December 1934, p. 1; The Automobile Official American Automobile Association 1908 Blue Book, p. 576.

6. Booklet, York, Maine (1896); Spiller, 350 Years as York, p. 287; booklet, Souvenir of Old York (c. 1900), p. 28; Bardwell,

A History of York Harbor, pp. 71, 73; Viele, The Origins of Modern York, p. 2.

7. Spiller, 350 Years as York, pp. 36, 165; booklet, Ocean House, York Beach, Me. (c. 1888); York Weekly, 23 January 1985, pp. 3, 21; booklet, Ocean House, York Beach, Maine (c. 1930); Souvenir of Old York (c. 1900), p. 46.

8. Bardwell, Old York Beach, p. 15; booklet, York, Maine (1896); DeLuxe Hotels of New England (1914); booklet, Young's Hotel, York Beach, Maine (c. 1900).

9. Waite, Guide Book for the Eastern Coast of New England (1871 ed.), p. 145; Baker, Woven Together in York County, Maine, p. 287; Hand-Book of Travel Over the Eastern & Maine Central Railroad Line (1875), p. 37; Bachelder, Popular Resorts, Routes to Reach Them (1873 ed.), pp. 47–48; Northern New England and Canada Resorts (1877 ed.), p. 51; Shelley, My Name Is Wells, pp. 243, 255. Images and descriptions suggest that the Island Ledge House had bedroom space for at least 200 people.

10. Shelley, My Name Is Wells, pp. 244, 256; booklet, York and Ogunquit, Maine, as a Summer Residence (c. 1897); Bardwell, Ogunquit-By-The-Sea, pp. 46–48; Seaman and Seaman, A Pictorial History of Ogunquit, Maine, 1870–1950, n.p.; booklet, Sparhawk Hall, Ogunquit, Maine (1924); brochure, Sparhawk Hall, Ogunquit, Maine (c. 1950).

11. Seaman, Ogunquit, Maine, 1900–1971, p. 44; Bardwell, Ogunquit-By-The-Sea, pp. 48–49; booklet, Ogunquit Village by the sea (c. 1915); booklet, York and Ogunquit, Maine, as a Summer Residence (c. 1897); flyer, "The Lookout—Ogunquit Club" (1950).

12. Varrell, Summer-by-the-sea, pp. 126–28; Murphy, Colonial Revival in Maine, p. 36; Official Hand-Book of the Boston and Maine Railroad (1877), p. 27.

13. Magnuson, Quiet, Well Kept, for Sensible People, pp. 47–48, 50, 58, 64, 65, 68, 71, 73, 75, 80, 81.

14. Magnuson, Quiet, Well Kept, for Sensible People, p. 82; booklet, Kennebunkport and Kennebunk Beach (New York: Geo. W. Richardson, c. 1922); Burr, The Kennebunks in Season, p. 45; booklet, The Atlantis, Kennebunk Beach, Maine (c. 1960); Boston & Maine and Maine Central Summer Resorts (c. 1891), p. 82.

15. Magnuson, Quiet, Well Kept, for Sensible People, p. 83; Portland Press Herald, 21 October 1985, p. 15; York County Coast Star, 27 July 1983, p. 8; booklet, Narragansett-By-The-Sea, Kennebunk Beach, Maine (c. 1929).

16. Boston & Maine and Maine Central Summer Resorts (c. 1891), pp. 81, 82; Burr, The Kennebunks in Season, pp. 90–91; Snow's Hand Book: Northern Pleasure Travel (1879 ed.), advertisement, p. 8; Leading Business Men of Kennebunkport,

Kennebunk and Old Orchard Beach . . . , p. 15; Joy, *The Kennebunks*, p. 95; [Clayton], *History of York County, Maine*, p. 441; *The Wave*, Midsummer Edition, 1902; broadside, "Ocean Bluff Hotel, Cape Arundel, Kennebunkport, Maine" (c. 1874); Butler, *Kennebunkport Scrapbook*, pp. 49–50; Baker, *Woven Together in York County, Maine*, pp. 284–85.

17. Burr, *The Kennebunks in Season*, p. 91; *The Eastern Star*, 15 April 1881; Beckford, *Leading Business Men of Kennebunkport, Kennebunk and Old Orchard Beach*, p. 19; *The Wave*, 5 July 1902 and 21 July 1906; Murphy, *Colonial Revival in Maine*, pp. 71–73; Murphy, "William E. Barry, 1846–1932," *A Biographical Dictionary of Architects in Maine*, no. 6 (1984).

18. *Half Hour Detours in the Four Kennebunks*, p. 41; booklet, *Kennebunkport and Kennebunk Beach* (c. 1922), advertisement; e-mail, Roz Magnuson (Old Brick Store Museum, Kennebunk, Maine) to Bryant F. Tolles, Jr., 25 July 2006; brochure, *The Glen Haven Hotel, Kennebunkport, Maine* (n.d.).

19. *Kennebunkport and Kennebunk Beach* (c. 1922), advertisement.

20. *The Eastern Star*, 13 September 1901; *The Wave*, 11 July 1903; Burr, *The Kennebunks in Summer*, pp. 94–95; *Kennebunkport and Kennebunk Beach* (c. 1922), advertisement; booklet, *Old Fort Inn, Kennebunkport, Me.* (c. 1903); brochure, *Old Fort Inn on Cape Arundel, Kennebunkport, Maine* (c.1952).

21. Murphy, *Colonial Revival in Maine*, pp. 132–33, essay by Kim Lovejoy; *Kennebunkport and Kennebunk Beach* (c. 1922), advertisement; Burr, *The Kennebunks in Season*, pp. 92–93; *Kennebunk Items*, 30 June 1917; "Staying With History," *Preservation* 56, no. 3 (May/June 2004): 28; booklet, *Breakwater Court, Kennebunkport, Maine* (c. 1925); brochure, *Breakwater Court, Kennebunkport, Maine* (c. 1915); brochure, *Breakwater Court, Kennebunkport, Maine* (c. 1918); brochure, *The Colony, Kennebunkport, Maine* (c. 1950). The Colony Hotel is listed with the "Historic Hotels of America," National Trust for Historic Preservation, and is currently owned by Jestena Boughton.

22. *Northern New England and Canada Resorts* (1877), p. 51; *Field's Hand-Book of Travel* (1873 ed.), pp. 19–20; Locke, *Shores of Saco Bay: A Historical Guide* (1880), p. 96.

23. Butler, *Biddeford*, p. 101; photographs and captions, Ocean View Hotel, McArthur Library, Biddeford, Maine; booklet, *The Ocean View Hotel, Biddeford Pool, Maine* (c. 1912); flyer, "Ocean View Hotel, Biddeford Pool, Maine" (c. 1930).

24. Grieve, *The New England Coast* (1892 ed.), pp. 100–101; *The Great Vacation Route* (1891), pp. 59–60; Hatch, ed., *Maine: A History*, p. 906; *Gateways of Tourist Travel: Pen and Camera Pictures* (1898), p. 63; *"Away Down East": My Unexpected Vacation* (1883), p. 17; Baker, *Woven Together in York County, Maine*, pp. 278, 281–82; *The White Mountains of New Hampshire and the Coast and Woods of Maine* (1890 ed.), p. 22; Barry and Verrier, "Sun, Sand, Sea — and Neon," *Down East* 29, no. 12 (July 1983).

25. *Glimpses of the Great Pleasure Resorts of New England* (c. 1895), p. 52; Locke, *Historical Sketches of Old Orchard and the Shores of Saco Bay* (1884 ed.), pp. 44–45; Elwell, *Portland and Vicinity*, p. 132; Bachelder, *The Great Steel Pier*, pp. 4–5; *New England: A Handbook for Travelers* (1873 ed.), p. 283; Locke, *Old Orchard Beach, Maine* (1879), p. 28; *The Maine Democrat*, 29 July 1875; *Morris' Tourist Hand Book* (c. 1891), pp. 154–55. The first Old Orchard House fire occurred on 21 July 1875.

26. *Keyes' Hand-Book of Northern Pleasure Travel* (1874 ed.), advertisement, p. 202; Dominque, *Greetings from Old Orchard Beach, Me.*, p. 17; booklet, *Old Orchard House, Old Orchard Beach, Maine* (c. 1900); booklet, *Old Orchard House, Old Orchard Beach, Maine* (1910); *Boston & Maine and Maine Central Summer Resorts* (c. 1891), pp. 88–89.

27. Booklet, *Sea-Shore House, Old Orchard Beach, Maine* (c. 1896); Locke, *Shores of Saco Bay: A Historical Guide* (1880), p. 104; *Boston & Maine and Maine Central Summer Resorts* (c. 1891), advertisement, p. 86.

28. Locke, *Shores of Saco Bay: A Historical Guide* (1880), pp. 97, 99, 100; *American Seaside Resorts* (1882 ed.), p. 23; *The Great Vacation Route* (1891), p. 58; Locke, *Historical Sketches of Old Orchard and the Shores of Saco Bay* (1884 ed.), pp. 101–2.

29. *Pleasant Days in Pleasant Places*, p. 17; booklet, *Hotel Fiske, Old Orchard Beach, Maine* (c. 1895); *Biddeford (Maine) Daily Journal*, 16 August 1907, p. 1; booklet, *Old Orchard Beach: A Series of Comparative Sketches* (n.d.), pp. 9–10; Beckford, *Leading Business Men of Kennebunkport, Kennebunk and Old Orchard Beach* (1888), pp. 54–55; Scully, *The Old Orchard*, pp. 30, 48; Dominque, *Greetings from Old Orchard Beach, Me.*, p. 75; Locke, *Historical Sketches of Old Orchard and the Shores of Saco Bay* (1884 ed.), p. 98.

30. Dominque, *Greetings from Old Orchard Beach, Me.*, pp. 36, 46; Scully, *The Old Orchard*, pp. 31, 32; booklet, *The Velvet Hotel, Old Orchard Beach, Maine* (c. 1898); booklet, *Hotel Velvet, Old Orchard Beach, Maine* (c. 1900); brochure, *Old Orchard . . . Hotel Velvet* (1902); viewbook, *Old Orchard Beach, Maine* (1900), p. 66; Bachelder, *The Great Steel Pier*, pp. 51–53.

31. Dominque, *Greetings from Old Orchard Beach, Me.*, pp. 35, 39; *Old Orchard Beach Hotel Guide* (1910).

32. *Boston & Maine and Maine Central Summer Resorts* (c. 1891), pp. 90–91; *Hand-Book of Travel Over the Eastern & Maine Central Railroad Line* (1875), p. 41; *The Great Vacation Route* (1891), p. 57; Waite, *Guide Book for the Eastern Coast of New England* (1871), pp. 156–57; Elwell, *Portland and Vicinity*,

p. 110; Laughton, *Scarborough*, pp. 32–36; Hutchinson, "Atlantic House: A Summer Refuge," *Down East* 21, no. 9 (June 1975): 50–55; *One Hundred Years of a Maine Hotel, 1850–1950*, pp. 4–5; "Historic Hotel Coming Down," *Portland Press Herald*, 29 May 1987.

33. *Boston & Maine and Maine Central Summer Resorts* (c. 1891), p. 91; Laughton, *Scarborough in the Twentieth Century*, p. 32; Laughton, *Scarborough*, pp. 41–42; Frank Hodgdon, "The Jocelyn Hotel" (www.scarboroughmaine.com/historical/jocelyn.html).

34. Davidson et al., *Frederick Church, Winslow Homer and Thomas Moran*, pp. 51–53; Frank Hodgdon, "The Checkley House" (www.scarboroughmaine.com/historical/checkleyhouse.html); Laughton, *Scarborough*, pp. 43–44; booklet, *The Checkley, Prout's Neck, Maine* (c. 1925); booklet, *The Checkley and The West Point House, Prout's Neck, Maine* (c. 1896); booklet, *Black Point Inn at Prout's Neck, Maine* (1938).

35. Letter, Barbara R. Sanborn (Cape Elizabeth Historical Preservation Society) to Bryant F. Tolles, Jr., 9 August 2005; Willis, *Guide Book for Portland and Vicinity* (1859), pp. 36, 39; Jordon, *A History of Cape Elizabeth, Maine*, pp. 132–55; *American Seaside Resorts* (1882 ed.), p. 21; Sweetser, *Book of Summer Resorts* (1868), pp. 54–55; *Cape Elizabeth, Past to Present*, pp. 85, 87; Roerden, *Collections from Cape Elizabeth, Maine*, pp. 81, 83.

CHAPTER 8. MAINE: FROM CASCO BAY TO NEW BRUNSWICK

1. Grieve, *The New England Coast* (1892), p. 166; booklet, *Portland and the Scenic Gems of Casco Bay* (1896), pp. 35, 41, 43, 48; Hull, ed., *Hand-Book of Portland, Old Orchard Beach, Cape Elizabeth and Casco Bay* (1888 ed.), pp. 180–81, 205–7, 211, 213–14; *Gateways of Tourist Travel* (1898), pp. 59–61; Hatch, ed., *Maine: A History*, p. 907; *Boston & Maine and Maine Central Summer Resorts* (c. 1891), pp. 96–104; Bachelder, *Popular Resorts and How to Reach Them* (1876 ed.), pp. 76–77.

2. Hatch, ed., *Maine: A History*, pp. 907–8; Moulton, *An Informal History of Four Islands*, p. 10; Elwell, *Portland and Vicinity* (1876), pp. 88–91; *New England: A Handbook for Travellers* (1873 ed.), p. 275; Sargent, *An Historical Sketch, Guide Book, and Prospectus of Cushing's Island* (c. 1886), pp. 86–88; Hull, *Hand-Book of Portland, Old Orchard Beach, Cape Elizabeth and Casco Bay* (1888 ed.), p. 207.

3. Booklet, *Portland and the Scenic Gems of Casco Bay* (1896), p. 35.

4. Hull, *Hand-Book of Portland, Old Orchard Beach, Cape Elizabeth and Casco Bay* (1888 ed.), p. 207; *Gateways of Tourist Travel* (1898), pp. 61–62; *Portland and the Scenic Gems of Casco Bay* (1896), p. 36; Barry and Ward, "Portland's Most Exclusive Enclave," *Down East* 35, no. 2 (September 1988): 80–84; Judd, Churchill, and Eastman, eds., *Maine: The Pine Tree State from Prehistory to the Present*, p. 432.

5. Front elevation perspective drawing, "Hotel Cushing's Island, Maine," by Clarence Luce, New York City, *Building* 7, no. 4 (23 July 1887); Moulton, *An Informal History of Four Islands*, p. 10.

6. *Glimpses of Portland* (c. 1895), p. 60; Elwell, *Portland and Vicinity*, pp. 96, 97, 100; Sweetser, *Cumberland, Maine*, pp. 111–14; Innes, *Some Momentos of Little Chebeague's Waldo Hotel*, p. 1; Vietz, "Rock On, Rock On" (Chebeague Inn), *Down East* 42, no. 11 (June 1996): 46–49.

7. Booklet, *Freeport, the Birthplace of Maine* (c. 1936); Reed, "William R. Miller, 1866–1929," *A Biographical Dictionary of Architects in Maine* 5, no. 14 (1988); Henderson, "Casco Castle," *Down East* 10, no. 10 (July 1964): 42–43; "Casco Castle Was One of the Finest," *The Brunswick (Maine) Record*, 29 November 1962; William C. Purington, "Old Casco Castle in Freeport Was Once a Unique Attraction," *Coastal Advertiser* (Bath, Maine) 1, no. 4 (6 August 1969): 1; Henry Milliken," Stone Tower All That Remains of Casco Castle," *Lewiston (Maine) Evening Journal Magazine Section*, 20 March 1971, p. 4A; booklet, *Casco Castle, So. Freeport, Maine* (c. 1910); booklet, *Casco Castle, South Freeport, Maine* (c. 1912). Architectural drawings for Casco Castle by William R. Miller are in the archives of the Freeport (Maine) Historical Society.

8. *Glimpses of the Great Pleasure Resorts of New England* (c. 1895), pp. 67–68; Duncan, *Coastal Maine*, pp. 495–97; Hatch, ed., *Maine: A History*, pp. 910–11.

9. Hatch, ed., *Maine: A History*, p. 910; *Gems of the Northland* (1898 ed.), pp. 30, 145; *Morris' Scenic Guide* (c. 1902), n.p.; letter, Ada M. Haggett to Bryant F. Tolles, Jr., 8 August 2005; Lapham, *Popham Beach as a Summer Resort . . .* , pp. 1, 7; Dozois, *Phippsburg*, pp. 111–12; "A Trip Down Our Blue River to Popham," *The Bath (Maine) Independent*, 27 July 1895; "A Summer Resort," *The Bath (Maine) Independent*, 22 October 1881; booklet, *The Rockledge Hotel, Popham Beach, Maine* (1900); booklet, *The Rockledge, Popham Beach, Maine* (1914).

10. Hatch, ed., *Maine: A History*, p. 910; Duncan, *Coastal Maine*, pp. 495–96; Clifford, *The Boothbay Region, 1906–1960*, pp. 117–18; Greene, *History of Boothbay, Southport and Boothbay Harbor, Maine, 1623–1905*, pp. 416–17; booklet, *Oake Grove Hotel* (c.1900); brochure, *Oake Grove Hotel* (c. 1905); booklet, *Oake Grove Hotel* (1916); booklet, *The Beginning of Oake Grove Hotel . . . Was in 1894* (c. 1925); *Boothbay (Maine) Register*, 7 January and 18 February 1965.

11. Hatch, ed., *Maine: A History*, p. 910; Clifford, *The Booth-bay Harbor Region, 1906 to 1960*, pp. 117–18; Greene, *Souvenir Hand-Book of Boothbay-Harbor-and-Vicinity*, n.p.; broadside, "Samoset House, Mouse Island, Boothbay Harbor, Maine" (c. 1881); flyer, "Samoset House and Rosewood Cottage, Mouse Island, Boothbay Harbor, Maine" (c. 1880); booklet, *The Samoset and Stone Cottage* (c. 1903); booklet, *The Samoset, Mouse Island, Maine* (c. 1910); *The Boothbay (Maine) Register*, 5 November 1959; Joshua F. Moore, "Hotel Inferno," *Down East* 51, no. 1 (August 2004): 126.

12. Duncan, *Coastal Maine*, pp. 495–96; Hatch, ed., *Maine: A History*, p. 910; Greene, *Souvenir Hand-Book of Boothbay-Harbor-and-Vicinity*, n.p.; Greene, *History of Boothbay, Southport and Boothbay Harbor, Maine, 1623–1905*, pp. 412–13; Merrills, ed., *Squirrel Island, Maine*, pp. 4, 44; McLane, *Islands of the Mid-Maine Coast*, vol. 4, p. 97; booklet, *Squirrel Inn, Squirrel Island, Maine* (c. 1900).

13. Duncan, *Coastal Maine*, p. 497; Hanna, "The Pemaquid Peninsula of Maine," pp. 171–74; booklet, *Holly Inn and Annex, Christmas Cove, Maine* (c. 1925); David Andrews, "The Heyday of Hotels, South Bristol, Maine," 2004 presentation, South Bristol (Maine) Historical Society, p. 7; Vincent, comp., *Down on the Island, Up on the Main*, pp. 192–93; booklet, *New Holly Inn and Rutherford House* (c. 1915); Wells, *The Christmas Cove Improvement Association, 1900–2000*, pp. 5, 22; H. Landon Warner, "A History of the Houses and Cottages in Christmas Cove," unpublished transcript, South Bristol (Maine) Historical Society. Formerly situated across John's Bay from Christmas Cove on Pemaquid Point was the Edgemere House (Windemere) (1885–86), a small, 80-guest, Second Empire–style summer hostelry closely resembling much larger hotels of the same era on the New England coast.

14. Thompson, ed., *Maine Forms of American Architecture*, pp. 206–7; Haynes, *The State of Maine in 1893*, p. 51; *Gems of the Northland* (1895 ed.), p. 31; "Old Time Tourism Set High Standards," *The Courier-Gazette* (Rockland, Maine), 24 February 1983; Harden, ed., *Shore Village Album*, p. 160; "The Sage of the Samoset," *Maine Times*, 13 October 1978, p. 3; *The Woods, Lakes, Sea-Shore, and Mountains* (1896), pp. 80–81; Withey and Withey, *Biographical Dictionary of American Architects (Deceased)*, p. 138; Tolles, *The Grand Resort Hotels of the White Mountains*, pp. 21–22. Normally associated with Rockland, the Samoset property is, in fact, divided between Rockland and Rockport to the northeast.

15. Harden, ed., *Shore Village Album*, p. 160; "The Saga of the Samoset," *Maine Times*, 13 October 1978, p. 3; booklet, *The SamOset, Rockland Breakwater, Maine* (1903); booklet, *The SamOset, Rockland Breakwater, Maine* (1904); Thompson, ed., *Maine Forms of American Architecture*, p. 207.

16. Booklet, *The SamOset, Penobscot Bay, Rockland Breakwater, Maine* (c. 1906); booklet, *The SamOset, Penobscot Bay, Rockland Breakwater, Maine* (1908); booklet, *The SamOset By The Sea, Rockland Breakwater, Maine* (c. 1916); booklet, *The SamOset By The Sea, Rockland Breakwater, Maine* (c. 1917); booklet, *The SamOset By The Sea, Rockland Breakwater, Maine* (c. 1919); booklet, Maine Central Railroad, *Vacation Board and Summer Tours in Maine and New Hampshire* (1920 ed.), advertisement; Gregory, "The Shingle Style," *Down East* 32, no. 7 (February 1986): 71. The Stevens drawings for the 1916–17 modifications to the Samoset are in the archives of the Maine Historical Society, Portland.

17. *Samoset Anniversary Special* (The Courier-Gazette, Rockland, Maine), 11 June 1994, pp. 3, 25; Harden, ed., *Shore Village Album*, pp. 86, 161; *The Courier-Gazette*, 29 January 1970, p. 1; *The Courier-Gazette, Samoset Pictorial Souvenir*, October 1972; *The Courier-Gazette*, 14 October 1972, p. 1; *Maine Sunday Telegram*, 8 August 1980, pp. 1D, 3D, 10D; *Maine Sunday Telegram*, 25 July 1989, pp. 1C, 3C; *The Courier-Gazette*, 13 October 1992, pp. 1, 14.

18. Shettleworth, *The Summer Cottages of Islesboro, 1890–1930*, pp. 20–23; *History of Islesboro, Maine, 1893–1983*, pp. 91–93; Farrow, *History of Islesborough, Maine*, pp. 305–11; Barger, *Facts and Fancies and Repetitions about Dark Harbor*, pp. 5–9, 17, 45–49; booklet, *Islesboro, Maine* (c. 1891); Withey and Withey, *Biographical Dictionary of American Architects (Deceased)*, pp. 201, 648; Jensen, "Edmund M. Wheelwright, 1854–1912," *A Biographical Dictionary of Architects in Maine* 4, no. 13 (1987); *Gems of the Northland* (1895 ed.), p. 34; *Glimpses of the Great Pleasure Resorts of New England*, pp. 69–70; *Mount Desert (Maine) Herald*, 4 July 1890.

19. Shettleworth, *The Summer Cottages of Islesboro, 1890–1930*, pp. 23–24; booklet, *Islesboro Inn, Dark Harbor, Maine* (Boston: C. B. Webster & Co., c. 1920). After the demolition of the second hotel, a separate ballroom building on the grounds was converted to a residence and survives today.

20. Shettleworth, "Joseph W. Thompson, 1822–91," *A Biographical Dictionary of Architects in Maine* 2, no. 1 (1985); Ellis, *The Story of Stockton Springs, Maine*, pp. 186–88; booklet, *Fort Point Hotel, Fort Point, Stockton Springs, ME.* (c. 1896). During its existence, the hotel was also referred to as the "Fort Point House (Hotel)" and "The Woodcliff." Outbuildings included an octagon-shaped dance hall, built late in the hotel's history.

21. Wheeler and Bartlett, *History of Castine, Penobscot and Brooksville, Maine*, p. 402; Wheeler, *Castine, Past and Present*,

p. 100; *Castine*, p. 20; booklet, *The Acadian, Castine, Maine* (1905); booklet, *The Acadian, Castine, Maine — On Penobscot Bay* (1910); booklet, *The Acadian, Castine, Maine* (c. 1917); *Glimpses of the Great Pleasure Resorts of New England* (c. 1895), advertisement, p. 91. Not included in this treatment of Maine coastal resort hotels because of its limited size (about 100 capacity) is the Blue Hill Inn, once situated at nearby Blue Hill on an inland rise with partially obscured views of the ocean. Erected from 1891 to 1892 from plans by the distinguished Boston architect William Ralph Emerson, this significant, Shingle-style building remained open until 1935, when it burned (see Reed, *A Delight to All Who Knew It: The Maine Summer Architecture of William R. Emerson*, pp. 98–105).

22. *Vacation and Summer Tours in Maine and New Hampshire* (Maine Central Railroad, 1920), pp. 8–10; *Gems of the Northland* (1895), pp. 37–38; *Gateways of Tourist Travel: Pen and Camera Pictures* (Grand Trunk System, 1898), p. 63; Hatch, ed., *Maine: A History*, pp. 912–13; *The Great Vacation Route* (1891), pp. 65–70; *American Seaside Resorts* (1882 ed.), pp. 25–26; Sweetser, *Book of Summer Resorts* (1868), pp. 55–60; Ingersoll, *Down East Latch Strings* (1887 ed.), pp. 53–56; *Field's Hand-Book of Travel* (1873 ed.), pp. 41–42; McQuill [Bruce], *From New York to the Summer Resorts of New England* (1880 ed.), pp. 61–62.

23. Hatch, ed., *Maine: A History*, pp. 913–14; Savage, "Bar Harbor: The Hotel Era, 1868–1880," *Maine Historical Society Newsletter* 10, no. 4 (May 1974): 101–7; Street, *Mount Desert: A History*, pp. 323–36; McAllister, "The History of Bar Harbor and Mount Desert Island," pp. 18–25; Seligmann, "Bar Harbor — From Eden to Tourism," *Down East* 4, no. 1 (August 1957): 25–26. Bar Harbor's first hotel was the Agamont House, erected in 1855 by Tobias Roberts.

24. Sweetser, *Chisholm's Mount-Desert Guide-Book* (1888), p. 16; Helfrich and O'Neil, *Lost Bar Harbor*, pp. 88–89; *Bangor (Maine) Daily News*, 19 October 1906; [Lapham], *Bar Harbor and Mount Desert Island* (1886), p. 5; *The Bar Harbor Blue Book and Mount Desert Guide* (1881), p. 22; McAllister, "The History of Bar Harbor and Mount Desert Island," pp. 37–38, 55; Sherman, *A Souvenir of Bar Harbor, Maine* (c. 1895), pp. 67–68.

25. *The Bar Harbor Blue Book and Mount Desert Guide* (1881), p. 23; Brechlin, *Bygone Bar Harbor*, n.p.; Helfrich and O'Neil, *Lost Bar Harbor*, pp. 90, 94, 101; booklet, *Newport House, Newport Annex and Cottages, Bar Harbor, Maine* (c. 1912); booklet, *The Newport House, Newport Annex and Cottages* (c. 1921).

26. Helfrich and O'Neil, *Lost Bar Harbor*, p. 95; Sweetser, *Chisholm's Mount-Desert Guide-Book* (1888), p. 16; Brechlin,

Bygone Bar Harbor, n.p.; [Lapham], *Bar Harbor and Mount Desert Island* (1886 ed.), p. 5; Sherman, *A Guide to Bar Harbor, Maine* (c. 1897), p. 75.

27. Turner, *When Bar Harbor Was Eden*, p. 76; Withey and Withey, *Biographical Dictionary of American Architects (Deceased)*, pp. 21, 320, 496; Bryan, *Maine Cottages*, p. 281; Sweetser, *Chisholm's Mount-Desert Guide-Book* (1888), p. 16; Brechlin, *Bygone Bar Harbor*, n.p.; Helfrich and O'Neil, *Lost Bar Harbor*, pp. 92–93; *The Woods, Lakes, Sea-Shore and Mountains* (1896), pp. 85–86; Haynes, *Maine Resorts*, advertisement, p. 19; booklet, *The Louisburg, Bar Harbor, Maine* (c. 1925); *Hotels of New England* (1915), p. 23.

28. Hill, *Discovering Old Bar Harbor*, p. 75; Helfrich and O'Neil, *Lost Bar Harbor*, p. 96; *The Bar Harbor Blue Book and Mount Desert Island* (1881), p. 22–23; Turner, *When Bar Harbor Was Eden*, p. 78; Sherman, *A Souvenir of Bar Harbor, Maine* (1893), p. 50.

29. Sweetser, *Chisholm's Mount-Desert Guide-Book* (1888), p. 16; *The Bar Harbor Blue Book and Mount Desert Island* (1881), p. 23; Sherman, *Sherman's Bar Harbor Guide* (1891), advertisement, p. 78; Scully, *The Shingle Style* (1955 ed.), p. 77; Reed, "Bruce Price, 1845–1903," *A Biographical Dictionary of Architects in Maine* 3, no. 5 (1986); Thompson, ed., *Maine Forms of American Architecture*, p. 205; *American Architect and Building News* 5, no. 161 (25 January 1879), West End Hotel front elevation perspective and description; booklet, *West End Hotel, Bar Harbor, Maine* (c. 1890).

30. Helfrich and O'Neil, *Lost Bar Harbor*, pp. 102–4; Turner, *When Bar Harbor Was Eden*, pp. 74, 88; booklet, *The Malvern, Bar Harbor, Maine* (c. 1925); Bryan, *Maine Cottages*, p. 281; Sherman, *A Souvenir of Bar Harbor* (1893 ed.), n.p.; *Boston & Maine and Maine Central Summer Resorts* (c. 1891), pp. 125–26.

31. McAllister, "The History of Bar Harbor and Mount Desert Island," pp. 31, 33–35, 85–86; Brechlin, *Bygone Bar Harbor*, n.p.; *Boston & Maine and Maine Central Summer Resorts* (c. 1891), pp. 10, 11, 127–28; Baedeker, ed., *The United States* (1904 ed.), p. 138; Shettleworth and Vanderberg, *Mount Desert Island*, pp. 27, 62–69; *Morris' Tourist Hand Book* (c. 1891), pp. 169, 210; Thorton, *Traditions and Records of Southwest Harbor and Somesville, Mount Desert Island, Maine*, p. 174.

32. Shettleworth and Vanderberg, *Mount Desert Island*, pp. 84–91; McAllister, "The History of Bar Harbor and Mount Desert Island," pp. 38–39, 84–85; Brechlin, *Bygone Bar Harbor*, n.p.; Baedeker, ed., *The United States* (1904 ed.), pp. 137–38; Street, *Mount Desert: A History*, pp. 337–40, 342–43; *Boston & Maine and Maine Central Summer Resorts* (c. 1891), pp. 214–15,

217; Baldwin, "The Man Who Built Northeast Harbor," *Down East* 42, no. 7 (February 1996): 34–35; Bryan, *Maine Cottages*, pp. 168–73, 281; Sweetser, *Chisholm's Mount-Desert Guide-Book* (1888), pp. 57–58, 62–64; booklet, *Rock-End Hotel* (c. 1905); booklet, *The Rock-End Hotel, Northeast Harbor, Maine* (c. 1920); *Bangor Daily News*, 24 August 1966, p. 10; *Bangor Daily News*, 27–28 August 1966, p. 10; *Morris' Tourist Hand Book* (c. 1891), p. 208; Vanderberg and Shettleworth, *Revisiting Seal Harbor and Acadia National Park*, pp. 16–17, 20, 74; Jellison, *Hancock County*, p. 161. Somesville, located at the north end of Somes Sound, became the locus of a small summer colony, possessing a few small hotels not of the same scale as many at the other island communities discussed in this chapter.

33. Phippen, *The Sun Never Sets on Hancock Point*, vol. 1, p. 320; *Hancock History Book* (1978), pp. 73–74; [Waldron], *The Front Dooryard of Our Country*, pp. 33–34; "Mt. Desert Ferry," *Bar Harbor Record*, 16 January 1915, p. 3.

34. *Morris' Tourist Hand Book* (c. 1891), p. 170; [Waldron], *The Front Dooryard of Our Country*, pp. 33–34; *Boston & Maine and Maine Central Summer Resorts* (c. 1891), pp. 130–32; Cooper, ed., *A Bicentennial History of Sullivan, Maine*, pp. 194–95; *Bar Harbor Register*, 27 June 1906, p. 1; Herson, *Sorrento*, pp. 27–28, 33, 45; booklet, *A Summer at Sorrento* (Boston: Collins Press, c. 1893); *Frenchman's Bay and Mt. Desert Land and Water Company, Sorrento, Maine* (Boston: John A. Lowell & Co., c. 1896). Another resort hotel, owned briefly by Frank Jones, was the smaller Waukeag House (1876; demolished, 1895) at Sullivan, just north of Sorrento at the head of the bay. A Second Empire–style building, it was similar in appearance to the larger Island House at Southwest Harbor (see Cooper, ed., *A Bicentennial History of Sullivan, Maine*, pp. 183–85).

35. *Boston & Maine and Maine Central Summer Resorts* (c. 1891), pp. 135–36; *Morris' Tourist Hand Book* (c. 1891), p. 170; Hahn, *A History of Winter Harbor, Maine*, pp. 9, 18–20; Fahlman, "Lindley Johnson, 1854–1937," *A Biographical Dictionary of Architects in Maine* 6 (1991); Gouldsboro Land and Improvement Company, *Grindstone Inn and Lands; Grindstone Neck, Winter Harbor, Maine* (c. 1891 and 1892 eds); *The Gouldsboro Land Improvement Company, Winter Harbor, Maine (1890)*, p. 11; booklet, *The Grindstone Inn, Winter Harbor, Maine* (c. 1910); *Bar Harbor Record*, 14 November 1890, p. 3. The Grindstone Inn's opening in June 1891 was fortuitously timed, for it filled the void created by the destruction by fire of the 150-capacity Hotel Beacon (1887) that same month in nearby Winter Harbor Village.

36. Sullivan, *The Algonquin, St. Andrews, N.B.*, pp. 23, 25, 26–33, 71–73, 83–101, 104; *The Algonquin History* (St. Andrews, N.B.:Algonquin Hotel, c. 1988); *New England: A Handbook for Travellers* (1873 ed.), p. 322; *New England: A Handbook for Travellers* (1885 ed.), p. 426 ; Haynes, *Souvenir of New England's Great Resorts* (1891 ed.), n.p.; *Boston & Maine and Maine Central Summer Resorts* (c. 1891), pp. 162–63; *The Woods, Lakes, Sea-Shore, and Mountains* (1896), p. 87; Wells, *Campobello: An Historical Sketch*, pp. 46–47; Nowlan, *Campobello: The Outer Island*, pp. 90–93; Withey and Withey, *Biographical Dictionary of American Architects (Deceased)*, pp. 154, 446, 486, 544, 590; booklet, *Campobello Island* (n.d.), pp. 3–7 and perspective drawings.

Bibliography

This bibliography is organized by general categories and lists printed materials that have been utilized in the researching and compilation of this book. Included are selected book, booklet, brochure, magazine, journal, and newspaper titles. Citations for infrequently used printed materials, as well as manuscripts, visuals, letters, e-mails, Web sites, oral interviews, and some ephemera items, are not included in this bibliography but are contained in the preceding chapter notes.

I. REFERENCE WORKS

Avery Index to Architectural Periodicals (Columbia University). 2nd ed., enl. and rev., 15 vols. Boston: G. K. Hall & Co., 1973. Also first supplement, 2nd ed., enl. and rev., 1975; second supplement, 2nd ed., enl. and rev., 1977; third supplement, 2nd ed., enl. and rev., 1979; and fourth supplement, 1979–82, 4 vols., 1985.

Avery Obituary Index of Architects (Columbia University). 2nd ed. Boston: G. K. Hall & Co., 1970.

Blumenson, John J. G. *Identifying American Architecture: Pictorial Guide to Styles and Terms, 1600–1945.* Rev. and enl ed. Nashville, Tenn.: American Association for State and Local History, 1981.

Coffin, Marie M., comp. *The History of Nantucket Island: A Comprehensive Bibliography of Source Material with Index and Inventory.* Bethlehem, Pa.: Laros Printing Co., 1970.

Cyclopedia of Architecture, Carpentry and Building: A General Reference Work. 10 vols. Chicago: American Technical Society, 1909.

Dunning, Glenna, comp. *Resort Hotels in the Eastern United States: An Annotated Bibliography.* Monticello, Ill.: Vance Bibliographies, 1987.

Feintuch, Burt, and David H. Watters, eds. *The Encyclopedia of New England: The Culture and History of an American Region.* New Haven, Conn., and London: Yale University Press, 2005. "Architecture of Tourism" and "Grand Resort Hotels" by Bryant F. Tolles, Jr.

Francis, Dennis Steadman. *Architects in Practice, New York City, 1840–1900.* New York: Committee for the Preservation of Architectural Records, 1979.

Hardenbergh, Henry J. "Hotel," *Dictionary of Architecture and Building,* ed. Russell Sturgis. 3 vols., 1901–2. Reprint, Detroit: Gale Research, 1966.

Harris, Cyril M. *American Architecture: An Illustrated Encyclopedia.* New York and London: W. W. Norton & Co., 1998.

———, comp. and ed. *Dictionary of Architecture and Construction.* New York: McGraw-Hill, 2000.

Haskell, John D., T. D. Seymour Bassett, and Roger Parks, comps. Bibliographies of New England History [series]. Vols. 1–4 (Massachusetts, Maine, New Hampshire, and Vermont). Boston: G. K. Hall & Co., 1976–81. Vols. 5–7 (Rhode Island, Connecticut, and New England). Hanover, N.H., and London: University Press of New England, 1983–89.

Historic Hotels of America. Washington, D.C.: National Trust for Historic Preservation, 2005. Listing of member hotels.

Hitchcock, Henry-Russell. *American Architectural Books: A List of Books, Portfolios, and Pamphlets on Architecture and Related Subjects Published in America before 1895.* Enl. ed. New York: DaCapo Press, 1976.

Johnson, Allen, et al. *Dictionary of American Biography.* 20 vols. New York: Charles Scribner's Sons, 1928–36. Also supplementary volumes, 1–8, 1944–88; and index volume, 1990.

Leonard, John W., et al. *Who's Who in America.* Vols. 1–20. Chicago: A. N. Marquis & Co., 1899–1938.

Maddox, Diane, ed. *Built in U.S.A.: American Buildings from Airports to Zoos.* Washington, D.C.: Preservation Press of the National Trust for Historic Preservation, 1985. See "Resort Hotels," by Jeffrey W. Limerick, pp. 144–47.

———. *Master Builders: A Guide to Famous American Architects.* Washington, D.C.: Preservation Press of the National Trust for Historic Preservation, 1985.

Marquis, Alfred N. *Who's Who in New England*. Chicago: A. N. Marquis & Co., 1909.

McAlester, Virginia, and Lee McAlester. *A Field Guide to American Houses*. New York: Alfred A. Knopf, 1984.

The National Cyclopedia of American Biography. 62 vols. New York and Clifton, N.J.: James T. White & Co., 1898–1984. Current volumes, A–N, 1930–63. Index volume, 1984.

Parks, Roger, comp. *Bibliographies of New England History: Further Additions to 1994*. Vol. 9 of Bibliographies of New England History. Hanover, N.H., and London: University Press of New England, 1995.

———, comp. *New England: Additions to the Six State Bibliographies*. Vol. 8 of Bibliographies of New England History. Hanover, N.H., and London: University Press of New England, 1989.

———, comp. *Writings on New England History: Additions to the Bibliographies of New England History Series (to 2001)*. Vol. 10 of Bibliographies of New England History. Boston: Massachusetts Historical Society, 2003.

Pevsner, Nikolaus, John Fleming, and Hugh Honour. *A Dictionary of Architecture*. Woodstock, N.Y.: Overlook Press, 1976.

Placek, Adolf K., ed. *Macmillan Encyclopedia of Architects*. 4 vols. New York: Free Press, Macmillan Publishing Co., 1982.

Poppeliers, John C., S. Allan Chambers, Jr., and Nancy B. Schwartz. *What Style Is It?: A Guide to American Architecture*. Washington, D.C.: Preservation Press for the Historic American Buildings Survey and the National Trust for Historic Preservation, 1983.

Public Ledger Resort Directory. Philadelphia: Public Ledger, 1910. National in focus.

Rifkind, Carole. *A Field Guide to American Architecture*. New York: New American Library, 1980.

Schrock, Nancy C., ed. *Architectural Records in Boston: A Guide to Architectural Research in Boston, Cambridge and Vicinity*. New York and London: Garland Publishing Co. for the Massachusetts Committee for the Preservation of Architectural Records, 1983.

———, ed. *Dictionary of Boston Architects, 1846–1970*. Cambridge, Mass.: Massachusetts Committee for the Preservation of Architectural Records, 1984.

Sokol, David M. *American Art and Architecture: A Field Guide to Information Sources*. Detroit: Gale Research Co., 1976.

Tatman, Sandra L., and Roger W. Moss. *Biographical Dictionary of Philadelphia Architects: 1730–1930*. Boston: G. K. Hall & Co., 1985.

Tishler, William H. *American Landscape Architecture: Designers and Places*. Washington, D.C.: Preservation Press of the National Trust for Historic Preservation and the American Society of Landscape Architects, 1988.

Van Vynckt, Randall J. *International Dictionary of Architects and Architecture*. Vol. 1, *Architects*. London and Washington, D.C.: St. James Press, 1993.

Ward, James A. *Architects in Practice, New York City, 1900–1940*. New York: Committee for the Preservation of Architectural Records, 1994.

Whiffen, Marcus. *American Architecture Since 1780: A Guide to the Styles*. Rev. ed. Cambridge, Mass., and London: MIT Press, 1992.

Whiffen, Marcus, and Frederick Koeper. *American Architecture, 1607–1976*. Cambridge, Mass.: MIT Press, 1981.

Who Was Who in America: Historical Volume, 1607–1896. Chicago: A. N. Marquis Co., 1963.

Who Was Who in America. Vols. 1–3. Chicago: A. N. Marquis Co., 1943–60. Index volume, Chicago: Marquis Who's Who, 1983.

Wilson, James G., and John Fiske, eds. *Appleton's Cyclopedia of American Biography*. 6 vols. New York: D. Appleton and Co., 1888–89.

Withey, Henry F., and Elsie R. Withey. *Biographical Dictionary of American Architects (Deceased)*. Los Angeles: Hennessey & Ingalls, 1970.

Woodhouse, Lawrence. *American Architects from the Civil War to the First World War: A Guide to Information Sources*. Detroit: Gale Research Company, 1976.

II. GENERAL WORKS

Abbott, Karl P. *Open for the Season*. New York: Doubleday & Company, 1950.

Amory, Cleveland. *The Last Resorts*. New York: Harper and Brothers, 1952.

The Architecture of the American Summer: The Flowering of the Shingle Style. Introduction by Vincent J. Scully, Jr. New York: Rizzoli International Publications, 1989.

Aron, Cindy S. *Working at Play: A History of Vacations in the United States*. New York and Oxford: Oxford University Press, 1999.

Barnes, Christine. *Great Lodges of the National Parks*. Bend, Ore.: W. W. West, 2002.

Barrett, Richmond B. *Good Old Summer Days: Newport, Narragansett Pier, Saratoga, Long Branch, Bar Harbor*. New York and London: D. Appleton–Century Company, 1941. Boston: Houghton Mifflin, 1952.

Blackmar, Betsey, Alf Evers, Elizabeth Cromley, and Neil Harris. *Resorts of the Catskills*. New York: St. Martin's Press for the Architectural League of New York and Gallery Association of New York, 1979.

Boeschenstein, Warren. *Historic American Towns Along the Atlantic Coast*. Baltimore and London: The John Hopkins University Press, 1999.

Braden, Susan R. *The Architecture of Leisure: The Florida Resort Hotels of Henry Flagler and Henry Plant*. Gainesville, Fla.: University Press of Florida, 2002.

Bryant, William Cullen, ed. *Picturesque America; or, The Land We Live In*. 2 vols. New York: D. Appleton and Company, 1872 and 1874.

Buckell, Betty Ahern. *Old Lake George Hotels: A Pictorial Review*. Lake George, N.Y.: Buckle Press, 1986.

Burchard, John, and Albert Bush-Brown. *The Architecture of America: A Social and Cultural History*. Boston: Little, Brown and Company, 1961.

Condit, Carl. *American Building Art: The Nineteenth Century*. New York: Oxford University Press, 1960.

Cook, Joel. *America: Picturesque and Descriptive*. Vol. 3. Philadelphia: Henry T. Coates & Co., 1900.

Corbett, Theodore. *The Making of American Resorts: Saratoga Springs, Ballston Spa, Lake George*. New Brunswick, N.J.: Rutgers University Press, 2001.

Davidson, Gail S., et al. *Frederick Church, Winslow Homer and Thomas Moran: Tourism and the American Landscape*. New York and Boston: Bulfinch Press for the Cooper-Hewitt National Design Museum, Smithsonian Institution, 2006.

Donzel, Catherine, Alexis Gregory, and Marc Walter. *Grand American Hotels*. New York: Vendome Press, [c. 1990].

Dorsey, Leslie, and Janice Devine. *Fare Thee Well: A Backward Look at Two Centuries of Historic American Hostelries, Fashionable Spas and Seaside Resorts*. New York: Crown Publishers, 1964.

Dulles, Foster Rhea. *A History of Recreation: America Learns to Play*. 2nd ed. New York: Appleton-Century-Crofts, 1965.

Dunbar, Seymour. *History of Travel in America*. New York: Tudor Publishing Company, 1937.

Ferris, George T., ed. *Our Native Land: Glances at American Scenery and Places. . . .* New York: D. Appleton and Company, 1889.

Funnell, Charles E. *By the Beautiful Sea: The Rise and High Times of That Great American Resort, Atlantic City*. New Brunswick, N.J.: Rutgers University Press, 1983.

Gerlernter, Mark. *A History of American Architecture: Buildings in Their Cultural and Technological Context*. Hanover, N.H., and London: University Press of New England, 1999.

Gill, Brendon, and Dudley Witney. *Summer Places*. New York: Methuen, 1978.

Gillon, Edmund V., Jr. *Early Illustrations and Views of American Architecture*. New York: Dover Publications, 1971.

Greiff, Constance M. *Lost America: From the Atlantic to the Mississippi*. Princeton, N.J.: Pyne Press, 1971.

Grover, Kathryn. *Hard at Play: Leisure in America, 1840–1940*. Amherst: University of Massachusetts Press, and Rochester, N.Y.: Strong Museum, 1992.

Hamlin, Talbot F. *Greek Revival Architecture in America, Being an Account of Important Trends in American Architecture and American Life prior to the War between the States*. New York: Oxford University Press, 1944; reprint, New York: Dover Publications, 1964.

Handlin, David P. *American Architecture*. New York: Thomas and Hudson, 1985.

Hepburn, Andrew. *Great Resorts of North America*. Garden City, N.Y.: Doubleday & Company, 1965.

Hewitt, Mark A. *The Architect & the American Country House, 1890–1940*. New Haven, Conn., and London: Yale University Press, 1990.

Hitchcock, Henry-Russell. *Architecture: Nineteenth and Twentieth Centuries*. 3rd ed. Baltimore: Penquin Books, 1968.

Kramer, J. J. *The Last of the Grand Hotels*. New York: Van Nostrand Reinhold Co., 1978.

Lawliss, Chuck. *Great Resorts of America*. New York: Holt, Rinehart and Winston, 1983.

Lemson, Rod. *America's Grand Resort Hotels*. Charlotte, N.C.: East Woods Press, 1985.

Lencek, Lena, and Gideon Bosker. *The Beach: The History of Paradise on Earth*. New York: Viking, 1998.

Lewis, Arnold, and Keith Morgan, eds. *American Victorian Architecture: A Survey of the 70s and 80s in Contemporary Photographs*. New York: Dover Publications, 1975. Originally published as *L'Architecture Americaine* (Paris: Andre, Daly fils Cie, 1886).

Limerick, Jeffrey W. "The Grand Resort Hotels of America." *Perspecta 15: The Yale Architectural Journal* (1975): 87–109.

———. "Resort Hotels." *Built in U.S.A.: American Buildings from Airports to Zoos*, ed. Diane Maddox. Washington, D.C.: Preservation Press, 1985.

Limerick, Jeffrey W., Nancy Ferguson, and Richard Oliver. *America's Grand Resort Hotels*. New York: Pantheon Books, 1979.

Loth, Calder, and Julius Trousdale Sadler, Jr. *The Only Proper Style: Gothic Architecture in America*. Boston: New York Graphic Society, 1975.

Ludy, David. *Historic Hotels of the World: Past and Present.* Philadelphia: David McKay Company, 1927.

McGinty, Brian. *The Palace Inns: A Connoisseur's Guide to Historic American Hotels.* Harrisburg, Pa.: Stackpole Books, 1978.

Morgan, H. Wayne, ed. *The Gilded Age: A Reappraisal.* Syracuse, N.Y.: Syracuse University Press, 1963.

Newton, Roger Hale. "Our Summer Resort Architecture — An American Phenomenon and Social Document." *Art Quarterly* 4, no. 4 (Autumn 1941): 297–321.

Platt, Frederick. *America's Gilded Age: Its Architecture and Decoration.* South Brunswick, N.J., and New York: A. S. Barnes and Co., 1976.

Rinehart, Floyd, and Marion Rinehart. *Summertime: Photographs of Americans at Play, 1850–1900.* New York: Clarkson N. Potter, Publishers, 1978.

Roth, Leland M. *A Concise History of American Architecture.* New York: Harper & Row, Publishers, 1979.

———. *Shingle Styles: Innovation and Tradition in American Architecture, 1874 to 1982.* New York: Harry N. Abrams, 1999.

Schlereth, Thomas J. *Victorian America: Transformations in Everyday Life, 1876–1915.* New York: Harper Collins, 1991.

Scully, Vincent J., Jr. *The Shingle Style and the Stick Style: Architectural Theory and Design from Downing to the Origins of Wright.* New Haven, Conn., and London: Yale University Press, 1971. 1st ed., 1955.

Sears, John. *Sacred Places: American Tourist Attractions in the Nineteenth Century.* New York: Oxford University Press, 1989.

Shaffer, Marguerite S. *See America First: Tourism and National Identity, 1880–1940.* Washington, D.C., and London: Smithsonian Institution Press, 2001.

Steele, David M. *Vacation Journeys East and West: Descriptive Stories of American Summer Resorts.* New York: G. P. Putnam's Sons, 1918.

Sterngass, Jon. *First Resorts: Pursuing Pleasure at Saratoga Springs, Newport & Coney Island.* Baltimore and London: The Johns Hopkins University Press, 2001.

Tackack, James. *Great American Hotels: Luxury Palaces and Elegant Resorts.* New York: Smithmark Publishers, 1991.

Tolles, Bryant F., Jr. *Resort Hotels of the Adirondacks: The Architecture of a Summer Paradise, 1850–1950.* Hanover, N.H., and London: University Press of New England, 2003.

Upton, Dell. *Architecture in the United States.* Oxford and New York: Oxford University Press, 1998.

Van Zandt, Roland. *The Catskill Mountain House.* New Brunswick, N.J.: Rutgers University Press, 1966.

Whiffen, Marcus, and Frederick Koeper. *American Architecture, 1607–1976.* Cambridge, Mass.: MIT Press, 1981.

White, Arthur. *Palaces of the People: A Social History of Commercial Hospitality.* New York: Toplinger Publishing Co., 1970.

Williamson, Jefferson. *The American Hotel: An Anecdotal History.* New York: Alfred A. Knopf, 1930.

Willis, Nathaniel P., with views by William H. Bartlett. *American Scenery.* 2 vols. London: George Virtue, 1838–40.

Wilson, Richard Guy, ed. *Victorian Resorts and Hotels: Essays from a Victorian Society Autumn Symposium.* Philadelphia: Victorian Society of America, 1982. Originally published in *Nineteenth Century* 8, nos. 1–2 (1982).

Withey, Lynne. *Grand Tours and Cook's Tours: A History of Leisure Travel, 1750–1915.* New York: William Morrow, 1997.

III. GUIDEBOOKS

All-Round Route and Panoramic Guide of the St. Lawrence. Montreal, P.Q.: International Railway Publishing Co., 1912.

American Seaside Resorts: A Hand-Book for Health and Pleasure-Seekers. . . . New York: Taintor Brothers, Merrill & Co., 1882.

Appletons' General Guide to the United States and Canada. Part I. New England and the Middle States and Canada. New York: D. Appleton and Company, 1886.

Appletons' Hand-Book of American Travel. Northern and Eastern Tour. . . . New York: D. Appleton and Company, 1870. Also 1871 ed.

Appletons' Illustrated Hand-Book of American Summer Resorts. New York: D. Appleton and Company, 1876. Also 1877, 1878, 1879, 1880, 1881, 1882, 1883, 1884, and 1889 eds.

Appletons' Illustrated Hand-Book of American Travel. Part I. The Eastern and Middle States, and the British Provinces. New York: D. Appleton & Co., 1857.

Appletons' Railway and Steam Navigation Guide. 2nd ed. New York: D. Appleton & Co., July 1857.

Atlantic Coast Guide: A Companion for the Tourist between Newfoundland and Cape May. New York: E. P. Dutton, 1873.

The Automobile Official AAA 1908 Blue Book. Vol. 2. *New England.* New York: Class Journal Company, 1908.

"Away Down East" or My Unexpected Vacation. New York: Publication Department, Leve & Alden, 1883.

Babcock, Louis M., ed. *Our American Resorts For Health, Pleasure, and Recreation: Where to Go and How to Get There.* Washington, D.C.: National News Bureau, 1883. Also 1884 ed.

Bachelder, John B. *Popular Resorts, Routes to Reach Them.* Boston: John B. Batchelder, Publisher, 1873.

———. *Popular Resorts and How to Reach Them.* Boston: John B. Bachelder, Publisher, 1874. Also 1875 and 1876 eds.

Baedeker, Karl, ed. *The United States With an Excursion Into Mexico: Handbook for Travellers.* Leipsic, Ger.: Karl Baedeker, Publisher, 1893. Also 1899, 1904, and 1909 eds.

The Bar Harbor Blue Book and Mount Desert Guide. Boston: Albert W. Bee, 1881.

Boston & Maine and Maine Central Summer Resorts. Boston and Portland, Maine: Skillings and Howard, [c. 1891].

Boston and Maine Railroad Summer Excursions to the White Mountains, Mt. Desert, Winnepesaukee, Rangley and Moosehead Lakes and New England Beaches. Boston: Passenger Department, Boston & Maine R.R., 1887. Also 1889, 1893, and 1894 eds.

Bradford's Hotel Guide to the United States and Canadas. Chicago: Jas. B. Bradford, Publisher, 1875.

Bragdon, Joseph H. *Seaboard Towns; or Traveller's Guide Book From Boston to Portland. . . .* Newburyport, Mass.: Moulton & Clark, Publishers, 1857.

[Chase, Fred D., Jr.]. *Newport, Block Island and Narragansett Pier. Illustrated.* Boston: Botolph Press, 1895.

Chisholm's All Round Route and Panoramic Guide of the St. Lawrence. . . . Montreal, P.Q.: Chisholm & Co., 1873. Also 1874 ed.

Chisholm's All Round Route and Panoramic Guide of the St. Lawrence. . . . Montreal, P.Q.: C. R. Chisholm & Bros., 1875. Also 1876 ed.

Chisholm's All-Round Route and Panoramic Guide of the St. Lawrence . . . and Western Tourist's Guide. . . . Chicago and Montreal, P.Q.: C. R. Chisholm and Co., 1881.

Denison, Rev. Frederic. *New Bedford, Martha's Vineyard and Nantucket. . . .* Providence, R.I.: J. A. & R. A. Reid, Printers, 1879. Also 1880 ed.

———. *The Past and the Present: Narragansett Sea and Shore.* Providence, R.I.: J. A. & R. A. Reid, Publishers, 1879. Also 1880 ed.

The Fall River and Newport Routes between New York and Boston. A Descriptive Guide with Sketches of Narragansett Bay, Newport and Its Attractions. . . . New York: Taintor Brothers, 1884.

Field's Hand-Book of Travel Over the Eastern and Maine Central Railroad Line, to the Shore Watering Places, White Mountains and Lower Provinces. Boston: Passenger Department, Eastern and Maine Central Railroad Line, 1873.

Gage, William C. *"The Switzerland of America." A Popular Guide Book to the Scenery of New Hampshire.* Manchester, N.H.: Steam Press of C. F. Livingston, 1875. Also 1878 ed., Manchester, N.H.: Thomas W. Lane, and 1879 ed., Providence, R.I.: J. A. and R. A. Reid, Publishers.

Gateways of Tourist Travel: Pen and Camera Pictures of Scenery Reached By The Grand Trunk Railway System and Connections. N.pl.: Passenger Department, Grand Trunk Railroad System, 1898.

Gems of the Northland: A Guide to the White Mountains of New Hampshire, Coast and Woods of Maine, the Entire Vacation Region Between Nova Scotia and Niagara Falls. Portland, Maine: Maine Central Railroad, 1898.

Glimpses of Camden and the Coast of Maine. Newtonville, Mass.: J. R. Prescott, 1904.

Glimpses of Portland and Casco Bay, Maine. Portland, Maine: G. W. Morris, [c. 1895].

Glimpses of the Great Pleasure Resorts of New England Embracing the Mountains of New Hampshire, also the Hunting, Fishing, and Sea-Shore Resorts of Maine. Portland, Maine: G. W. Morris, Publisher, [c.1895].

Godfrey, Edward K. *The Island of Nantucket. What It Was and What It Is, Being a Complete Index and Guide to this Noted Resort. . . .* Boston: Lee and Shepard, Publishers, 1882.

The Great Resorts of America (Illustrated). Together with Places of Interest in Colorado, New York, Maine, New Hampshire and Canada. Portland, Maine: Wilbur Hayes, 1894.

The Great Vacation Route. Chicago, Niagara Falls, White Mountains and Portland Line. Portland, Maine: H. Wilbur Hayes, Publisher, 1891.

Grieve, Robert, ed. *Guide Book to the Mountains of New Hampshire and the Shores of Southern New England.* Providence, R.I.: Journal of Commerce Co., 1899.

———. *The New England Coast: Its Famous Resorts.* 2nd ed. Providence, R.I.: J. A. & R. A. Reid, Publishers, 1892.

———. *Picturesque Narragansett: An Illustrated Guide to the Cities, Towns and Famous Resorts of Rhode Island.* 2nd ed. Providence, R.I.: J. A. & R. A. Reid, Printers and Publishers, [c. 1889].

Guide to Historic Plymouth. Plymouth, Mass.: A. S. Burbank, 1900.

A Guide to Narragansett Bay: Newport, Narragansett Pier, Block Island, Watch Hill, Rocky Point, Silver Spring, and all the Famous Resorts Along the Shore. . . . Providence, R.I.: J. A. & R. A. Reid, Printers and Publishers, 1878.

A Handbook of New England: An Annual Publication. Boston: Porter E. Sargent, 1916. Also 1917 and 1921 eds.

Hand-Book of the Portland and Ogdensburg Railroad. Portland, Maine: G. W. Morris, Publisher, [c. 1888].

Hand-Book of Travel Over the Eastern & Maine Central Railroad Line to the Shore Watering Places, White Mountains, and the Lower Provinces. . . . Boston: Passenger Department of the Eastern and Maine Central Railroad Line, 1875.

[Haynes, George H.]. *Seaside, Mountain, and Lake Summer Resorts . . . on the Line of the Maine Central Railroad*. . . . Lewiston, Maine: Journal Press, [c. 1886].

Hill, Benj. D., and Winfield S. Nevins. *The North Shore of Massachusetts Bay. An Illustrated Guide*. Salem, Mass.: Salem Press, 1879. Also 1880, 1881, 1882, 1883, 1884, 1885, 1886, 1888, 1889, 1890, 1891, 1892, 1893, and 1894 eds., Salem, Mass.: various publishers.

Homes on the Sound for New York Business Men: A Description of the Region Contiguous to the Shore of Long Island Sound. . . . New York: George L. Catlin, 1875.

Illustrated Souvenir Guide Book of Kennebunkport and Kennebunk Beach. . . . Kennebunkport, Maine: John Collins Emmons, [c. 1890].

Ingersoll, Ernest. *Down East Latch Strings; or Seashore, Lakes and Mountains by the Boston & Maine Railroad*. Boston: Passenger Department, Boston & Maine Railroad, 1887.

James, Bushrod W. *American Resorts, with notes upon their climate*. Philadelphia: F. A. Davis, 1889.

Keyes' Hand-Book of Northern Pleasure Travel to the White and Franconia Mountains, St. Lawrence and Saugenay Rivers. The Northern Lakes, Montreal and Quebec. Boston: George L. Keyes, Publisher, 1874.

King, Moses, ed. *King's Handbook of the United States*. Buffalo, N.Y.: Moses King Corporation, 1891.

[Lapham, W. B.]. *Bar Harbor and Mount Desert Island*. New York: Press of Liberty Printing Company, 1886; 2nd ed., Bar Harbor, Maine: n.pub., 1887; 3rd ed., Augusta, Maine: Farmer Job Print, 1888.

Lapham, W. B. *Popham Beach as a Summer Resort*. . . . Augusta, Maine: Farmer Job Print, 1888.

Livermore, Samuel T. *Block Island. I. A Map and Guide. II. A History (Abridged)*. Hartford, Conn.: Press of the Case, Lockwood & Brainard Company, 1882. Also 1886 ed.

Locke, J. S. *Shores of Saco Bay. A Historical Guide to Biddeford Pool, Old Orchard Beach, Pine Point, Prout's Neck*. Boston: J. S. Locke and Company, Publishers, 1880.

Martin, Clara Barnes. *Mount Desert, on the Coast of Maine*. Portland, Maine: Loring, Short & Harmon, 1874. Also 5th ed., 1880.

McQuill, Thursty [Wallace Bruce]. *From New York to the Summer Resorts of New England . . . to the White Mountains and the Seashore*. New York: New York News Company, 1880.

———. *The White and Green Mountains and Routes Thereto via Newport, Boston, Plymouth, Portland, Harlem and Connecticut Valleys*. New York: n.pub., 1872. Also 1873 ed.

Morris' Scenic Guide: Embracing the Famous Hunting and Fishing Territory, and all the Great Summer Resorts at the Mountains, Lakes, Woods, Springs and Sea Shore. Portland, Maine: G. W. Morris, Publisher, [c. 1902].

Morris' Tourist Hand Book. Illustrated. With Descriptive Matter of Interest of Mountains, Lakes, Rivers, and Sea Shore. Portland, Maine: G. W. Morris, Publisher, [c. 1891].

"Mush, Ben." *Block Island: A Hand-Book with Map*. . . . Norwich, Conn.: James Hall, 1877.

The Narragansett: A Guide to the Famous Resorts and Places of Rhode Island. Providence, R.I.: J. A. & R. A. Reid, Publishers, 1887.

The Narragansett Blue Book: A Summer Souvenir and Hotel Guide. . . . Hartford, Conn.: American Book Exchange, 1900.

New England: A Handbook for Travellers. Boston: James R. Osgood and Company, 1873. Also 1876 and 1880 eds.; 1885 ed., Boston: Ticknor and Company.

Newport, Block Island and Narragansett Pier. Illustrated. Boston: J. F. Murphy, N.Y., N.H. and H. R.R., 1897.

Newport and Narragansett Bay. A Guide. . . . Providence, R.I.: Tillinghast & Mason, 1870. Also 1874 ed.

Northern New England and Canada Resorts. A Hand-Book for Tourists and Travelers. New York: Taintor Brothers, Merril & Co., 1877. Also 1884 and 1886 eds.

The Northern Traveller, and Northern Tour. New York: J. & J. Harper, 1831.

Norton, Charles L. *American Seaside Resorts from the St. Lawrence River to the Gulf of Mexico*. New York: Taintor Brothers, 1877.

Official Hand-Book of the Boston and Maine Railroad, to the Sea-Shore, Lakes, and the White Mountains. Boston: Batchelder, Amidon & Co., 1877.

The Old Colony; or, Pilgrim Land, Past and Present. Boston: Fall River Line and Old Colony Railroad, 1886. Also 1889 ed.

The Old Colony Railroad: Its Connections, Popular Resorts, and Fashionable Watering Places. Boston: Press of Rand, Avery and Company, 1874. Also 1876 ed.

Pettee, Edward E. *Block Island, R.I. Illustrated: With a Descriptive Sketch and Outline of History*. Boston: Press of Deland & Barta, 1884.

Pleasant Days in Pleasant Places; The Question "Where to Go This Summer" Answered to the Satisfaction of All. New York: Imprinted for the Pratt Manufacturing Company, 1886.

Ramblings Along the Eastern Shore of New England. Boston:

Passenger Department of the Eastern Railroad Company, 1879.

Red Book Interstate Automobile Guide . . . New England. Worcester, Mass.: F. S. Blanchard & Company, 1909.

[Reid, James Allan]. *The Narragansett Blue Book: A Summer Souvenir and Guide . . . Narragansett Bay. . . .* Providence, R.I.: American Book Exchange, 1896. Also 1897 ed.

Richards, T. Addison, ed. *Appletons' Companion Hand-Book of Travel . . . United States and Canadas.* New York: D. Appleton & Company, 1866.

——, ed. *Appleton's Illustrated Hand-Book of American Travel: A Full and Reliable Guide. . . .* Part I. "The Eastern and Middle States, and the British Provinces." New York: D. Appleton & Company, 1857.

Rollins, Frank West. *The Tourists' Guide-Book to the State of New Hampshire.* Concord, N.H.: Rumford Press, 1902. Also 2nd ed., 1902.

Roads, Samuel, Jr. *A Guide to Marblehead.* 5th ed. Marblehead, Mass.: Merrill H. Graves, [c. 1883]. Also, c. 1902 and c. 1906 eds.

Russell, William S. *Guide to Plymouth and Recollections of the Pilgrims.* Boston: published for the author by George Coolidge, 1846.

Sea-Shore, Lakes and Mountains. Descriptive of the Sea-Shore, Lake and Mountain Resorts on the Boston and Maine Railroad and Immediate Connections. Boston: Passenger Department of the Boston and Maine Railroad, 1886. Also 1888 ed.

Sherman, W. H. *A Guide to Bar Harbor, Maine.* Boston: n.pub., [c. 1897].

——. *Sherman's Bar Harbor Guide: Business Directory and Reference Book.* Portland, Maine: Brown Thurston Company, 1891.

——. *Sherman's Guide to Bar Harbor and Mt. Desert Island, Me.* Portland, Maine: Smith & Sale, 1892.

——. *A Souvenir of Bar Harbor, Maine.* Boston: H. G. Collins, 1893. Also c. 1895, c. 1896, and 1897 eds.

Simonton, Thaddeus R. *Tourist's Guide of Picturesque Camden on the Coast of Maine.* Camden, Maine: Camden Herald Print, 1886.

Snow's Hand Book. Northern Pleasure Travel. Worcester, Mass.: Noyes, Snow & Company, 1876. Also 1879 ed.

Southeastern Massachusetts: its Shores and Islands, Woodlands and Lakes, and How to Reach them. . . . Boston: Press of G. H. Ellis for the Old Colony Railroad, 1878.

Springs, Water-Falls, Sea-Bathing Resorts, and Mountain Scenery of the United States and Canada. New York: Published by J. Disturnell, 1855.

Sproul, Arthur E. *Tourists' Guide to Nantasket Beach, Downer Landing, Martha's Vineyard, Nantucket, Plymouth . . . and the summer resorts of Cape Cod and the South Shore of Massachusetts.* Boston: Everett & Zerrahn, 1881.

Stanhope, Clarence. *In and Around Newport.* Newport, R.I.: Daily News Job Print, 1891.

Stork's Popular Summer Tours: From Baltimore to New York, Newport, Martha's Vineyard, Nantucket, Boston, Mt. Desert, White Mts., Etc. Baltimore: Stork's Summer Tours, 1881.

Stork's 1700 Mile Summer Tours: From Baltimore to New York, Newport, Martha's Vineyard, Nantucket, Boston, Mt. Desert, White Mts., Etc. Baltimore: Stork's Summer Tours, 1879.

Summer in New England. Boston: Passenger Traffic Department, Boston and Maine Railroad, 1927. Also 1929 and c. 1932 eds.

A Summer Note-Book. Detroit: Michigan Central Railroad, 1897.

Summer Resorts of the New York, Providence and Boston Railroad, or Places in Rhode Island and Connecticut. . . . New York: Passenger Department, 1885.

Summer Resorts of the South and Summer Resorts of New England. Boston: George H. Chapin, 1896.

Summer Resorts Reached by the Grand Trunk Railway and Its Connections. Montreal, P. Q.: Passenger Department, Grand Trunk Railway, 1888.

Sweetser, Charles H. *Book of Summer Resorts . . . A Complete Guide for the Summer Tourist.* New York: "Evening Mail" Office, 1868.

Sweetser, Moses F. *Chisholm's Mount-Desert Guide-Book.* Portland, Maine: Chisholm Brothers, Publishers, 1888.

——. *Here and There in New England and Canada. All Along the Shore.* Boston: Passenger Department, Boston & Maine Railroad, 1889.

——. *King's Handbook of Boston Harbor.* Cambridge, Mass.: Moses King, Publisher, 1882.

The Tourist Guide to Nantucket and Martha's Vineyard. Boston: John F. Murphy, [c. 1902].

Tourists' Guide to Down the Harbor, Hull and Nantasket, Downer Landing, Hingham, Cohasset, Marshfield, Scituate, Duxbury, "The Famous Jerusalm Road," "Historic Plymouth," Cottage City, Martha's Vineyard, Nantucket, and the Summer Resorts of Cape Cod and the South Shore of Massachusetts. Boston: John F. Murphy, Publisher, 1890.

The Tourists' Guide to the Shore Resorts of Narragansett Bay. Boston: published for John F. Murphy, [c. 1906].

Waite, Otis F. R. *Guide Book for the Eastern Coast of New England.* Concord, N.H.: Edson C. Eastman and Company;

Boston: Lee & Shepard; New York: Lee, Shepard & Dillingham, 1871.

[Waldron, Holman D.]. *The Front Dooryard of Our Country and What It Contains . . . Maine and the Provinces.* Portland, Maine: Passenger Department of the Maine Central Railroad, 1888.

Where to Stay in Vacation Land. Boston: Passenger Traffic Department, Boston and Maine Railroad, 1916.

The White Mountain Guide Book. Concord, N.H.: Edson C. Eastman, 1858.

The White Mountains of New Hampshire and the Coast and Woods of Maine. Portland, Maine: Maine Central Railroad, 1890. Also 1891 ed.

Williams, Wellington. *Appletons' Northern and Eastern Traveller's Guide. . . .* New York: D. Appleton & Company, 1850. Also 1853 and 1854 eds.

———. *Appletons' Railroad and Steamboat Companion.* New York: D. Appleton Company, 1848. Also 1849 ed.

Willis, William. *Guide Book for Portland and Vicinity.* Portland, Maine: B. Thurston and J. F. Richardson, 1859.

York, Maine. York, Maine: Bureau of Information, 1896.

IV. NEW ENGLAND

Andrews, Wayne. *Architecture in New England: A Photographic History.* Brattleboro, Vt.: Stephen Greene Press, 1973.

Attractive Bits Along the Shore: Rye Beach, Portsmouth, Isles of Shoals, Old York, Kittery Point. Portland, Maine: H. Wilbur Hayes, [c. 1890].

Brown, Dona. *Inventing New England: Regional Tourism in the Nineteenth Century.* Washington, D.C.: Smithsonian Institution Press, 1995.

Bullard, Frederic L. *Historic Summer Haunts from Newport to Portland.* Boston: Little, Brown, 1912.

Coolidge, A. J., and J. B. Mansfield. *A History and Description of New England, General and Local. Vol. 1. Maine, New Hampshire and Vermont.* Boston: Austin J. Coolidge, 1859.

Davis, William T., ed. *The New England States: Their Constitutional, Judicial, Educational, Commercial, Professional and Industrial History.* 4 vols. Boston: D. H. Hurd & Co., 1897.

DeLuxe Hotels of New England: Containing Photographic Views and Description of Some of the Famous Hostelries and Beauty Spots of the Playground of America. Boston: C. B. Webster & Co., 1914.

Drake, Samuel Adams. *Nooks and Corners of the New England Coast.* New York: Harper & Brothers, Publishers, 1875.

Evans, Walker. "Summer North of Boston." *Fortune* 40 (August 1949): 74–79.

Haynes, George H. *Souvenir of New England's Great Resorts.* 2nd ed. New York: Moss Engraving Company, 1891.

Hotels of New England: Containing Photographic Views and Description of Some of the Famous Hostelries and Beauty Spots of the Playground of America. Boston: C. B. Webster & Co., 1915.

Kay, Jane Holtz. *Preserving New England.* New York: Pantheon Books, 1986.

Marnell, William H. *Vacation Yesterdays of New England.* New York: Seabury Press, 1975.

New England's Summer and America's Leading Winter Resorts. New York: G. Frederick Kalkhoff, 1897.

Robinson, William F. *Coastal New England: Its Life and Past.* Boston: New York Graphic Society, 1983.

Varrell, William. *Summer by-the-sea: The Golden Era of Victorian Beach Hotels.* Portsmouth, N.H.: Strawberry Bank Print Shop, 1972.

The Woods, Lakes, Sea-Shore, and Mountains. Portland, Maine: G. W. Morris, Publisher, 1896.

Wriston, John C., Jr. *Vermont Inns and Taverns, Pre-revolutionary to 1925 — An Illustrated and Annotated Checklist.* Rutland, Vt.: Academy Books, 1991.

Zaitsevsky, Cynthia, and Myron Miller. *The Architecture of William Ralph Emerson, 1833–1917.* Cambridge, Mass.: Fogg Art Museum, 1969.

V. CONNECTICUT

Atwan, Robert, ed. *Greenwich, An Illustrated History: A Celebration of 350 Years.* Greenwich, Conn.: Historical Society of the Town of Greenwich and Greenwich Times, 1990.

[Brainard, Newton C.]. *Fenwick.* Hartford, Conn.: Case, Lockwood & Brainard Co., 1944.

Caulkins, Frances M. *History of New London, Connecticut.* New London, Conn.: H. D. Utley, 1895.

Churchill, Sarah P. "The Pequot Colony." *Tidings* (September/October 1987): 14–21.

Clark, William J. *Greenwich.* Images of America. Charleston, S.C.: Arcadia Publishing, 2002.

Decker, Robert Owen. *The Whaling City: A History of New London, Connecticut.* Chester, Conn.: Pequot Press, 1976.

Dorman, Bennett W. *Savin Rock: An Illustrated History.* North Haven, Conn.: Photo Restoration and Design, 1998.

Durbrow, Mitzie. "The Birdsall House." *New Canaan Historical Society Annual* 9, no. 2 (1982): 10–15.

Farnham, Thomas J. *Fairfield: The Biography of a Community, 1639–2000.* 2nd rev. ed. West Kennebunkport, Maine: Phoenix Publishing for the Fairfield Historical Society, 2000.

Ferguson, Henry L. *Fishers Island, N.Y., 1614–1925.* New York: privately printed, 1925.

Fort Griswold House (Eastern Point), New London, Conn. New York: Liberty Printing Company, 1886.

Galvin, Mary C. "Riches to Rubble." *The Greenwich Review* (April 1986): 29. Edgewood Inn.

Gibbs, James. *The City of Groton: Historical & Architectural Resources Survey Report, Phase III–Volume III-1.* Groton, Conn.: Town of Groton Planning Department, 1996.

Grant, Marion Hepburn. *The Fenwick Story.* Hartford, Conn.: Connecticut Historical Society, 1974.

"The Griswold—A Study in Summer Hotel Building." *The Architectural Record* 19, no. 5 (May 1906): 344–60.

Hanna, Archibald. *A Brief History of the Thimble Islands in Branford, Connecticut.* Branford, Conn.: Archon Books for the Branford Historical Society, 1971.

Helander, Joel E. *Oxpasture to Summer Colony: The Story of Sachem's Head in Guilford, Connecticut.* Guilford, Conn.: by the author, 1976.

Hill, Everett G. *A Modern History of New Haven and Eastern New Haven Colony.* 2 vols. New York and Chicago: S. J. Clarke Publishing Company, 1918.

History of Middlesex County, Connecticut. New York: J. B. Beers & Co., 1884.

Hubbard, Frederick A. *Greenwich History: The Judge's Corner.* Ed. Frank Nicholson. Greenwich, Conn.: Round Hill Publications, 2001.

Hughes, Arthur H., and Morse H. Allen. *Connecticut Place Names.* Hartford, Conn.: Connecticut Historical Society, 1976.

Johnson, Gilbert, comp. *Savin Rock Remembered—1985.* West Haven, Conn.: Kramer Printing Company, [c. 1985].

Jones, Dick, et al. *Black Rock: A Bicentennial Picture Book.* Bridgeport, Conn.: Black Rock Civic and Businessmen's Club, 1976.

Justinius, Ivan O. *History of Black Rock.* Bridgeport, Conn.: Antoniak Printing Service for the Black Rock Civic and Business Men's Club, 1955.

Kimball, Carol W., et al. *Groton.* Images of America. Charleston, S.C.: Arcadia Publishing, 2004.

King, Mary Louise. *Portrait of New Canaan: The History of a Connecticut Town.* New Canaan, Conn.: New Canaan Historical Society, 1981.

Norton, F. C. *History of Sachem's Head.* N.pl.: privately published, 1902.

Palmer, Henry Robinson. "Stonington, Connecticut." *The New England Magazine* n.s. 20, no. 2 (April 1899): 225–44.

———. *Stonington By the Sea.* Stonington, Conn.: Palmer Press, 1957.

Read, Eleanor B. "Mystic Island." *Historical Footnotes: Bulletin of the Stonington Historical Society* 21, no. 2 (February 1984): 1–3, 5, 8, 9.

Richardson, Susan, ed. *Greenwich Before 2000: A Chronology of the Town of Greenwich, 1640–1999.* Greenwich, Conn.: Historical Society of the Town of Greenwich, 2000.

Rockey, J. L. *History of New Haven County, Connecticut.* 2 vols. New York: W. W. Preston & Co., 1892.

Ruddy, John J. *New London.* Images of America. Dover, N.H.: Arcadia Publishing, 1998.

Ryerson, Kathleen H. *A Brief History of Madison, Conn.* New York: Pageant Press, 1960.

Saxton, Diane B. "Old Greenwich Inn on the Sound." *The Greenwich Review* (April 1987): 18–19.

Seymour, George Dudley. *New Haven.* New Haven, Conn.: privately printed for the author, 1942.

Stark, Charles R. *Groton, Conn., 1705–1905.* Stonington, Conn.: Palmer Press, 1922.

Starr, W. H. *A Centennial History of the Town of New London.* New London, Conn.: Charles Allyn, 1876.

Stevens, Edna S. *History of Sachem's Head.* Guilford, Conn.: Dorothy Whitfield Historical Society, 1951.

Towne, Richard R. "Good Bye to the Grand Old Greenwich Hotel." *Yankee* 33, no. 4 (April 1969): 66–73, 136–37.

"Wadawanuck House." *Historical Footnotes: Bulletin of the Stonington (Conn.) Historical Society* 5, no. 1 (November 1967): 1.

Witkowski, Mary K., and Bruce Williams. *Bridgeport on the Sound.* Images of America. Charleston, S.C.: Arcadia Publishing, 2001.

VI. RHODE ISLAND

Atlas of Newport, Jamestown, Middletown & Portsmouth, Rhode Island. New York: Sanborn Map Company, 1921.

Atlas of the City of Newport, Rhode Island. . . . Philadelphia: G. M. Hopkins, C. E., 1883.

Atlas of the City of Newport and Towns of Middletown and Portsmouth, Rhode Island. Springfield, Mass.: L. J. Richards & Co., 1907.

Atlas of the State of Rhode Island and Providence Plantations. Philadelphia: D. G. Beers & Co., 1870.

Bayles, Richard M., ed. *History of Newport County, Rhode Island.* New York: L. E. Preston, 1888.

Beckwith, Henry Truman. *The History of Block Island*. N.pl.: n.pub., [c. 1873].

Belcher, Horace G. "Old Rocky Point." *Rhode Island History* 7, no. 1 (January 1948): 32–50.

Benson, Frederick J. *Research, Reflection and Recollections of Block Island*. Westerly, R.I.: Utter Co., 1977.

Block Island: Hotels, Residences and Places of Interest. Providence, R.I.: David Rubin, 1900.

The Book of Rhode Island. Providence, R.I.: Rhode Island State Bureau of Information and Rhode Island Conference of Business Associations, 1930.

Boss, Judith A. *Newport: A Pictorial History*. Norfolk and Virginia Beach, Va.: Donning Company, Publishers, 1981.

Brownell, W. C. *Newport*. America Summer Resorts. New York: Charles Scribner's Sons, 1896.

Buffum, Robert C. *The Weekapaug Inn: The Best of All Possible Worlds, 1899–1999*. Weekapaug, R.I.: Weekapaug Inn, 1999.

Buttrick, James C. *Jamestown*. Images of America. Charleston, S.C.: Arcadia Publishing, 2003.

Carroll, Charles. *Rhode Island: Three Centuries of Democracy*. 4 vols. New York: Lewis Historical Publishing Company, 1932.

———. "Sketch of Narragansett Pier." *Harper's New Monthly Magazine* 59 (July 1879): 161–77.

City Atlas of Newport, Rhode Island. Philadelphia: G. M. Hopkins, C. E., 1876.

Cole, J. R. *History of Washington and Kent Counties, Rhode Island. . . .* New York: W. W. Preston & Co., 1889.

[Collins, John]. *The City and Scenery of Newport, Rhode Island*. Burlington, N.J.: n.pub., 1857.

Cotter, Betty J. *South Shore of Rhode Island*. Images of America. Charleston, S.C.: Arcadia Publishing, 1999.

Crandall, William C. *A Sketch of Narragansett Pier, including Rambles Through South Kingston*. 2nd ed. Wakefield, R.I.: n.pub., [c. 1884].

D'Amato, Donald A. *Warwick: A City at the Crossroads*. Making of America. Charleston, S.C.: Arcadia Publishing, 2001.

D'Amato, Donald A., and Henry A. L. Brown. *Block Island*. Images of America. Charleston, S.C.: Arcadia Publishing, 1999.

Davidson, W. B. *Views of Watch Hill, R.I. and the Neighboring Shore of Little Narragansett Bay*. Westerly, R.I.: O. Stillman, Bookseller & Stationer, [c. 1891].

Demars, Stamford E. "19th century shore resorts on Narragansett Bay." *New England–St. Lawrence Valley Geographic Society Proceedings* 5 (1975): 51–55.

Dow, Charles H. *Newport: The City by the Sea*. Newport, R.I.: J. P. Sanborn, 1880.

Downie, Robert M. *Block Island—The Land*. Block Island, R.I.: Book Nook Press, 1999.

Downing, Antoniette F., and Vincent J. Scully, Jr. *The Architectural Heritage of Newport, Rhode Island, 1640–1915*. 2nd ed., rev. New York: Clarkson N. Potter, Publisher, 1967.

Grieve, Robert. *Newport: Its Approaches by Sea and Land*. Providence, R.I.: J. A. & R. A. Reid, 1889.

Grosvener, Richard. *Newport: An Artist's Impression of Its Architecture and History*. Beverly, Mass.: Commonwealth Editions, 2002.

Hammett, Charles E., Jr. *A Hand-Book of Newport, and Rhode Island*. Newport, R.I.: C. E. Hammett, Jr., 1852.

Haun, Eugene. "Jamestown, R.I., 1657–1961." *Yankee* 25, no. 5 (May 1961): 60–67.

Historic and Architectural Resources of Block Island, Rhode Island. Providence, R.I.: Rhode Island Historical Preservation Commission, 1991.

Historic and Architectural Resources of Jamestown, Rhode Island. Providence, R.I.: Rhode Island Historical Preservation & Heritage Commission, 1995.

Historic and Architectural Resources of Narragansett, Rhode Island. Providence, R.I.: Rhode Island Historical Preservation Commission, 1991.

Historic and Architectural Resources of Westerly, Rhode Island: A Preliminary Report. Providence, R.I.: Rhode Island Historical Preservation Commission, 1978.

History of the State of Rhode Island. With Illustrations from Original Sketches. Philadelphia: Hoag, Wade & Co., 1878.

Hitchcock, Henry-Russell. *Rhode Island Architecture*. New York: Da Capo Press, 1968.

Howard, John H. *100 Years in Jamestown: From Destination Resort to Bedroom Town*. [Jamestown, R.I.]: Jamestown Historical Society, 2000.

Hunter, Anna F. "A Decade of Newport As Seen by Two Wandering Sons." *Bulletin of the Newport Historical Society*, no. 53 (April 1925): 1–23.

Jordy, William H. *Buildings of Rhode Island*. Buildings of the United States. Oxford and New York: Oxford University Press, 2004.

Jordy, William H., and Christopher P. Monkhouse, eds. *Buildings on Paper: Rhode Island Architectural Drawings, 1825–1945*. Providence, R.I.: Brown University, the Rhode Island Historical Society, and the Rhode Island School of Design, 1982.

Kelch, Kristen. "The Glitter is gone, but there is life yet in Oakland Beach." *Rhode Islander*, 27 June 1982, pp. 6–8, 12.

Lang, Derryl G. "The Development of a Summer Resort: Watch Hill, Rhode Island." Ph.D. dissertation, Columbia University, 1988.

Latimer, Sallie W. *Narragansett-By-The-Sea.* Images of America. Dover, N.H.: Arcadia Publishing, 1997.

Livermore, Samuel T. *A History of Block Island. . . .* Hartford, Conn.: Case, Lockwood & Brainard Co., 1877.

Maden, Sue. *The Building Boom in Jamestown, Rhode Island, 1926–1931.* Jamestown, R.I.: West Ferry Press, 2004.

———. *Greetings from Jamestown, Rhode Island: Picture Post Cards, 1900–1950.* Jamestown, R.I.: West Ferry Press, 1988.

———. *Jamestown News Items, 1873–1899.* Jamestown, R.I.: Jamestown Historical Society and the Jamestown Press, 1995.

Maden, Sue, and Patrick Hodgkin. *Jamestown Affairs: Miscellany of Historical Flashbacks.* Jamestown, R.I.: West Ferry Press, 1996.

"'The Mathewson,' Narragansett Pier, R.I.—C. P. H. Gilbert, Architect." *American Architect and Building News* 59, no. 1157 (26 February 1898).

Mendum, Samuel W. "Block Island." *The New England Magazine* n.s. 16, no. 6 (August 1897): 738–51.

Moulton, F. I., comp. *Newport and the Resorts of Narragansett Bay. . . .* Providence, R.I.: J. A. & R. A. Reid, Printers, 1877.

Munro, Wilfred H. *Picturesque Rhode Island. Pen and Pencil Sketches. . . .* Providence, R.I.: J. A. & R. A. Reid, Publishers, 1881.

Narragansett Pier. Evansville, Ind.: Unigraphic, 1980. Reproduced booklets.

"Narragansett Pier." *Harper's New Monthly Magazine* 59, no. 350 (July 1879): 161–75.

Narragansett Pier: The Ideal Summer Resort. New Haven, Conn.: New York, New Haven and Hartford Railroad Company, 1915.

Narragansett Pier, Narragansett, Rhode Island: Statewide Historical Preservation Report W-N-1. Providence, R.I.: Rhode Island Historical Preservation Commission, 1978.

Narragansett Pier, Rhode Island: Street Scenes, Hotels, Residences and Places of Interest. Boston: Heliotype Printing Co., 1899. Also 1900 ed., Providence, R.I.: David Rubin.

Narragansett Pier, R.I., Illustrated. N.pl.: Hotel Men's Association, 1891.

Narragansett Pier, R.I.: Photo-Gravures. Brooklyn, N.Y.: A. Witteman, 1898.

Newport. Season of 1874. Newport, R.I.: Davis & Pitman, [c. 1874].

Newport and its Points of Interest, Embracing Also Jamestown, Wickford, Wakefield and Peacedale. New York: Mercantile Illustrating Company, [c. 1894].

Ocean View Hotel, Block Island, R.I. Boston: Deland & Barta, Printers, [c. 1882].

Odiseos, Phyllis. "The Resort Hotels of Block Island, 1862–1911." M.A. thesis, Columbia University, 1969.

Panaggio, Leonard J. *Portrait of Newport.* Providence, R.I.: Mowbray Company—Publishers, for the Savings Bank of Newport, 1969.

Peck, Regenald E. *Early Land Holders of Watch Hill.* Westerly, R.I.: Utter Co., 1936.

Perry, Charles E., ed. *Block Island: An Illustrated History, Map and Guide. By Rev. S. T. Livermore, A. M.* Rev. ed. Providence, R.I.: Snow & Farnham for C. C. Ball, 1901.

———. "Block Island's Story. . . ." *New England Magazine* 30, no. 5 (July 1904): 515–24.

Reid's Illustrated Sea-Side Souvenir. . . . Providence, R.I.: J. A. & R. A. Reid, [c. 1900].

Robson, Lloyd. "The Hotel Period (1844–1865)." Unpublished booklet of magazine and newspaper article transcripts, n.d. Newport Historical Society, R.I.

———. "Newport, One Hundred Years Ago." *Bulletin of the Newport Historical Society,* no. 106 (July 1961): 3–18.

Rush, Barbara J. *The Narragansett Pier Towers & Casino at the Turn of the Century.* Wakefield, R.I.: Wilson Publishing Company, 1983.

Schreier, Barbara, and Michele Major. "The Resort of Pure Fashion: Newport, Rhode Island, 1890–1914." *Rhode Island History* 47 (February 1989): 22–34.

Simpson, Richard V. *Bristol, Rhode Island.* Images of America. Dover, N.H.: Arcadia Publishing, 1986.

A Sketch of Narragansett Pier: Its Past, Present and Future. Wakefield, R.I.: Narragansett Times, 1888.

Smith, Brigid R. *Watch Hill: By River and By Sea.* Images of America. Charleston, S.C.: Arcadia Publishing, 1999.

Snow, Bradford E. "They go to join the Larkin." *Rhode Islander,* 4 September 1966, pp. 4–6.

Snydacker, Daniel. "The Great Depression in Newport." *Newport History* 58, part 2, no. 198 (Spring 1985): 42–55.

[Snydacker, Daniel, et al.]. "The Business of Leisure: The Gilded Age in Newport." *Newport History* 62, part 3 (Summer 1989): 97–126.

Souvenir of Conanicut. Providence, R.I.: Providence Heliograph Co., [c. 1900]. Jamestown, R.I.

State of Rhode Island and Providence Plantations: Preliminary Survey Report, Town of Tiverton. Providence, R.I.: Rhode Island Historical Preservation Commission, 1983.

State of Rhode Island and Providence Plantations: Preliminary Survey Report, Town of Westerly. Providence, R.I.: Rhode Island Historical Preservation Commission, 1978.

Tallman, Mariana M. *Pleasant Places in Rhode Island, and How to Reach Them.* Providence, R.I.: Providence Journal Company, 1893. Also 1894 ed.

Travis, Donna, et al. *History of Oakland Beach, Then and Now.* Warwick, R.I.: Warwick Historical Society, [c. 1987].

Turner, Henry E. "Newport, 1800–1850." *Newport Daily News,* March 24 and 25, 1897.

Utter, George H. *Old Pictures of Westerly, Rhode Island.* Westerly, R.I.: Utter Company, 1991.

Views of Narragansett Pier. Providence, R.I.: Tibbitts & Preston, 1884.

Views of Newport, R.I. and the Neighborhood. London, Edinburgh, and New York: Thomas Nelson and Son, n.d.

Warwick, Rhode Island: Statewide Historical Preservation Report K-W-1. Providence, R.I.: Rhode Island Historical Preservation Commission, 1981.

Watch Hill, Rhode Island, and its Attractions as a Summer Resort. Cincinnati, Ohio: Robert Clarke & Co., 1886. Also 1887 ed. Republished as the "Historical Souvenir of Watch Hill R.I." Watch Hill, R.I.: Book and Tackle Shop, 1977.

Watson, Irving. *Narragansett Pier As A Fashionable Watering Place and Summer Residence.* Providence, R.I.: A. Crawford Greene, Steam Book and Job Printer, 1873.

Watson, W. L. *History of Jamestown on Conanicut Island in the State of Rhode Island.* Providence, R.I.: John F. Greene Co., 1949.

Westerly, Rhode Island. New York: C. G. Dunn, [c. 1900].

What a Difference a Bay Makes. Providence, R.I.: Rhode Island Historical Society, 1993.

Wyatt, Donald W. *Rocky Point: A Rhode Island Treasure.* Warwick, R.I.: Beacon Communications, [c. 1997].

Yarnell, James L. *Newport through Its Architecture: A History of Styles from Postmedieval to Postmodern.* Newport, R.I.: Salve Regina University Press, 2005.

VII. MASSACHUSETTS

Abbott, Gordon, Jr. *Jeffrey's Creek: A Story of People, Places and Events in the Town That Came to Be Known as Manchester-by-the-Sea.* Manchester-by-the-Sea, Mass.: Manchester Historical Society, 2003.

Anderson, Dorothy M. *The Era of the Summer Estates: Swampscott, Massachusetts, 1870/1940.* Canaan, N.H.: Phoenix Publishing, 1985.

Arrington, Benjamin F., ed. *Municipal History of Essex County, Massachusetts.* 4 vols. New York: Lewis Historical Publishing Company, 1922.

Ayer, Silas Hibbard. *Souvenir of Bass Rocks, Gloucester, Mass.* Boston: Bass Rocks Improvement Association, 1905.

Babson, John J. *History of the Town of Gloucester, Cape Ann, Including the Town of Rockport.* Reprint of 1860 ed. Gloucester, Mass.: Peter Smith, 1972.

Baker, James W. *Plymouth.* Images of America. Charleston, S.C.: Arcadia Publishing, 2002.

Banks, Charles E. *The History of Martha's Vineyard, Dukes County, Massachusetts.* 3 vols. Boston: G. H. Dean, 1911–25.

Barber, Laurence L. *West Yarmouth: A Village Ignored, 1639–1939.* Yarmouth Port, Mass.: Historical Society of Old Yarmouth, 1999.

Bergan, William M. *Old Nantucket.* North Quincy, Mass.: Christopher Publishing House, 1968.

[Brown, Eugene H., comp.]. *Sketches of Nahant: Showing Many Points of Interest.* Boston: Atlantic Printing Company, 1911.

Brown, Richard D., and Jack Tager. *Massachusetts: A Concise History.* Amherst, Mass.: University of Massachusetts Press, 2000.

Carlisle, Robert D. B. *Weathering A Century of Change: Chatham, Cape Cod.* Chatham, Mass.: Chatham Historical Society, 2000.

Chesbro, Paul L. *Osterville: A History of the Village.* Vol. 1. Taunton, Mass.: William S. Sullwold, Publishing, 1988.

Committee for the Preservation of Hull's History. *Hull and Nantasket Beach.* Images of America. Charleston, S.C.: Arcadia Publishing, 1999.

——. *Hull and Nantasket Beach.* Scenes of America. Charleston, S.C.: Arcadia Publishing, 2006.

——. *Then & Now: Hull and Nantasket Beach.* Charleston, S.C.: Arcadia Publishing, 2001.

Cook, Louis A. *History of Norfolk County, Massachusetts, 1622–1918.* 2 vols. Boston: S. J. Clarke, 1918.

Cutter, William R. *Genealogical and Personal Memoirs Relating to Boston and Eastern Massachusetts.* 4 vols. New York: Lewis Historical Publishing Co., 1908.

Daly, Janet M. *Chatham.* Images of America. Charleston, S.C.: Arcadia Publishing, 2002.

"Dedicated to Innkeepers of the Past: An Historical View." *2005 Annual Report — The Cape Cod Five Cents Savings Bank.* Orleans, Mass.: Cape Cod Five Cents Savings Bank, 2005.

Deyo, Simeon L. *History of Barnstable County, Massachusetts.* New York: H. W. Blake & Co., 1890.

Douglas-Lithgow, R. A. *Nantucket: A History.* New York and London: G. P. Putnam's Sons, 1914.

Dyer, Arnold W. *Hotels & Inns of Falmouth: A Survey of 17th, 18th and 19th Century Accommodations.* Falmouth, Mass.: Falmouth Historical Society, 1993.

Eldridge, George W. "Martha's Vineyard, Gem of the North Atlantic." *New England Magazine* n.s. 40 (1909): 163–79.

"An Exclusive North Shore Hotel: The Famous New Ocean

House at Swampscott." *The North Shore Reminder* 6, no. 10 (31 August 1907): 3–6.

Falmouth-by-the-Sea: The Naples of America. Falmouth, Mass.: Board of Trade and Industry, 1896. Reprinted, with additions, Falmouth Chamber of Commerce, 1976.

"A Famous North Shore Resort: The New Ocean House, Swampscott, Massachusetts." *The North Shore Reminder* 6, no. 4 (20 July 1907): 2–7.

Faught, Millard C. *Falmouth, Massachusetts: Problems of a Resort Community*. New York: Columbia University Press, 1945.

Fawsett, Marise. *Cape Cod Annals*. Bowie, Md.: Heritage Books, 1990.

Fifty Glimpses of Nantucket Island from Recent Photographs. Chicago and New York: Rand, McNally & Co. for John F. Murphy, Boston, 1897.

Floyd, Frank L. *"Manchester-by-the-Sea."* 2nd ed. Manchester, Mass.: Floyd's News Store, 1945.

Foley, Joanne S. *Lynn*. Images of America. Dover, N.H.: Arcadia Publishing, 1995.

Foster, Mrs. E. G., and Alice W. Foster. *The Story of Kettle Cove*. Magnolia, Mass.: n.pub., 1899.

Freeman, Frederick. *The History of Cape Cod: The Annals of Barnstable County, Including the District of Mashpee*. 2 vols. Boston: George C. Rand & Avery, 1858–62.

Fuess, Claude M., ed., and Scott H. Paradise, comp. *The Story of Essex County*. 4 vols. New York: American Historical Society, 1935.

Galluzzo, John. *The Golden Age of Hull: Old Home Week, Neighbors and Gala Days*. Charleston, S.C.: The History Press, 2006.

Garland, Joseph E. *Boston's Gold Coast: The North Shore, 1890–1929*. Boston and Toronto: Little, Brown and Company, 1981.

———. *Boston's North Shore: Being an Account of Life Among the Noteworthy, Fashionable, Wealthy, Eccentric and Ordinary, 1823–1890*. Boston and Toronto: Little, Brown and Company, 1978.

———. *Eastern Point: A Nautical, Rustical, and Social Chronicle of Gloucester's Outer Shield and Inner Sanctum, 1606–1950*. Dublin, N.H.: William L. Bauhan, Publisher, 1971.

———. *Eastern Point Revisited: Then and Now, 1899–1989*. Gloucester, Mass.: Association of Eastern Point Residents, 1989.

———. *The Gloucester Guide: A Retrospective Ramble*. Gloucester, Mass.: Gloucester 350th Anniversary Celebration, 1973.

———. *The Gloucester Guide: A Stroll through Place and Time*. Rockport, Mass.: Portean, 1990.

Garrett, Edmund H. *Romance & Reality of the Puritan Coast*. Boston: Little, Brown & Co., 1897.

Gilbreth, Frank B. *Inside Nantucket*. New York: Crowell, 1954.

Gille, Frank A., ed. *Encyclopedia of Massachusetts*. New York: Somerset Publishers, 1984.

Gott, Lemuel, and Ebenezer Pool. *History of the Town of Rockport*. Rockport, Mass.: Rockport Review Office, 1888.

Gould, James W., and Jessica R. Grassetti. *Contuit and Santuit*. Images of America. Charleston, S.C.: Arcadia Publishing, 2003.

Guba, Emil Frederick. *Nantucket Odyssey: A Journey into the History of Nantucket*. 2nd ed. Waltham, Mass.: n.pub., 1965.

"The Harbor View Hotel, Now 100 Years Old." *Dukes County Intelligencer, Dukes County (Mass.) Historical Society* 32, no. 4 (May 1991): 172–80.

Hart, Hildegarde T. *Magnolia Once Kettle Cove*. Magnolia, Mass.: Peter Smith Publishing, 1962.

Hart, Lorena L., and Francis R. Hart. *Not All Is Changed: A Life History of Hingham*. Hingham, Mass.: Hingham Historical Commission, 1993.

Hawes, Charles B. *Gloucester, By Land and Sea: The Story of a New England Seacoast Town*. Boston: Little, Brown, 1923.

Hercher, Gail Pike. "Cat Island: A History of Kings, Captains, and Kids." *Marblehead Magazine* 2, no. 2 (1981): 31–34.

Herihy, Mark Allen. "Leisure, Space, and Collective Memory in the 'Athens of America': A History of Boston's Revere Beach." Ph.D. dissertation, Brown University, 2000.

Herrick, Paul F., and Larry G. Newman. *Old Hyannis Port, Massachusetts: An Anecdotal, Photographic Panorama*. New Bedford, Mass.: Reynolds-DeWatt, 1968.

History of the Town of Hingham, Massachusetts. 3 vols. Hingham, Mass.: published by the town, 1893.

Hobbs, Clarence W. *Lynn and Surroundings*. Lynn, Mass.: Lewis & Winship, 1886.

Hough, Henry Beetle. *Martha's Vineyard: Summer Resort, 1835–1935*. Rutland, Vt.: Tuttle Publishing Company, 1936.

Hoyt, Edwin P. *Nantucket: The Life of an Island*. Brattleboro, Vt.: Stephen Greene Press, 1978.

Hurd, D. Hamilton, ed. *History of Bristol County, Massachusetts. . . .* Philadelphia: J. W. Lewis & Co., 1883.

———, ed. *History of Essex County, Massachusetts. . . .* 2 vols. Philadelphia: J. W. Lewis & Co., 1888.

———, ed. *History of Norfolk County, Massachusetts. . . .* Philadelphia: J. W. Lewis & Co., 1884.

———, ed. *History of Plymouth County, Massachusetts*. Philadelphia: J. W. Lewis & Co., 1884.

Hutt, Frank W., ed. *A History of Bristol County, Massachusetts*. 3 vols. New York: Lewis Historical Publishing Co., 1924.

Jenkins, Candace. "The Development of Falmouth as a Summer Resort, 1850–1900." *Spritsail: A Journal of the History of Falmouth and Vicinity* 6 (Winter 1992): 2–34.

Keene, Betsey D. *History of Bourne from 1622 to 1937.* Yarmouthport, Mass.: C. W. Swift, 1937.

Kittredge, Henry C. *Cape Cod: Its People and Their History.* 2nd ed. Boston: Houghton Mifflin Company, 1968.

Knapton, Ernest John. *Chatham Since The American Revolution.* Chatham, Mass.: Chatham Historical Society, 1976.

Krusell, Cynthia H., and Betty M. Bates. *Marshfield: A Town of Villages, 1640–1990.* Marshfield Hills, Mass.: Historical Research Associates, 1990.

Lamson, Darius F. *History of the Town of Manchester, Essex County, Massachusetts.* Manchester, Mass.: by the town, [c. 1895].

Lancaster, Clay. "Charles H. Robinson." *Historic Nantucket* 38 (Fall 1990): 46–47; (Winter 1990): 52–55. Builder (1829–1915).

———. *Holiday Island: The Pageant of Nantucket's Hostelries and Summer Life From Its Beginnings to the Mid–Twentieth Century.* Nantucket, Mass.: Nantucket Historical Association, 1993.

———. *Nantucket in the Nineteenth Century.* New York: Dover Publications, 1979.

Leonard, Henry C. *Pigeon Cove and Vicinity.* Boston: F. A. Searle, 1873.

Lewis, Alonzo. *The Picture of Nahant.* Lynn, Mass.: Thos. Herbert and Company, 1855.

Lewis, Alonzo, and James R. Newhall. *History of Lynn, Essex County, Massachusetts. . . .* 2 vols. Lynn, Mass.: G. C. Herbert, 1890–97.

Lovell, Russell A., Jr. *Sandwich: A Cape Cod Town.* Sandwich, Mass.: Sandwich Archives and Historical Center, 1984.

Magnolia Souvenir. Boston: Frank Wood, Printer, 1889.

Maloney, Joan M. *Community Life, 1855–1955: Harwich and the Cape Cod Savings Bank.* Harwich, Mass.: Harwich Historical Society and the Cape Cod Five, 2000.

———. *Harwich.* Images of America. Charleston, S.C.: Arcadia Publishing, 2001.

Martin, Roger. *A Rockport Album: Photographs of Bygone Days.* Gloucester, Mass.: Curious Traveller Press, 1998.

———. *Rockport Remembered.* Gloucester, Mass.: Curious Traveller Press, 1997.

Mathias, Christopher R., and Kenneth C. Turino. *Nahant.* Images of America. Charleston, S.C.: Arcadia Publishing, 1999.

McCalley, John W. *Nantucket: Yesterday and Today.* New York: Dover Publications, 1981.

McCauley, Peter E., II. *"Revere Beach Chips": Historical Background from The Revere Journal.* Revere, Mass.: by the author, 1979. Centennial ed., Revere, Mass.: Revere Society for Cultural and Historic Preservation, 1996.

McChristal, Joseph F. *Revere: 100 Years, 1871–1971.* Revere, Mass.: City of Revere, 1972.

Monbleau, Marcia J. *At Home: Harwich, Cape Cod, Massachusetts.* Harwich, Mass.: Harwich Historical Society, 1993.

Morgan, William C. *Beverly, Garden City by the Sea. . . .* Beverly, Mass.: Amos L. Odel, 1897.

Morley, Arthur P. *Rockport: A Town of the Sea.* Cambridge, Mass.: Murray Printing Company, 1924.

Mowry, William A. "Martha's Vineyard." *New England Magazine* n.s. 16 (1897): 543–60.

The New Ocean House Book. Swampscott, Mass.: E. R. Grabow Company, 1911.

North and South Shore Views. N.pl.: Forbes Co., 188?.

O'Connell, James C. *Becoming Cape Cod: Creating a Seaside Resort.* Hanover, N.H., and London: University Press of New England, 2003.

O'Gorman, James F. *This Other Gloucester: Occasional Papers on the Arts of Cape Ann, Massachusetts.* Boston: for the author, 1976.

Parsons, Eleanor. *Rockport: The Making of a Tourist Treasure.* Rockport, Mass.: Twin Lights Publishers, 1998.

Paterson, Stanley, and Carl G. Seabury. *Nahant on the Rocks.* Nahant, Mass.: Nahant Historical Society, 1991.

Perley, Sidney. "Fountain Inn, Marblehead." *Essex Antiquarian* 2 (1898): 125–27.

Perry, E. G. *A Trip Around Cape Cod: Nantucket, Martha's Vineyard, South Shore, and Historic Plymouth.* 3rd ed. Boston: by the author, 1898.

Photographic History of Gloucester. 4 vols. Gloucester, Mass.: Gloucester Historical Reproductions, 1976–79.

Picturesque Cape Ann. Gloucester, Mass.: E. C. McIntire, 1911. Also 1912 ed.

Pratt, Burtram J. *A Narrative History of the Town of Cohasset, Massachusetts.* Cohasset, Mass.: Committee on Town History, 1956.

Pratt, Walter M. *Seven Generations: A Story of Prattsville and Chelsea.* N.pl.: privately printed, 1930.

Pringle, James R. *History of the Town and City of Gloucester, Cape Ann, Massachusetts.* Gloucester, Mass.: n.pub., 1892.

Railton, Arthur R. *The History of Martha's Vineyard.* Beverly, Mass.: Commonwealth Editions and the Martha's Vineyard Historical Society, 2006.

Ray, Mary. *Gloucester, Massachusetts, Historical Time-Line,*

1000–1999. Ed. Sarah V. Dunlap. Gloucester, Mass.: Mary Ray, with the Gloucester Archives Committee, 2002.

Reed, Roger. *Building Victorian Boston: The Architecture of Gridley J. F. Bryant.* Amherst and Boston: University of Massachusetts Press, 2007.

Reid, Nancy T. *Dennis, Cape Cod: From Firstcomers to Newcomers, 1639–1993.* Dennis, Mass.: Dennis Historical Society, 1996.

Revere: 100 Years, 1871–1971. Revere, Mass.: n.pub., [c. 1972].

Richards, Lysander S. *History of Marshfield.* 2 vols. Plymouth, Mass.: Memorial Press, 1901–5.

Roads, Samuel, Jr. *The History and Traditions of Marblehead.* Marblehead, Mass.: Press of N. Allen Lindsey & Co., 1897.

Rockport As It Was . . . A Book of Pictures. Rockport, Mass.: n.pub., 1975. Reprinted, 1992.

Rogers, Patricia H. *Three for a Nickel: Martha's Vineyard Postcards, 1900–1925.* Cambridge, Mass.: Aqua Press, 2002.

Rogers, Rebecca M. "Resort Architecture at Nahant, 1815–1850." *Old-Time New England* 45, nos. 1–2 (July–December 1974): 12–31.

Ryan, Barbara M., et al. *Images in Time: Cape Cod Views from the Historical Society of Old Yarmouth.* Yarmouth Port, Mass.: Historical Society of Old Yarmouth, 2003.

Schneider, Paul. *The Enduring Shore: A History of Cape Cod, Martha's Vineyard, and Nantucket.* New York: Henry Holt, 2000.

Scituate Historical Society. *Scituate.* Images of America. Charleston, S.C.: Arcadia Publishing, 2000.

Searle, Richard W. "History of Catta Island off Marblehead." *Essex Institute Historical Collections* 83, no. 4 (October 1947): 308–52.

Sears, Ann, and Nancy Kougeas. *Falmouth.* Images of America. Charleston, S.C.: Arcadia Publishing for the Falmouth Historical Society, 2002.

The Seven Villages of Barnstable. Barnstable, Mass.: Town of Barnstable, 1976.

Shilham, Michael J. *When I Think of Hingham.* 2nd ed. Hingham, Mass.: Hingham Historical Society and Hingham Historical Commission, 2002.

Shurtleff, Benjamin. *The History of the Town of Revere.* Boston: Beckler Press, 1937.

Sigler, Ruth. "The Resorts of Marblehead." *Marblehead: A Quarterly Magazine* 1, no. 2 (Summer 1980): 25–27, 66.

Smith, Mary Lou, ed. *The Book of Falmouth: A Tricentennial Celebration, 1686–1986.* Falmouth, Mass.: Falmouth Historical Commission, 1986.

———, ed. *Woods Hole Reflections.* Woods Hole, Mass.: Woods Hole Historical Collection, 1983.

Smith, William C. *A History of Chatham, Massachusetts. . . .* 4 vols. Hyannis, Mass.: F. B. & F. P. Goss, 1909–47.

Snow, Caleb H. *A History of Boston, The Metropolis of Massachusetts, From Its Origins to the Present. . . .* Boston: Abel Bowen, 1825.

Snow, Edward Rowe. *The Islands of Boston Harbor, 1630–1971.* New York: Dodd, Mead & Company, 1971.

Starbuck, Alexander. *The History of Nantucket, County, Island, Town. . . .* Boston: C. E. Goodspeed, 1924.

Stoddard, Chris. *A Centennial History: Cottage City.* Oak Bluffs, Mass.: Oak Bluffs Historical Commission, 1980.

Swampscott, Massachusetts Celebrating 150 Years, 1852–2002. Swampscott, Mass.: Swampscott Historical Commission, 2002.

Swan, Marshall W. S. *Town on Sandy Bay: A History of Rockport, Massachusetts.* Canaan, N.H.: Phoenix Publishing for the Town History Committee, 1980.

Swift, Charles F. *Cape Cod, The Right Arm of Massachusetts, An Historical Narrative. . . .* Yarmouth, Mass.: Register Publishing, 1897.

———. *History of Old Yarmouth, Comprising the Present Towns of Yarmouth and Dennis. . . .* Yarmouthport, Mass.: n.pub., 1884.

Thompson, Carolyn, and Jim Thompson. *Cape Ann in Stereo Views.* Images of America. Charleston, S.C.: Arcadia Publishing, 2000.

Thompson, Elroy S. *History of Plymouth, Norfolk and Barnstable Counties, Massachusetts.* New York: Lewis Historical Publishing, Company, 1928.

Thompson, Waldo. *Swampscott: Historical Sketches of the Town.* Lynn, Mass.: Press of Thos. P. Nichols, 1885.

Three Centuries of Cape Cod County, Barnstable, Massachusetts, 1685–1985. Barnstable, Mass.: Butterworth, 1985.

Trayser, Donald G., ed. *Barnstable: Three Centuries of a Cape Cod Town.* Hyannis, Mass.: F. B. & F. P. Goss, 1939.

Turino, Kenneth C., and Christopher R. Mathias. *Swampscott.* Images of America. Dover, N.H.: Arcadia Publishing, 1996.

Vuilleumier, Marion. *The Town of Yarmouth, Massachusetts: A History, 1639–1989.* South Yarmouth, Mass.: Historical Society of Old Yarmouth, 1989.

Webber, C. H., and W. S. Nevins. *Old Naumkeag: An Historical Sketch of Salem, and the Towns of Marblehead, Peabody, Beverly, Danvers, Wenham, Manchester, Topsfield and Middletown.* Salem, Mass.: A. A. Smith & Company, Publishers, and Boston: Lee & Shepard, 1877.

Webber, John S., Jr. *In and Around Cape Ann: A Hand-Book of Gloucester, Mass., and Its Immediate Vicinity. . . .* Gloucester, Mass.: Cape Ann Advertiser Office, 1885.

Weiss, Ellen Barbara. "Wesleyan Grove and Oak Bluffs: From Camp Meeting to Summer Resort." Ph.D. dissertation, University of Illinois, 1984.

Wilson, Fred A. *Some Annals of Nahant, Massachusetts.* Boston: Old Corner Book Store, 1928.

Wood, Edward F. R., Jr. *Old Mattapoisett: A Summer Portrait.* Mattapoisett, Mass.: Quadequina Publishers, 1995.

Woodman, Betsy. "Salisbury Beach (1638–1913): A Place to Gather." *Essex Institute Historical Collections* 124, no. 1 (January 1988): 38–74.

Wright, John Hardy. *Gloucester and Rockport.* Images of America. Charleston, S.C.: Arcadia Publishing, 2000.

———. *Marblehead.* Vol. 1. Images of America. Dover, N.H.: Arcadia Publishing, 1996.

———. *Marblehead.* Vol. 2. Images of America. Charleston, S.C.: Arcadia Publishing, 2000.

Youngman, Elsie P. *Summer Echoes from the 19th Century: Manchester-by-the-Sea.* Rockport, Mass.: Don Russell for the Manchester Historical Society, 1984.

VIII. NEW HAMPSHIRE

Adams, Rachel. "Star of the Sea: Restored, the Wentworth reopens at last." *Preservation* 55, no. 2 (March/April 2003): 28.

Albee, John. *New Castle, Historic and Picturesque.* Boston: Rand Avery Supply Company, 1884.

Aykroyd, Elizabeth, and Betty Moore. *Hampton and Hampton Beach.* Postcard History Series. Charleston, S.C.: Arcadia Publishing, 2005.

Ballingall, H. M. S. "Mr. and Mrs. Smith and the Gala Days of the Wentworth-by-the-Sea." *New Hampshire Profiles* 35, no. 5 (May 1986): 34–37.

Bardwell, John D. *The Isles of Shoals: A Visual History.* Portsmouth, N.H.: for the Portsmouth Marine Society by Peter E. Randall, Publisher, 1989.

Barker, Shirley F. "The Heyday of the Grand Hotel." *New Hampshire Profiles* 5, no. 8 (August 1956): 18–21, 43; no. 9 (September 1956): 26–28, 47–48.

Bigelow, Rev. E. Victor. *Brief History of the Isles of Shoals.* Star Island, Isles of Shoals, N.H.: Congregational Summer Conference, 1923.

"Boar's Head, Hampton Beach, N.H." *Granite Monthly* 9, nos. 1 and 2 (January and February 1886): 75–77.

"Boar's Head Hotel." *Granite Monthly* 10, no. 4 (April 1887): 153–55.

Candee, Richard. *Building Portsmouth: The Neighborhoods and Architecture of New Hampshire's Oldest City.* Portsmouth, N.H.: Portsmouth Advocates, 1992.

Chadwick, John W. "The Isles of Shoals." *Harper's New Monthly Magazine* (October 1874): 663–76.

Cornish, Louis C. *The Story of the Isles of Shoals.* Boston: Beacon Press, [c. 1936].

Dow, Joseph. *History of the Town of Hampton, New Hampshire . . . From Its Settlement in 1638 to the Autumn of 1892.* Salem, Mass.: Salem Press Publishing and Printing Company, 1893.

Gage, William L. *The Isles of Shoals in Summer Time.* Hartford, Conn.: Case, Lockwood & Brainard, 1875.

Garvin, James L., and Donna-Belle Garvin. *On the Road North of Boston: New Hampshire Taverns and Turnpikes, 1700–1900.* Concord, N.H.: New Hampshire Historical Society, 1988.

Gilmore, Robert, and Bruce Ingmire. *The Sea Coast, New Hampshire: A Visual History.* Norfolk, Va.: Donning Company, Publishers, 1989.

Hazlett, Charles A. *History of Rockingham County, New Hampshire, and Representative Citizens.* Chicago: Richmond-Arnold Publishing Co., 1915.

Hobbs, Stillman M., and Helen D. Hobbs. *The Way It Was in North Hampton.* Seabrook, N.H.: Withey Press, 1978.

Hurd, D. Hamilton. *History of Rockingham and Strafford Counties, New Hampshire. . . .* Philadelphia: J. W. Lewis & Co., 1882.

Karabatsos, Lewis T. *Rye and Rye Beach.* Postcard History Series. Charleston, S.C.: Arcadia Publishing, 2004.

Koch, Lou. "Wentworth Hotel, Past and Present." *The Shoreliner* [1] (July 1950): 24–27.

Laighton, Oscar. *Ninety Years at the Isles of Shoals.* Andover, Mass.: Andover Press, 1929.

Lakes and Summer Resorts of New Hampshire. Manchester, N.H.: John B. Clarke, Public Printer, 1891. Also 1892 ed., Concord, N.H.: Ira C. Evans, Public Printer, for the Board of Agriculture.

Lane, L. K. H. "Gems of the New Hampshire Shore." *Granite Monthly* 19, no. 1 (July 1895): 8–38.

———. "Historic Hampton." *Granite Monthly* 21, no. 1 (July 1896): 1–21.

Metcalf, H. H. "The Story of the Isles of Shoals." *Granite Monthly* 46, no. 8 (August 1914): 231–45.

"New Castle." *Granite Monthly* 3, no. 10 (July 1880): 446–48.

"New Castle and the Piscataqua." *Granite Monthly* 13, nos. 3–4 (March/April 1890): 73–88.

Parsons, Langdon B. *History of the Town of Rye, New Hampshire.* Concord, N.H.: Rumford Printing Company, 1905.

Pillsbury, Hobart. *New Hampshire: Resources, Attractions and People, A History*. 8 vols. New York: Lewis Historical Publishing Co., 1927–28.

"Popular Summer Resorts in New Hampshire." *Granite Monthly* 13, nos. 3–4 (March/April 1890): 92–96.

Randall, Peter E. *Hampton, A Century of Town and Beach, 1888–1898*. (*History of Hampton, New Hampshire, 1638–1988*, vol. 3). Hampton, N.H.: for the Town of Hampton by Peter E. Randall, Publisher, 1989.

Randall, Peter E., and Maryellen Burke, eds. *Gosport Remembered: The Lost Village at the Isles of Shoals*. Portsmouth, N.H.: Published for the Portsmouth Marine Society by Peter E. Randall, Publisher, 1997.

Robinson, J. Dennis. *Wentworth By The Sea: The Life and Times of a Grand Hotel*. Portsmouth, N.H.: Peter E. Randall, Publisher, 2004.

Rutledge, Lyman V. *The Isles of Shoals in Lore and Legend*. Barre, Mass.: Barra Publishers, 1965. 2nd ed., Boston: Star Island Corporation, 1971.

Rutledge, Lyman V., et al. *Ten Miles Out: Guide Book to the Isles of Shoals, Portsmouth, New Hampshire*. 5th ed. Boston: Isles of Shoals Association, 1972. Also 6th ed., 1984.

Squires, J. Duane. *The Granite State of the United States: A History of New Hampshire from 1623 to the Present*. 4 vols. New York: American Historical Company, 1956.

St. John, Helen. *Inalong, Outalong, Downalong: Reminiscences of New Castle, New Hampshire*. Portsmouth, N.H.: Peter E. Randall, Publisher, 1985.

Stackpole, Everett S. *History of New Hampshire*. 5 vols. New York: American Historical Society, [c. 1916].

A Stern and Lovely Scene: A Visual History of the Isles of Shoals. Durham, N.H.: University Art Galleries, University of New Hampshire, 1978.

Teschek, William H. *Hampton and Hampton Beach*. Images of America. Dover, N.H.: Arcadia Publishing, 1997.

Tolles, Bryant F., Jr., ed. and contributor. *The Grand Resort Hotels and Tourism in the White Mountains*. Concord, N.H.: New Hampshire Historical Society, 1995. Proceedings of the third Mount Washington Observatory Symposium, Bretton Woods, N.H., 24–25 June 1994.

— —. *The Grand Resort Hotels of the White Mountains: A Vanishing Architectural Legacy*. Boston: David R. Godine, Publisher, 1998.

———. *New Hampshire Architecture: An Illustrated Guide*. Hanover, N.H.: University Press of New England for the New Hampshire Historical Society, 1979. Reprt., 2004.

———. *Summer Cottages in the White Mountains: The Architecture of Leisure and Recreation, 1870 to 1930*. Hanover, N.H., and London: University Press of New England, 2000.

Town and City Atlas of the State of New Hampshire. Boston: D. H. Hurd & Co., 1892.

Varrell, William M. "The Golden Era of Rye Beach." *New Hampshire Profiles* 8, no. 9 (September 1959): 20–23, 51.

———. *Rye and Rye Beach*. Images of America. Dover, N.H.: Arcadia Publishing, 1995.

———. *Rye on the Rocks: The Tale of a Town*. Portsmouth, N.H.: Strawberry Bank Print Shop, 1962.

"Wentworth By the Sea, A Marriot Hotel and Spa." Advertising Supplement to *The Boston Globe Magazine*, 4 May 2003.

Whittaker, Robert H. *Land of Lost Content: The Piscataqua River Basin and the Isles of Shoals. The People, Their Dreams, Their History*. Dover, N.H.: Alan Sutton Publishing, 1993.

Wood, James A. *New Hampshire Homes*. Concord, N.H.: n.pub., 1895. Section titled "Leading Hotels of New Hampshire."

IX. MAINE

Abbott, John S. C. *The History of Maine, From the Earliest Discovery of the Region . . . Until the Present Time. . . .* Boston: B. B. Russell, and Portland, Maine: John Russell, 1875.

Art Work of York County, Maine. Chicago: W. H. Parish Publishing Company, 1894.

Atlas of York Co., Maine. Philadelphia: Sanford, Everts & Co., 1872.

Bachelder, Peter Dow. *The Great Steel Pier: An Illustrated History of the Old Orchard Beach Pier*. Ellsworth, Maine: Breakwater Press, 1998.

Baker, Madge. *Woven Together in York County, Maine: A History, 1865–1900*. Shapleigh, Maine: Wilson's Printers, 1999.

Balanger, Pamala J. *Inventing Acadia: Artists and Tourists at Mount Desert*. Hanover, N.H., and London: University Press of New England, 1999.

Baldwin, Letitia. "The Man Who Built Northeast Harbor." *Down East* 42, no. 7 (February 1996): 32–35; 57–59. Fred L. Savage.

Bardwell, John D. *A History of York Harbor and the York Harbor Reading Room*. Portsmouth, N.H.: Peter E. Randall, Publisher, for the Old York Historical Society, 1993.

———. *Ogunquit-By-The-Sea*. "The Old Photographs Series." Augusta, Maine: Alan Sutton, 1994.

———. *Old Kittery*. Images of America. Dover, N.H.: Arcadia Publishing, 1995.

———. *Old York Beach*. The Old Photographs Series. Augusta, Maine: Alan Sutton, 1994.

———. *Old York Beach.* Vol. 2. Images of America. Dover, N.H.: Arcadia Publishing, 1996.

Bargen, Edna H. *Facts and Fancies and Repetitions about Dark Harbor.* N.pl.: privately printed, 1935. Islesboro Island, Maine.

Barry, William D., and Debra Verrier. "Sun, Sand, Sea — and Neon: Old Orchard Beach Celebrates One Hundred Years of Summer Fun." *Down East* 29, no. 12 (July 1983): 66–72, 104.

Barry, William D., and Ellen M. Ward. "Portland's Most Exclusive Enclave." *Down East* 35, no. 2 (September 1988): 80–84. Cushing's Island, Casco Bay.

Beckford, William H. *Leading Business Men of Kennebunkport, Kennebunk and Old Orchard Beach. . . .* Boston: Mercantile Publishing Company, 1888.

Beem, Edgar Allen. "America's Summer Playground." *Down East* 51, no. 9 (April 2005): 74–77, 107.

Bibber, Joyce K. *Harpswell.* Images of America. Dover, N.H.: Arcadia Publishing, 1996.

Billings, Richard W. *The Village and the Hill: Growing Up in Seal Harbor, Maine, in the 1930s.* Augusta, Maine: Day Mountain Publishing Company, 1995.

Bradbury, Tom, and Pamela Wood, eds. *Across Generations: 350 Years of Life in Kennebunkport.* Kennebunkport, Maine: by the town, 2003.

Brechlin, Earl. *Bygone Bar Harbor: A Postcard Tour of Mount Desert Island & Acadia National Park.* Camden, Maine: Down East Books, 2002.

Bryan, John M. *Maine Cottages: Fred L. Savage and the Architecture of Mount Desert.* New York: Princeton Architectural Press, 2005.

Burr, Steven. *The Kennebunks in Season.* Postcard History Series. Charleston, S.C.: Arcadia Publishing, 2005.

Butler, Charles J., Jr. *Biddeford.* Images of America. Charleston, S.C.: Arcadia Publishing, 2003.

Butler, Joyce. *A Kennebunkport Album.* Kennebunk Landing, Maine: Rosemary House Press, 1984.

———. *Kennebunkport Scrapbook.* Kennebunk, Maine: Thomas Murphy, Publisher, 1977.

Cape Elizabeth, Past to Present. Cape Elizabeth, Maine: Cape Elizabeth Historical Preservation Society, 1991.

Castine. Images of America. Dover, N.H.: Arcadia Publishing, 1996.

Clark, Charles E. *Maine: A Bicentennial History.* New York: W. W. Norton & Company for the American Association for State and Local History, 1977.

Clarke, Grace O. *One Hundred Years of a Maine Hotel, 1850–1950.* Scarborough Beach, Maine: Atlantic House, 1950.

[Clayton, W. W.]. *History of Cumberland Co., Maine.* Philadelphia: Everts & Peck, 1880.

———. *History of York County, Maine.* Philadelphia: Everts & Peck, 1880.

Clifford, Harold B. *The Boothbay Region, 1906 to 1960.* Freeport, Maine: Bond Wheelwright Co., 1961.

Clough, Annie L. *Head of the Bay: Sketches and Pictures of Blue Hill, Maine, 1762–1962.* Woodstock, Vt.: Elm Tree Press for the Congregational Church of Blue Hill, 1963.

Coe, Harrie B. *Maine: Resources, Attractions, and Its People.* 5 vols. New York: Lewis Historical Publishing Company, 1928.

Cole, John N. *Summer Hotel: The Claremont Story, 1884–1994.* Southwest Harbor, Maine: Claremont Hotel, 1994.

Cooper, S. Josephine, ed. *A Bicentennial History of Sullivan, Maine.* Sullivan, Maine: Sullivan-Sorrento Historical Society, 1989.

DeCosta, Benjamin F. *Rambles in Mount Desert: With Sketches of Travel on the New England Coast, From Isles of Shoals to Grand Mahan.* New York: A. D. F. Randolph & Co., 1871.

———. *Sketches of the Coast of Maine and Isles of Shoals, with Historical Notes.* New York: by the author, 1869.

Dibner, Martin, ed. *Portland.* Portland, Maine: Greater Portland Landmarks, 1972.

Doiron, Paul. "The Black Point Inn." *Down East* 48, no. 9 (April 2002): 31–32, 34.

Dole, Nathan Haskell. *Maine of the Sea and Pines.* Boston: L. C. Page & Company, 1928.

Dominique, Robert A. *Greetings From Old Orchard Beach, Me.: A Picture Post Card History.* Wilmington, Mass.: Hampshire Press, 1986.

Dozois, Elin B. *Phippsburg.* Images of America. Charleston, S.C.: Arcadia Publishing, 1999.

Drake, Samuel Adams. *The Pine-Tree Coast.* Boston: Estes & Lauriat, 1894.

Duncan, Roger F. *Coastal Maine: A Maritime History.* New York and London: W. W. Norton & Company, 1992.

Dyer, Barbara. *Camden and Rockport.* Images of America. Dover, N.H.: Arcadia Publishing, 1995.

———. *Vintage Views of Camden, Maine.* Camden, Maine: Camden Printing Company, 1987.

Elkins, L. Whitney. *The Story of Maine: Coastal Maine.* Bangor, Maine: Hillsborough Company, 1924.

Ellis, Alice V. *The Story of Stockton Springs, Maine.* Stockton Springs, Maine: Historical Committee, 1963.

Elwell, Edward H. *Portland and Vicinity.* Portland, Maine: Loring, Short & Harmon, and W. S. Jones, 1876.

Emery, Carl S. *Forest City (Portland, Maine)*. Portland, Maine: Carl S. Emery, 1948.

Emery, George A. *Ancient City of Gorgeana and Modern Town of York (Maine)* . . . . 2nd ed. York Corner, Maine: Courant Steam Job Print, 1894.

Ernest, George. *New England Miniature: A History of York, Maine*. Freeport, Maine: Bond Wheelwright Company, 1961.

Fahlman, Betsey. "Lindley Johnson, 1854–1937." *A Biographical Dictionary of Architects in Maine* 6, ed. Earle G. Shettleworth, Jr., and Roger G. Reed. Augusta, Maine: Maine Historic Preservation Commission, 1991.

Fairfield, Ray P. "The Old Orchard 'Set-Off.'" *New England Quarterly* 27, no. 2 (June 1954): 227–42.

Farrow, John P. *History of Islesborough, Maine*. Bangor, Maine: Thomas W. Burr, 1893. Reprint, Camden, Maine: Camden Herald Publishing Co. for the Islesboro Historical Society, 1965.

Fillmore, R. B. *Chronicles of Knox County*. N.pl.: n.pub., 1922.

——. *Chronicles of Lincoln County*. Augusta, Maine: Kennebec Journal Press Print Shop, 1924.

Freeport. Images of America. Dover, N.H.: Arcadia Publishing, 1996.

Gouldsboro Land and Improvement Company. *Grindstone Inn and Lands; Grindstone Neck, Winter Harbor, Maine*. Winter Harbor, Maine: Grindstone Land Improvement Company, [c. 1891]. Also [c. 1892] ed.

The Gouldsboro Land Improvement Company, Winter Harbor, Maine. Winter Harbor, Maine: G. L. I. Co., 1890.

Grant, Alec J. *A Guide to Bar Harbor, Mount Desert Island, Maine*. Bar Harbor, Maine: W. H. Sherman, Printer, 1901.

Greene, Francis B. *History of Boothbay, Southport and Boothbay Harbor, Maine, 1623–1905*. Portland, Maine: Loring, Short & Harmon, 1906. Reprint, Somersworth, N.H.: New England History Press, 1984.

——. *Souvenir Hand-Book of Boothbay-Harbor-and-Vicinity.* . . . Boothbay Harbor, Maine: Register Job Print, [c. 1896].

Gregory, Jane. "The Shingle Style." *Down East* 32, no. 7 (February 1986): 49–51, 69, 71, 110. John Calvin Stevens, architect.

Hahn, Nathalie. *A History of Winter Harbor, Maine*. Winter Harbor, Maine: by the author, 1974.

Hale, Richard W., Jr. *The Story of Bar Harbor*. New York: Ives Washburn, 1949.

Half Hour Detours in the Four Kennebunks. Kennebunk, Maine: Publicity Bureau of the Kennebunk Chamber of Commerce, 1927.

Hanna, Joshua. "The Pemaquid Peninsula of Maine: A Study of Economic and Community Development, 1815–1915." Undergraduate honors thesis, Dartmouth College, 1994.

Harden, Brian R., ed. *Shore Village Album: A Photographic Tour of Rockland, Maine, 1880–1930*. Rockland, Maine: Shore Village Historical Society, 1977.

Harden, Brian R., et al. *Shore Village Story: An Informal History of Rockland, Maine*. Rockland, Maine: Rockland Bicentennial Commission, 1976.

Hatch, Louis C., ed. *Maine: A History*. New York: American Historical Society, 1919.

Haynes, George H. *The Islands and Shore Gems of Beautiful Casco Bay*. New York: Moss Engraving Co., 1892.

——. *Maine Resorts: Health, Pleasure and Sporting*. New York: Press of Andrew H. Kellogg, 1894.

——. *The State of Maine in 1893*. New York: Moss Engraving Company, 1893.

Hebert, Richard A. *Modern Maine: Its Historic Background, People and Resources*. 4 vols. New York: Lewis Historical Publishing Company, 1951.

Helfrich, G. W., and Gladys O'Neil. *Lost Bar Harbor*. Camden, Maine: Down East Books, 1982.

Henderson, Ruth. "Casco Castle." *Down East* 10, no. 10 (July 1964): 42–43.

Herson, Catherine O'Clair. *Sorrento: A Well-Kept Secret*. Sorrento, Maine: privately published, 1995.

Hill, Ruth Ann. *Discovering Old Bar Harbor and Acadia National Park: An Unconventional History and Guide*. Camden, Maine: Down East Books, 1996.

History of Islesboro, Maine, 1893–1983. Islesboro, Maine: Islesboro Historical Society, 1984.

Hornsby, Stephen J. "The Gilded Age and the Making of Bar Harbor." *Geographical Review* 83 (October 1993): 455–68.

Hull, John T., ed. *Hand-Book: Portland, Old Orchard, Cape Elizabeth and Casco Bay*. Portland, Maine: Southworth Brothers, 1888.

Hutchinson, Gloria. "Atlantic House, A Summer Refuge." *Down East* 21, No. 9 (June 1975): 50–55.

Ingleheart, Elizabeth. "Cushing's Island, Maine: A Planned Summer Colony." M.A. thesis, Columbia University, 1984.

Innes, Richard B. *Little Chebeague Island: Its History from 1874 to 2002*. Portland, Maine: by the author, 2002.

——. *A Partial History of Little Chebeague Island, Casco Bay, Maine*. N.pl.: n.pub., 1995. Covers period 1813 to 1876.

——. *Some Mementos of Little Chebeague's Waldo Hotel*. N.pl.: n.pub., 2000.

Jellison, Connee. *Hancock County: a rock-bound paradise—A Bicentennial Pictorial*. Norfolk and Virginia Beach, Va.: Downing Company, 1990.

Jensen, Carole A. "Edmund M. Wheelwright, 1854–1912." *A Biographical Dictionary of Architects in Maine* 4, no. 13, ed. Earle G. Shettleworth, Jr., and Roger G. Reed. Augusta, Maine: Maine Historic Preservation Commission, 1987.

Jordon, William B., Jr. *A History of Cape Elizabeth, Maine.* Portland, Maine: House of Falmouth, 1965.

Joy, Kenneth. *The Kennebunks: "Out of the Past."* Freeport, Maine: Bond Wheelwright Company, 1967.

Judd, Richard W., Edwin A. Churchill, and Joel W. Eastman, eds. *Maine: The Pine Tree State from Prehistory to the Present.* Orono, Maine: University of Maine Press, 1995.

Kocher, Paula H. *Having a Great Time! Postcards of Ogunquit, Wells, the Yorks and the Kennebunks, 1900–1930.* Malvern, Pa.: Poverty Ridge Stone Co., 1989.

Kramer, Barbara. *Belfast and Searsport.* Images of America. Dover, N.H.: Arcadia Publishing, 1997.

Laughton, Rodney. *Scarborough.* Images of America. Dover, N.H.: Arcadia Publishing, 1996.

———. *Scarborough in the Twentieth Century.* Images of America. Portsmouth, N.H.: Arcadia Publishing, 2004.

Locke, John Staples. *Historical Sketches of Old Orchard and the Shores of Saco Bay, Biddeford Pool, Old Orchard Beach, Pine Point, Prout's Neck.* Enl. ed. Boston: C. H. Woodman & Co., Publishers, 1884.

———. *Old Orchard, Maine. Pen and Pencil Sketches.* Boston: Graves, Locke & Co., 1879.

Lovering, Frank W. "Watering Places of the Gay Nineties." *Down East* 6, no. 1 (August 1959): 16–19.

MacIsaac, Kimberly E. *The Casco Bay Islands, 1850–2000.* Images of America. Charleston, S.C.: Arcadia Publishing, 2004.

Magnuson, Rosalind. *Quiet, Well Kept, for Sensible People: The Development of Kennebunk Beach from 1860–1930.* Kennebunk, Maine: Brick Store Museum, 2000.

McAllister, Timothy E. "The History of Bar Harbor and Mount Desert Island: A Century as a Summer Resort." Honors thesis, Williams College, 1978.

McLane, Charles B. *Islands of the Mid-Maine Coast: Pemaquid Point to the Kennebec River.* Gardiner, Maine: Tilbury House, and Rockland, Maine: Island Institute, 1994.

Meara, Emmett. "It Breaks a Feller's Heart." *Yankee* 36, no. 4 (April 1972): 38–46. Samoset Hotel, Rockland, Maine.

Memories of Camden. Camden, Maine: Camden Bicentennial Committee, 1991.

Merrill, John P., and Suzanne Merrill, eds. *Squirrel Island, Maine: The First Hundred Years.* Freeport, Maine: Bond Wheelwright Company for the Squirrel Island Village Corporation, 1973.

Moody, Edward C. *Handbook History of the Town of York From The Earliest Times to the Present.* Augusta, Maine: Kennebec Journal Company [c. 1921].

Moore, Joshua F. "Hotel Inferno." *Down East* 51, no. 1 (August 2004): 126. The Samoset, Mouse Island, Southport, Maine.

Moulton, John K. *An Informal History of Four Islands: Cushing, House, Little Diamond, Great Diamond.* Yarmouth, Maine: n.pub., 1991.

———. *Peak's Island: An Affectionate History.* Yarmouth, Maine: n.pub., 1993.

Murphy, Kevin D. *Colonial Revival in Maine.* New York: Princeton Architectural Press, 2004.

———. "William E. Barry, 1846–1932." *A Biographical Dictionary of Architects in Maine,* no. 6, ed. Earle G. Shettleworth, Jr. Augusta, Maine: Maine Historic Preservation Commission, 1984.

Myers, Denys Peter. "Isaiah Rogers, 1800–1869." *A Biographical Dictionary of Architects in Maine* 3, no. 2, ed. Earle G. Shettleworth, Jr., and Roger G. Reed. Augusta, Maine: Maine Historic Preservation Commission, 1986.

Neagle, Majorie S. "Appledore—Maine's House of Entertainment." *Down East* 9, no. 10 (July 1963): 34–37, 60. Isles of Shoals.

Neal, John. *Portland Illustrated.* Portland, Maine: W. S. Jones, Publisher, 1874.

Nowlan, Alden. *Campobello: The Outer Island.* Toronto and Vancouver: Clarke Irwin & Company, 1975.

One Hundred Years of a Maine Hotel, 1850–1950. Scarborough Beach, Maine: Atlantic House, [c. 1950].

Phippen, Sanford E., ed. *The Sun Never Sets on Hancock Point: An Informal History.* 2 vols. Hancock, Maine: Historical Society of the Town of Hancock, Maine, 2000.

Portland . . . and the Scenic Gems of Casco Bay. Portland, Maine: G. W. Morris, 1896.

Prouts: Then and Now, 1888–1970. Scarborough, Maine: Prouts Neck Association, 1971.

Reed, Roger G. "Bruce Price, 1845–1903." *A Biographical Dictionary of Architects in Maine* 3, no. 5, ed. Earle G. Shettleworth, Jr., and Roger G. Reed. Augusta, Maine: Maine Historic Preservation Commission, 1986.

———. *A Delight to All Who Knew It: The Maine Summer Architecture of William R. Emerson.* Augusta, Maine: Maine Historic Preservation Commission, 1990.

———. *Summering on the Thoroughfare: The Architecture of North Haven, 1885–1945.* Portland, Maine: Maine Citizens for Historic Preservation, 1993.

———. "William R. Miller, 1866–1929." *A Biographical Dictionary of Architects in Maine* 5, no. 14, ed. Earle G. Shettleworth, Jr., and Roger G. Reed. Augusta, Maine: Maine Historic Preservation Commission, 1988.

Rich, Louise Dickinson. *The Coast of Maine: An Informal History.* 3rd ed. New York: Thomas Y. Crowell Company, 1970.

Richards, David L. *Poland Spring: A Tale of the Gilded Age, 1860–1900*. Hanover, N.H., and London: University Press of New England, 2005.

Ritter, Chris. *Ogunquit, Maine — A Photographic Essay*. Ogunquit, Maine: Pinetree Designs Gallery, [c. 1966].

Robinson, Revel. *History of Camden and Rockport, Maine*. Camden, Maine: Camden Publishing Company, 1907.

Roerden, Chris. *Collections from Cape Elizabeth, Maine*. Cape Elizabeth, Maine: by the town, 1965.

Rolde, Neil. *Maine: A Narrative History*. Gardiner, Maine: Harpswell Press, 1990.

———. *York is Living History*. Brunswick, Maine: Harpswell Press, 1975.

Samoset Anniversary Special. Rockland, Maine: Courier-Gazette, 11 June 1994.

The SamOset By the Sea, Rockland Breakwater, Maine. Portland, Maine: Ricker Hotel Company, [c. 1914].

Samoset Pictorial Souvenir: The End of an Era. Rockland, Maine: Courier-Gazette, 1972. Documents the 1972 burning of the Samoset Hotel.

Sargent, William M. *An Historical Sketch, Guide Book, and Prospectus of Cushing's Island, Casco Bay, Coast of Maine*. New York: American Photo-Engraving Company, [c. 1886].

Savage, Richard A. "Bar Harbor: A Resort is Born." *New England Galaxy* 18, no. 4 (Spring 1977): 11–22.

———. "Bar Harbor: The Hotel Era, 1868–1880." *Maine Historical Society Newsletter* 10, no. 4 (May 1971).

Scott, Connie P. *Kennebunkport*. The Old Photographs Series. Augusta, Maine: Alan Scott, 1994.

Scully, Jeffrey A. *It Happened Right Here: . . . Biddeford, Saco and Old Orchard Beach*. Saco, Maine: Doodlebug Publishing, 1999.

———. *The Old Orchard*. Images of America. Dover, N.H.: Arcadia Publishing, 1995.

Seaman, Charles L. *Ogunquit, Maine, 1900–1971*. Ogunquit, Maine: C & D Publications, 2001.

Seaman, Charles L., and Dorothy A. Seaman. *A Pictorial History of Ogunquit, Maine, 1870–1950*. Ogunquit, Maine: by the authors, 1993.

Seligmann, Herbert J. "Bar Harbor — From Eden to Tourism." *Down East* 4, no. 1 (August 1957): 24–29, 45–46.

Shelley, Hope M. *Beaches of Wells*. Images of America. Charleston, S.C.: Arcadia Publishing, 1997.

———. *My Name Is Wells: I Am the Town: A History of Wells, Maine. . . .* Wells, Maine: Penobscot Press for the 350th Celebration History Committee, 2002.

———. *Wells*. Images of America. Charleston, S.C.: Arcadia Publishing, 1996.

Shettleworth, Earle G., Jr. "Joseph W. Thompson, 1822–1891."

A Biographical Dictionary of Architects in Maine 2, no. 1, ed. Earle G. Shettleworth, Jr., and Roger G. Reed. Augusta, Maine: Maine Historic Preservation Commission, 1985.

———. *The Summer Cottages of Islesboro, 1890–1930*. Islesboro, Maine: Islesboro Historical Society, 1989.

Shettleworth, Earle G., Jr., and Lydia B. Vanderbergh. *Mount Desert Island, Somesville, Southwest Harbor, and Northeast Harbor*. Images of America. Charleston, S.C.: Arcadia Publishing, 2001.

Smith, David C., and Edward O. Schriver. *Maine: A History Through Selected Readings*. Dubuque, Iowa: Kendall/Hunt Publishing Company, 1985.

A Souvenir of Bar Harbor and Mount Desert Island. Bar Harbor, Maine: Bar Harbor Historical Society, 1996. Reprint of work published by W. H. Sherman, Bar Harbor, 1893.

Spend Your Vacation at Old Orchard Beach, Maine. Old Orchard Beach, Maine: P. R. Rich, Resort Advertising, 1920.

Spiller, Virginia S. *350 Years As York: Focusing on the Twentieth Century*. York, Maine: Town of York 350th Anniversary Committee, 2001.

Sprague, John Francis. "Mount Kineo and the Maine Summer Resort Industry." *Sprague's Journal of Maine History* 2, no. 1 (May 1914): 10–16.

Stevens, John Calvin, II, and Earle G. Shettleworth, Jr. *John Calvin Stevens: Domestic Architecture, 1890–1930*. Scarborough, Maine: Harp Publications, 1990.

Stimpson, Mary S. "Rockland, Rockport and Camden." *New England Magazine* 31, no. 1 (September 1904): 3–15.

Street, George E. *Mount Desert: A History*. Boston and New York: Houghton, Mifflin and Company, 1905.

Sullivan, David. *The Algonquin, St. Andrews, N.B. on Passamaquoddy Bay*. St. Andrews, N.B.: Pendlebury Press, 2005.

Sweetser, Phyllis S. *Cumberland, Maine, in Four Centuries*. Cumberland, Maine: Town of Cumberland, 1976.

Thompson, Deborah, ed. *Maine Forms of American Architecture*. Camden, Maine: Downeast Magazine for the Colby Museum of Art, 1976.

Thorton, Nellie C. *Traditions and Records of Southwest Harbor and Somesville, Mount Desert Island, Maine. . . .* Southwest Harbor, Maine: n.pub., 1938.

Turner, Loretta M. *When Bar Harbor Was Eden*. Images of America. Dover, N.H.: Arcadia Publishing, 1995.

Vanderbergh, Lydia, and Earle G. Shettleworth, Jr. *Revisiting Seal Harbor and Acadia National Park*. Images of America. Dover, N.H.: Arcadia Publishing, 1997.

Viele, S. Thompson. *The Origins of Modern York*. York, Maine: Old York Historical Society, 2004.

Vietze, Andrew. "Rock On, Rock On . . . Chebeague Inn." *Down East* 42, no. 11 (June 1996): 46–49.

Vincent, Ellen, comp. *Down on the Island, Up on the Main: A Recollected History of South Bristol, Maine.* Gardiner, Maine: Tilbury House Publishers for the South Bristol Historical Society, 2003.

Ward, Ellen M. "Ninety-Day Wonder." *Down East* 47, no. 2 (September 2000): 66. Passaconaway Inn, Cape Neddick, Maine.

Wells, Kate G. *Campobello: An Historical Sketch.* Boston: n.pub., [c. 1893].

Wells, Stan, and Ellen Wells. *The Christmas Cove Improvement Association, 1900–2000: A Centennial History.* So. Bristol, Maine: Christmas Cove Improvement Association, 2000.

Wheeler, George A. *Castine, Past and Present. . . .* Boston: Rockwell and Churchill Press, 1896.

Wheeler, George A., and Louise Wheeler Bartlett. *History of Castine, Penobscot and Brooksville, Maine.* Cornwall, N.Y.: privately printed, 1923.

Williamson, Joseph, and Alfred Johnson. *History of the City of Belfast in the State of Maine.* Vol. 2, 1875–1900. Boston and New York: Houghton Mifflin Company, 1913.

Wood, Esther. *Deep Roots: A Maine Legacy.* Camden, Maine: Yankee Books, 1990. Blue Hill, Maine.

York, Maine, Then and Now: A Pictorial Documentation. York, Maine: Old Gaol Museum Committee and Old York Historical and Improvement Society, 1976.

Index

Page numbers in *italics* refer to illustrations.

Acadian Hotel (Castine, Maine), 164–65, *165*

Ainsile, Allen, 93

"Aladdin's Palace." *See* Hotel Nantasket

Alden, Henry Bailey, 79

Algonquin Hotel (St. Andrews, New Brunswick, Canada), *12*, 177–79, *178*

Americus Club, 16–17

Appledore House (Appledore Island, Maine), *8*, *120*, 120–21

archery, 12

architectural style: overview, 3–4; economic considerations in, 5; post–Civil War prosperity and, 9; public-building architecture, 41, 139; social class and, 1–2. *See also particular styles*

Arts and Crafts movement, 13

Asher Benjamin's Exchange Coffee House (Boston), 6

Asticou Inn (Northeast Harbor, Maine) — second, *172*, 172, *Plate 14*

Astor House (New York City), 6–7

Atlantic House (Bar Harbor, Maine) — second, 168

Atlantic House (Hull, Massachusetts), 66–67, *67*

Atlantic House (Marshfield, Massachusetts; orig. Pioneer Cottage), 70

Atlantic House (Narragansett Pier, Rhode Island), *46*, *46*

Atlantic House (Newport, Rhode Island), 36–37

Atlantic House (Rye Beach, New Hampshire), 111

Atlantic House (Scarborough, Maine), 148

Atlantic House (Watch Hill, Rhode Island; later Colonial House), 52, 54, *56*

Atlantic House (Wells Beach, Maine), 133

Atlantis Hotel (Kennebunk Beach, Maine), *135*, 135

Atwood House (Narragansett Pier, Rhode Island), 46

Austin, Henry, 184n14

automobiles: automobile-accessible porches, 18; automobile touring as marketing appeal, 12; chauffeur dormitories, 160; effect on resort industry, 179

Bachelder, John, 83, 111–12, *133*

badminton, 12

Baedeker, Karl, 38

Bailey's Island, Maine, 152

Baker, D. C., 90

Ball, Nicholas, 57, 59, *59*

ballrooms and dance halls, 23, 31, 55, 114, 121, 127, 141, 155, 157, 198n20

Ballston Spa, New York, 7

Balsams, the (White Mountain region, New Hampshire), 101, 158

barber shops, 138

Bar Harbor, Maine, 45, 165–70, *166*, 179

Barker, Elias W., 131

Barker, John W., 184n16

Barnum, P. T., 20

Barrett, Nathan Franklin, 176

Barry, William E., 137

baseball, 12

basketball, 64

Bass Rock House (Gloucester, Massachusetts; orig. Whitings), 104, *104*

bathhouses and beach facilities, 20, 23, 40, 65, 75, 81, 84, 101, 102, 103, 105, 110, 114, 115, 126, 157. *See also* swimming areas and pools

bathrooms: hot and cold water, 44, 90, 102, 126; piped water systems, 7, 29, 64; private indoor facilities, 6, 18; stacked bathrooms, 32

Bay Point Hotel (Rockland, Maine). *See* Samoset Hotel

Bay View Hotel (Ferry Beach, Maine; later Ocean Crest Manor), 143

Bay View House (Bar Harbor, Maine), 168

Bay View House (Jamestown, Rhode Island), *41–43*, 41–43, 186–87n15

Bay View House (Watch Hill, Rhode Island), 52

Bay Voyage Hotel (Jamestown, Rhode Island), 187n18

Beach House (Siasconset, Massachusetts), 82, *82*

Beach House (Swampscott, Massachusetts), 93

Beal, J. Williams, 73

Beaux Arts style, 13

bedrooms. *See* guest rooms

Bellevue Hotel (Bar Harbor, Maine; orig. St. Sauveur Hotel), 167

Belle Vue House (Newport, Rhode Island), *36*

Benedict, Eliss C., 16

Bentley, William, 89

Bergengren, Roy F., 92

Beverly, Massachusetts, 95, 98

Bevins, Charles L., 43

Biddeford Pool, Maine, 139–40

billiards, 17, 24, 31, 40, 64, 65, 66, 80, 90, 110, 115, 121, 127, 157, 160

Bishop, John, 26

Black Point, Maine (later Prouts Neck, Maine), 148–49

Black Point Inn (Scarborough, Maine; orig. Southgate House), 149

Black Rock House (Cohasset, Massachusetts), 68–69, *69*

Blaisdell, Edward B., 129, 131

Blanchard House (Old Orchard Beach, Maine), 143, *143*

Block Island, Rhode Island, 57–62

Blue Hill Inn (Blue Hill, Maine), 199n21

Bluffs, the (Mount Desert Ferry, Maine), 11, *175*, 175

Blynman, the (Magnolia, Massachusetts; orig. the Crescent Beach), 99

Boar's Head Hotel (Hampton, New Hampshire; orig. Hampton Beach Hotel), 109–10, *110*

boating facilities, 20, 94, 96–97, 115, 121, 126, 157

Booth, Junius Brutus, Jr., 98–99

Boothbay Harbor, Maine, 156–58

Bowen, Patrick, 65

bowling, 12, 18, 24, 40, 65, 75, 80, 90, 103, 110, 115, 121, 157

Brackett, Gilbert, 96

Brackett, Paul, 96

Branford Point House (Branford, Connecticut), 22, *22*, 29

Breakwater Court (Kennebunkport, Maine; later Colony Hotel), 138–39, *139*

brick construction, 127

Bridge, Robert C., 95
Brinton, G. H., 82
Brown, Dona, 74, 82
Brown, Mrs. E. G., 104
Bryan, William A., 22
Bryant, Gridley J. F., 90
Buckley, Morgan G., 24
Bufford, John H., 111
Bugbee, S. Charles, 103
Burns, J. G., 47

Campbell, Charles E., 115
Cape Cod, Massachusetts, 63, 74–79
Cape Cod Bay House (Dennis, Massachu-
    setts; later Nobscusett House), 76, 76–77
Cape Codder (Falmouth, Massachusetts;
    orig. Sippewissett Hotel), 76
Cape Cottage (Cape Elizabeth, Maine), 150
Cape Elizabeth, Maine, 150
Cape May, New Jersey, 7
Carpenter, E. T., 81
Carpenter, William D., 82, 85
Carter, R. W., 93
Casco Bay Islands, Maine, 151–54
Casco Castle (South Freeport, Maine),
    154–55, 155
Casino and Towers (Narragansett Pier,
    Rhode Island), 47–49, 48
casinos, 18, 27, 64, 75, 105, 114
Castine, Maine, 164–65
Catskill Mountain House (New York), 7
Central House (Old Orchard Beach, Maine),
    143, 143
Chalfonte Hotel (Cape May, New Jersey), 11
Champernowne Hotel (Kittery, Maine), 125,
    125–26
Chase, Daniel, 115
Chase House (Squirrel Island, Maine; later
    Squirrel Inn), 157
Chatham, Massachusetts, 77–79
Chatham Bars Inn (Chatham, Massachu-
    setts): overview, 78–79; as Colonial
    Revival style example, 13, 79; illustrations,
    4, 79, Plate 4; as surviving hotel, xv, 63,
    79, 180
Checkley House (Prouts Neck, Maine), 149,
    149
Cheney, Oren B., 157
Christmas Cove, Maine, 158, 198n13
Churchill, George, 70
Churchill Hotel (Marshfield, Massachusetts),
    70, 71, 74
City Hotel (Baltimore), 6
Claremont Hotel (Southwest Harbor, Maine),
    171
Clark, Deacon Henry H., 171
Clark, Henry Paston, 139
Clark, John E., 167, 173, 175
Clark, M. P., 95
class. See social class

Cleaves Hotel (Old Orchard Beach, Maine),
    145
Clemens, Samuel, 184n14
Clergue, Francis H., 175
Cleveland, Grover, 65
Cleveland Hotel (Falmouth, Massachusetts;
    orig. Sippewissett Hotel), 76
Cliff Cottage (Cape Elizabeth, Maine), 150
Cliff Hotel (Scituate, Massachusetts), 70, 70
Cliff House (Kennebunkport, Maine), 136,
    136–37
Clifford House (Plymouth, Massachusetts;
    later Hotel Pilgrim), 72, 72–73
Clifton House (Northeast Harbor, Maine), 172
Cobb, Francis, II, 159
Cohasset, Massachusetts, 68–69
Cole, J. R., 39–40
Colonial Arms Hotel (Gloucester, Massa-
    chusetts): overview, 105–8; as Colonial
    Revival style example, 13; exceptional
    extravagance of, 87; illustrations, 6, 106–7;
    roof design, 79
Colonial House (Watch Hill, Rhode Island;
    orig. Atlantic House), 52
Colonial Revival style: in the Kennebunk-
    port, Maine, area, 135; on the Massachu-
    setts coastline, 63, 74; origin of, 13;
    Palladian windows, 117; roof styles, 17,
    96; use in university buildings, 139; wall
    balconies, 17
    —Examples: CONNECTICUT — Hotel
    Griswold, 32. MAINE — Cliff House, 137;
    Colony Hotel, 139; Holly Inn (second),
    158; Hotel Alberta, 147; Islesboro Inn
    (second), 163; Kimball House, 173;
    Marshall House (second), 127; Nar-
    ragansett Hotel, 135–36; Oceanic Hotel,
    137; Samoset Hotel, 160; Sparhawk
    Hall, 134; Squirrel Inn, 157–58. MASSA-
    CHUSETTS — Cliff Hotel, 70; Colonial
    Arms, 13, 106; Harbor View Hotel, 85;
    Hotel Belmont, 77; Hotel Mattaquason,
    78; Hotel Pilgrim, 72; Mayflower Hotel,
    73; New Ocean House, 13, 94; Peace
    Haven Hotel, 70; Rockmere Inn, 96;
    Sippewissett Hotel, 75; Sippican Hotel,
    74; Turk's Head Inn, 13, 108. NEW
    HAMPSHIRE — Hotel Wentworth, 117,
    119. NEW YORK — Mansion House, 33.
    RHODE ISLAND — Ocean House (Watch
    Hill) veranda, 54, 54; Rockingham,
    the, 47–48; Weekapaug Inn (second),
    188n31
Colony Hotel (Kennebunkport, Maine; orig.
    Breakwater Court), xv, 137, 138–39, 139,
    180, Plate 12
Columbus Hotel (Narragansett Pier, Rhode
    Island), 48, 51
Continental Hotel (Narragansett Pier, Rhode
    Island; later Hotel De La Plage), 46, 46–47

Coombs, George M., 159
cottages: effect on resort industry, 179;
    private cottages near resorts, 16; in resort
    complexes, 14, 20, 61; upscale cottage
    communities, 38–39, 57, 85. See also resort
    communities
Crescent Beach, the (Magnolia, Massachu-
    setts; later the Blynman), 99
Crocker, Henry Scudder, 27
croquet, 12, 23, 29, 157
Crossways Inn (Greenwich, Connecticut), 16
Cummings, Charles A., 85, 177
Curtis, John, 135
Cushing, Lemuel, 152
Cushing's Island, Maine, 152–54

Damon, J. Linfield, 66
Damon, John L., 66
David Irving Company, 73
Davis, Alfred, 133
Davis, Harrison, 133
Day, John W., 100–101, 103–4, 106
Delavan House (Narragansett Pier, Rhode
    Island), 46, 48
Dennis, Massachusetts, 76
Devnell, George A., 136
Dickens Inn (Watch Hill, Rhode Island), 52
Dillon, Nicholas, 43
dining facilities: banquet facilities, 160;
    farm and garden operations, 18, 20, 40;
    separate dining facilities, 18
    —Examples: CONNECTICUT — Edgewood
    Inn, 20; Fenwick Hall, 25; Hotel
    Griswold, 31. MAINE — Old Orchard
    House, 143; Samoset Hotel, 161.
    MASSACHUSETTS — Hotel Nantasket,
    65; Magnolia Hotel, 102; Rockmere Inn
    (Fo'cas'le), 97
Doane, Ralph Harrington, 188n31
Dooley, Charles, 73, 76
Douglas, Frank A., 85
Douglas, Perry, 26
Downing, Antoinette F., 35, 36–38
Drew, J. W., 85
Drew, Phineas, 90
Dumas, Stebbins H., 110
Dunning, Benjamin Franklin, 155

Eagle Rock House (Kennebunk Beach,
    Maine), 135
Ecole des Beaux-Arts, 13
Edgartown, Massachusetts, 85
Edgecomb, Roswell S., 27
Edgecomb House (New London, Connecti-
    cut; later Fort Griswold House), 27–29, 28
Edgemere House (Pemaquid Point, Maine),
    198n13
Edgewood Inn (Greenwich, Connecticut), 13,
    18, 19, 20
Edwards, Jesse B., 117

Eldredge, Marcellus, 78

Eldridge, B. F., 137

electric bells, 70, 93, 97, 126

electric generators, 75

electric lights, 44, 65, 97, 102, 107, 126, 138

elevators, 29, 32, 44, 66, 92, 93, 102, 107, 115, 121, 138

Elmwood Hotel (Narragansett Pier, Rhode Island), 48

Emerson, the (Old Orchard Beach, Maine; orig. Hotel Velvet), 145

Emerson, William Ralph, 199n21

Emerson House (York, Maine), 127

English Tudor Revival style, 162

environmental design: development of farmland, 41; farm and garden operations, 18, 20, 40; greenhouses, 24; landscaping, 32; oceanfront settings, 4–5; panoramic views, 4–5, 29, 40, 55, 73, 92, 102, 103, 110, 112, 129, 131, 150, 157; rusticity as resort theme, 40–41; sea water/air health qualities, 12, 61, 110

Evans, Edmund C., 163

Evans, Thomas, 140

Fairmount Hotel (York, Maine), 133

Falmouth, Massachusetts, 74–76

Falmouth Arms Hotel (Falmouth, Massachusetts; orig. Sippewissett Hotel), 76

family-oriented hotels, 68, 160

Farragut House (Rye Beach, New Hampshire) — first, 112, 112

Farragut House (Rye Beach, New Hampshire) — second, 11, 111, 112–14, 113, Plate 6

Fenno, William, 93

Fenwick Hall (Saybrook, Connecticut), 10, 24–26

Ferguson, Edmund M. and Walter, 33

fire hoses/alarms, 18, 29

Fisher's Island, New York, 32–34

fishing, 110, 121, 126

Fiske, C. H. and A. H., 143

floor plans: overview, 9; crescent-shaped plans, 34, 79, 105; double-loaded corridors, 5; E-shaped floor plan, 108; H-shaped floor plan, 147; kitchen facilities, 31; L-shaped floor plan, 17, 21, 25, 28, 41, 52, 53, 69, 70, 105, 110, 115, 127, 137–38, 141, 157, 159, 168, 175; of Narragansett Pier structures, 47, 48; T-shaped floor plan, 20, 47, 52, 57, 59, 62, 74, 78, 97, 111, 126, 170; U-shaped floor plan, 49, 176; V-shaped floor plan, 18, 112. See also guest rooms
   — Examples: CONNECTICUT — Fenwick Hall, 25; Fort Griswold House, 28; Hotel Griswold, 30–31. MAINE — Hotel Fiske, 144; Hotel Velvet, 146; Islesboro Inn (first), 163; Marshall House (second), 127; Oceanic Hotel, 138; Old Orchard House, 142; Samoset

Hotel, 161. MASSACHUSETTS — Hotel Masconomo, 99; Lincoln House, 92; Sippewissett Hotel, 75. NEW BRUNSWICK, CANADA — Algonquin Hotel, 177. NEW HAMPSHIRE — Hotel Wentworth, 115. RHODE ISLAND — Bay View House (Jamestown), 43; Ocean View Hotel, 60; Watch Hill House, 56

Florence, the (Bar Harbor; orig. Hotel Porcupine), 170

Folger, Clifford, 82

Footman, Fred N., 115, 117

Fort Griswold House (New London, Connecticut; orig. Edgecomb House), 27–29, 28–29, 185n24–25

Foss, Ira C., 149

Fox, DeGrasse, 170

Freeman, E. S., 70

Frenchman's Bay, Maine, 175–76

Frey, Dorothy Wilkey, 78

Frisbee, Jesse E., 125

Fuller, Daniel W., 99–100

Gardner, Mr. and Mrs. Stephen, 43

Gardner House (Jamestown, Rhode Island), 41, 43, 43

Garland, Joseph, 105

George Hotel (Bridgeport, Connecticut), 20, 21

Georgian Revival style, 186n9

Gerald, Amos F., 154

Gerald Hotel (Fairfield, Maine), 155

Gibson, Robert W., 31

Giddings, George L., 74

Gilbert, C. P. H., 49

gingerbread architecture, 145

Gladstone Hotel (Narragansett Pier, Rhode Island), 48, 48

Glen Cove House (Seal Harbor, Maine), 173

Glen Haven Hotel (Kennebunkport, Maine; orig. Oceanic Hotel, later Colony Hotel), 137, 137–38

Glen House (White Mountain region, New Hampshire) — second, 11

Gloucester, Massachusetts, 102–8

golf courses, 12, 18, 64, 72, 75, 94, 160

Gothic Revival style, 27, 38, 150

Grabow, Edward, 93

Grand Central Hotel (Bar Harbor, Maine), 168, 168

grand hotels: defined, xvi; list of prominent examples, 4; list of surviving hotels, xv, 180; modernism as impulse for, 12; Queen Anne style supplanted by, 12–13; social status of patrons, 1. See also hotels; resorts

Grand Union Hotel (Saratoga Springs, New York), 9–10

granite construction, 176

Granite Spring Hotel and Casino (Long Island, Maine), 154, 154

Granite State House (Kennebunk Beach, Maine), 135

Great Chebeague Inn (Great Chebeague Island, Maine), 154

Great Northern Hotel (Millinocket, Maine), 155

Greek Revival style: overview, 36
   — Examples: MASSACHUSETTS — Old Colony House, 67. NEW HAMPSHIRE — Winnicumet House, 109. NEW YORK — Catskill Mountain House, 7. RHODE ISLAND — Atlantic House, 37; Ocean House (first), 36, 38; Stone Bridge House, 186n5

Greene's Inn (Narragansett Pier, Rhode Island), 48–49, 50

Greenwich, Connecticut, 16–19. See also Edgewood Inn; Indian Harbor Hotel

Griffing, Nathaniel, 23

Grindstone Inn (Winter Harbor, Maine), 176, 176, 200n35

Griswold Hotel. See Hotel Griswold

Grove Hill House (Kennebunk Beach, Maine), 135

guest rooms: connecting suites, 25, 127; descriptions of, 29, 55, 138; guest room layout, 5, 9; private lockable bedrooms, 6; telephones, 18, 32, 44. See also floor plans
   — Examples: CONNECTICUT — Edgecomb, 29; Hotel Griswold, 32. MAINE — Hotel Velvet, 145–47, 146; Old Fort Inn, 138. RHODE ISLAND — Larkin House, 55

guidebooks: Cape Cod described in, 74; Cohasset, Massachusetts, described in, 68; Old Orchard Beach described in, 141. See also marketing; tourism
   — Hotels described: CONNECTICUT — Edgecomb, 29. MAINE — Appledore House, 121; Cape Cottage, 150; Seaside Hotel, 173. MASSACHUSETTS — Hotel Pemberton, 66; Hotel Pines, 88; Magnolia Hotel, 102; Nahant Hotel, 90; Rockmere Inn, 96–97; Sea View House, 83. NEW HAMPSHIRE — Farragut House (second), 112, 114; Ocean House, 111–12. RHODE ISLAND — Larkin House, 55; Ocean House, 38–39

Hadley, Charles H., 61

Hamilton Hotel (Great Chebeague Island, Maine), 154

Hammond, George F., 80

Hampton, New Hampshire, 109–10

Hampton Beach Hotel (Hampton, New Hampshire; later Boar's Head Hotel), 109–10

Hancock, Maine, 175

Harbor View Hotel (Edgartown, Massachusetts), xv, 63, 85–86, 180, Plate 5

Hawthorne Inn (Gloucester, Massachusetts), 103–4, *104*

Haynes, John C., 75

Hazlett, W. C., 106

health and fitness movement, 11–12, 61

Hesperus House (Magnolia, Massachusetts), 99–100, *100*

Heywood House (Bar Harbor, Maine; later West End Hotel), 169

Highland House (Kennebunkport, Maine)—second, 139–40, *140*

Highland House (Vineyard Highlands, Massachusetts), *84*, 84

Hildreth, Herbert L., 145

Hill, Benjamin, 88

Hilton, Frank, 115

Hingham, Massachusetts, 67–68

Historic Hotels of America, 79

historic preservation: Historic Hotels of America, 79; Hotel Wentworth preservation initiative, 114–15, 119–20; National Register of Historic Places, 148, 171; National Trust for Historic Preservation, 79

Hitchcock, Henry-Russell, 35

Hobson, C. L., 74

Holly Inn (Christmas Cove, Maine), 158, *158*

Holt, Selden W., 147

Homer, Winslow, 148

Hoppes, Maria Bodine, 33

Horgan, Patrick H., 43

Horgan Hotel. *See* Hotel Thorndike

horse and carriage facilities, 20, 24, 27, 75, 94, 110, 115

hospitality tourism, 63, 69, 95

Hotel Alberta (Old Orchard Beach, Maine), 145, *147*, 147

Hotel Albracca (York, Maine), *131*, 131, 133

Hotel Beacon (Winter Harbor, Maine), 200n35

Hotel Belmont (West Harwich, Massachusetts), *77*, 77

Hotel Berwick (Narragansett Pier, Rhode Island; orig. Mount Hope House), 46

Hotel Chatham (Chatham, Massachusetts), 13, 77–78, *78*

Hotel Cushing's Island (Cushing's Island, Maine; Ottawa House alternate name), 152, *153*

Hotel De La Plage (Narragansett Pier, Rhode Island; orig. Continental Hotel), 46

Hotel Everett (Old Orchard Beach, Maine), *147*, 147–48

Hotel Fiske (Old Orchard Beach, Maine), 10, 143–45, *144*

Hotel Goodwood (Revere, Massachusetts; orig. Robinson Crusoe Hotel, then Ocean House), 88

Hotel Griswold (New London, Connecticut), 29–31, *29–32*

Hotel Harwarden. *See* Hotel Thorndike

Hotel Humarock (Scituate, Massachusetts), 69, 69–70

Hotel Manisses (Block Island, Rhode Island), 58, *59*

Hotel Masconomo (Manchester, Massachusetts), 98–99, *99*

Hotel Mattaquason (Chatham, Massachusetts), 78, *79*

Hotel McSparren (Narragansett Pier, Rhode Island; later Rockingham Hotel), 47

Hotel Moorland (Gloucester, Massachusetts), 104–5, *105*

Hotel Nantasket (Hull, Massachusetts), 4, 10, 26, 65, *65*

Hotel Nantucket (Nantucket, Massachusetts), 80, 80–81

Hotel Pemberton (Hull, Massachusetts), 65–66, *66*

Hotel Pilgrim (Plymouth, Massachusetts; orig. Clifford House), 72, 72–73

Hotel Pines (Revere, Massachusetts), 88–89

Hotel Porcupine (Bar Harbor, Maine; later the Florence), 170

Hotel Preston (Swampscott, Massachusetts), 92–93

Hotel Sorrento (Sorrento, Maine), *175*, 175–76

Hotel Thorndike (Jamestown, Rhode Island)—first, 13, *41*, 43–45, *44*, 152

Hotel Thorndike (Jamestown, Rhode Island)—second, 44–45

Hotel Thorwald (Gloucester, Massachusetts), 105, *105*

Hotel Velvet (Old Orchard Beach, Maine; later the Emerson), *145*, 145, *147*

Hotel Waldo (Little Chebeague Island, Maine), 154

Hotel Wentworth (New Castle, New Hampshire): overview, 114–20; exceptional extravagance of, 10, 95, 109; Frank Jones as owner, 175; illustrations, *7*, *115–19, Plates 7–9*; modernization of, xv, 194n20; nearby attractions, 194n20; other comparable hotels, 139; as Queen Anne style example, 11; as surviving hotel, xv, 180

hotels: historical overview, 6–14; appeal to business class, 3; European urban model, 6; family-oriented hotels, 68, 160; hospitality tourism, 63, 69, 95; list of surviving hotels, xv, 180–81. *See also* grand hotels; resorts

Hull, Massachusetts, 63–67, 88

Humphrey, Charles, 76

Hunt, Richard Morris, 13

Hygeia, the (Block Island, Rhode Island), 59, *61*, 61–62

Idunda Springs Hotel (York, Maine), 133

Imperial, the (Old Orchard Beach, Maine; orig. Ocean House), 141

Imperial Hotel (Narragansett Pier, Rhode Island), 51, *52*

Indian Harbor Hotel (Greenwich, Connecticut), *2*, *16–17*, 16–18, 183n5

Island House (Southwest Harbor, Maine), 171, *171*

Island Ledge Hotel (Wells Beach, Maine), 133

Islesboro Inn (Islesboro Island, Maine)—first, 161–63, *162–63*

Islesboro Inn (Islesboro Island, Maine)—second, 163–64, *164*, 198n19

Islesboro Island, Maine, 161–64

Isles of Shoals (Maine and New Hampshire), 120–23

Italianate style: Atlantic House (Watch Hill, Rhode Island), 52; Hamilton Hotel (Great Chebeague Island, Maine), 154; in Pequot Colony, Connecticut, 27; Rocky Point Hotel (Warwick, Rhode Island), 40

Italian Revival style, 17, 111

Jackman, Eli, 105

Jacobs, Nehemiah P. M., 134

Jamestown, Rhode Island, 40–45, *41*, 187n18

Jenness, Job, 111, 136

Jenness, Jonathan Rollins, 111

Jocelyn House (Prouts Neck, Maine), 11, *148*, 148–49

John Hinkley & Sons, 76

Johnson, Andrew L., 97

Johnson, Benjamin, *77*

Johnson, Lindley, 176

Jones, Frank, 115–16

Jordan, Eben, *77*

Jordy, William H., 35, 40–41, 49

Keith, Elijah J., *73*

Kelley, Samuel D., 76

Kelsey, George R., 21

Kennebunk Beach, Maine, 134–36

Kennebunkport, Maine, 134–35, 136–40

Killam, Lewis, 135

Kimball, Daniel and Loren, 172

Kimball House (Northeast Harbor, Maine), 172–73, *174*

Kirkwood Inn (Scarborough, Maine), 148

Kittery, Maine, 125–26

Knowles, Adolphus, 41

Knowles, William H., 41

Krewson, George C., Jr., 101

Laighton, Thomas B., 120

Lamprey, Jerry, 109

Lancaster, Clay, 81–82

Larkin, Daniel F., 54

Larkin House (Watch Hill, Rhode Island), 10, 54–55, *55*, 57

Larrabee, E. N., 137

Leavitt, Ebenezer, 110

LeFavour, Israel, 98

Lennox House (Greenwich, Connecticut), 16

Lewis, Alonzo, 90

Lewis, Ion, 95

libraries, 6, 18

lighthouses, 57

Limerick, Jeffery W., 1–2, 12

Lincoln, S. W., 25

Lincoln House (Swampscott, Massachusetts), 91–92, *91–92*

Linwood Hotel (Rockport, Massachusetts), 108

Littlefield, Joseph Mendum, 136

Littlefield, N. S., 43

Long Branch, New Jersey, 7

Long Island, Maine, 154

Lookout Hotel (Ogunquit, Maine), *134,* 134–35

Lougee, George G., 114

Louisburg Hotel (Bar Harbor, Maine), 167–68, *168*

Lovejoy, Kim, 139

Lowell Island House (Marblehead, Massachusetts), 97, *97–98*

Luce, Clarence, 152

Luce, Joe Snow, 74

Lyles Beach Hotel (Fisher's Island, New York). *See* Munnatawket Hotel

Magnolia, Massachusetts, 99–102

Magnolia House (Magnolia, Massachusetts), 11, 87, 102

Malvern Hotel (Bar Harbor, Maine), 170, *170*

Manchester, Massachusetts, 95, 98–99

Manhattan Beach Hotel (Coney Island, New York), 11

Mansfield, Erastus G., 115

Mansion House (Fisher's Island, New York), 32–34, *33*

Mansion House (Hull, Massachusetts), 65

Maples, the (Greenwich, Connecticut), 16

Marblehead, Massachusetts, 95–98

Marie Joseph Spiritual Center, 140

Marion House (Marion, Massachusetts), 73

marketing: advertising broadsides, 24, *24*; automobile touring as marketing appeal, 12; promotional booklets, 18, 152; tourist publications, 12–13. *See also* guidebooks; tourism

Marlborough House (Bar Harbor, Maine), 167

Marshall family, 127, 129

Marshall House (York, Maine)—first, 10, *126,* 126–27, 133

Marshall House (York, Maine)—second, 127–29, *127–30,* 133, 148

Marshfield, Massachusetts, 70

Marston, Abraham, Jr., 109

Martha's Vineyard, Massachusetts, 63, 82–86

Martin, C. B., 108

Mason, George C., Jr., 187n18

Mason, Sidney, 103

Massasoit Hotel (Narragansett Pier, Rhode Island; orig. Maxson House), 46

Mathewson, S. W., 48

Mathewson House (Narragansett Pier, Rhode Island)—first, 48–49, *49*

Mathewson House (Narragansett Pier, Rhode Island)—second: overview, 46, 49–51; illustrations, *3, 50–51*; other comparable hotels, 44, 152; as Shingle style example, 13

Mattakeset Lodge (Edgartown, Massachusetts), 65, *85,* 85

Maxson House (Narragansett Pier, Rhode Island; later Massasoit Hotel), 46

Mayflower Hotel (Falmouth, Massachusetts; orig. Sippewissett Hotel), 76

Mayflower Hotel (Plymouth, Massachusetts), 73, *73,* 76

Menawarmet Hotel (Boothbay Harbor, Maine), 157

Metatoxet House (Narragansett Pier, Rhode Island; later Beachwood Hotel), 46, *46*

Miller, William Robinson, 155

Minot House (Cohasset, Massachusetts), 76

Mitchell, Horace M., 125

Monkhouse, Christopher, 49

Monononnotto Inn (Fisher's Island, New York), 32–34, *34*

Montowese House (Branford, Connecticut), 22–23, 184n14

Morton House (Greenwich, Connecticut), 16

Mountain View House (White Mountain region, New Hampshire), 22

Mount Desert Ferry, Maine, 175

Mount Desert Island, Maine, 165–75

Mount Hope House (Narragansett Pier, Rhode Island; later Hotel Berwick), 46–47, *47*

Mount Kineo House (Moosehead Lake, Maine), 158

Mount Vernon Hotel (Cape May, New Jersey), 8–9

Mount Washington Hotel (White Mountain region, New Hampshire), 31, 95, 101, 158

Mouse Island, Maine, 157

Munnatawket Hotel (Fisher's Island, New York; orig. Lyles Beach Hotel), 32–34

Murphy, Kevin, 139

Nahant, Massachusetts, 7, 89–90

Nahant Hotel (Nahant, Massachusetts), 89–90, *89–90*

Nanepashemet Hotel (Marblehead, Massachusetts), 95

Nantucket Island, Massachusetts, 63, 80–82, 190n17

Narragansett Bay, 35, 39

Narragansett Hotel (Kennebunk Beach, Maine), *135,* 135–36, *Plate 11*

Narragansett House (Narragansett Pier, Rhode Island), 45–46

Narragansett House (Watch Hill, Rhode Island), 52

Narragansett Pier, Rhode Island, 45–51, 57; functional Second Empire style at, 5

Nash, George M., 53

Nash, Jonathan, 52, 55

Nash, Nathan, 52

Nash, Winslow, 52

National Hotel (Block Island, Rhode Island), 40, 57, 58

National Register of Historic Places, 148, 171, 188n31

National Trust for Historic Preservation, *79*

neo-Adamesque style, 117

Neoclassical style, 31

Nevins, Winfield, 88

New Barker Hotel (Guilford, Connecticut), 184n16

New Brunswick, Canada, 177–79

Newhall, F. S., 90

New Ocean House (Swampscott, Massachusetts), 5, 13, 87, 93–95, *94*

Newport, Rhode Island, 7, 36–39, 186n5, 186n9

Newport Hotel (Bar Harbor, Maine), *167,* 167, 170

New Shoreham, Rhode Island, 57–62

Newton, Dudley, 38

New Watch Hill House (Watch Hill, Rhode Island), 55–57, *56*

New York City Hotel (New York City), 6

Nobscusett House (Dennis, Massachusetts; orig. Cape Cod Bay House), 76, *76–77*

Norman style, 154–55

Northeast Harbor, Maine, 171–72

Norton, Ruel W., 138

Nourse, Henry N., 177

Nudd, David, 109

Nudd, Stacy, 110

Nye, Walter A., 51

Oak Bluffs, Massachusetts, 82–83, 85

Oake Grove Hotel (Boothbay Harbor, Maine), *156,* 157

Oakland Beach Hotel (Warwick, Rhode Island), *40,* 40

Ocean Bluff Hotel (Kennebunkport, Maine), 9, 136, 136–37

Ocean Crest Manor (Ferry Beach, Maine; orig. Bay View Hotel), 143

Ocean House (Narragansett Pier, Rhode Island), 46

Ocean House (New London, Connecticut), 29, 185n23

Ocean House (Newport, Rhode Island)—first, 36, *37*

Ocean House (Newport, Rhode Island)—second, *3,* 29, 36–39, *37–39*

Ocean House (Old Orchard Beach, Maine; later the Imperial), 141

Ocean House (Revere, Massachusetts; orig. Robinson Crusoe Hotel), 88
Ocean House (Rye Beach, New Hampshire)—first, *110–11, 110–11,* 120
Ocean House (Rye Beach, New Hampshire)—second, *111, 111*–12
Ocean House (Southwest Harbor, Maine), *171*
Ocean House (Swampscott, Massachusetts)—first, 91, 93
Ocean House (Swampscott, Massachusetts)—second, 93
Ocean House (Watch Hill, Rhode Island), 52–54, *53–55,* 57, Plates 1–2
Ocean House (Wells Beach, Maine), 133
Ocean House (York Beach, Maine), *132,* 133
Oceanic Hotel (Kennebunkport, Maine; later Glen Haven Hotel, then Colony Hotel), 137, *137*–38
Oceanic Hotel (Star Island, New Hampshire)—first, *121–22, 121–23*
Oceanic Hotel (Star Island, New Hampshire)—second, xv, *121–23, 122, Plate 10*
Ocean Manor (Marblehead, Massachusetts; orig. Nanepashemet Hotel), 96
Oceanside Hotel (Magnolia, Massachusetts): overview, 100–102; exceptional extravagance of, 10, 87; illustrations, *5, 100–101*; as Queen Anne style example, 11
Ocean View Hotel (Biddeford Pool, Maine), 140, *140, Plate 13*
Ocean View Hotel (Block Island, Rhode Island), 59, *59–61, 60*
Ocean View House (Popham Beach, Maine; later Rockledge), *156, 156*
Ocean View House (Rockport, Massachusetts), 108
Ocean Wave House (North Beach, New Hampshire), 193–94n14
octagonal style: Bluffs tower, 175; Champernowne Hotel tower cupolas, 125; of Edgewood Inn tower, 18; Hotel Masconomo observatory, 99; Hotel Moorland corner tower, 105; Kimball House tower, 173; Larkin House cupolas, 55; Ocean House (second) cupola, 38; Passaconaway Inn towers, 129; Rocky Point Hotel observation tower, 40; Sippewissett Hotel cupolas, 76; Turk's Head Inn tower, 108
O'Gorman, James, 103
Ogunquit, Maine, 133
Old Colony House (Hingham, Massachusetts), 67, *68*
Old Fort Inn (Kennebunkport, Maine), 137, *139, 139*
Old Greenwich Inn (Greenwich, Connecticut), 16
Old Orchard Beach, Maine, 5, 45, 88, 124, 140–48
Old Orchard House (Old Orchard Beach, Maine)—second, 141, *142*

Olmstead, Frederick Law, 152
Oregon House (Hull, Massachusetts), *64,* 64
Oriental Hotel (Coney Island, New York), 11
Ottawa House (Cushing's Island, Maine)—first, *152, 152*
Ottawa House (Cushing's Island, Maine)—second, *11, 13, 44,* 152, *153*
Owen, the (Campobello Island, New Brunswick, Canada), 177

Paige, Orra, 100
Parker, George, and family, 22
Parker House (Kennebunkport, Maine), 139
Park Field Hotel (Kittery, Maine), 125
Parsons, Edward P., 104
Passaconaway Inn (York, Maine): overview, 129, 131; illustrations, *131*; other comparable hotels, 44, 152; as Shingle style example, *13,* 133
Pavilion Hotel (Gloucester, Massachusetts; later Surfside, the), *103,* 103
Payne, William, 89
Peace Haven Hotel (Marshfield, Massachusetts), 70, *71*
Peak's Island, Maine, 152, 154
Peak's Island House (Peak's Island, Maine), 154
Pepperrell House (Kittery, Maine), 125
Pequot House (New London, Connecticut), *2, 26–27, 26–27,* 184–85n20
Perkins, Thomas Handasyd, 89–90
Perkins House (Magnolia, Massachusetts), 100
Perry, Agnes, 98–99
Peterson, John R. and Shirley, 76
Pettee, Charlotte W., 81
Philbrick family, 112
Phippsburg, Maine, 156
piazzas. *See* verandas
Pickwick House (Falmouth, Massachusetts; later Vineyard Sound Hotel), 74–75
Pigeon Cove House (Rockport, Massachusetts), 108
Pioneer Cottage (Marshfield, Massachusetts; later Atlantic House), 70
pistol galleries, 40
Plant, Morton F., 29, 32
Plimpton, Andrew S., 52
Plimpton House (Watch Hill, Rhode Island), *52,* 52
Plymouth, Massachusetts, 70–73
Pocahontas, the (Kittery, Maine), *126,* 126
Poland Spring House (South Poland, Maine), 29–30, 95, 101, 158, 159–60
Pollard, Gorham L., 97
polo, 12
Poor, John R., 121
Popham Beach, Maine, 156
Potter, William T., 36
Pratt, S. F., 85

Preston, Andrew, 92
Preston, William G., 49, 177
Price, Bruce, 169
Profile House (Franconia Notch, New Hampshire), 101
Prospect House (Adirondack region, New York), 11
Prouts Neck, Maine (orig. Black Point, Maine), 148–49
Putnam, Pickering, 65

Queen, the (Beverly, Massachusetts), 98
Queen Anne style: overview, 11; features of, 101. *See also* vernacular style
—Examples: MAINE—Bluffs, the, 11, 175; Champernowne Hotel, 125; Cliff House, 137; Highland House, 140; Jocelyn House, 11, 149; Kimball House, 173; Samoset Hotel, 160; Seaside Inn, 11, 175. MASSACHUSETTS—Atlantic House, 66; Churchill Hotel, 70; Hesperus House, 100; Hotel Moorland, 105; Hotel Pemberton, 65–66; Hotel Pines, 88; Hotel Preston, 93; Lincoln House, 92; Magnolia Hotel, 11, 102; New Ocean House, 94; Oceanside Hotel, 11, 100; Queen, the, 98; Sea Cliff Inn, 81. NEW BRUNSWICK, CANADA—Tyn-y-Coed, 177. NEW HAMPSHIRE—Farragut House (second), 11, 112; Glen House (second), 11; Hotel Wentworth, 11, 115. NEW JERSEY—Chalfonte Hotel, 11. NEW YORK—Manhattan Beach Hotel, 11; Oriental Hotel, 11; Prospect House, 11; Sagamore Hotel, 11. RHODE ISLAND—Bay View House (Jamestown), 41

railroad travel, 47, 64, 70, *77,* 87, 91, 103, 126, 141, 149, 151, 165, 175, 179
Ralph Waldo Emerson Inn (Rockport, Massachusetts; orig. Pigeon Cove House), 108
Reed, Roger G., 169
resort communities: insular community design plan, 14; Pequot House Colony, 27; storefront verandas, 44; upscale cottage communities, 38–39, 57, 85. *See also* cottages; resorts
resorts: as antithesis of urban/suburban life, 2–3; business facilities in, 3, 18; cultural significance of, 1, 7; decline of New England coastal resorts, 179; distinguished visitors, 61, 65, 89, 94; floor plans, 9; health and fitness facilities, 11–12, 61; overview of architectural styles, 3–4; post–Civil War large resorts, 9–10, 38; pre–Civil War large resorts, 8–9; social class and, 1–2; spas and mineral springs, 7; vulnerability of, 2. *See also* grand hotels; hotels; resort communities

Revere, Massachusetts, 88–89

Revere House (Narragansett Pier, Rhode Island), 46

Richards, Keyes H., 157

Ridgewood, the (Kennebunk Beach, Maine), 135

Ripley, Nehemiah, 64

Roads, Samuel, Jr., 96–97

Robinson, Charles H., 81, 82

Robinson, George C., 48

Robinson Crusoe Hotel (Revere, Massachusetts; later Ocean House, then Hotel Goodwood), 88

Rock End Hotel (Northeast Harbor, Maine), 135, 172, *173*

Rockingham, the (Narragansett Pier, Rhode Island; orig. Hotel McSparren), *47–48*, 47–48

Rockland Café (Hull, Massachusetts), *4*, 65

Rockland House (Hull, Massachusetts), *64*, 64–65

Rockmere Inn (Marblehead, Massachusetts; orig. the Fo'cas'le, later Hotel Marblehead), 13, 96–97, *96–97*

Rockport, Massachusetts, 108

Rocky Point Hotel (Warwick, Rhode Island), *39*, 39–40

Rodick, David, Jr., 165–66

Rodick House (Bar Harbor, Maine), 10, 165–68, *167*

Rogers, Isiah. *See* Tremont House

rooms. *See* guest rooms

Roosevelt, Theodore, 89

Rose Standish House (Hingham, Massachusetts), 67–68, *68*

Royal Poinciana (Florida), 101

Russell, John, 139

Rye Beach, New Hampshire, 110–14

Sachem's Head House (Guilford, Connecticut), 23–24, *24*, 184n16

Safford, Edward, 125

Sagamore Hotel (Adirondack region, New York), 11

Sagamore Hotel (Kennebunk Beach, Maine), 135

Sagamore Hotel (Odiorne's Point, New Hampshire), 193–94n14

Salem, Massachusetts, 95

Samoset Hotel (Rockland, Maine; orig. Bay Point Hotel), 13, 127, 148, 158–61, *159–61*

Samoset House (Mouse Island, Maine), 157, *157*

Samoset House (Plymouth, Massachusetts), 72

"Saratoga by the Sea." *See* Ocean House (Newport, Rhode Island) — second

Saratoga Springs, New York, 7, 9, 166

Sargent, Rufus, 111

Savage, Augustus C., 172

Savage, Fred L., 163, 168, 170, 172

Savage, Herman L., 172

Savin Rock (West Haven, Connecticut), 20–21, *21*

Scarborough, Maine, 148–49

Scituate, Massachusetts, 69–70

Scranton, Horace Lee, 23–24

Scully, Vincent J., Jr., 13, 35, 36–38, 44, 169

Sea Cliff Inn (Nantucket, Massachusetts), 81–82

Seal Harbor, Maine, 173–74

Sears, Williard T., 177

Seashore House (Old Orchard Beach, Maine), 141, *143*, 143

Seaside Hotel (Seal Harbor, Maine; later Seaside Inn), 173

Seaside House (Kennebunk Beach, Maine), 135

Seaside Inn (Seal Harbor, Maine; orig. Seaside Hotel), 11, 173–75, *174*

Sea View Hotel (Rye Beach, New Hampshire), *114*, 114, 193–94n14

Sea View House (Kennebunk Beach, Maine), 135

Sea View House (Oak Bluffs, Massachusetts): overview, 82–83, *83*; Mattakeset Lodge as competitor, 85; mentioned, 84; as Stick style example, 10, 26, 65

Sea View House (West Haven, Connecticut), 21, *21*

Second Empire style: on Block Island, 57, 61–62; functional emphasis in, 5; on New England coast, 164; Queen Anne style as alternative to, 11; roof style of, 41, 57, 110, 115, 154

— Examples: CONNECTICUT — Edgecomb House, 27; George Hotel, 20; Indian Harbor Hotel, 17; Pequot House Colony, 27; Sea View House, 21. MAINE — Bay View Hotel, 143; Blanchard House, 143; Central House, 143; Edgemere House, 198n13; Granite Spring Hotel and Casino, 154; Highland House, 140; Island House, 171; Island Ledge Hotel, 133; Marshall House, 127; Newport Hotel, 167; Ocean House, 141; Ocean View House, 156; Parker House, 139; Peak's Island House, 154; Rodick House, 166; Wassaumkeag Hotel, 164; Waukeag House, 200n34. MASSACHUSETTS — Bass Rock House, 104; Churchill Hotel, 70; Clifford House, 72; Hesperus House, 100; Highland House, 84; Hotel Masconomo, 99; Hotel Preston, 93; Rockland House, 64. NEW HAMPSHIRE — Boar's Head Hotel, 110; Hotel Wentworth, 115, 119; Oceanic Hotel (first), 121; Sea View Hotel, 114. NEW YORK — Mansion House, 33. RHODE ISLAND — Bay View House

(Jamestown), 41; Gardner House, 43; Mathewson House (first), 48; Ocean View Hotel, 59; Rocky Point Hotel, 40

Shaw, O. M., 169

sheet music cover illustrations, 3, *7*, *83*, *90*

Shingle style: on Cape Cod, Massachusetts, 74; characteristics of, 152, 154, 170; influence on Colonial Revival style, 13; in Kennebunkport, Maine, area, 135; in Narragansett Pier structures, 48–49

— Examples: CONNECTICUT — Edgewood Inn, 13, 18; Pequot Casino, 27. MAINE — Blue Hill Inn, 199n21; Florence, the, 170; Hotel Albracca, 133; Islesboro Inn (first), 162; Malvern Hotel, 170; Old Fort Inn, 137–38; Ottawa House (second), 13, 152, 154; Passaconaway Inn, 13, 129, 133; Pocahontas, the, 126; Stanley House, 171; West End Hotel, 169. MASSACHUSETTS — Beach House, 82; Black Rock House, 69; Hawthorne Inn, 103; Hesperus House, 100; Hotel Moorland, 105; Nanepashemet Hotel, 95–96; New Ocean House, 94. NEW BRUNSWICK, CANADA — Algonquin Hotel, 177, 179. NEW YORK — Mansion House, 33; Mononotto Inn, 33–34. RHODE ISLAND — Casino and Towers, 48; Greene's Inn, 48–49; Hotel Thorndike, 13, 44; Mathewson House (second), 13, 49; Weekapaug Inn (first), 188n31

Simpson, Edward C., 136

Sippewissett Hotel (Falmouth, Massachusetts; later Cleveland Hotel, Falmouth Arms, Mayflower Hotel, then Cape Codder), *75*, 75–76

Sippican Hotel (Marion, Massachusetts; orig. Bay View House), 73–74, *74*

Skowhegan, Maine, 157

Slade, Robert A., 81

Smith, Al, 65

Smith, Sarah R., 69

Smith, Wesley G., 143

social class: in Jamestown, Rhode Island, resorts, 40–41; in Kennebunkport, Maine, 135; less-exclusive/reclusive hotels, 88–89; post–Civil War prosperity and, 9, 11; privacy vs. social display and, 1–2; upscale cottage communities, 38–39, 57, 85

Somerville, Maine, 200n32

Sorrento, Maine, 175–76

South Freeport, Maine, 154–55

Southgate House (Scarborough, Maine; later Black Point Inn), 149

Southwest Harbor, Maine, 171

Spanish Colonial Revival style, 135, 172

Sparhawk Hall (Ogunquit, Maine), *134*, 134

Sprague, Frank, 102

Spring House (Block Island, Rhode Island), xv, 57–59, *58*, 180, *Plate 3*

Squirrel Inn (Squirrel Island, Maine; orig. Chase House), 157, *158*

Squirrel Island, Maine, 157–58

stables. *See* horse and carriage facilities

Stacy, George O., 103–5, 107

staff dormitories, 18, 176, 187n18

Stage Neck Inn (York, Maine), 129

Stanley House (Southwest Harbor, Maine) — second, *171*

Staples, Ebenezer C., 141

Starkweather, W. S., 140

St. Cloud House (Old Orchard Beach, Maine), 143

steamboat travel, 22, 26–27, 41, 64, 126, 151, 175

steam heat, 44, 64, 70, 102, 107, 126

Stephenson, H. M., 108

Stevens, John Calvin, 66, 127, *129*, 148–49, 152, 160

Stevens, John Howard, 160

Stevens, Paran, 90

Stick style: overview, 10; Queen Anne style as alternative to, 11; tower styles of, 168
— Examples: CONNECTICUT — Fenwick Hall, 10, 24–26. MAINE — Claremont Hotel, 171; Cliff Cottage, 150; Grand Central Hotel, 168; Hotel Everett, 147; Hotel Waldo, 154; Ocean View Hotel, 140; West End Hotel, 169. MASSACHU-SETTS — Hotel Nantasket, 10, 26, 65; Hotel Pines, 88; Mattakeset Lodge, 85; Pickwick House, 74; Sea View House, 10, 26, 83. NEW HAMPSHIRE — Sea View Hotel, 114. RHODE ISLAND — Hygeia, the, 62

Stockton Springs, Maine, 164

Stokes, Edward D., 24

Stone Ridge House (Newport, Rhode Island), 186n5

Straitsmouth Inn (Rockport, Massachusetts), 108

St. Sauveur Hotel (Bar Harbor, Maine; later Bellvue Hotel), *167*, 167

Sturtevant, A. P. and J. D., 29

Surf Hotel (Block Island, Rhode Island), 57, *57*

Surfside, the (Gloucester, Massachusetts; orig. Pavilion Hotel), 103

Swampscott, Massachusetts, 91–95

Sweetser, Moses F., 64, 66, 173

swimming areas and pools, 72, 115, 194n20. *See also* bathhouses and beach facilities

Taylor, Bertrand E., 177

telegraph service, 70, 115, 127

telephone service, 18, 32, 44, 94, 102, 107, 127, 138

tennis, 12, 18, 23, 64, 75, 94, 96, 101, 157

Thaxter, Celia, 120

Thaxter, Levi, 120

Thayer, Samuel J. F., 112

theater, 23

Thompson, Joseph W., 164

Thorpe, Albert T., 158

Tobey, Charles and Francis, 76

Tontine Hotel (New Haven, Connecticut), 23

tourism: automobile touring, 12; cultural significance of, 1, 7; at Narragansett Pier, Rhode Island, 45–46; at Newport, Rhode Island, 38; tourist publications, 12–13. *See also* guidebooks; marketing

Tower Hill House (Narragansett Pier, Rhode Island), 46–47, *47*

towers: CONNECTICUT — Edgecomb House, 29; Edgewood Inn, 18; Indian Harbor Hotel, 17. MAINE — Bay Point Hotel, 159; Bluffs, the, 175; Champernowne Hotel, 125; Grand Central Hotel, 168; Kimball House, 173; Oake Grove Hotel, 157; Pocahontas, the, 126; Samoset Hotel, 160; Sparhawk Hall, 134. MASSA-CHUSETTS — Black Rock House, 69; Highland House, 84; Hotel Chatham, 78; Hotel Masconomo, 99; Hotel Moorland, 105; Hotel Nantasket, 65; Lincoln House, 92; Mattakeset Lodge, 85; Thorwald Hotel, 105; Turk's Head Inn, 108. NEW BRUNSWICK, CANADA — Algonquin Hotel, 177; Tyn-y-Coed, 177. NEW HAMP-SHIRE — Farragut House — second, *112*, 112; Hotel Wentworth, 117, *118–19*. RHODE ISLAND — Bay View House (Jamestown), 41; Hotel Thorndike, 44; Mathewson House — second, 49; Mount Hope House, 47; Rockingham, the, 47; Tower Hill House, 47

Towle, Amos, III, 109

Tremont House (Boston), 6–7

Turk's Head Inn (Rockport, Massachusetts), 13, 108, *108*

Twain, Mark, 184n14

Tweed, William Marcy "Boss," 16

Tyn-y-Coed (Campobello Island, New Brunswick, Canada), 177

Tyn-y-Maes (Campobello Island, New Brunswick, Canada), 177

United States Hotel (Saratoga Springs, New York), 10

Upham, A. E., 140

Upton, George A., 100–101

vegetable gardens, 18

verandas: as display areas, 2; first-floor storefront verandas, 44; functions of, 5; stacked verandas, 21, *39*, 66, 114, 176;

wraparound verandas, 55, 57, 61, 70, 88, 91–92, 96, 114, 121, 133, 167, 177
— Examples: CONNECTICUT — George Hotel, 20; Hotel Griswold, 32; Indian Harbor Hotel, 17; Montowese House, 22; Sachem's Head House, 24; Savin Rock, 20; Sea View House, 21. MAINE — Hotel Sorrento, 176; Island Ledge Hotel, 133; Newport Hotel, 167. MASSACHUSETTS — Hotel Nantucket, 80; Hotel Pines, 88; Hotel Preston, 93; Sea View House, 83. NEW BRUNSWICK, CANADA — Algonquin Hotel, 177. NEW HAMPSHIRE — Oceanic Hotel (second), 122; Sea View Hotel, 114. NEW YORK — Mononotto Inn, 34. RHODE ISLAND — Hotel Thorndike, 44; Hygeia, the, 61; New Watch Hill House, 57; Ocean House (second (Newport)), 38; Ocean House (Watch Hill), 54, *54*

vernacular style: economic considerations in, 5; exposed rafters, 23; in grand hotels, xvii; post–Civil War romanticism and, 10–11; predominant in early period, 3. *See also* Queen Anne style
— Examples: CONNECTICUT — Mon-towese House, 22–23. MAINE — Ocean View Hotel, 140. MASSACHUSETTS — Lowell Island House, 97; Nahant Hotel, 89–90. NEW HAMPSHIRE — Boar's Head Hotel, 110

Victorian eclectic styles: overview, 10
— Examples: CONNECTICUT — Pequot House Colony, 27. MAINE — Ocean Bluff Hotel, 136; Seashore House, 141, 143

Viking Hotel (Newport, Rhode Island), 186n9

Vineyard Sound Hotel (Falmouth, Massa-chusetts; orig. Pickwick House), *74*, 74–75

Walker, Forest, 160

Walker, Thomas J., 85

Wardwell family, 91, 93

Warren, Russell, 37

Warren, Whitney, 186n9

Warwick, Rhode Island, 39–40

Wassaumkeag Hotel (Stockton Springs, Maine), 164, *165*, 198n20

Watch Hill, Rhode Island, 51–57

Watch Hill House (Watch Hill, Rhode Island), 52, *53*, *56*

Waukeag House (Sullivan, Maine), 200n34

Weaver, John G., 37

Weekapaug Inn (Weekapaug, Rhode Island), 188n31

Weir, J. T., 18

Wells, George A., 20

Wells Beach, Maine, 133

Wentworth, Owen, 135

Wentworth-by-the-Sea. *See* Hotel Wentworth

Wentworth Hotel (Kennebunk Beach, Maine), 135

Wesley House (Oak Bluffs, Massachusetts), 85

West End Hotel (Bar Harbor, Maine; orig. Heywood House), 10, 168–70, *169*

Westerly, Rhode Island, 51–57

West Harwich, Massachusetts, *77*

Wetherill, J. M., 108

Wheelwright, Edmund M., 162

Wilkenson, Ella S., 108

Wilkey, Frederick, 78

William McKenzie & Company, 66

Willis, William, 150

Wilson, Fred A., 89

Winnicumet House (Hampton, New Hampshire), 109

Winter Harbor, Maine, 176

Witherell, Nathaniel, 18

wood construction: flexibility of design and, 38; use of prefabricated lumber, 115; vulnerability to decline, xv, 2, 179

Worster, William A., 133

Yeaton, Philip, 110

York, Maine, 126–33

Young's Hotel (York Beach, Maine; orig. Thompson House), *132*, 133

Zerrahn, Franz Edward, 77

zoos, 155

1. Ocean House (south view), Watch Hill, R.I. Photograph, 2004, by the author.

2. Ocean House (southwest view), Watch Hill, R.I. Photograph, 2004, by the author.

3. Spring House Hotel (main building), Block Island, R.I. Photograph,
c. 2006. Courtesy of Michael Melford, the Spring House Hotel, Block Island, R.I.

4. Chatham Bars Inn, Chatham, Cape Cod, Mass. Photograph, 2007, by Carolyn K. Tolles.

5. Harbor View Hotel, Edgartown, Martha's Vineyard, Mass. Photograph, 2007, by Carolyn K. Tolles.

6. The Farragut House, Rye Beach, N.H. Photograph, 1973, by the author.

7. Wentworth-By-The-Sea, New Castle, N.H. Photograph, 1968, by the author.

8. Wentworth By-The-Sea, New Castle, N.H. Photograph, 1999, by the author.

9. Wentworth-By-The-Sea, New Castle, N.H. Photograph, 2004, by the author.

10. Second Oceanic Hotel (Star Island Conference Center), Star Island, Isles of Shoals, N.H. Photograph, 2007, by Carolyn K. Tolles.

11. Narragansett Hotel (Condominiums), Kennebunk Beach, Maine. Photograph, 2006, by the author.

12. The Colony Hotel (Breakwater Court), south façade, Kennebunkport,
Maine. Photograph, 2006, by the author.

13. Ocean View Hotel
(Marie Joseph Spiritual
Center), Biddeford
Pool, Maine. Photo-
graph, 2006, by the
author.

14. The second Asticou Inn, Northeast Harbor, Mount Desert Island,
Maine. Photograph, 2006, by the author.